JAN DE VRIES: A LIFE IN HEALING

OTHER TITLES BY THE SAME AUTHOR

BY APPOINTMENT ONLY SERIES
Arthritis, Rheumatism and Psoriasis
Asthma and Bronchitis
Cancer and Leukaemia
Do Miracles Exist?
Heart and Blood Circulatory Problems
Migraine and Epilepsy
Neck and Back Problems
New Developments for MS Sufferers
Realistic Weight Control
Skin Diseases
Stomach and Bowel Disorders
Stress and Nervous Disorders
Traditional Home and Herbal Remedies
Viruses, Allergies and the Immune System

NATURE'S GIFT SERIES
Air – The Breath of Life
Body Energy
Food
Water – Healer or Poison?

WELL WOMAN SERIES
Female Cancers
Menopause
Menstrual and Pre-Menstrual Tension
Mother and Child
Pregnancy and Childbirth

JAN DE VRIES HEALTHCARE SERIES
Healing in the 21st Century
Hidden Dangers in What We Eat and Drink
How to Live a Healthy Life
Inner Harmony
My Life with Diabetes
Questions and Answers on Family Health
The Five Senses
Treating Body, Mind and Soul

NATURE'S BEST SERIES
10 Golden Rules for Good Health

THE JAN DE VRIES PHARMACY GUIDEBOOK SERIES
The Pharmacy Guide to Herbal Remedies

ALSO BY THE SAME AUTHOR
Life Without Arthritis – The Maori Way
The Jan de Vries Guide to Health and Vitality
Who's Next?

JAN DE VRIES

A LIFE IN HEALING

Jan de Vries

MAINSTREAM
PUBLISHING
EDINBURGH AND LONDON

First published in Great Britain in 2006 by
MAINSTREAM PUBLISHING COMPANY (EDINBURGH) LTD
7 Albany Street
Edinburgh EH1 3UG

ISBN 978 1 84596 141 1 (from January 2007)
ISBN 1 84596 141 2

A catalogue record for this book is available from the British Library

Typeset in Cheltenham and Futura

Printed and bound in Great Britain by
William Clowes Ltd, Beccles, Suffolk

Contents

PART ONE A STEP AT A TIME

	Foreword	9
1	Second Fiddle to the Ironing Board	13
2	Batten Down the Hatches	17
3	The Reluctant Scholar	26
4	Janny Beuze – 'The Boss'	32
5	Nunspeet – A Profitable Village	36
6	Four-Leaf Clover	44
7	Mokoia – 'Island of Rest'	50
8	Alfred Vogel – A Genius	54
9	Auchenkyle – 'Beneath the Kyles'	60
10	Healing Instead of Blundering	69
11	For Goodness Sake	80
12	The Flying Dutchman	89
13	The Media – Friend or Foe?	102
14	Pioneers and Fighters for Truth and Freedom	112
15	The Other Side of the Coin	122

PART TWO FIFTY YEARS FIGHTING

1	My Fight for Freedom of Choice in Medicine	135
2	My Fight against Degenerative Diseases	146
3	My Fight against the Media	152
4	My Fight against Addictions Today	158
5	My Fight against Poison and Pollution	168

6   My Fight for Complementary Medicine Education   178
7   My Fight for Understanding   185
8   My Fight for Peace and Love   191
9   My Fight for Truth, Honesty and Reality   201
10   My Fight for Compassion   213
11   My Fight for Vision   223

PART THREE **MY LIFE AND WORK WITH ALFRED VOGEL**

       A Note from Alfred Vogel   235
1   'Good health should be treasured and never abused ...' 239
2   'Illness and suffering are caused by imbalance and
           disharmony ...'   249
3   'Happiness is the soothing balm for a sick heart ...' 256
4   'By trying to help others, we, in turn, help ourselves.' 262
5   'Foresight is the source of health and happiness.'   267
6   'The physician or therapist is like a mountain guide ...' 278
7   'My home is our planet.'   288
8   'Each plant is complete in itself ...'   296
9   'In all your striving, let love be your guide ...'   306
10   'There is nothing common about common sense.'   312
11   'Questions lead to wisdom.'   318
12   'Man has not one body but three ...'   325
13   'It is very important to be in tune with your body.'   334
14   'Nature always overrules science.'   339

AFTERWORD   345

PART ONE

A STEP AT A TIME

Foreword

You will treasure this book. The life of Jan de Vries is enthralling. More importantly, his philosophy of life and healing are of the utmost value.

Jan de Vries was born in a small Dutch town in 1937. Under the Nazi occupation, he helped his mother find food for people she was hiding. Little Jan ran horrific risks; he still carries the mark of an explosion and he has a couple of squint fingers because his hands were frozen as he waited for hours in a queue for prunes for his grandmother. At one point in this hell, the child prayed that if his mother and he were saved, he would care about the well-being of people for the rest of his life.

Jan gained his degree when he was 21. He continued to pursue a special interest in pharmacy. In 1959 he was in Amsterdam, and he happened to go to a lecture that touched on homoeopathy.

'What do you think?' asked the man in the next seat.

'This is for spinsters and old wives,' said Jan.

'You must have a very small mind,' came the reply.

This was one of those moments that can galvanise and define a life. The man in the next seat was Alfred Vogel, the great authority on herbs, natural healing and homoeopathy. Jan's heart and instincts, despite what he had said to Vogel, were passionately against the small-minded, and this passion is part of Jan's creative life force today as much as when he was a student. Jan went on to study osteopathy in Germany and Holland. He managed to get into China, where he studied acupuncture. He worked in Taiwan. All his life, he has explored different modes of healing. He also worked with Vogel, who had challenged him at the lecture; indeed, Jan became the only pupil whom Vogel 'really taught'.

Some 40 years after the lecture in Amsterdam, Jan de Vries was in London. He made time in a crowded schedule for a stranger who had no appointment. That stranger was me. I had just been diagnosed with a malignant cancer of which a textbook writes that 'the median survival time is under a year in untreated patients, and two to three years with treatment'. I was in despair. But I happened to read Jan de Vries's book, *Cancer and Leukaemia*, and its account of an elaborate Chinese breathing exercise with visualisations. I tried the exercise and had a hunch that it was helping me. So I tracked down Dr de Vries.

I describe the meeting in my book, *Living Proof: A Medical Mutiny*:

> When my turn comes to see him, de Vries writes notes, as if there is not a second to spare, but he scarcely looks at the pad.
>
> His eyes focus on mine.
>
> For a whole minute.
>
> Perhaps more.
>
> I can hear his pen scratching, otherwise we might be anywhere. Then there is a shutdown of his concentration and he writes a prescription.
>
> 'One look at you, and you do not need chemotherapy.'
>
> I am so surprised that I do not ask why. Dr de Vries's extra-sensory minute, if it was that, is over. He is recharging his energy for the next patient …
>
> 'You can sort out this melanoma. Goodbye.'

At the time of this meeting with Jan, five cancer specialists, independently of each other, were urging me to start chemotherapy: if I did not, they said, the probability was that I would be dead in a year. But I decided to follow the contrary advice of Jan. I felt, by instinct, that something radical had occurred during our meeting, an inner world had been pierced – I write about it further in *Living Proof: A Medical Mutiny*. Jan also prescribed potassium drops (to help alkalise the body) and endorsed the Chinese breathing exercises and nutritional therapies which I was starting to follow.

Eight years on, I still have not had chemotherapy or radiotherapy. And I continue to do my job.

Living Proof: A Medical Mutiny, was published in March 2002. Jan read it and was astonished when he came to my account of our meeting because he discovered that I am the first patient, to his knowledge, to suspect that he has an extra sense of intuition that assists him in his work.

So this was another chance meeting that produced great results. Jan's generosity in 1994, when he fitted in a stranger with no appointment, helped to save my life, just as he helped his mother – although in a different way – to save lives when he was a boy under the Nazis. Also, *Living Proof* sparked off this magnificent autobiography by Jan, *A Step at a Time*.

A Step at a Time reveals that Jan became aware as a boy, at the age of about four or five, of his extra-sensory gifts. Yet, as I read his pages, I also think of the parable of the talents in Matthew 25. Jan was accorded a gift, but he turned it into an achievement. He treasured God's blessing but he also studied pharmacy, osteopathy, acupuncture, herbalism and many other approaches to healing. Like the good servants in Matthew, he laboured with hard work and humility to double the talent he was given. 'Well done, thou good and faithful servant,' says the Lord when he returns from the far country where he had travelled. And he also says to the servants who had worked, 'Enter thou into the joy of the Lord.'

Jan's sense of joy in life was clear to me even in his hurried consultation over my cancer. His joy was a presence, a psychic reality, a catalyst for healing, an unspoken celebration. I wrote at the time that 'de Vries is generous', as in one of my favourite texts: 'So let him give, not grudgingly or of necessity, for God loveth a cheerful giver.' (2 Corinthians 9:7) It is a quality you will find on every page of *A Step at a Time*.

Jan was a turning point in my own struggle with cancer, and I can try to state his philosophy by linking him with my next turning point, the senior Professor of Medicine in the University of Oxford, Sir David Weatherall FRS. In *Living Proof*, I describe how I sat in the Institute of Molecular Medicine, a world centre of advanced research, and told Sir David about Jan and the various therapies of diet and visualisation that I followed.

> 'Do you think I am mad to try what I am doing?' I ask.
> Sir David Weatherall is a man who thinks for as long as he wishes before he speaks. A minute or two pass.
> 'What you must understand, Mr Gearin-Tosh, is that we know so little about how the body works.'
> I am astonished.

Sir David repeats his remark.
'We know so little about how the body works.'
Nine short words.

It is in the context of these nine short words that doctors of vision, dedication and humility are so crucial. Jan pleads in *A Step at a Time* for so-called orthodox and complementary medicine to work together. He aptly quotes the biblical expression 'where there is no vision, the people perish' (Proverbs 29:18). Sir David wrote for *Living Proof*, 'Though I do believe passionately in scientific medicine, I have not got to the stage of being so blinkered that I cannot believe that at least some aspects of the more complementary approach to medicine may have a lot to offer. I think they could be put to scientific test, and should be, but whether this will happen is far from clear.'

Mankind has always needed men and women of vision who step ahead of their time and who have the courage to do so. *A Step at a Time* is Jan's wise, proportionate and modest title. But its inner meaning is that of Sir David Weatherall: a step *ahead* of time. A step ahead of mere convention. A step, certainly, ahead of small-mindedness, the peril which Alfred Vogel articulated to Jan almost half a century ago at that lecture in Amsterdam. A step that leads into the unknown. A step that others should follow.

Steps that lead forward have never been more necessary than they are today. They are the value and joy of Jan's life and of *A Step at a Time*.

Michael Gearin-Tosh,
St Catherine's College,
University of Oxford.

1

Second Fiddle to the Ironing Board

On a wintry, snowy day in January 1937 (and in Holland winter can be very, very cold), my mother started a chore that she had hated all her life but, nevertheless, always did herself – ironing! This was a job she really loathed, and in the company of a pound of cherry chocolates perched on the end of the ironing board, she tried to get through the pile of clothes as quickly as possible. However, right in the middle of this, she realised that she was going into labour. She sent my brother Nicolas, who was 13 at the time, to ask the local midwife (who lived just round the corner) to come. She hurried immediately to the house and not long after, at ten past four in the afternoon, I was born. (At that time in Holland, babies were always born at home.) There, by the River IJssel, which was completely frozen, in Voorstraat 51, a very healthy boy arrived. My mother's friend came in to help and, as soon as she got things settled, she left and walked up to my father's factory to tell him that he was richer by one son.

I was wanted very much by my mother when I was born, but I was a great disappointment to my father, because he had wanted a daughter. He was making his way home from work when my mother's friend met him in the street and told him the wonderful news. He was so disappointed that he went back to the factory straight away.

My father was very set in his ways and, although he was a proper gentleman, he lived in his own world, dominated by music and religion. My mother, who had a very friendly, gentle character, coped with my father's ways. Nevertheless, she had to take the lead. She was a great personality and I was very close to her as I grew up. My mother was also a very hard-working woman, whilst my father went at a slower pace.

The little place in which I was born, Kampen, had a tremendous history. Although my father's profession – cigar-making – was the main industry of the area, enamel pots and pans were also manufactured, and agriculture played an important part too, being carried on from one generation to the next. Several large buildings – for instance, the local council hall and the church (which was almost as big as a cathedral) – dominated the town. There was a lot of life in that little place as people busied themselves with their merchandise. It was also a very close community. The people of Kampen are fiercely loyal to each other. Even today, if an outsider criticises a Kampenaar to another local, he will loyally defend him.

The IJssel was very busy with ships going up and down the river. Money was spent on treasures that were housed in the old council hall and the church, thus helping to preserve the past for future generations, giving a picture of what life was like for their ancestors. Some very valuable pieces are still there today which show that, at the time, Kampen was one of the richest Hanze cities. The cigar industry was widespread and I remember well the hundreds and hundreds of cigar-makers who ensured that they produced the very best – even the cigars that Churchill smoked were made in our little town.

A number of very famous people were born in this town, including Professor Kolff, who invented the kidney dialysis machine in the 1940s, and whom I will talk more about later. It was well known for its two theological universities. Religion caused a lot of strife in the town and, although largely Protestant, there were large groups of many different religious bodies in Kampen. At one time, standing on a bridge in the town, you could count 12 different places of worship and I don't know how many manses for ministers and lay preachers. There were many divisions, and conflict about moral issues, right and wrong, dominated people's thoughts. Perhaps that was the reason I began to question these things later on in life.

A military high school was located in the town, and some of my uncles (who were military officers) underwent training there. It became a very famous school as, even before the war, Germany sent soldiers there for training. Overall, our little town was booming and it certainly had a lot of positive energy.

My family's roots were there. Many generations, both from my father's and mother's side, were born and brought up in Kampen, and they had a great influence on its history. The IJssel, stemming from the Rhine, was a great river for sailing along. I remember my father and I sailing there, enjoying the beauty of the scenery and the town.

My father was the product of a Jewish family from the beautiful town of Amsterdam. Although in her day it was somewhat unusual, my grandmother had married a much younger man; she was very good-looking. I remember her as a very kind-hearted person and, if we went to visit her on a Saturday, she would give us one or two pennies to make sure that we had enough money to buy some apples or other fruit when we returned – she didn't like us to buy sweets. It was always a delight to visit my grandmother and see my grandfather smoking his very long pipe in the cosy atmosphere of their home. My grandfather on my mother's side was in the cigar industry, and my grandmother was a great source of information. We loved to go and visit her and, later on in life, although she was nearly blind and we were grown up, she was still of tremendous help in answering any questions we had about our youth, as she was a fount of information. I used to kneel on the floor, listening to her for hours, as she was also a wonderful storyteller. She told us all about the little town where I was born, and its rich history. She had a tremendous interest in military life and, because all her sons were in the army, she hoped that they would become military men of courage. She proudly told us that all her brothers were involved in music. One was a music teacher and the other two were conductors of well-known bands, and, during their lifetimes, their music was often to be heard on the radio. I still have some adverts which promoted them as being the best flute players in the country, and I thought I would take the opportunity to show one of these here.

J.H. Dekker was my grandmother's oldest brother, who was quite a famous musician in his day. He, together with two other brothers, also founded the City Music Orchestra.

My grandmother also related stories about her own life, especially about the time when she was employed as a nanny to care for the Lord Provost of Delft's family. In those days, when she was young, that was quite an achievement. She would tell us some memorable stories about the times when King William III visited the Lord Provost Seimensvaders. When the old king died, she recalled, the students climbed onto the roof of the house to see him being buried in the cathedral in Delft, and she remembered all the shouting and screaming that went on. When I think back to that story, I realise not a lot has changed. My grandmother was a wonderful cook, too, and we often enjoyed sumptuous meals with her.

I feel privileged to have had grandparents who took an interest in us as youngsters, and also to have been born in Kampen, which had a charm and vibrancy that is still very much in evidence today. I am always happy to return. However, not long after I was born, dark clouds slowly came over Holland as the Second World War loomed. It was not an easy world in which to grow up.

2

Batten Down the Hatches

The war started and misery was everywhere. Food was very restricted and the nights were dark, with no lights. People had no idea what was happening and I was too young to understand what was going on. However, as the war began to take its toll, I also came to experience the unhappiness that everybody was talking about. My father and brother were taken away by the Germans and deported. First of all, my father was sent to Apeldoorn in Holland and then Nicolas, my brother, was deported to Germany.

My mother, being kind-hearted, helped everybody around her and had a lot of people in danger from the Nazis staying in the house, even hiding them under the floorboards when she knew the Germans were after them. She was quite a forceful woman and, as she was very much against the Nazi regime, people from all sides turned to her for help. In her own quiet way, she worked tirelessly to ensure people's safety and played an important role in providing a safe shelter – not only in the short term, but sometimes also for longer periods.

Because I was very young – still only eight when the war ended – and could easily walk along the streets without causing suspicion, I was able to help in many ways and worked very hard to assist my mother. My mother knew of various sources she could rely on to obtain some food for the people she was hiding. One day, she told me to go to a certain farm – no questions asked, I was just told to do it. I was informed that the farmer would be waiting for me with his hay cart and I was to direct him to our house. It is quite interesting to note that farms were very often located in the middle of our town and shelter was provided for the cattle in the backs of houses. People were

17

accustomed to seeing hay being hauled up and put through upstairs windows to be used for feeding the animals. This was very much the done thing in those days, so a farmer with a full load of hay going through the streets was a common sight. The particular farmer I was sent to meet had a cart laden with hay, pulled by two horses. However, unknown to me, a Jewish girl was hiding among the hay and had to be transported to our house, where she remained in safety for quite some time. I never realised at that time that I was actually helping with the underground work, but in so doing I saved this girl's life, because she managed to survive the war without being caught. My mother took situations like this in her stride and we luckily managed to get enough food for the people living with us.

Food was hard to come by. As I mentioned earlier, my father was in the tobacco industry and a lot of people knew him. So, at around the age of five, I was frequently sent to try and get some milk from the nearby farms so that my mother could feed the people she was hiding. The farmers knew my father well and I was often lucky enough to get some milk from them, but it was a very, very sad time.

Two things happened during the Second World War that made me determined to help others. At the age of about four or five, I remember very clearly going with my mother one Sunday afternoon to visit an uncle of hers (a brother of my grandmother). I always loved to visit my great-uncles because they were, as I have said, very good musicians and all of them could play an instrument of some sort. It was marvellous to hear them playing the flute, the violin and the trumpet. Sadly, the uncle we had gone to visit that day was quite ill and, while I was at his house, something happened which has stayed with me all my life. Because I had never visited a seriously ill person before, I was surprised when a very bitter taste suddenly came into my mouth, and I had to ask my mother if we could leave as I thought I was going to be sick. I was not actually sick at all, but the bitter taste remained in my mouth until we had returned home. The next day, my great-uncle died.

Later in life, I realised that a bitter taste always appears in my mouth when somebody is dying. I really didn't understand its significance at first, but then I noticed that, wherever we were, if there was somebody there who was very ill and I got this taste in my mouth, then usually the next day that person would die. It is a great gift, because if I meet patients and am uncertain about their health, but get that taste in my mouth, I always send them immediately to their doctor or the hospital. Very often, I have not even needed to examine these patients or manipulate them in any way, because I knew that they were very seriously ill. This particular phenomenon has stayed with me throughout my life.

Another very peculiar thing happened during the winter of 1944. At that time, we often had to live in darkness. When there was a threat of bombardment, we were naturally completely cut off from electricity. In addition to this, our windows had to be covered with thick black paper during the black-out so that no light was visible from the houses. We had no candles to provide us with light. We did, however, have a little windmill at home, which helped a bit with this problem. During air raids we were locked in underground shelters. I noticed that when I was sitting across from people, if it was pitch dark, I could see colours around them. Later on in life, when I learned that everybody has an aura, I realised that was what I could see. Occasionally some people can see these colours. When I learned about Kirlian photography (which can be used to photograph auras), I realised that this was not so odd, but a science that existed, although auras are not seen by everybody. I was aware that these things were gifts that God had entrusted to me, which I could use in the future to benefit others. My perception of things became so strong that usually I could intuitively tell my mother when there was danger around.

Because I was very underweight and, as the doctor had told my mother, completely undernourished, I became quite nervous. As a result of this nervous condition, I often became uncontrollable and difficult to handle. In fact, I was always looking for something to do, as I got bored very quickly. I realised what the Germans were capable of, though, and knew very well that I could not do anything wrong or they would shoot me. I became more aware of this when I heard of acquaintances of my mother's who were shot because of their underground work in the Resistance. My mother had to be very careful of the dangers involved when protecting others against the enemy.

One day, I put the whole town under tremendous stress. My mother, who was trying to get coupons for the many people she was looking after, was standing in a queue at the distribution office. As my father's youngest brother was a civil servant and in charge of distributing these coupons, I knew that he would help my mother to the best of his ability. Naturally, after a while of waiting in the queue, I got very bored. I noticed a bell quite high up by a drainpipe and, to relieve my boredom, quickly climbed up the pipe and pressed the bell. It turned out to be an air raid alarm and the whole town was thrown into a state of panic.

The Germans were raging and everybody was greatly distressed. My uncle, I remember, came out of his office, shouting about what could have happened. They knew that as the alarm had gone off from that distribution office, somebody must have touched the bell. Until today, nobody ever found out who did it because I was like quicksilver, and speedily hid myself under my mother's big raincoat! The newspapers reported the alarm but, as nobody knew who had set it off, luckily I escaped notice.

That was the sort of thing I got up to and my mother, I am sure, had quite a job keeping me under control. When it came to pestering the Germans, I was always number one, because I really hated them, knowing how much harm they were doing to our town and its people. Usually, when they marched along the street, as boys we would yell at them, singing '*Tom Tom kijk eens om, kijk eens naar beneden. Kijk eens naar die grote stad. Heel Berlin is plat.*' The words meant that when the English (Tommies) flew over our town, they were to look down, see what the Germans had done and then go and flatten Berlin. This made the Germans absolutely furious and usually we had to run away very quickly, otherwise they would have shot us. At the beginning of the war they were not so vicious, but as the war heightened they became more and more frightening.

Food was always in short supply. I remember once, when we were very hungry, I heard that a greengrocer had prunes. I had never seen a prune in all my life but stood the whole day in the fierce cold waiting in a queue to get some as a surprise for my grandmother. After standing there all morning and afternoon, at seven o'clock at night, I was so disappointed when the greengrocer's wife told all the people who had been waiting patiently in the cold that her husband hadn't come back, so there would be no prunes for them. When I went to my grandmother's house, she noticed that both my little fingers were almost frozen and managed to save them, although they have been squint ever since. If anybody asks me why I don't have straight pinkies, I explain to them that it happened during the war.

The war kept raging on. Things became more and more difficult and many Dutch people were half-starved. Schooling was almost impossible. My school was taken over by the Germans and used as a pigsty, so it became redundant. In the midst of all this turmoil, there was a little bright point. On a very wintry day, during an air raid, my little sister was born. I knew there was something going on as I was put out of the house. A short time later, I heard that I had a little sister, which would have delighted my father but, by this time, he had been taken away by the Germans, together with my brother. I can still remember the posters that were put up on noticeboards throughout the town decreeing that all men under the age of 65 had to enlist with the Germans, either in Holland or in Germany. Although a lot of men were deported to Germany, many remained in Holland. However, those who did not enlist ran the risk of being picked up and classed as an anti-Nazi. The difficult part was recognising collaborators, as you never knew who they were. They would then report you to the Germans for not having signed up and these people were then caught and deported, like my father and brother – some of them had to endure great hardship.

Everybody was delighted by the birth of my sister, until clouds gathered over that happiness. The doctor who was in charge of the birth found that she had been born with a cancerous tumour on her back. My mother, being as strong as ever, arranged a meeting that morning, took things in hand and said to the doctor that she would try and get some advice from Professor Kolff, a well-known surgeon and the inventor of the artificial kidney machine, now known as kidney dialysis. He examined my sister and told my mother that the tumour had been caused by an unbalanced food pattern – the result, in other words, of the limited variety of food available during the war. This had made our diet very one-sided. I often thought later that he was one of the first orthodox doctors who recognised how important food was in relation to good health, and that unbalanced food patterns can cause problems and possibly disease.

Our doctor and Professor Kolff decided that my sister would have to go to nearby Zwolle for treatment. Unfortunately, the doctor sympathised with the Germans but, fortunately for my mother, he managed to get transport to take my sister there, where she became the youngest person in the world to receive radium treatment, which was successful. My sister was saved, and is still alive and kicking.

After the birth of my sister, when things got back to normal a bit, I had more and more free time and was usually quick to get into mischief. One day I had a tremendous shock when some boys and I were searching for food. I remember being very hungry, because I had been sitting on the refuse heap at the local milk factory all morning looking for little pieces of black coal that had not been burned, so that I could give these to my poor old grandmother. I sat there for many hours and came home with no more than a pound of little pieces of black coal. In the afternoon, we went around rooting for food and I remember, as so often happened, that I had been eating grass to keep my rumbling tummy quiet. During our search, we came across an enormous car, full of food. I was amazed at what was in that car and had never seen the likes of it before – there were tins and packets, sugar and butter of unknown quantity. It was like paradise, and not a German in sight. Because I was small and very quick, I went into the car and started to throw out the food. After a while, planes came over and started to shoot at the car. Our lives were really in danger at that moment, and we crawled to the river where we hid ourselves in the rushes, terrified that they would find us and we would be shot. That experience left me with a small dent in my head where one of the grenade pieces hit it but I was lucky because it did not do any real damage. Amazingly, that was the only physical war wound I received. Often when people make fun of alternative medicine, I say to them, 'This is one of the reasons I have a hole in my head,' and let them feel the dent on top of my skull.

There were many great miracles in the Second World War, and one I shall never forget happened very late one night. At the time my mother was hiding quite a number of people in the house. The doorbell rang and I awakened to hear my mother going to the door. There stood a man wearing one clog and one normal shoe. He took a piece of paper out of his pocket and said to my mother that he had been given her address as a safe place to go to, and could he please come in as he had escaped from a ship which was taking him to a concentration camp. My mother let him in. He had scabies from top to toe, but she covered him with ichthyol ointment, which is still used today for scabies. It was lucky that she dealt with the man so quickly, because my aunt came over to warn my mother of a commotion in the street. The Germans were looking for a man who had escaped. My mother hid him under the floorboards, where he joined the other people already hiding there, and said to me, 'Now we have to go down on our knees and pray very hard that God will save us.' The Germans were going around like lions turning over every house from top to bottom. Then the miracle happened. Although they turned over every other house, they never even touched our front door – one of the real miracles that I experienced during the war.

Not long after, my mother was asked to go to Arnhem Oosterbeek to help out in a home for elderly people. Although there were people in our home being hidden from the Germans, my mother was needed there, so we had to go. We went to Arnhem Oosterbeek, where my mother's friend was the assistant matron; she also played a role in the work of the Resistance.

This brought about a turning point in my life. Again, there was no school there for me to attend, but next to the house was a big monastery which housed a lot of monks, and I got friendly with one of them. He played a great part in my young life. I must have been intelligent enough to take in what he said as he taught me a lot and made a very big impression on me. Although I was only very young, while we stayed there I went to help him in the herb garden every day. He told me all about herbs and plants, roots and trees, and what they were used for. With great passion, he taught me of God's creation and the wonders of nature. This instilled in me a great love for man and nature.

I still remember how heartbreaking it was when my mother came one day and said that we had to move, and fast. I never saw a place empty so quickly as then, which was very sad, but right under the eyes of the Germans everybody was led to safety for another day. Hitler bombarded Oosterbeek nearly to the ground. The house we had been living in was completely flattened. I remember a little friend, who was really good to me and still is. She and I were allowed, after these great bombardments, to see the damage. The death and destruction that the Nazis had wreaked was overwhelming. With my instilled love for God and creation, I could not understand why this was happening. That same day I promised God that if my mother and I were saved from this terrible hell, I would care about the well-being of people for the rest of my life. I hope I have kept that promise in the many years I have devoted to helping people and I will continue to do so until my dying day – I want to fulfil that promise to do what I can to help the less privileged, not only in this country but in others as well, and especially in the Third World.

The war raged on, but Hitler was losing ground. Finally, on 17 April 1945, our little town of Kampen was liberated by the Canadian and Scots troops. I can still picture them coming in their jeeps. That was the first time in my life that I had seen chocolate. When I was given some by one of the soldiers I took it home and showed it to my mother! She broke off a little piece and said 'Taste it!' I told my mother how wonderful it was and she said to me, 'Respect it all your life and never eat too much of it.' Nowadays, when I see the half- or one-metre bars of chocolate people buy, I still get shocked.

I remember my father came back from Germany in very poor health, his arms and legs thinner than a baby's. However, my mother fed him up as best she could from the little food we had and he survived. Every day, I went onto the street to watch people arriving back from concentration camps and places they had been hiding, and every day I looked to see if my brother was amongst them. Every day, I returned home without my brother and saw my mother crying in the hope that one day he would return. Finally, when he did come home, holding a bundle of coupons in his hand, he looked as if there had never been a war. He told my mother that he had been to every distribution office, telling them that he had just come back from Germany and needed coupons. He told my mother that we could have a big party now, as we had plenty of coupons.

He had been very lucky. Because he had told the Germans that he was a first-class cook, he landed work in the kitchen. Uppermost in his mind at that time was that he had to be able to eat if he was to survive his time in Germany, so he ended up in the best place.

I remember the marvellous party there was after we were all reunited and the war was over. The whole Dutch nation was full of promise – everybody wanted a united Holland, with one religion, one political party and the guarantee that there would never be a war again. People were so thankful that the war had ended that there was much harmony and togetherness. When I think of those parties and the wonderful festivities we had at that time, and the religious battles that Holland has had over the years and the tremendous number of political parties now, it is clear that those promises have long been forgotten. Holland is more divided now than it ever was before the Second World War.

When I see how people take food for granted and their disrespect for it, I still remember the days when we would have been so happy just to have a crumb to eat. Nowadays people throw away good food with no gratitude for what they have been given and no thought of the many people in the world suffering from hunger, who would give anything for that food. Important lessons have to be learned.

I suppose that my experiences during the war, of which I have given only a few examples in this chapter, taught me to respect life and to fight for it. Life is very valuable. When I look around and see how life is taken for granted in many people's eyes, I am often reminded of those days when life was so precious and how many people were cut down in their prime by the Nazi monsters. As the war progressed, things got so difficult that people started to eat tulip bulbs – and even their own dogs and cats – because they were so hungry. Luckily, by this stage the war was coming to an end.

Before it ended, however, something happened which would determine my future. It was an accident which took place during the summer of 1943. I never would have thought then, because of that accident, I would end up spending most of my life in Britain. I must have been about six years of age when we saw a bomber on fire going down over our town. The plane took a nosedive into the beautiful IJssel. When the bodies were dredged from the water, I saw the full horror: the six military men in the plane, who had been transporting bombs, had been shot down by the Germans and lost their lives. They were buried in the nearby cemetery and, after some time, I was asked to look after the grave of the navigator, Charlie Young. His full title was Flying Officer C.W.R. Young, Air Bomber, Royal Air Force, who died 13 June 1943, aged 27. I did this faithfully, and every Sunday went up to the cemetery, taking some flowers with me. With great devotion, I took this job upon myself and looked after that grave with great care. There were simple little crosses upon each grave, and flowers on each one. Later on, proper gravestones replaced these crosses, very nicely done and all in keeping with each other. The inscriptions on every grave read 'Sunshine and shadows by turn but always love', which reminded me of other young people who had lost their lives in their fight for freedom during that war.

Years later, I understood much better than I ever could as a child the words from the Bible: 'It is not in man that walketh to direct his steps.' (Jeremiah 10:23) Later it would become quite clear why this job had been entrusted to me.

Now that the war was over, I had to restart my education, which was very difficult. It wasn't easy to get me to attend school because I simply hated it. However, although I'd had broken years at kindergarten and the first classes of school (I missed primary two to primary four almost entirely), I was determined to work hard and make up for lost time. I really had to discipline myself to make up for those wasted years.

3

The Reluctant Scholar

By the time the war was over, I dreaded the thought of going back to school. My past experience of school made me almost hate it. I had also become used to a certain measure of freedom during the war. In Holland, education is very different to Britain. There are religious schools with biblical lessons and non-religious schools. My father was a very strict, religious man, and before the war he insisted that I go to the Christian school for infants, where they put great emphasis on the Bible. Because I was too young to understand what this was all about, I went to school quite happily at first. I attended a small school on the Ebbinge Straat. The schoolmistress there was Miss Aman. I just loved Miss Aman – she really impressed me. She had a very old-fashioned hairstyle and looked lovely. She was also a good storyteller and in the morning I loved to listen to her as she told us stories from the Bible – until somebody in our neighbourhood died and I heard people saying that he was going to heaven. Miss Aman used to tell us all sorts of wonderful stories from the Bible and about people going to heaven or to hell, so I was very intrigued by the whole subject. Being inquisitive, this led me to ask questions, and I kept asking questions until one day Miss Aman went to see my father and mother and told them that it would probably be better if I went to a school where they did not teach the Bible as she felt that the Bible stories were really troubling me, and that the questions I kept asking were really not suitable for the other children to hear.

I was moved to another school where the headmistress was called Miss de Groot. She was a much stricter headmistress and it was a much bigger school but, nevertheless, I loved to go to this school with my cousins in the Panjansteeg. I went faithfully and quite enjoyed my time there until the Germans took the building over and the school had to be closed. By that time, I had managed to learn a little bit from primary one. My father then wanted me to go to another religious school. I did quite well there and my new teacher, Miss Nip, was quite understanding but, again, my questions about the Bible came to the fore. She decided to talk to me at lunchtime and made such an impression on me that we remained friends all our lives. Suddenly, that school was taken over by the Germans to be used as a pigsty so, basically, from primary two until primary four, I received no formal education apart from an occasional day here and there in a church or in a hall, but it was so sporadic that I had to have extra teaching at home.

Back in primary four, after the war we all had to work very hard to make up for lost time. The Julianna School had quite a few good teachers then and Miss van Dyk was especially kind to me. She often came to school in a horse and carriage and bribed me by saying that if I was extremely good and obedient she would take me home in her horse and carriage, as she lived near me. This was, of course, a very exciting experience and I enjoyed it so much that I started to love school, until a gentleman teacher replaced Miss van Dyk. He was very strict and realised that I had a lot to learn so, of course, I began to hate school again. Nevertheless, I had no choice but to get on with it as I realised my mother was monitoring the whole situation. One day I went home with a bad report and I will never forget how terribly angry she was. The mark I had received for behaviour was very low. At that time, my father was still in Germany, where he had been deported.

The headmaster took the next class I went into. He was a real tyrant and, at one point, I remember only too well that when he talked about the Church, history or religion, he spoke at great length about Roman Catholics and how they had tortured the Protestants. I said in the class that I had also read of the followers of Calvin and Zwingli burning Catholics alive. This made him very angry and my punishment was to sit and work on my own in one of the classrooms for two weeks. He asked how I dared criticise the great reformers. Until this day, I still don't understand the behaviour of that headmaster as I knew only too well, even as a young boy, that when two people fight both are at fault. By that time I had started to form my own opinions on religion, being from a Protestant family on my father's side and a Catholic family on my mother's. After forming my own opinion on the whole matter, I decided to talk to the assistant headmaster, who took my class in primary six and was a wonderful person. His name was Mr Nijboer. He had a great influence on my life and I still regard him as a great philosopher and a most understanding teacher. With a lot of encouragement, he helped me and, again, I became very friendly with him. He had a small farm, where I was always made very welcome on my free days, and where he gave me a lot of private tuition to improve my levels at school. Although the headmaster had told him not to waste his time on me because I would never amount to anything and would be of no use to society, Mr Nijboer worked hard to prove him wrong and he certainly succeeded. He was very patient with me and, to this day, I am grateful for the contribution he made during my formative years.

Now that the first part of my education had finished, I had to go to secondary school. Here again, my impatient nature got the better of me and the headmaster had great problems with me, especially as he was influenced by the headmaster of my previous school. He was advised not to waste time on me and just to let me 'get on with things'.

Although I hated going to school, there were certain subjects I worked very hard at. Believe it or not, I was top of my class for poetry, singing and drama and was awarded first prize in most competitions. This made me feel as if I was somebody important. Luckily, experience soon knocked that out of me.

On one special evening, when almost the whole town was present, I was assigned three very special roles – the first of these was to sing on my own, the second was to play the main role in a short drama and the third was to recite a beautiful piece of poetry. The singing went perfectly, as did the drama. Finally came the piece of poetry. I recalled often seeing my father looking very intently at his watch while holding a meeting. While standing on the platform, I made the big mistake of copying my father by looking at my watch before starting to recite the poetry. That was frowned on in those days, and the audience all booed me. The next day, the local papers said how wonderful my singing and acting had been, but I got no sympathy when it came to the poetry as it was felt I had been too big for my boots! I also had to face my mother, who humbled me in such a way that I lost my confidence. The entire experience affected me to such an extent that it took a long time before my self-confidence returned and, even now, I catch a glimpse of this at times when I am lecturing in front of very large audiences, especially in the United States where I often come face-to-face with thousands of people. Nevertheless, I gained one thing from that experience which I have kept at the forefront of my mind all my life, and that is to remain humble, think of the simple things in life and never boast. Boasting is something that I hate hearing, which is probably due to the fact that I tried too hard in my younger days to impress people, but my own stupidity on the platform that evening brought me back down to earth.

Despite the many punishments I received for being naughty – which often led to the headmaster calling on my parents to complain – I still managed to progress through my school years.

Fortunately, I managed to find a lot of work outside school because I felt there was more to life than just homework and hanging about. By pure luck, one day I stepped into a bookshop and asked the owner if he could give me some work on Saturdays or in the evenings as I wanted to make a few pennies. Mr de Jong said he would think about it and asked me to go back the next day. I met his wife and I think she must have liked me, because I was offered the job of keeping his library of books in order, which I did with great enthusiasm.

This couple had a lot of business interests, including a printing company and, without my realising it, Mr de Jong was gradually familiarising me with all matters relating to his businesses. He even brought me to the printing company, where one of the foremen taught me all about printing. I had a whale of a time and decided I wanted to leave school as soon as possible. Of course, this was out of the question, as my parents would not allow it. Undeterred, one evening Mr and Mrs de Jong came to my parents' home and pleaded – especially with my mother – to permit them to train me in all aspects of their businesses, as they had no children of their own and felt I would be the perfect person to take over the running of their businesses one day. They added that they wanted to educate me in order to prepare me for this responsible position. Somehow, I felt that I could not do this.

However, I enjoyed being with them and loved them dearly. I looked after their dog, did a lot of tidying up for them and even worked late at night window-dressing. One particular occasion made Mr de Jong even more certain that he wanted to keep me in his business. That was on the Queen's birthday. It was a wonderful day and, as one of his shops sold things like lanterns, trumpets, hats and so on, he asked me to go there in the morning to sell these as we had a free day from school. As very little was being sold in the shop, I asked the manageress if I could set up a table outside and take all the goods out onto the street to see if I could sell more that way. By 12 o'clock I had sold the entire stock and when Mr de Jong arrived he was so happy that he hugged me. This convinced him that I was definitely the right person to run his businesses, and he made me a great offer. I felt awful because, in my heart, I realised that my future did not lie in that direction and so I declined all the offers made by Mr and Mrs de Jong. Sadly, following that difficult decision, I felt I could not continue working for them as a bad atmosphere developed.

One morning, on my way to school, I went to collect a little friend from her home. The whole area was blocked off as the house, with 13 people in it, had completely burnt down and was totally in ashes. This was an enormous shock to me and, although I was very young, this tragedy brought me to my senses. At that time, there were strong religious views being aired regarding this family which I was really too young to understand. There was much religious conflict in my home town and many teachings, due to the presence of the theological universities, and the many different religions that existed in the town. I made up my young mind then (and still believe today) that if you keep to the simplicity of the teachings of Christ, then you cannot go wrong. All thoughts of the reformers and the many people who had their own views on religion went to the back of my mind and I felt that if I could hold on to that belief, things would turn out all right.

I managed to get another good job when I was asked to arrange guided tours of our local church, which was almost as big as a cathedral. I studied the church's history and my guided tours became quite well known. These took place on Saturdays and in the evenings, and the pocket money and gifts that people gave me helped greatly towards my studies. I often had money left over, so I gave this to my mother who then shared it equally with others who were less privileged than us.

There was a pharmacy situated across the road from our house. Somebody new had taken over the business and was rebuilding the whole shop. I took a great interest and, as I knew quite a bit about pharmacy, asked the owner if I could help. The lady who owned the shop was very grateful for any help I could give her. I helped out whenever I could, after attending to the other little jobs I had. Believe it or not, due to our hard work, that particular pharmacy became one of the best in town. The owner encouraged me to study pharmacy and to get a degree in this field, so that I could work for her. The stories she told me about her underground work were absolutely fascinating. I respected this lady for the way in which she had stood up to the Germans as much as she could and, under their very eyes, did so much for the underground movement. Unfortunately, this took such a toll on her health that she became a very serious diabetic. Many people will remember her as a very bossy lady, but I got on with her well and she helped me a lot when I studied pharmacy which was, in those days, not very easy. In the next chapter, I shall share with you some of my experiences in that pharmacy, where I worked until after I graduated.

4

Janny Beuze – 'The Boss'

There I was, totally involved in pharmacy. This was something that my family approved of very much. I had to study extremely hard to obtain my degree and, because I also worked hard at the weekends to build up the pharmacy to be the best in town, it all became too much for me. I had very little time for any private life at all, as I studied and worked hard, but I must say that I got a lot of help from the boss, Janny Beuze. She was known throughout Holland for the part she played in the underground work during the Second World War, and she often told me gruelling stories from that period of her life. She was really on the front line, hence the reason for her being greatly honoured by Churchill and Eisenhower. Helping so many people and standing up to the Nazis had, sadly, taken its toll on her health during those years, and, for that reason, I often felt sorry for her. She certainly wasn't easy to work for, though – in fact, she was very difficult – but I learned then that diabetics were not always the easiest people to deal with. If she wasn't satisfied with something I did, I sometimes had to repeat the job over and over again until I perfected it. She examined any ointment I made in the mortar about ten times before it received her approval. Any other concoctions I made were also very sharply criticised.

However, her strict training was instrumental in me becoming a very good pharmacist, and I profited greatly from this experience. I travelled to do my studies and luckily, in July 1958, I got my degree. I remember that I fell down the stairs, with my certificate under my arm, right in the street in Amsterdam. That day eight of us had gone to sit the exams. In those days they were very difficult, which was emphasised by the fact that of those who sat the exams, only two of us succeeded.

I couldn't believe my ears when I heard I had passed. I arrived back in my home town to be greeted by a local fanfare and was treated like a king. Although my head was bursting with knowledge, I had no idea what the future would hold for me but, with the tremendous welcome I received on coming home, I decided that whatever I did, I would try hard to make a good job of it.

Next year, I went to the Krasnapolsky Hotel in Amsterdam to listen to a lecture being given by a German professor on homoeopathy – Professor Zabel – and sat next to an older gentleman. We talked about homoeopathy and when this gentleman asked me what I thought about it, I told him that it was good for spinsters and old wives. He looked at me and said, 'You must have a very small mind.' That really struck home. I started to talk to him and became very interested in what he had to say. I discovered who he was – Alfred Vogel from Switzerland, a guru of homoeopathic medicine in his time. He told me that he had just come back from a meeting with his best friend, Albert Schweitzer. What he had to say was completely enthralling and I felt that this meeting could open a door for me, so I wanted to keep in contact with him. When I went back to our pharmacy in Kampen, Janny Beuze, who had already made her business into a limited company of which I was a shareholder, was very happy.

When I told my friends about Vogel, nobody was interested. Homoeopathy was taboo in Holland at that time. Nobody wanted to hear about it. Because of the German occupation, anyone involved in homoeopathy had a bad name as Hitler and Himmler were great followers of it and helped homoeopathic doctors (those whose allegiance was with the Germans) in Holland during the war in all kinds of ways. Therefore, after the war anybody who had an interest in homoeopathy was looked on as yet another collaborator. When I shared with others the fascinating facts that Vogel had told me about, I lost most of my friends, even my girlfriend, who said this was the quickest route to quackery and I should certainly not get involved in it!

The principles of alternative medicine, however, were very attractive to me and, although I lost most of my friends and became very depressed about that, I wanted to pursue my interest. It was a very lonely battle and I was so down that Janny Beuze suggested I should take a break. This was an ideal opportunity for me to go to Scotland, which I had always wanted to do.

Why Scotland? Remember the plane that was brought down in flames in our town in 1943 and landed in the IJssel, and the navigator's grave I tended with so much care as a child? Well, his family had asked me many times to go over and meet them. So I thought the time was now right as I had always promised them that I would go after I graduated. Never did I think for one minute that my visit to Scotland would bring such an enormous change to my life.

I travelled to Scotland first by boat and then by train, and finally arrived in Edinburgh to be met by the father of the dead navigator, Charlie Young. It was a wonderful journey overall and the start of a much-needed break after such a lot of hard work. Before leaving Holland, my aunt handed me a letter and asked if I could deliver it to two ladies who lived in Edinburgh. When we arrived at my host's home, I met Charlie Young's mother and also his widow. She was a lovely lady who had only been married for six weeks when her husband lost his life in my country. We all had a wonderful time and got on so well together. We became very fond of each other. When I told Mr Young about the letter to be delivered to the two ladies, he said that it was amazing because they lived just up the hill at Royal Terrace, so we could go the following afternoon and deliver it.

When we arrived there the next day, the maid who opened the door said that the ladies were at their sister-in-law's house in Inverleith Place. Mr Young suggested that we deliver the letter to them there. When we arrived at this charming house, the lady who opened the door asked me to come in and introduced me to several people. Unfortunately, my English was very bad. When she asked me when I had arrived in Scotland, I replied, 'I comes tomorrow and here I is.' That was how bad it really was! Out of politeness, they didn't laugh at me but, some time later, we had quite a laugh about it. The ladies who lived in Royal Terrace asked me if I would like to have lunch or dinner with them. I asked my host, who had accompanied me, and it was arranged that I would go to their house for supper on the Sunday evening, this being the most convenient time.

When I arrived on the Sunday night, there were about 26 people already there. While I was sitting talking about Holland (to the best of my ability!), three younger ladies arrived and sat just across from me. One of them especially caught my eye. When we were asked to go through for dinner, I sat across from her. We talked together and I had a great time. Later on in the evening, when it was time to leave, it was decided that the three young ladies would take me. As fate would have it, a car picked up two of the young ladies and I was left alone with the other one.

As she was going in the same direction as me, she said she would show me the way back to where I was staying. We talked a lot and she impressed me so much that I asked if I could meet her again. So we met again the following Tuesday. By then, I had learned that the lady who had asked me when I had arrived and I had replied, 'I comes tomorrow, here I is,' was the mother of the girl who walked home with me. To cut a long story short, we became very friendly. I invited the family to come to Holland and, when they arrived about six months later, I got engaged to her. She is now my wife and has given me four daughters and we have ten grandchildren. Another great thing that the war had done for me!

I had the most wonderful time in Scotland and realised then that changes had to be made. This came about when my girlfriend came to Holland and we got engaged, because Janny Beuze became very angry and jealous of my new-found love and things became absolutely impossible between us. She apparently wanted me for herself and did not like the thought that someone else had come along with whom I wanted to share the rest of my life. She was overcome with jealousy, but thought that this relationship with my girlfriend would never last because, as she always said, there is a large sea between Holland and Scotland. She also felt quite secure in the fact that I was close to her, taking care of business matters and, because of the war, I had to carry a lot of responsibility. I certainly could not go on working there and, as I had acquainted myself with Alfred Vogel, I decided that I would take up his offer to work with him in Nunspeet to help him establish the first clinic for natural cures in Holland, which soon became one of the best places to go to for health and fitness.

On my second visit to Edinburgh, I was so amazed at the splendour of that beautiful city. On one occasion, between Christmas and New Year, I took a bus which, in those days, used to have a conductor on board. As the bus went round a corner, there was a man hanging around a lamppost completely drunk. The conductor went to the driver and said, 'Look at him.' The bus driver looked and said, 'Oh my, what a pity it is not me. Never mind, it is my turn next week.' I knew that Scotland had quite a reputation for drink and much later, when treating patients who were alcoholics, I realised just how big that problem actually is in Scotland.

5

Nunspeet – A Profitable Village

There are many people who think that I have made a lot of money in Scotland and in alternative medicine. That is not really true, but I do admit that we made a lot of money in pharmacy in a small village called Nunspeet. Let me tell the story.

On 2 January 1960, I went by train from my birthplace of Kampen to Nunspeet. I had a special mission as I was to meet Alfred Vogel, the man I had met in 1959 and with whom I had since been in contact in Holland. Vogel had just bought a house called Roode Wald, a lovely old mansion with a lot of wooded grounds. With the help of others, his ambition was to set up the first nature cure clinic in Holland. That day, he asked me if I could help as it was essential that he employed someone who was qualified to dispense medicines and also he wanted us to work together to make his clinic successful. It had all the necessary requisites to become an absolutely wonderful clinic, so I decided to accept his offer and, with the help of others, turn this building into a magnificent place.

Roode Wald became a marvellous clinic. In the early stages when we were trying to build up the business, the general manager, a charming gentleman (who was also friendly with Vogel), and his wife dealt with the day-to-day running of the business, while I concentrated on dealing with the treatments and medicines. I foresaw lots of difficulties though – the nurses were not always the easiest people to deal with, and there were also some very dishonest staff ranging from housekeepers to domestic staff, so we had great problems. The positive side of all this was the focus on the remedies made by Vogel, and on some of the remedies we made together. They started to become well known in Holland and, in turn, the business started to flourish. However, I realised that the management of the clinic could not continue as it was although, despite the many difficulties we had (which mainly centred on the staff), the care and attention given to the patients was not affected and their health was helped greatly.

One night, the head nurse called me to come over as something disastrous had happened. The general manager was at a conference in Germany and, that night, his wife had run away with many of their possessions. He was so devastated when he returned that he felt like giving up. With no government help or grants, it was very difficult to keep the business operating.

A lot of the staff we employed were not as caring or devoted to people's health as they could have been. The staff problems – drunken nurses, theft and unreliable doctors – created a difficult situation. Dutch law stipulated that a medically qualified doctor had to be in charge of the therapies. However, we soon realised that medical doctors specialising in alternative medicine were very scarce in those days, and we therefore had no alternative but to employ some unsavoury characters sometimes. I remember one who had long hair, tied back with a pink ribbon. Eventually it got so dirty that it was almost black and we realised that he could not be allowed to treat patients. Then we employed another doctor who developed a phobia of sunshine and would always walk around wearing dark glasses. I remember he once visited my wife on a wintry, snowy day wearing sandals without socks, and asked her if he could sit on the terrace outside to have his cup of tea. We employed some very eccentric characters; but although these doctors didn't really do any work, we had to take them on in order to satisfy the authorities. My book *Who's Next?*, which I wrote some time ago, is full of very funny stories about characters like these and also about patients I have treated over the years. Some of these stories are really unbelievable.

Being Vogel's friend, I advised him that it would be better if he sold the business as, the way things were at that time, there was no future for Roode Wald. On the other hand, I felt it would be a good idea to continue producing the remedies so that the Dutch people could still benefit from them. So, after running the business for three years, we finally reached the decision to close the clinic but continue to manufacture the remedies.

After leaving Roode Wald, the first thing we did was to set up a sales office in Nunspeet and then one in The Hague. I was appointed director of the whole operation and things improved greatly from then on. Bioforce – or Biohorma in Dutch – became very well known. We then concentrated on building up the little business we had in The Hague, which was being managed by Mr Bolle. I shall never forget when Mr Bolle, Mr Drenth (one of the directors of Bioforce in Holland) and myself met in Utrecht and, on the stairs of Hotel Terminus, made a decision to establish a factory at Elburg in Holland. We initially set up business in the house next to where Mr Bolle lived and later gradually started to build up the company in Elburg which, with a workforce of nearly 500 and a large turnover, became one of the biggest and most successful businesses in Holland. That was something to be really proud of.

That was not the only wonderful thing that happened in Nunspeet. As the village was such a lovely place to holiday in and had a beautiful hotel called Hotel Ittmann, I thought it would also make a charming place to get married. My future wife and I were very lucky because I had heard about a piece of land (roughly two acres) which I could buy extremely reasonably. We built our first house there and called it Tukien.

It was a glorious summer's day when we got married in Nunspeet and, as I had already made a name for myself, it was a very big wedding, where the police had to direct the traffic outside the hotel because a lot of well-wishers had come along. We treasured the little house we had built, and three of our children were born there. It was a marvellous way for us to start married life. Everything went well, there in the woods of Holland with its beautiful scenery, not far from the secret village I wrote about in *Do Miracles Exist?* We were both very busy and, although I was building up Vogel's business, something else happened that brought us a lot of money. The biggest pharmacy in the province was located in this village. It was well known throughout Holland for the many different items it sold. The owners were delightful people and Mr Hiddink, its owner, who was also a famous artist, had an interesting circle of friends. They were all local artists and we soon became friendly with this wonderful bunch of people. Although perhaps not famous in Holland at that time, they certainly became famous later as artists – people like Jos Lussenburg, Chris ten Bruggenkate, Briett and others. Mr and Mrs Hiddink had a daughter called Herma. She became like a sister to me as we worked together sometimes. Mr Hiddink wanted to devote more of his time to painting and, as he knew I was a pharmacist, asked if I would be interested in taking over their business. It was a difficult decision as we had just got married and had little money but, after a lot of consideration, we decided to take the plunge. After we took over the business we had lots of fun running it, and I rebuilt it three times during our ownership. It expanded into five businesses under one roof, employing a staff of almost 30 people. Not only was it a pharmacy, but it was also the biggest photographic business in the district and the first place in Holland where films were developed and photographs ready within a few hours. It became well known and the turnover was astonishing. In all fairness, we made a lot of money there.

In the '60s, we opened another two pharmacy businesses and Joyce, my wife, took control of the photography side. She cleverly completed a four-year course in photography in just one year and became very well known in this field.

Running these businesses was very time-consuming but, on top of that, I still found time to work with Vogel building up his company, Bioforce. However, business was not really my forte: I have always said that I am not a businessman. My heart was with people and my aim in life was to help others. Although I worked hard to help people in the course of my work in the pharmaceutical business, I felt I wanted to do more, so I started lecturing on health, and these talks were very well attended. In between, I managed to visit countries throughout the world with Vogel, where we studied the way in which people from other countries lived, what they did and why certain illnesses were unheard of in certain parts of the world. I had already studied the Vogel philosophies and the way in which he produced the medicines. We had even been to Switzerland several times to study the manufacturing process of medicines. I advised Vogel that this was the only way in which we could make his business profitable. I was therefore the first person to set up a manufacturing plant in Holland. We started on a small scale, but the plant soon grew and is now so big that it also makes herbal remedies for other companies and is a great success.

I wanted to study more and go to China, and so I came out of the Dutch operation for a period in 1962 with enough money to enable me to further my studies. I wanted to know all about osteopathy (which I studied in Germany and then later in Holland). At the end of 1959, I had treated a Roman Catholic priest with very severe neck pain. During the course of our conversation, he mentioned that he sometimes worked in China and told me all about the philosophies of acupuncture. This whetted my appetite so much that I had a strong desire to go to China and learn about it. The priest said that this would be very difficult to do, but that through the Red Cross it could probably be arranged for me to go to a place where acupuncture was studied. I waived his fee of course, and much later, thinking about this conversation, I wrote to him. Lo and behold, he managed to get me into China, for which I shall always be very grateful. Anyone who wants to know about acupuncture needs to understand the philosophies behind it. I had first-class masters to help me with this, especially Professor Tsjang, who was of great assistance during my career and was the first man in the world who could show the existence of meridians. I gathered quite a lot of knowledge on this subject during my time there. I also worked with a Dr Tan in Kowloon, Hong Kong. Dr Tan adapted acupuncture so that it could be used to treat Westerners.

However, I think I gained most knowledge while working in the Veterans' Hospital in Taipei, Taiwan. I had the most wonderful time there and, along with the other students, learned not only about classic acupuncture but also about homoeopuncture – the method of dipping needles into homoeopathic solutions and inserting them in the acupuncture points. Although we would never be permitted to practise acupuncture in this country as we did in the Veterans' Hospital, it was still great experience. I remember very clearly working with a doctor who gave me the opportunity of gaining some practical experience in this field. She said I could take the cases I wanted, plus some of the difficult ones, which I was very pleased about. At one point, I was most astonished when the doctor brought a patient with Bell's palsy before me. She asked me how I treated people with Bell's palsy in Britain, and when I told her a smile appeared on her face. She asked the patient to lie down and then took an enormous, long needle, inserted it at the side of the patient's cheek, behind the eye, right to the brain, twiddled the needle a bit and then pulled it out. The Bell's palsy had disappeared! I nearly fainted in disbelief at what I had just witnessed and asked the doctor what would have happened if this woman had developed a haematoma. She said in China that is the patient's responsibility. Fortunately, in most other countries, the minute a patient walks through the doctor's door, the doctor is responsible for the well-being of that patient.

I saw quite a few amazing things and at the same time learned a lot. I felt very privileged that the Chinese disclosed their secret knowledge of some very important acupuncture points to me as there is still a great deal of secrecy in China concerning the various acupuncture points they have discovered and worked with. That was a most interesting time in my life, and was to be of great assistance in my career.

Here we are, back in Nunspeet in 1963. It is an absolutely wonderful place which brought us as a family a lot of prosperity. Nunspeet had so much to offer and I will always remember the many happy times we had there.

One particularly happy moment was when the village celebrated its freedom from the Nazis. Because of my British connections, the provost of the village asked if I could find out the name of the captain or commander in charge who finally freed Nunspeet from the Germans. This was a difficult job, but I finally traced this gentleman to Kent and asked him if he could come over to parade through the village in a Polar Bear Brigade jeep, giving the 'V' for Victory sign to show that we had been freed from the Germans. This he agreed to do. My friend Jos Lussenburg and I had a discussion and agreed to organise an enormous festival in the local Orange Park, where the flame of freedom that Captain Strawson was to ignite was positioned. Not long after we had organised this event, we managed to find out the original base of the Polar Bear Brigade. We had a great time re-enacting how Nunspeet was freed from the Nazis in 1945. Our local circle of friends all had a wonderful time and when Captain Strawson went through the village in the front of the jeep giving the 'V' sign, with Jos Lussenburg and me sitting in the back, we really had a lot of fun. Nunspeet certainly brought us a lot of happiness and, in addition to this, as I have already said, we had a lot of good fortune in business, turning the local pharmacies into the biggest in the district.

Of course, building up Bioforce and the pharmacies took a lot of time. During the years that we worked and lived in Nunspeet, even although we were both very busy, we still managed to have all of our four children there. The first to be born was Fiona, in April 1961. My father and mother were still alive then and, as they also lived in the same village, they were of great help to us in looking after the children. Fiona qualified in nursing and went to work for the health service. Later on, she worked as a health visitor before securing an important post in London. She now has two children, both very gifted in music.

Our second daughter, Janyn, was born in April 1963 and, as we were convinced that she was going to be a boy, up until the moment she was born we didn't have a name for her. I remember going into Angelicq's house (our friend who lived across the road) and my wife, Joyce, and I looked at each other when she asked me what we were going to call the new baby. I replied 'Janyn' and Joyce said, 'Funnily enough, that was the name I had in mind.' Janyn studied science and is now married to Dr Jen Tan. They both later took over and became managing directors of Bioforce UK, after Jen had helped me to run my practices in Scotland. Janyn and Jen have three very intelligent children.

Our third daughter, Tertia ('the third'), was born in February 1967 and married a Dutchman. She studied as a medical herbalist and manages one of our clinics. Tertia and her husband, Michiel, are also very happily married and have two lovely children. Michiel worked in the same place as I did when I was later in Holland.

By the time Mhairi, our youngest daughter, was born in August 1969, we had moved to a new home which was called de Berken. She studied osteopathy and married one of her lecturers in that subject. They now have a big practice in London and three wonderful boys.

So, Nunspeet was not only prosperous financially, but was also prosperous in that it gave us four wonderful daughters of whom, along with their families, we are very proud.

As life went on, we began to feel that we wanted to spend a bit more time with our daughters. We considered taking a sabbatical and going over to Scotland to my wife's family home, to spend at least a year with the children. We decided to keep our house in Holland and possibly return to live there after our sabbatical had come to an end. However, when we arrived in Scotland in 1970, I fell totally in love with the country. We bought a huge property in Troon which we decided to call Mokoia. It had about 40 rooms and, because it was so big, we felt that the most practical thing to do was to convert it into flats. However, when Alfred Vogel came over and set eyes on Mokoia, he had different ideas. He said, 'This is a wonderful place – why don't we set up a residential clinic here? It would be a great opportunity for people who live in this part of the world to be given the chance of being introduced to nature cures.' I looked at the magnificent property and realised he was right. Why should we keep such beauty to ourselves? Why not get the whole place sorted out and open it as a clinic? Over the years, I had studied widely in alternative treatments and was particularly interested in such areas as homoeopathy, osteopathy, acupuncture and naturopathy. I had also undertaken several studies on these subjects. I felt I had to think about Vogel's suggestion seriously.

This was emphasised when God sent a little angel to see me one very rainy Sunday afternoon. A lady stood at the front door and asked my name. She said that we had studied certain forms of homoeopathy and breathing exercises under the same professor in Germany. That was Professor von Durckheim. We had a wonderful conversation and realised we had a lot in common. Many Scottish people will still know this lady – Dr Annelie Hennessy. Not only was she very well respected in Glasgow, but she was also a consultant at the Homoeopathic Hospital. Dr Hennessy thought that Mokoia would make a wonderful place in which to treat patients and that I should start a residential clinic there as soon as possible. I grew even more determined to do so. We thought long and hard about it and decided to get the property completely in order. As it transpired, the chosen name for the house was very apt, as Mokoia means 'Island of Rest'.

We made up our minds to set up this new clinic in Troon and to say goodbye to good old Nunspeet. This was very difficult because we had to leave all our friends and family there, but I really felt that setting up this clinic in Scotland was my calling. I loved the people, I loved the country and, once more, that old biblical saying 'It is not in man that walketh to direct his steps' (Jeremiah 10:23) came to mind. The decision was made to take the first step into a completely new and unknown venture. We had to start from scratch, but the business soon began to grow and continued to expand on an unbelievable scale.

But now, I would like to say a little more on my children and grandchildren.

6

Four-Leaf Clover

Some time ago, an elderly lady sat in my waiting room, clutching her handbag on her lap. I could see she was unsteady on her feet, so I helped her to a chair in my consulting room and said I would see her after tending to a patient in the treatment room. As it was a particularly busy day, and as I was so absorbed in other things, I felt terribly embarrassed when I realised that I had actually forgotten she had been waiting to see me. She must have been sitting there for about half an hour before I returned and, on entering the room, I could see that she was looking intently at the family photograph hanging behind my desk. After apologising profusely, she said not to worry, as she had been engrossed in looking at the photograph. She then enquired if she could ask me a question. In her broad Scottish accent, she asked if all those children were mine. I replied that, yes, I had four daughters, four sons-in-law and 10 grandchildren. With unconscious humour, she replied, 'My, my, isn't it wonderful to see what a wee man like you is capable of.' It made me smile for the remainder of the day.

Indeed, we have been richly blessed with four beautiful daughters, each with her own charm. At each birth, I wondered if this time it would be a boy. However, they were all girls and this was probably lucky; they have all given us such a lot of pleasure and, as daughters are usually very devoted to their fathers, I am very fortunate. They are a nice mixture of nationalities, with Dutch, German, Jewish, English, Scottish and Irish blood. I suppose the combination of genes was helpful as they all did well at school and, thankfully, were never any trouble to Joyce or myself.

Because my wife had worked in education and knew more about

44

child psychology than I did, I told her she could take the lead and that she could rely on my total support in their upbringing. They were a real pleasure as they were growing up. As they are now all married, our lives have been further enriched by the addition of ten grandchildren – all with a wonderful mixture of Dutch, Scottish, English, Irish, German, Jewish, Chinese and Singaporian blood.

I treasure every one of my daughters and each has such great qualities. They all played their part in helping me in the clinic as they were growing up and I encouraged them all to do a stint at the reception desk when I was practising. This brought them into contact with people and, during their school holidays, they were very helpful in assisting me whenever necessary. This did not always meet with the greatest enthusiasm because they felt their father was strict and Victorian, but that was the way I was brought up and I tried to instil in them that life was not easy and could sometimes be quite difficult.

Sometimes it was with great hilarity that they undertook their work and I well remember the time when my eldest daughter, Fiona – who was still at school when she helped with reception work – once knocked on my door and, with a long face, showed in a very nice female patient whom she thought was after her father. She opened the door for this lady and said, 'Daaaad, this is your next patient, but Mum needs you.' This was to make absolutely certain that the well-dressed and made-up lady knew I was married. I later asked Fiona why she had said that and she told me that she had become suspicious because the lady in question had been in the cloakroom for about half an hour putting on her make-up and dolling herself up. This was just one of the funny things that happened when my daughters attended to patients at the reception desk.

When she grew up, I was so proud to see Fiona succeeding in her nursing career and later on, with her nursing degree, she obtained a very responsible job in London. I was happy that she too wanted to help others. She married Peter, a very good artist who came from Dorset and set up a successful business in Troon – a framework gallery that not only showcases his own work but also that of other artists. He handles some of the most beautiful paintings, which is lucky for me as I have a weakness for paintings. They are blessed with two wonderful children. The oldest one, Michael, has an exceptional aptitude for music and plays the violin and piano. The genes of both my family and his father's family are evident in him. As there were so many well-known musicians in my family, Michael has inherited a talent going back generations on both my mother's and father's side. I can never overestimate how proud I am when I see him performing in big halls full of people and the applause that he gets for his talents. His younger sister, Rachel, very clever at school, also has a gift for music.

My second daughter, Janyn, to whom I have been very close since the day she was born, developed a strong flair for business that became evident from an early age. She had a little friend called Freddy. One day, they disappeared together and we could not find them anywhere. We were almost frantic with worry until they eventually returned with a bag full of coins. Janyn had suggested to her little friend that they look for acorns, gather them in big bags and sell them to the farmers, demonstrating a business aptitude when they were still at nursery and very young! It is therefore not surprising that she graduated with a degree in science and business studies and is now the managing director of Bioforce, the British arm of Biohorma, the company set up by Alfred Vogel and me. When I told the story to Vogel, he thought it was amazing that she had such flair. I thought it would be an excellent idea to put these business skills to good use in forming what was to become a leading company in herbal and homoeopathic medicine. Janyn married a very clever young doctor, who had great prospects in medicine but, luckily, they were both so business-minded that he joined her and together they have built up a very big business which is not only of great assistance to the well-being of many people, but also to the entire industry, as the research they undertake with their company benefits the field of alternative medicine and also provides employment for many people.

My first grandchild, Li-Anna, was a product of these two. Li-Anna was a most wonderful baby and when she was born it sank in that I was now a grandfather for the first time. I did not like the thought of that at all! Having a Peter Pan complex of always wanting to feel young, I had to get used to the idea. I have often heard parents saying what a marvellous feeling it is when they become grandparents. I never really understood that fully until Li-Anna was born, when I enjoyed the gift of my first grandchild. I have found having grandchildren to be one of the most wonderful experiences in my life. As Li-Anna was growing up and starting to talk, it was suggested that she called us Grandma and Granddad, but my wife and I did not want this at all. My daughter then said to me, 'You must not be so grumpy' and, from that moment, we were called 'Mumpy' and 'Grumpy'. As Li-Anna couldn't say the word 'Grumpy', she called me 'Dumpy' instead and, to this day, every grandchild I have calls me 'Dumpy'. She is now studying medicine. She was always very caring and I experienced that while in the process of writing this autobiography. Her parents were abroad on business and their nanny was looking after all three of the children at home. On one particular Saturday afternoon, when I was busy attending to many patients at my clinic at Auchenkyle, I suddenly saw Li-Anna floating around outside my consulting room window. When she caught my eye, she came to the window and said, 'Dumpy, I came to see if you were all right.' As a grandparent, it tugs at your heartstrings when a young girl, then just 14, cares so much for her grandfather that she has to come and make sure he is all right. It is a feeling that is difficult to put into words but, nevertheless, so heart-warming to experience. Joni, her little brother, who is named after me, has a great technical brain. He loves playing with his train set and planes, just as I used to do as a boy. The youngest one, Harriet, is a most humorous child who always amazes me with the way she chooses her words. Looking at this happy family, I am grateful for these great gifts.

My third daughter, Tertia, resembles me in looks the most and is also identical in character. She was in the limelight shortly after she was born when she appeared in the local newspapers as the best-looking baby in the town and was pictured being held by Miss Holland. As a baby she was photographed many times. She has a tremendous sense of humour and a gift for cheering people up when they are depressed or down and, because she works with me, she is greatly loved by the patients. When I went to Holland to undertake my research work, Tertia came with me to assist with the project to test allergies, as she was a qualified medical herbalist. She was of great help in the clinical and research work we set up in Holland. There was a wonderful boy, Michiel, who worked at that clinic during his holidays, a very serious fellow who worked with great devotion. He became attracted to Tertia, with her usual charm, and it was a surprise to me when she told me that they both wanted to talk to my wife and myself about their friendship. They got on very well together and, after a while, became engaged and, later on, got married. They then announced that they were going to Canada where Michiel, a real Dutchman, had a business in snowmobiles. They went to Bathurst where they started their business and were there for a number of years before returning to Holland. Thankfully, they now live quite near us. Their first baby was called Gemma. She stole our hearts and I have written about her in many of my books. She was a little miracle, as she weighed only 1lb 8oz when she was born. However, she has grown up to be the most loving girl and is now doing very well. Some time later, her little brother, Dale, was born. He is the image of his mother and, therefore, of myself. It is amazing how you can see yourself in your children and grandchildren, and he is exactly like us in many ways. Even when he was only a year old, I could still see some of my mannerisms in him. They very much enjoy family life and it is a great delight to see the children playing together. Dale has a mischievous nature similar to his mother's as she was growing up. I remember when we were staying in the Grand Hotel in Toronto that Tertia, at about the age of five, sneakily turned around all the 'Do Not Disturb' signs on the bedroom doors so that they read 'Please Make Up The Room'. The chambermaids wakened up all the confused guests, who managed to see the funny side when they realised what Tertia had done. On another occasion, when we went to the Deer Park at Loch Lomond, she turned round all the signs to point in the opposite direction and that caused great chaos. These were some of the little sneaky things she did that made everyone laugh.

My fourth daughter, Mhairi, was also born in Nunspeet. She was the least good-looking when she was born. My friend, the doctor who was there at the birth, said that she would be very beautiful one day, and he was right. She is now the best-looking girl of the four, and the older she gets the more beautiful she becomes. Every time I see her, I can hardly believe she is my daughter. She has a very serious character and was therefore very precise at school, very correct in her speaking and writing. Nowadays, she often writes for magazines and newspapers. She, of course, came from Holland to Scotland and it was quite funny when she mixed English nouns with Dutch grammar and verbs. Her teacher would often laugh, telling her colleagues that Mhairi had said, 'That's how you *don't* do it.' She went on to study osteopathy and her lecturer, a very lovely young man, recognised her beauty. When we were told that her lecturer had fallen in love with her and they both wanted to tell us how happy they were, they hoped we would give them our approval. Marcus, now her husband, is a great friend to me. We do a lot of things together and, as he has his own clinic, I often help him and vice versa. On the many times that we travel to and from the airport, we have the most interesting discussions and the most profitable business meetings, where we talk about our ideas, the formulation of remedies and compare these with patients' results. Mhairi and Marcus produced three good-looking boys, all very sporty. One of them, Jonathan, is already very advanced at playing tennis. Cameron, serious like his mother, is very thoughtful. It was an emotional moment when he thought I was very worried about something. He came up to me and put his arm around me and said, 'Dumpy, I love you.' The youngest, Oliver, is a bit like myself – always on the go, in perpetual motion and full of mischief. The three of them once appeared on television with me on *This Morning* with Richard and Judy. They behaved unbelievably well when they were asked lots of questions.

It is amazing to see how my grandchildren have developed. Although all ten have different qualities and characteristics, there are similarities between them.

My daughters were all born in Holland and could only speak Dutch when they came to Britain. My wife and I were often criticised for not hiring the services of an English tutor. We actually did this on purpose. Being in the teaching profession, my wife had often seen how quickly children pick up a new language in the classroom, and learn much quicker that way, so we decided to let our daughters learn like that rather than putting the extra burden on them of having a tutor teach them a foreign language. The wisdom of that decision was evident when they obtained very high grades in their English Highers.

So, we have been very fortunate with our children and grandchildren, who are all so happy and healthy. When I cast my mind back to the days when my children were small and I took them out with their bicycles or for little walks, I often regret that I was not able to spend more time with them. My work has taken up such a lot of my time that perhaps my family life was sacrificed a little. In retrospect, I now feel I should have given more time to my children. As one gets older, there is nothing more regrettable than not having made more of life and enjoying family life to the full when one's children are small. To have healthy children is a great gift. Now my daughters have all established themselves so well, and life has so much to offer them.

7

Mokoia – 'Island of Rest'

Mokoia was a beautiful mansion overlooking the Clyde, with the most marvellous features and a library like I have never seen before, built from the roots of a walnut tree. There is a love story about the island of Mokoia in New Zealand, where Hinemoa, a Maori prince, finds his princess on the island of Rotorua. It is such a beautiful story and very touching. The spirit of the house was very invigorating and the atmosphere of the whole place was like a breath of fresh air.

However, to bring the house up to the standard required to transform it into a clinic, a great deal of work had to be done. A lot of refurbishment took place and we worked for a whole year to get the property in order. After all the work had been completed, we thought it would make a wonderful clinic. It was therefore a great shock to me when – after all the work had been completed, with everything looking absolutely beautiful, and we were ready for business – there was no interest in it at all. Many days I prayed very hard for God to send patients because I was itching to get started, after the busy times that I previously had in Holland, where I led a very full life.

The children had all gone to school – some to nursery, others to primary school – and my wife felt that as all our money had gone into renovating the property, she had to go back to teaching in order to help financially, and so she took up a job as a teacher.

Gradually, the Scottish people became curious about what we had to offer and soon people started to stream in. As well as the residential clinic, we also had a day clinic. The residential clinic soon became full and the day clinic also started to get busier and busier. I managed to find some great staff to help me, especially my physiotherapist, Janice

Thompson, and later Teresa Sampson. We also arranged seminars and it gives me a lot of pleasure to think back to the great days when we gave yoga and teaching seminars. A few of our successes became known and many people then wanted to be helped. The osteopathic and acupuncture clinics grew very quickly and we soon had our hands full.

In those early days, I remember one of the female patients we had who was quite ill and had been confined to her bed for years. After treatment, she was like a new person and was able to return home. A lot of other patients then followed, as this was seen as a miracle. A young Rangers footballer who had given up playing also came to me for help. After he had completed his treatment at the clinic, the papers were full of stories of how this young man had regained his health. Another lady, who came from the Isle of Arran and had to be brought in on a stretcher, returned home after three weeks of receiving treatment and was able to walk again. After that miracle, nearly half of Arran became patients!

Things were going very well and, as we needed healthy food for the kitchen at the clinic, I went to the local health food store. They never usually stocked the items we needed, so I tried to get the addresses of their suppliers from the lady who owned the shop. She asked if I would be interested in taking over her business, and that was how I bought my first health food store. I had planned to close it but, one evening after I had taken over, the lady who worked there came to my door and asked if I would keep it going as she loved working there and would do her best to run the shop, so I would have no problems. I decided to give it a try. I helped her a little bit and, after we started work on it, the store grew. It enabled us to provide the right products at the right time.

Strangely, similar problems arose at the residential clinic as had come up in Holland. We had many problems finding domestic staff to do the cleaning and staff to look after the patients. This made things very difficult and, for almost the same reasons as Alfred Vogel and I had to close the Dutch clinic, we decided to close the residential clinic in Scotland. I found this a very difficult decision. However, I still wanted to be able to help patients, so we reopened as a day clinic only, which was a great success and very busy. We opened this six days a week from 7 a.m. to 10 p.m. Patients came from all over the world and, as these included a lot of famous people, the clinic soon developed a reputation and we were sometimes so busy that I could hardly cope.

We already used some of Vogel's remedies that I had brought from

Holland, but we wanted to be able to stock the whole range of his products. As Vogel had an importer in England, Joe Bennett, from Chorley in Lancashire, I contacted him to see if he could provide the extra medicines I needed to treat all my patients. We met on a Monday morning at Carlisle station, together with his friend, Bert Barlow. We discussed different options and Joe finally offered me the whole range of Vogel's imported remedies if I was willing to take a clinic once a month in his premises in Chorley. I naturally accepted his offer and still honour it now, more than 30 years later, by regularly taking clinics there.

I have many memories of these monthly visits as, when I started there in the '70s, a lot of time was spent travelling to and from the clinics. I used to leave on the night train on Sunday about 11 o'clock and arrive in Carlisle at around 1 o'clock in the morning. On my arrival at Carlisle station in the middle of the night, I sometimes had to spend three-quarters of an hour – or sometimes even a full hour – waiting for a connection to Preston. Because of these long waits, I sometimes witnessed such disturbing scenes – fights and other unspeakable things – in the waiting-room that I had to leave. On one particular night I was nearly attacked by a drunken youth and had to leave very quickly.

When I arrived at Preston the first time, Joe Bennett was there to meet me. Having had just a few hours' sleep, I started the clinic at 7 a.m. for 7.30 a.m. When I arrived at the clinic, the place was usually as packed as Lourdes. My practice was open all day, plus the evening, and then I had to leave in the middle of the night to go back to Troon and see patients that morning. This was a very hectic time, but travel has improved greatly since then and I still attend the clinic so as not to disappoint patients.

Mokoia was growing bigger and, after Joe had given us the import of the Bioforce products, we formed a company called Swiss Health Products. We initially promoted the business by advertising the wonderful remedies that Vogel made and, with a lot of work, we built up this company, until my second daughter, Janyn, who by now had a degree in business science, started Bioforce UK in the 1980s.

Mokoia was a busy place and it was with great regret that, because of overheads, we had to sell. As it was such a big place, a local builder who had inspected the property felt that it could be converted into flats. At the time we opened Mokoia as a residential clinic, we had also bought a house in Ottoline Drive in Troon and moved our family there. The property was quite small, and our lawyer mentioned that he had heard there was a house situated in part of an estate called Auchenkyle which was for sale. On a lovely Sunday morning, we went to have a look at this property and, indeed, South Auchenkyle was for sale. My mother was visiting us at that time. She had a strong sense of intuition, and felt that we should buy this property. I too felt that it would be a very good choice. Many times in life I have followed my intuition, and it has never failed me.

There are five tangible senses – vision, hearing, taste, smell and touch. However, there is also a sense which often is said to be a 'clairvoyant' sense. I disagree with this, as I believe it is actually intuition. There is a theory that this sense has a lot to do with breathing and, as I have always said, the way we breathe is a very important part of life and has a tremendous effect on life in general. The sense of intuition has been, for me, of great importance throughout my life and, not only has it been of great help to me when treating patients, but in other areas too, and it has never let me down. The decision to purchase South Auchenkyle was the right one to make and I will go into this in more detail in Chapter Nine.

During the latter part of the time we lived in Mokoia, Alfred Vogel depended on me and I had to go to Switzerland several times to help him with business matters and also to advise him on many of the Bioforce affairs. Although I thought I knew this little man very well already, I got to know him much better during that period and also started to lecture throughout the world with him. I learned more about his philosophies and his lifestyle during my travels with him.

8

Alfred Vogel – A Genius

Alfred Vogel was a remarkable little man. Wherever he went, he always had an audience. I have spoken about him earlier in this autobiography, but Vogel played a great role in my life. He often said that we clicked at that very first meeting, and I totally agree with him. Usually at his big lectures, he would talk to me and ask me what I thought about certain things, as he knew he had found a true follower in me. I was the only person in the world that he really taught. Because he was so busy attending to people's health, he never had enough time to devote to teaching, which was a great pity, although he imparted a lot of his knowledge to others through his books and lectures, and was never afraid to share his thoughts about life in general. There were generations of wise people in his family, who come from a little place called Aesch, right across from the Ida Wegmann Institute, the Anthroposophical Institute of Rudolph Steiner, where Vogel was born. This little place holds lots of memories of Vogel. There is a museum in honour of him, to which he gifted many artefacts that he collected from other countries during his travels. He learned a lot from his grandmother, a great lady who knew a tremendous amount about herbs. His whole heart and soul was devoted to nature cure. From a young age, it was all he was interested in. His enormous knowledge and thirst for what nature had to offer took him to many underdeveloped countries in the world, where he loved to study methods used by other nationalities. He also tried to discover why certain illnesses were unheard of in certain countries. He gained a tremendous amount of information from his family while he was growing up, and then began to treat people himself.

He bought a little house right on the hill overlooking Teufen near St Gallen. During his travels throughout the world he gathered a lot of knowledge and I still remember busloads of people coming to his first little clinic. Like myself, he started with a small residential clinic, but later became so busy with patients that he had to close the residential side. He also wanted to produce his own medicines for his patients and to manufacture these to the very highest quality. He and his wife Sophie, whom I also greatly respected, did as much as they could to help others.

I would like to say a little about my first visit to Teufen, and later my last visit to Vogel's beautiful home, completely organically built, in Feusiberg. As I have said earlier, I met Alfred Vogel in Holland and worked with him at his first clinic of nature cure in Holland. I told him that, in order for his business to survive, we had to manufacture as many products as possible locally in order to reduce costs and allow the products to be easily accessible to patients. He agreed, and in 1961 I went to his home in Switzerland for a few months to learn about the procedures involved. I was newly married at that time and my wife decided to come with me. We arrived in Teufen, where other doctors were taking his clinics, as Vogel was completely involved in his organic garden, covering a field with manure himself, which was something he loved doing. He was not at all pleased by our arrival, as we were disturbing him and he wanted to get on with the garden. He really didn't make us feel very welcome and we were quite upset when his manager took us to a little hotel called Schafiliegg. As the Swiss people were very small, our heads could touch the ceiling of our room!

The next day, we went to start work and luckily Vogel was a little friendlier this time. However, before we started, we went to a lawyer and I became the only person in the world to have control over all the recipes and their manufacture. This was all signed and sealed and then we started work. It was very hard. Vogel taught us along with his doctor, Dr Reinmalt, and his fantastic manager, Herr Metler. We put a lot of energy into learning the processes and we not only had to write everything down, but we also had meetings and training sessions. Finally, because I was a pharmacist, I took the whole operation in hand, and went back to Holland to commence the manufacturing process, which is still done at Bioforce today.

Vogel and I became friends and trusted each other. We talked a lot and, as his ideas on business and religion were quite extreme, we had some heated discussions. This little man had a very sober lifestyle, kept strictly to a healthy diet and was very fit. He was usually in bed by nine o'clock in the evening, but then he would be in the clinic by four or five o'clock the next morning to deal with his massive correspondence. His staff found working for him very difficult. They all had to work extremely hard, which resulted in the highest standard of quality control I have ever seen. If anything was not up to standard, it had to be thrown away. He built up the business very well and gave it his full attention.

It was wonderful to listen to Vogel's poetry and wise sayings. A lot of these sayings were very dear to me and one which I remember was, 'In nature, everything is in harmony. Everything remains in harmony if man does not interfere.' He also had wonderful sayings about creation. Wherever he went, he was bursting with enthusiasm, telling people how to preserve their health.

We became very close, especially when we went up into the mountains to discover more plants and flowers. He taught me about the characteristics and signatures of plants, herbs, roots and leaves. Many times when we were in the mountains, he would say, 'Here is arnica. If you stand on it, it will talk back to you. This is a sign from God that it should be used to treat trauma – that is the reason it makes a noise when you step on it.' Even after all these years, I still prescribe arnica for trauma. I was very pleased when Her Majesty the Queen once told me personally that her grandfather used to carry arnica in his pocket, and would give it to people if he saw little accidents happening.

Vogel would fall to his knees and dig in the heavy lime clay in the Swiss Alps whenever he smelled wild garlic. He used to say to me, when it was very dirty and wet, 'Come and look at the garlic. Can you see that nothing of the earth will influence it? It is silvery white to show you that it is a great cleanser.' He also used to show me hypericum (St John's wort). Its leaves had little holes, filled with the wonderful St John's wort oil. This plant had the message: 'I am the plant of love. When you are depressed or even suicidal, take me with my loving signature, I want to heal you.' It was a wonderful experience. Later on, we went to other countries where he studied different plants, and every time when he returned after discovering new plants and flowers, he considered what ailment they could be used to treat.

Our best teachers, though, were the gypsies. They taught us more about herbs during the time we spent with them in the mountains than the best professors of pharmacology. They were masters not only in finding herbs, but also knew so much about them and shared their knowledge with us. Often, when we could not find them, Vogel knew where they would be and went to the local pub for them. Drink was their greatest friend and the minute Vogel had paid them, they would go off to the pub. They very seldom ate anything and when they were not with us in the mountains, they would drink gallons of Schuetzengarten beer. If we ever needed to find certain herbs and could not find the gypsies, one of the pubs could often tell us where they were, as they usually owed a lot of money. It was a wonderful time and we frequently stayed overnight in the mountains on warm summer evenings. For me, it was a great education.

Back in Holland, I remember that when Janyn, my second daughter, was born, Alfred Vogel held her in his arms and said, 'I wish you were a son so that you could become my successor. Now you will have to do it.' Little did he know then that Janyn would later become one of his best general managers.

In Holland, we had a lot of battles to fight building up Biohorma. I remember one day, after working very hard, Arie Drenth (a colleague of mine) and I went for something to eat. Vogel would usually only have a pear or an apple during the day, and would never think of taking time off to eat anything. He was almost completely addicted to helping people by creating more and more remedies.

We both worked very hard in Holland, giving lectures to big gatherings in health food stores in order to keep the message alive, and also working on a new edition of *The Nature Doctor* and its translation, which sold over half a million copies in Holland alone – hard work but, nevertheless, very rewarding. When we started working together in Great Britain, he had the same enthusiasm and when we met various people at universities, everybody was astonished by his knowledge. He was absolutely delighted when we started Bioforce UK in Cramlington in Newcastle, so that his remedies and his books could be accessible to people throughout the country. People hung on every word and many loved him.

I often think that his life story was very similar to that of the greatest Jewish king who ever lived, King David, as he was also greatly gifted. In many ways, he was eccentric and difficult to work with, as he was a very impatient person, but from experience I knew that he was a genius and had a very high IQ. I have often felt that his daughters – especially one who was mentally affected – were probably a result of this. Ruth, one of his daughters, was a great friend to me and later on I often tried to follow in Vogel's footsteps. We were very concerned about him when his first wife, Sophie, died. Vogel became very depressed about this great loss and it took a lot of gentle persuasion to encourage him to try and find another wife as he was not the type of man who liked being on his own. He was very much a social character, and also needed to be nurtured. Luckily, one of his former secretaries arrived on the scene and when he told me he was going to get remarried, I was very happy. As well as being a genius, Vogel was quite an eccentric man. I remember he once asked me to bring my daughter, Janyn, over to visit him because he wanted to discuss the future of Britain.

I came out of the company in 1988 for a lot of reasons, one being that I didn't feel comfortable at the thought of making money from promoting the products. I told Vogel that I did not want to stay in a company from which I was benefiting financially, and I felt that it would be better to leave it completely to my daughter and her husband to operate.

On one visit to Switzerland to meet Vogel, my daughter and I had just met at the airport in London when I discovered that I had forgotten my passport. To get into Switzerland without a passport is virtually impossible, but I decided to try because I did not have enough time to go back and collect it. I thought that I could speak to Vogel at the airport over a railing. My daughter and I were very worried because we knew how strict the Swiss were about passports.

A meeting had been arranged at Vogel's house in Riehen. At the end of the journey, we arrived at Zurich passport control. Of course, we had no chance of getting into Switzerland, but I knew that Vogel and his wife were on the other side of passport control to meet us and, when I was asked at the control point what I was going to do, I said that I would only be there for a day, that I would leave my luggage and everything else with him and that I had a meeting with Alfred Vogel. He said, 'Ah, Alfred Vogel from Teufen?' I confirmed that it was. He asked, 'Is this the man who wrote *The Nature Doctor*?' to which I replied, 'Yes. He is outside passport control. I know he is there waiting for us.' He kindly sent someone to find Vogel and his new wife and ask them to go to passport control, where Vogel confirmed that we had meetings arranged and promised that he would personally make sure I was brought back to the airport the same evening. Incredibly, Janyn and I were allowed through.

I wish you could have seen Vogel's reaction. For at least 15 minutes, he was incredulous that I had managed to get into Switzerland so easily. He said to me, 'If people can get into this country as easily as that, then what is this country coming to?' I told him that he should be proud of himself; it was because he had such a good name in Switzerland that my daughter and I had been allowed through. That finally settled him down and we had a wonderful meeting.

I could fill a whole book with the experiences that Vogel and I had wherever we travelled throughout the world. His sense of humour often managed to get us out of difficult situations. I dearly loved him and, when he went, I lost a very great friend.

Our last meeting was totally different from the first one. In 1996, a few weeks before he died, I spent a whole day with him. He was already not very well and, when I arrived, he became quite emotional. A lot of happy memories came into our minds and I was surprised at how sharp his mind was. He could still talk about our various business affairs throughout the world, the problems relating to medical acts and legal procedures, so he was well up to date. By the afternoon, he got a little tired, but he picked up when we started to talk about past experiences, and we had some good laughs. By five o'clock, it was time for me to leave. Before I left, I took a letter out of my pocket from the Royal Free Hospital in London. The letter related to a patient who had incurable cancer. Unfortunately, although this girl had been through all the medical processes, she had not improved. When I saw her I took her into my care, using a lot of Vogel's remedies and also his philosophies and, luckily, she steadily improved. At long last the tumour, which had nearly reached her brain, had shrunk to such an extent that she was told by the oncologist that she could live a normal life. The oncologist, however, wanted to know what she had done and, when she told him, he said that he would write to me. This was the letter I had just taken out of my pocket, in which he said that he was not only surprised but also had great admiration for the way she was treated. He had monitored this girl and the work that was carried out on her, and wanted to know more about the remedies used. He asked if I would go over to the hospital and do some lectures on this subject and also tell them exactly the methods I used to treat this unfortunate girl, who could now lead a normal life. I read this letter to Vogel before I left and I could see he was very moved. He embraced me and the feelings of nearly 40 years working together were very strong as, for the last time in this life, I had to say goodbye to him.

9

Auchenkyle – 'Beneath the Kyles'

Auchenkyle is the most beautiful place, set in 20 acres of woodland, looking over Auchenkyle Bridge to the Clyde with the beautiful Isle of Arran in the background. It is a place where many people have regained their health and found happiness. The Fraser family, in building Auchenkyle, spared no expense in making it a most attractive property, surrounded by rhododendrons, some of which are unique. When we first went there we lived in South Auchenkyle, but another family lived in North Auchenkyle, who did not appreciate its beauty and had done a lot of damage to the property. Some of its most beautiful trees had been felled like matchsticks and we could see, as neighbours, how much the place was being neglected. With a lot of diplomatic persuasion, I asked the owners of North Auchenkyle if they would consider selling. Finally, we were successful and bought it at a reasonable price. However, difficulties then arose in trying to get them to leave the property. Eventually my lawyer, John Mason, and I managed to get them out, but the damage that had been caused was quite extensive and it was necessary for many repairs to be carried out.

We renovated the property to its original state and started our clinic there after Mokoia had been sold. Patients could then attend Auchenkyle as a day clinic. The business rocketed and, from then to this day, I have had to work very hard from early morning until late evening in order to meet patients' needs. People come from all over the world to try to find help – the famous, the rich and the poor. We have had some wonderful successes, which I will write about in a later chapter, but the demands on me were so great that, regrettably, I had to curtail some of my other work. Unfortunately, I had to give up the clinic in Birmingham, which I really loved, but could no longer keep this going as other clinics had developed and I had to divide my time between them. Through my book writing, I then got involved in a tremendous amount of radio work, and television stations also urged me to take part in some of their programmes.

I started with Gloria Hunniford in 1982, who then broadcast on Radio 2. The programmes became a tremendous success and even more so after Gloria broke her arm during a tennis match and I was instrumental in helping to mend it very quickly. Gloria, who was initially quite sceptical about alternative medicine, became more and more interested. From 1982 until 1992, we did programmes together every month for Radio 2. They became so successful that, after one programme, nearly 10,000 letters were received. The demand became greater and greater.

While broadcasting these programmes, I usually stayed in the George Hotel, which was situated across from Langham Church. A funny thing happened when patients discovered where I was staying – they actually followed me there! On leaving the hotel early in the morning, on my way to the radio station to prepare for the programme at two o'clock, I was amazed to find the hotel restaurant packed full of patients. I managed to see people in a side room and gave them free advice. However, this unofficial clinic became so busy that the hotel manager came to me at one point and said, 'Listen, this place is beginning to look like a hospital, with wheelchairs and ill people – you take over the whole place when you are here. Although we love the extra business this brings us, there have been objections from some of the residents. Would you be interested in possibly taking two rooms upstairs, which we would be willing to give you for nothing, as a lot of your patients would then stay overnight here?'

Unfortunately, as some of my patients found using the lifts and stairs a problem, I had to look for alternative premises from which to consult and, in 1983, found a place at 10 Harley Street. This was a very prestigious building and although there were about 60 other doctors practising there at that time, I decided to consult there on two days a month. As my patients in the London area had increased so much, we needed at least two days there to meet their demands. Everybody was quite happy and, at No. 10, I saw a lot of famous people – from royalty and film stars to politicians as well as the general public. People came from all over the world and I met some very interesting people and had some wonderful results. I became very friendly with the owners, who asked me if I would join the governing body at 10 Harley Street to discuss its further development. It was most interesting to see orthodox and alternative medical practitioners working together, and it was controlled by ethics. I saw quite a few amazing things there. We had a great team and everything went absolutely fine.

As I was coming up the stairs one day, I remember meeting a lady whom I had treated years before and had not seen since. When I recognised her, I asked her why she was singing and looked so happy. 'Because,' she said, 'I came to you on a stretcher to Auchenkyle, brought by a private plane, with a letter from my doctor stating that I had a month to live.' She added that, after all these years, she was here to visit me just for a check-up. She said that I had cured her. I told her that I have never cured anyone – God cures, I only treat.

We saw many patients there. I loved the place and practised there with the greatest pleasure but, unfortunately, problems arose. On the two days when I was there, the consulting room was so full of my patients that the other doctors' patients couldn't find a seat. It was very sad, but we could find no other solution than to look for alternative rooms, which we later found at 53 Upper Montague Street – just a few streets away from Harley Street. However, the Harley Street premises were very much in my heart, as I remembered the many people I had seen there and how happy we had been. More work then came my way because of the publicity in newspapers and magazines, radio and television, and so we had to extend further.

Bioforce UK, which had established itself in Cramlington and was run by my daughter Janyn, also began to grow. Bioforce had got so much bigger that they needed some help. A lot of patients in the Newcastle area had also enquired about seeing me. As I was needed there at that time, it was decided that I would consult at Cramlington one day a month. Again, patients came from far and wide, and we were very busy there – so busy, in fact, that we again had to look for bigger premises, as Bioforce needed my consulting room to expand the business. I found rooms in a very busy general practice. This was the first time in my life that I had worked as a practitioner in a doctor's practice. The cooperation between the doctors and myself was absolutely brilliant and patients who consulted me there were delighted. It was quite a sacrifice, as I had to get up at 4.30 in the morning to go by car, with my assistant, Teresa, to Newcastle to start work there before 8 a.m. We did not finish until 7 p.m., after which

I then had to fly to London to consult at my Harley Street clinic after a hard day's work. However, we enjoyed it. We worked well together and learned such a lot from each other.

However, all the travelling made things very hard and, although we consulted at this clinic for many years, we got so busy and the travelling became so much more difficult due to congestion that we finally decided to give it up after being stranded on the A74 one evening. I shall never forget that evening – I have never seen so much ice and snow and misery. We were sandwiched between large lorries on the road and it made us realise how dreadful travelling could really be. So, after many years, we had to give up the Newcastle clinic which, again, I regretted as I always think of patients as part of myself. Luckily, patients from that area could still go to the Chorley clinic and, as I was still within travelling distance, I could see them there from time to time. I was sometimes also available to give people free advice while consulting in health food shops.

Auchenkyle became busier. I was well aware that some people had to travel from very far afield to get advice and, although I tried to introduce other practitioners, people still wanted to see me personally, possibly because of the many years I had been in practice. Auchenkyle grew very quickly and, after we introduced additional practitioners, it actually became too busy. At that particular point, when we really were at our peak, I received a visit from two important people from Holland who said that the time had now come for me to prove the efficacy of alternative medicine integrating with orthodox medicine. The Dutch Government had given a lot of money to aid this project and I was asked to work on it with the Dutch health service. It would be a great sacrifice to draw back from all my work in Britain, so I decided to do this part of the time and still keep on my clinics in Harley Street, Chorley and Auchenkyle, and allow about 70 per cent of my time to be taken up with the project in Holland. I looked into it and had a few talks with the Dutch health service, who were very interested in what I had to say, and we then started to plan a project of double-blind tests on patients who had osteoarthritis and rheumatoid arthritis. This would be monitored by one of the Dutch universities.

The project meant that my wife and I had to live in Holland and, fortunately, we managed to find a wonderful place near to where these trials had to be conducted. Right under the bridge featured in *A Bridge Too Far* was an estate (where my grandmother used to work as a nanny) overlooking the beautiful River Waal, in one of the nicest parts of Holland. The house, called Rozendal, had a rich history and still retained a lot of its original seventeenth century features, including a thatched roof, and it had a beautiful big pond at the foot of the hill. The minute I saw this house, full of character, I knew it was the place for us. My wife was over the moon about it and so the deal was done – we would live there and I would work on this research project to convince the orthodox medics that alternative medicine really worked.

An old monastery, set in over 300 acres of woodland, in which over 200 monks used to live, was offered to us as the perfect place to carry out the research. The buildings were ideal and, on the ground floor, there was the biggest kidney dialysis centre in Holland. We were very lucky to find an underground source of water that had beneficial properties for rheumatic and psoriatic patients. This was a most nerve-racking experience. It was known that there was water there, but digging deeper and deeper cost a lot of money. The manager nearly gave up, but after much blood, sweat and tears came success. After a long time, the water, which was like gold, was found. The minerals in this were so rich that a big thermal bath was built, which was also beneficial for our project and we started work. Professor Mazek, a very well-known rheumatologist who was completely against alternative medicine, headed the orthodox part of the project, while I headed the alternative part. It was most interesting that each time he came to lecture me about diet, etc., he seemed to become more fascinated. It was total ignorance on his part (and that of his wife, who was also a doctor) that made him doubt my work, which I have so often found to be the case. However, we did work very well together. The professor also worked in a nearby hospital. We compared a lot of notes and, next to a room with his patients, I also had a room with other patients. The health service invited me to conduct several lectures and to set up and monitor the development of the patients. In the first few weeks, the professor's section of patients got better much quicker than mine, but as time went on, my patients became much more pain free and, whilst his patients still had very limited movement, mine were much freer. He was very impressed and the orthodox team became more and more interested in what I was doing.

I loved this work, but I was very unhappy in Holland. I could not forget Britain – and especially Scotland – where my friends were and I was so happy each time I went back. We undertook a lot of important work in Holland, laid the foundation for these trials, which I am still happy about, and helped to build this tremendous place Klein Vink into a centre of excellence in Holland where patients can not only find relief for their aches and pains, but also regain health and vitality. The work we put in there has certainly been valued. Professor Mazek and his team became impressed to such an extent that his wife, who was also a doctor, wanted to work with me. What started as a very difficult relationship ended as a great friendship, and, although I was sorry to leave there, I had to tell them that I wanted to return to Scotland. On one return visit I remember being so homesick that, on the road to Troon, I stopped in Johnstone, where I used to work with Dr Sarah Marr in her practice, also with a lot of rheumatic patients. I just wanted to be there for a little while until my feelings of homesickness diminished. I was always happy during the times that I worked in England and Scotland in between my research work in Holland and that is the reason I carried on there for nearly seven years.

Luckily, I managed to convince my daughter and her husband to come to Scotland, where Dr Tan could take over my practice and, when the new Bioforce was built in Irvine, the two businesses complemented each other. Overall, this exercise has been of great benefit; I have learned a lot, and we have worked together a great deal. One cannot argue with results, as was proved to my orthodox colleagues in Klein Vink.

One day, a big Bentley drove up and out stepped a very important minister from another country flanked by two bodyguards. He came in and sat down. He was dying of a tumour in his throat and began to tell me a quite remarkable story. He had been to the dentist for some work on a tooth. After leaving the surgery, he had felt something in his throat. He had gone back the following day and the dentist had had a look at his throat, but could not find anything. He did nothing further for about two or three weeks. However, as he felt there was still something in his throat, he returned to the dentist who still could not find anything but advised him to go to his doctor. The doctor had a look, but could not find anything either. Nothing was found when the man returned a second time. Time went on, but he still felt there was something in his throat so he went back to the doctor who then sent him to an ear, nose and throat (ENT) specialist, who could not find anything either. Although the country he came from is very advanced in medicine, they could not get to the bottom of his problem – the ENT specialist even suggested that the problem was in his mind, and he should see a psychiatrist! He went to a psychiatrist, who told him that he was absolutely normal. He was then sent back to the hospital. More extensive tests were done and, by that time, because of the months that had elapsed since he first complained of the problem, a tumour had formed. He was told that if they operated, he would be left with no voice.

Disgusted, he looked for alternatives, and a friend, who was the president of a large car company and also a patient of mine, recommended that he came to see me – and here he was. I looked at him and could immediately see how distressed he was. I then proceeded to carry out a few tests. The dermatone tests showed up heavy metal, which made me think that there was a little truth in his theory about the dentist. I phoned the hospital where my friend Professor Mazek worked. We had a look and felt that the problem must have originated from a piece of amalgam which had come out of the tooth and lodged itself in the throat, where the cancerous process had started. I was told this was a very clever diagnosis but was asked what could be done about it. I took the man in hand, treated him and successfully managed to dissolve the little piece of amalgam, after which his tumour disappeared. The evidence is clear – he still holds a very important position and, throughout his treatment, continued to carry out his very responsible job successfully. A lot of orthodox doctors were impressed when they heard his story. He later invited me to dinner, along with his friend (the car company president). That was probably the best dinner I have ever had, because it had been such a remarkable recovery. When I thought about this situation, I realised that one sometimes has to be a detective to figure out what can be wrong with a patient.

Auchenkyle is indeed a lovely place. When we finally managed to get the gardens into order after the ruination caused by the previous owners, it became a very happy place. It took a lot of work to repair all the damage that had been done in the house. I am quite sure that the Frasers, who lived there for over 50 years, would have been proud of the restoration that took place. We then managed to buy the lodge house at the end of the road, which made the whole business complete. We also opened a wonderful little coffee shop. This has been a very welcome place for patients, who sometimes have to wait a long time. Many people will remember the great party we had in a marquee, set in the gardens, to celebrate my 25 years of being in practice in Scotland. People came from far afield – even from San Francisco, India, Sri Lanka and many other countries. This was a great event and now that I am reaching almost 50 years of being a practitioner, I look back appreciatively at the experiences that life has given me.

We have such a wonderful job. I remember a time while I was working in one of the GP practices, when the senior doctor confided in me that he had a young doctor working there who was very miserable. Because I was older, he asked if I could talk to her. I will never forget that experience because it reminded me very much of the fact that being in practice means 'service above self', and that this is not a job, but a calling. She was constantly so unhappy that all the other doctors did not know what to do. As I passed her room, I noticed her gazing miserably straight ahead. I went in to see her and asked her what was wrong. She answered, 'Nothing.' I commented that she looked very unhappy. 'None of your business,' was her reply. I said, 'Well, that is not really an answer – why are you so unhappy?' She then opened up to me. She said she had been on call a lot of weekends, sometimes being called out for nothing, often having to deal with difficult patients and nagging people – she just hated the job. I asked her why she had chosen to become a doctor if she hated it. 'None of your business' was the answer again. I then told her that I had been in practice for many years and that some of my sons-in-law were also in practice – in fact, she might know one of them, as he could have been at university at the same time as her. She then started to take an interest and realised that indeed she did know him. I told her that he was very happy helping others in the course of his work, but if she was not happy doing this job, then she would be better to give it up. She was still quite withdrawn, but I persevered and had a very good chat with her. By the time we had reached the end of our talk, I think she had changed her mind. Some of the other doctors asked me what I had done, as they said she was a different person after I had spoken to her. Sometimes in life you need to give things a little shake to realise what a wonderful job you have. If it becomes boring or a burden, then you know there is something wrong. If we are grateful for the life that we have and the creation we are part of, and can fill a little place, then things will be all right.

Auchenkyle kept growing and we treated patients from every corner of the world. Sometimes I am amazed when I look back at the work at the clinic that has been done to help alleviate human suffering, at the gifts that all of us have been given and how we have made use of these in helping other people. I was very grateful that others, especially my son-in-law, kept Auchenkyle going during the seven years I had been away in Holland. Although it was hard to leave the beautiful place in which we lived and the interesting job I had done there, I was happy to be back with my own patients in Scotland and that encouraged me to work even harder than I was already doing.

New treatments were developed and, because of the media attention we received, we needed to expand further afield in order to cope with demand. In order for us to reach most people who wanted help, we decided to create some new clinics, so that a lot more could be done to help those who needed it. When we bought a building in Ayr to transform into a clinic, I remember how much work had to be done to restore the property. We also set up a clinic in Edinburgh. Located in a prominent position in York Place, this clinic is doing very well. Later on, we opened one in Glasgow and, again, this great old mansion has been restored and is now a place where many people help to heal others. We also have affiliated clinics in the north of London, in Wheelton, and in Belfast. We have a total of eight clinics now, all with the aim of helping those in need. The Belfast clinic, which sometimes has a waiting list of three years for new patients, has been a great success. During the Troubles, I kept consulting there. It has certainly not gone unnoticed by me that many degenerative diseases and other illnesses developed in people there over the many years that the conflict went on. I saw the same when I opened the Dublin clinic. The enormously rapid growth of the economy there has affected people by causing stress and an inability to cope with these quick developments. It has left its mark on many people because they are constantly living with pressure, and have therefore paid the price for the rapid economic growth.

It is wonderful that I am able to travel to all the different clinics. Sorting out the misunderstandings the public and press have had about my work, and working towards integrating alternative and conventional medicine into a complementary system, have been difficult tasks. The example of the Dutch complementary medicine system, and my experience of this, has certainly been of the greatest help. Today, there are still enough evidential papers to show how alternative and conventional medicine have slowly married and been very beneficial to patients' health. However, the path towards a complementary system was not easy and, in the next chapter, I shall share a few good and bad experiences, and some interesting cases.

10

Healing Instead of Blundering

I once met Her Majesty the Queen of Great Britain at Holyrood Palace, and she told me she believes that it is most important for people in this country to have freedom of choice. This is a statement that has been made by many, but Her Majesty has a very open mind. With enormous intelligence, she has studied many subjects and, during the conversation that I was allowed to have with her, I was surprised at her wide knowledge of many forms of complementary medicine. Over the years that I have been working in this field, I think the most difficult part of my job has been talking to people with totally closed minds, who think that salvation is only to be found in orthodox medicine. I have a great respect for orthodox medicine and, as I have always said, what would we do without it? Nevertheless, it is great to have an open mind, at least to study the evidence and the efficacy of this tremendous subject.

Well over 200 years ago, our national poet, Robert Burns, wrote to Dr Moore, the well-known doctor and author of *A View of the Causes and Progress of the French Revolution*. This letter is very interesting to read. Basically, what he said is that the blunders and mistakes we make are through ignorance. I have come across this ignorance many times while lecturing to students and postgraduates. I remember giving a lecture once in a hospital where there were a lot of young student doctors. At that time, evening primrose oil was very much to the fore and one student ridiculed its properties. I asked him if he knew all about it and he shook his head. I told him that I had read of the benefits of evening primrose in books from the sixteenth and seventeenth centuries and, today, I have also seen through evidential trials how much evening primrose has to offer us. It is always a problem when one closes one's mind to something that might be of benefit in the future. Later in the book, I will discuss a few people who were thought to be complete nutcases and whose views were completely discredited, but who are highly esteemed today. Copernicus, when his views of the solar system became known, was also thought to be a nutcase in his own time, yet we still believe today that he was right.

When I think of the few extraordinary cases where it has been shown that healing was possible and blunders have been made, they were probably the result of a closed mind.

A short time ago, when I was working in Northern Ireland, a young girl appeared with her father, mother and both grandfathers and grandmothers. They actually came to thank me for the miraculous recovery of this young seventeen-year-old. A month earlier, her father had phoned the clinic from the hospital to ask if I could see his daughter. He said that they would bring her by ambulance as she was almost dying. I very seldom say 'yes' because of my busy practice, but somehow my intuition told me that I should see her, and so, the girl arrived. She could walk, but I saw straight away that her centre of gravity was very much out of line. I also noticed that her breathing was very heavy. I did my Chinese facial diagnosis and realised that this girl was indeed seriously ill. I asked her to lie on the bench and went to a certain spot right on the end of the gullet. It was actually quite obvious that that was where her problem was and, although she had had endoscopies and all kinds of tests, they had not found anything wrong and her parents were told that unfortunately she could not be helped as the doctors felt it was probably all in her mind. I used a very simple technique that I learned from Gonstead in the United States many years ago. He was a genius in bone symmetry and, by outwardly looking at the patient, could see what was out of line. The end of the gullet was almost bulging in this young patient and her rib cage was very much out of alignment. This procedure took me no more than three or four minutes in itself and I could then immediately see that this girl could breathe properly again.

Technically, she was in a very bad state. I told her father and mother that it wasn't in her mind, but there was a mechanical problem, and we could only hope and pray that this would be rectified. I sent her back to the hospital and asked her to eat very slowly and to have very small meals as I was not completely sure, without carrying out further tests, that she did not have a small hiatus hernia. She went back to the hospital and by the Monday she was much better. By Tuesday, the doctors who had seen her previously came back to look at her and they were quite surprised. By Wednesday, a professor came with some young graduates to see her and, in the presence of her parents, he told the young students, 'Here we have a typical example of a placebo. This girl had nothing wrong with her. It was all in her mind, but she went to a man who knows nothing about medicine. He did something with her and suddenly her mind told her that she was better.' Her father said, 'That is not true, because if you had looked at her chest, you would have seen that she was completely out of alignment and, mechanically, this man put her back into the right posture.' The professor smiled. When the father asked him why he could not have done that, he just walked away with his postgraduates, still of the opinion that this was only a placebo. How often have I seen over the years that that was not the case: people with slipped discs and even a prolapse of the intervertebral disc have told the same stories. It has taught me to be very careful what I say without knowing the truth of the matter. Only when we can honestly say that we have looked at a case from every angle can we be justified in making a statement.

I never like to mention names and adhere to strict confidentiality. I sometimes see doctors, especially complementary ones, mention famous names when they advertise. I can honestly say, unless the patient has requested this, I have never done so. One evening a very well-known Scottish footballer came in to my clinic with his trainer, who had persuaded the player to see me. He was one of Scotland's best and greatest footballers. At that time, I treated players from Celtic and Rangers, and also a lot of players from the English teams. This man was a much-admired footballer and I could see in his face that he was very worried about something. He had already undergone a few operations on his foot and the professor in question had told him that he would never play again. This, for him, was a huge shock. He then developed diabetes, which made things even more difficult – being diabetic myself, I can understand why, because of the terrible worry and the emotional slap in the face of having been told that he would never play again, he had developed the disease. His trainer, whom many people knew and who often asked me to mention his name if I wished, Jimmy Steele, was a great Celtic supporter and, before he died, he left his training suit to me. I had a good look at the player's foot and told him I would deal with it. I gave him acupuncture treatment with moxibustion, and also helped with his diabetes. He got so much better that after three treatments he started to play again. After the sixth treatment, he went to see the professor, who was absolutely furious and threatened me with legal action if I let him play, saying I was very irresponsible. I told him that I could see no reason why he could not play. He went on to become the club captain, and played better than ever before for many years after that. This is a good example of the importance of an open mind.

It is not always easy to help certain people when they have been told they will never recover, because their hope has been taken away. This reminds me of the case of a girl from East Kilbride who came to see me in a wheelchair. She was definitely a multiple sclerotic patient and I am the last person who would say he can 'cure' multiple sclerosis. You cannot – what is dead is dead. What I will say, however, is that one can control it. I do not know what caused this to happen but, on this girl's second visit, after I had given her some acupuncture treatment, as she was coming off the bed she told me that she felt some strength in her legs. On that particular day, I had not used the needles by the book. I had taken a completely different route. I asked her to hold my hands and see if she could stand, which she did. I then asked her to try and walk a little. Of course, she was very weak, and her muscles were also weak as she had not been walking for a long time, but she felt she could. She then went home. Three weeks later, I saw her sitting in the hall. I asked my assistant, Teresa, to look and see if her wheelchair was in the cloakroom. Naturally, I thought it was quite strange that she was sitting there without it. When Teresa came back and told me that there was no wheelchair there, I then called her name and, to my great surprise, she walked into the consulting room. Naturally, she was very happy and told me that she had experienced great benefits following the previous treatment and felt that she could walk again. On the fourth visit, she felt the same – until she had a visit from her neurologist. Her doctor, who was most surprised by her improvement (and has since sent quite a number of patients to consult me) had called the neurologist to see her. He was equally interested. He looked at her, then told her it was a welcome short remission and added that all he could do for her was to order her a chairlift, as she would soon be back in her wheelchair again. She was very distressed. A week later, she had regressed and could not walk, and had come back to see me. I sat her down. She was quite a religious lady, so I had a short talk with her, related a little Bible story about people who have no faith and, even worse, people who have lost their faith, not only in themselves but also in others. I told her that, because of her faith, she should not think negatively but be positive in her mind about walking again and, luckily, she did. She is now serving behind the counter in her husband's shop and feels a lot better than she ever did before.

It is wonderful to think of the power of nature to heal people. If you give nature a chance and stay positive – which is always very important – it can be done. It is also important that one accepts professional advice and does what is recommended. Experience has taught me what is right and what is wrong, and patients can improve by taking their doctor's or practitioner's advice, as they are doing their best to help the patient.

A very famous singer, probably one of the most famous in the country, came to see me once in Harley Street. She told me that, unfortunately, she had problems with her singing, which had deteriorated and, because of this, she had become very depressed. In talking to her, I could see that she had problems with the right side of her jaw. I asked her if she had been to the dentist recently and, indeed, she had. She told me that after seeing the dentist, she had experienced some problems. In a matter of seconds, I adjusted her jaw, which had been causing tremendous pressure on the tempero-mandibular joint. If pressure is there, it always affects the hyoid bone, which can affect speaking and singing. That was exactly what had happened in this case. I treated this lady very quickly, and she looked at me with great disbelief, wondering how this could have helped as she was in and out the door within five minutes. After a week, she phoned me to say that her singing had improved very much and her jaw felt a great deal better. She wondered whether she should come back and see me or not. I told her that I would like to see her once more to examine her and hopefully find that everything was all right. And it was. She is still singing and a lot of people in this country still enjoy her beautiful voice.

Another story comes to mind, this time about a lady who is related to royalty. She came into the clinic and told me that she felt very ill. I could smell candida. My extra sense, my intuitive sense, may have helped develop my breathing and sense of smell. This is a gift that perfumers are partially gifted with. When I smelled this candida, I knew that she spoke the truth – she was indeed ill. A lot of people think they have candida, but not all of them actually do. It is a yeast parasite that lives in all of us but is not always active. I told her that I wanted her to give up five foods – wine, cheese, mushrooms, yeast and sugar. She answered that she would omit four of them, but she would not give up her bottle or two of wine a day. I said, 'Then I am afraid I cannot help you.'

'I will show you that I can do it,' she said. After six weeks, she came back and the same candida smell was still evident. After the second visit, I told her not to waste her money and she said, in no uncertain terms, that I was a lousy practitioner and she was going somewhere else. Some time later, I got a letter from her, saying that she had gone to a doctor in America who allowed her to drink her daily quota of wine and he had cleared her candida. In other words, I was not a good practitioner – she just wanted to let me know this.

Half a year later, there she was back before me. I said to her, 'Let me have a little look in your eyes first of all.' As I was looking with my iridology apparatus, she told me that she did not believe in such things and this was not a scientific piece of equipment. Nevertheless, I looked into her eyes and asked her where her left kidney was. She asked if I had second sight. I said, 'No, I don't have second sight at all. I see in your left eye that there is no left kidney.' She told me that 27 years previously her left kidney had been removed. That gave her a bit of confidence in my ability. She told me that although she had spent thousands and thousands of pounds going to this doctor in America, who promised that he would get rid of her candida, it had returned and, this time, she would be willing to cooperate with me. I asked her to promise to do as I told her, and she did. Luckily, I got rid of the candida, after which the other doctor in America got a letter from her saying that *he* was a lousy doctor!

There is another case that I shall not easily forget. In front of me sat a beautiful princess. I could see that she had many problems and a lot of misunderstanding in her life. I agreed that, in her position, it was very difficult to work out what was the right thing to do. Her life was full of emotional ups and downs and she had to consider her position and the publicity she received, so it was difficult to advise what was best. Mistakes had been made by her advisors and others in the past. All that this girl needed to find the harmony within was understanding and compassion. But it is not always easy, and advice is not always appreciated. What worried me was that I sensed the way forward would not be a path of roses and instantly felt that she wouldn't have a long life. This decided me, at that time, to write my book *Inner Harmony* which, from all the letters I have received, has been of comfort for many. Patients have the right to confidentiality and therefore it is difficult for me to talk in depth about this case.

I also remember a duke who came to see me. He was so engrossed in his own health problems that, although he could easily have led a full life, he spoiled it by thinking of himself all the time. Every time he visited me, he talked and talked about all the terrible treatments he had received, the blunders that had been made in his treatment and wondered why his health never improved. I told him that the key to his own recovery was totally within himself but I couldn't open his mind. One day when he came to see me, I asked him to sit down and listen to me. I told him about the situation I had seen as a child, with the factory workers back in the cigar factory in my birthplace of Kampen, about the poverty of the people, followed by the Second World War and the tremendous suffering I had seen. I must say he listened intently. After I had finished, he said a very wise thing that showed he had changed his way of looking at things. He said that, while listening to my story of suffering, he realised that his problems were minute in comparison to the suffering I had seen in my life. I was happy when I later heard that he had got married and had something else on which to focus his attention, instead of thinking about himself all the time. How often do we see that, when people have too much money or time on their hands, they become so self-important that they forget to think of others, and to share. This is so important and something I learned from Mother Teresa when I worked with her in India. I once shared a platform at a conference in Bangalore with the Dalai Lama and Mother Teresa, and we had a wonderful talk. In our own ways, each of us was thinking about love and sharing it with others, trying to do what we could to help others. This is what life is all about and I always come back to my war story when, on seeing the utter misery, death and destruction, I promised God that I would share my life with others to the best of my ability. This is one of the most important things in life. One can get so involved in one's own problems that one does not see reality any more.

This reminds me of a girl who came to see me, telling me she had MS. I asked, 'Why do you think you have MS?' She said, 'Because one doctor thought I might have.' I did a Chinese facial diagnosis on her. This is something I often do. It has helped me tremendously in my busy practices, and has never failed me. Outwardly, the diagnoses are sometimes so clear as to where the problems lie and, in this case, I saw that this girl did not have MS. I asked her if she had had a lumbar puncture. She said, 'No, but I have had MRI scans and some white patches showed up.' So I told her that white patches can also indicate an ME patient, and that I personally did not think she had MS. She had imagined the pictures so well and had even adopted certain MS symptoms that she had read about. The mind is stronger than the body and the body will be obedient to the mind. This is very often the root of the problem. I then said to her, although I do not approve of it, that she should have a lumbar puncture to make absolutely sure. After she had the lumbar puncture, the doctor told her that indeed there were no indications that she had MS. This still did not convince her that she was healthy because she was now afraid that she couldn't have children. I sat her down and had a real chat with her, until I finally managed to convince her that she did not have MS. Once that penetrated her subconscious mind, she realised that I was right and improved from that day.

Often this happens with people who imagine that they are not capable of certain things and cannot do what others can. This reminds me of a very well known and much-loved BBC personality. For a long time she had tried to have a baby, but her subconscious mind told her that she could not conceive. I asked her husband and herself to come and see me. We had a long chat and there was absolutely no evidence on either side that this was not possible – he was perfectly all right, his sperm count was OK, motility OK, he hadn't had mumps; everything was fine. She was a very healthy woman, had no endometriosis, no other problems, was not too old to conceive, not overweight – everything pointed to the fact that they could have a baby. My intuition told me that they would conceive, and I am very happy to say that they now have two children and are the happiest family I deal with. In fact, their photograph is with me in my room to remind me that positive thinking is much better than negative, and it is a good idea to replace a negative thought with a positive thought and to say to oneself, 'I can do it.'

My dear mother always said, '"Cannot" lies in the cemetery and "will not" is its neighbour.' It is very important that we are positively minded in order to reach our goal.

The medical world is strange. Sometimes you need to be a detective to find out what is wrong with patients, sometimes you have to be a philosopher and, at other times, you have to use psychology to make your patients better. I once got a phone call from a doctor who had heard about me and the success we had at Roode Wald, our clinic in Nunspeet, from a colleague in Holland. She said she was very fond of one of her female patients, but she was also very worried about her because she could not walk, and medically there seemed to be no reason for this. I felt that she should come into the clinic to be examined and have tests. Perhaps by administering an acupuncture treatment I could do something to help. The lady was brought in on a stretcher and was taken straight up to one of the rooms. I had a good chat with her, tested all her reflexes and everything else I could think of, but could not find any reason for her paralysis. As it turned out, a psychological trauma was the cause. I felt it would be dishonest to give this lady a lot of treatments as I sensed that psychologically there was something far wrong with her. I gave it a lot of consideration and remembered an old professor I used to work with in Holland, who had a lot of ideas on dealing with patients with psychological problems, and I hoped that one of them would have the desired result in this case. I went to the health food shop, where I found a very big tablet called Ge Vee Tabs – only a vitamin pill! Then I returned home and told the lady I had found a tablet that could be the cure. I said I would give her this before she went to bed and that the next afternoon we would both have a walk through the garden, as her paralysis would be gone. This filtered through from her subconscious to her conscious mind, taking away the thought that was absolutely cemented in her mind that she could not walk. I prayed very hard that this would work, and the pill did its job. The following day at 2 p.m., I asked her to take my arm so that we could walk and, indeed, we walked round the garden. That particular lady has been walking ever since. Once a thought has become a reality in someone's mind, it often becomes so deeply ingrained that it is very difficult to remove unless it is replaced positively. That was what I managed to do with this lady and, of course, she stayed with us for a while to make sure that she did not regress. After having been brought to Mokoia on a stretcher and then going back home walking, she told everybody how wonderful the treatment had been and even today, 30 years later, we have a lot of patients from that part of the world who remember the miraculous recovery of that patient.

The mind is stronger than the body and it is often important, when sudden thoughts are accepted by the mind, to break through the barrier to dispel any negative thoughts, replace them with positive thoughts and then wait for the results. It is quite astonishing the difference that even one word can make.

A very famous horse rider, well known as one of the best horsewomen we have in this country, was doing well in her career. Unfortunately, while she was in trials, the famous horse she was riding fell and she fell with it, quite badly. Both the horse and the owner were very badly hurt. The vet was called, who said that the horse would have to be put down, which would have been a crime. The master of the hunt advised the rider to come and see me. She phoned and asked if I could please see them. I saw them both and took them into treatment straight away. The rider advised me that the next week she and the horse had to compete in the world championships in Germany. This 17-hand horse and its owner had to be treated, and I made it my responsibility to help them. I saw them every day. They went to the competition the week after, both well, and became champions. The pair won the championship in Germany. So, sometimes it can be done.

When trying to help others, it is very important that we keep an open mind and are not dogmatic or bigoted. On a very busy Saturday, a gentleman came into Auchenkyle. He looked very worried and I could see that he was in distress. I asked him what was wrong and he told me that on Monday he had to have his leg amputated, as there was a cancerous growth in his knee joint. I looked at him and couldn't see any of the 10 outward signs of cancer (cancer often can be identified by 10 or even 12 outward signs), such as a dryness of the skin or damage in the mucous membranes. Although I didn't have a lot of time, I asked him to step onto the plinth so that I could have a look at his knee. My first thought was that this man did not have cancer. When I looked carefully at the knee, I could not see a lot of limitations. I phoned our radiographer, who worked daily in a cancer hospital, to take some X-rays of this man's leg and especially his knee, to find out if there was in fact a cancerous growth. I told him to go to our X-ray centre and the negatives were made. I asked the gentleman to come back in the afternoon to see me, by which time I would have the results of the X-rays. My radiographer phoned me and said that she had scrutinised the negatives, but couldn't see that there was anything to worry about – just a little arthritis in the knee. So I asked this gentleman if I could speak to his doctor. I phoned the doctor who was very unsympathetic. In fact, he said to me, 'Do you bl**** think you know any better than the hospital?' He was not willing to listen to my advice. I told this doctor, in no uncertain terms, that if no further X-rays were made in the hospital for this gentleman, I would hold him totally responsible under the Human Rights Act for doing something that he shouldn't, and that seemed to do the trick. On the Monday, the gentleman went to the hospital in question. Another X-ray was made and, indeed, my radiographer had been right. The long and the short of the story was that the initial X-rays were from another patient and had got mixed up. It is quite frightening and it is often advisable to seek another opinion or a second diagnosis if there is any doubt about one's case. I never feel upset when people go for a second opinion. We can all make mistakes, although some are unforgivable. It is important to remember that we deal with life and life is very precious.

I saw a Rangers footballer not so long ago, who, like the player that I helped overcome a foot injury and diabetes, was in the depths of despair because he had suffered an injury which would put him out of the game. He had sought many opinions, none of which were the same. He was baffled. When he came over, I said, 'I will take you into treatment and prove to your coach, who has been very discouraging, that we will get your leg better.' His leg improved completely, but he could not get over the fact that he had been told that this injury was fatal to his career. It is therefore advisable to seek a second opinion before the door closes.

Often I feel that we have failed in medicine and, some years ago, when I did a talk in the House of Lords on some of my prison work, I made it very clear to the House that the importance of research is something that should have the full attention of the House of Lords and the House of Commons. I spoke about my work in male and female prisons. In female prisons, a lot of women are imprisoned because they have done something completely out of character due to a hormonal imbalance. They become like Jekyll and Hyde, and behave irrationally. Because of that, they have committed crimes that they have deeply regretted – even to the point of murdering someone they dearly loved. A lot more focus needs to be placed on aspects of health that are easily forgotten, such as hormones and allergies. With one prisoner I treated, before he committed his last murder, he actually ate and drank the things to which he was allergic. Not only did these make him high, but they also caused him to do things that were totally out of character and which he now deeply regretted. Other prisoners I have dealt with on this subject, where blunders were made in treating certain conditions and where healing has now taken place, have written a lot of letters to me stating that they only want to do better. There are cases that need further investigation and much more research. It is certainly of the greatest importance that we look at medicine and start at the grass roots. Where did things go wrong? Why did society fail to look at problems from a different angle? Life can be very sweet, but it can also be very bitter if it is full of misjudgements and misunderstandings, and loses its real purpose.

11

For Goodness Sake

It is with real pleasure that I look back on the day I acquired my first little shop on Templehill, in Troon. I mentioned this occasion earlier but would like to say more about it now. We needed health foods for the clinic and, as the shop was very small and did not always have room to stock the goods we required, I had to go in quite often and ask the owner if she could order various things for me. She said, 'Well, this shop is really not something that I want to keep on.' I looked around and said, 'Well, what if we do a deal? I will give you £1,000 for the stock and £1,000 for the counter, the till and the chair.' Her face lit up and she replied, 'The deal is done.'

Nothing was further from my mind than running a health food shop and I intended to shut it down straight away. However, I did need the addresses of the suppliers so that I could order the foods that were needed for the patients at Mokoia. I went into the shop the next day to do the stocktaking and, amazingly, the stock came to just over £890, so my estimate was good and my intuition did not disappoint me. But here I was, landed with a shop that I wanted to close.

The next day, a very friendly lady, of whom I became very fond, came to the door and told me that she often helped in the shop. She loved the customers coming in and offered them advice. Would I consider keeping the shop going? I said that I would give it some thought, and would meet her again that evening. As the weekly rent and rates were only £1 each, we decided to keep the shop open. Unfortunately, it only had a turnover of £40–45 per week. However, the lady in question was very keen, so I gave her some help in making the window look attractive to entice customers and the shop's trade began to grow and grow, until the premises became far too small and we had to start looking for larger ones. We found what we were looking for in Academy Street, a very big shop with lots of different goods, and things started to expand even further. The second shop I opened was in Kilmarnock, where the owner was too old to go on. The third shop to be opened was in Prestwick; the previous owners wanted to dispose of it. We expanded further by opening one in Largs, then Stranraer and later in Stewarton. Things mushroomed to such an extent that we eventually had ten shops. This reminded me of the time I had said, as a very small boy, to my mother, 'One day, mother, I will have at least ten shops.' Well, that was exactly what had happened, and it was really good fun. I remember one health food shop in particular which I didn't want to take over at all. It was owned and run by a farmer and his wife. However, they both went to a yoga seminar where his wife fell in love with the guru and the guru with her. She didn't want to come home and the poor man was then left with the shop. As he had a lot of work on his farm, he wanted to sell it. I phoned my marvellous right-hand man, Mr John McCallum, who was very loyal to me and we took over that particular shop.

We had completed quite a ring of shops in Scotland by that time. However, there was one shop we did not have; probably the biggest in Ayrshire. We didn't know if this shop would ever come on the market until one day, out of the blue, the owner and his wife came to see me and told me there was a chance they might sell out and wondered if we would be interested. However, in order to keep these shops trading and make them profitable, one needed a fairly big turnover. I listened and asked him what he was offering. To my great surprise, he took a Monopoly set out of his bag and put it in front of me. He then said, 'You have a lot of these – you even have Piccadilly Circus, but one shop that you haven't got is Park Lane – and I own that shop. We are offering it to you but, because it is Park Lane, we want a lot of money for it.' To cut a long story short, after protracted negotiations we bought that shop and to this day it still has the biggest turnover, although I don't actually own it any more.

That time holds a lot of fond memories, although we all had to work very hard to build the businesses up in the various towns and increase their turnovers. We had to introduce a lot of new items to sell in order to make them profitable. All the shops began to do well, however, especially the one in Ayr. I managed to get a baker to make certain breads to sell in the shops and, because of my days with the pharmacy,

I also made remedies under our own name, which were very much appreciated. So everything was going absolutely wonderfully.

Nearly 50 years ago, when I was in Edinburgh and not yet married, a relative of my wife had an extremely bad cough. I had two choices – I could go to a chemist, or I could go to a herbalist. In Bristo Place, I found a herbalist who had been trading there for decades. Although in those days the shop was not very busy, it had certain customers who went there for remedies, so it was a blessing to many people. I went into that little shop, which was quite dark, but nevertheless very attractive with its brass knobs and smell of a real herbal pharmacy. Everything shone. What a delight it was! It reminded me of the *pharmacognosie* studies that I had to attend for my degree in Holland. I felt right at home in that little shop and was happy to talk to the herbalist, whose name was John Napier. He was a delightful gentleman who carried out his work with great enthusiasm, and when I told him I was a pharmacist, he was very interested in my work and also in my interest in herbs. I told him about Alfred Vogel, of whom he had heard, and mentioned several of his friends who were in the same profession. We had a great talk. He prepared a wonderful prescription for me, which I gave to my wife's relative and, indeed, it helped her tremendously. I did not think for one minute that one day I would be the proud owner of that shop, nor did I realise how much it would come to mean to me.

It was many years later that the owners of Napier's, who by then were Gerard House, offered me the chance of taking over the business. I bought it from them lock, stock and barrel, not only because it had fascinated me so much all those years ago but also because of the recipes I thought I might find there. I took over the shop, renovated it from top to bottom and brought back the old philosophies of the Napier family who had operated this business since the seventeenth century. During those renovations, whilst breaking up a lot of the old cupboards which had degenerated over the years, I suddenly came upon a metal box full of real treasures, prescriptions that were used in the days of the plague and tuberculosis and all the different methods, plus a full book of remedies that had never been made. I felt as rich as a king. I saw remedies that had been long forgotten, and the tremendous work that the Napier family had put into this particular place over the years in order to help others. What I had found was fascinating. I also came across the written reports of a court case. This was a big case that took place in Edinburgh concerning a man who had been drunk and had been brought in with a badly damaged eye, which old Mr Duncan Napier treated with a particular ointment. It wasn't until the drunk man had sobered up that he thought he would try to get money out of Mr Napier, claiming his ointment had caused damage to his eye. This was a big court case for those days, and the bills and the countless papers from the case showed how much it had all cost. Luckily for Mr Napier, at the end of it all, it was established that while the man had been drunk, he had damaged his eye himself and Mr Napier was totally exonerated because the ointment could not have caused any harm at all, nor was Mr Napier at fault for the way in which the man had been treated. Because of the publicity surrounding the case, this man actually made Napier's of Edinburgh very famous.

I built the business up as much as I could and started doing consultations there. I was very happy with Napier's, until the call came for me to go to Holland and work on the project to show the efficacy of herbal medicine. Then I had to sell the business, although I retained the premises myself as a reminder of the good times I had had running it.

I was involved in another fascinating find, when many herbs, long forgotten, were discovered at the site of a very interesting pharmacy in a medieval hospital. This was in the Soutra Hills just south of Edinburgh. Aerial photographs that had been taken of a certain area of the Soutra Hills suggested that some form of habitation had existed there. The photographs showed foundations buried on land where cows and sheep now grazed. Excavations by archaeologists took place. The evidence showed that, in fact, there had been a medieval monastery on this site. In the twelfth century, the monks had provided a refuge and a hospital. When the English and Scots were fighting each other in the border wars, crossing the border at Jedburgh and then riding up to Edinburgh on what was known as The King's Road, they would come across this haven where they could be nursed and looked after medically before continuing on their journey. When the excavations started, Professor Brian Moffat, who was in charge of the whole operation, asked if I would like to go over and have a look at the excavation work. I felt very privileged to have been asked to be part of this and went along with my assistant, Teresa. We observed what was going on and were both very interested in what had been found. During the excavations, they discovered a church and, off to one side, what came to be recognised as an infirmary. A piggery was also discovered, almost intact, but the most interesting part for us was the area that had been used as a pharmacy, where they found herbs and prescriptions similar to those used at Napier's in Edinburgh. The pottery jars were the most amazing sight, with remnants of arnica, rosemary, skullcap, belladonna and all kinds of remedies that had been buried there since the twelfth century after the infirmary was burned to the ground. One fascinating discovery was the instruments that were used for bloodletting, and, even more interesting, a drain where layers of blood were still present after all these years. These findings were analysed in the laboratory and found to have traces of TB and typhus viruses present. In those days, after bloodletting the blood was disposed of in this large drain. Scientific analysis also showed the types of plants that were grown in that area at that time, many of which would have been used medicinally, such as flax, mustard, barley and tormentil. It was amazing to see this whole operation taking place and to witness this excavation. I had a great desire to set up a museum there and Professor Moffat and I talked a lot about it. The cost, however, would have been too great, plus the purchase of the land would have been too expensive to make the whole operation profitable. So, today the cows are grazing again on what was a valuable and most interesting part of Scotland.

We could have called this site 'For Goodness Sake', after the great love and devotion of the monks. They did so much to aid the sick. We could learn from them: so much work and time must have gone into preparing those remedies, to help people who were stranded and needed help to enable them to continue on their journey.

This was an interesting time. The whole health food industry, which was mainly based on good dietary management, herbal and homoeopathic medicine, started to spread across Britain very quickly. I gave many lectures at various shops and associations and talked on radio and television, as I wanted to bring this matter much more to the fore. The health food industry started to grow very fast as people became more and more conscious of the benefits of organically grown foods. It was amazing to see the acceleration of growth in an industry that, at one time, was almost completely dead. I vividly remember the large health food manufacturers' exhibitions in the old days at the Royal Lancaster Hotel in London, which later moved to Olympia, and I followed these with great interest. Things were very different in Holland, where there were pharmacists, druggists and 'reform' shops, which basically sold vitamins, minerals and trace elements, health foods, drinks and organically grown foods: health food shops in Britain showed a completely different picture. I was always amazed at how many people would turn up at the big lectures I held, especially in London. Many of them had a great desire to learn how to look after themselves, so they would ask a lot of questions. The public was beginning to realise the damage that could be done by E numbers, colourings and artificially grown foods that were sprayed with pesticides, herbicides or fertilisers.

When I worked in Teufen, I clearly remember Alfred Vogel growing his herbal plants, trees and shrubs organically. These really flourished. Not so terribly long ago, I was given an example of the importance of good healthy foods, and investing in one's health. Many years ago, Vogel planted two cherry trees. It is well known that cherry trees do not have a very long life. However, when I visited Teufen not long ago, it was interesting for me to see that after almost 40 years one of the trees was still alive. I asked the housekeeper, a very old lady, what had happened to the other one. Vogel had carried out an experiment with these trees. They had come from the same source and the same family. One of the young trees was planted in a small plot and artificial fertilisers, herbicides and pesticides were used to encourage its growth. He planted the other cherry tree further away from the first one, and grew it completely organically – it was fed organically and had no artificial manure. The first cherry tree bore fruit a lot quicker than the organically grown one. The fruit was also bigger and looked much better, but the odd thing was that it did not have the smell of a cherry. The cherries on the organically fed tree were not as big, they did not have such a wonderful colour, but the taste was gorgeous, and it had survived while the other had died. Many times, Vogel spoke about those two cherry trees. As he always used to say, 'You get out of it what you put into it.' The same applies to the human body and, in the long run, you will have a longer life if you feed it well.

I thought about this when I was there some time ago on an excursion, taking people through the old place where I used to work and where my heart still was, thinking how hard we worked to prove to the world that those philosophies were right. The philosophies of Vogel, Napier and Mr Abbott of Leigh are still valuable today. People must realise that life is valuable and we only get out of life what we put into it. As for the cherry tree, which was looked after with care and devotion, it was almost impossible to believe that it was still alive after all those years. It reminded me again that I should instil in people that we live in a time when a strong immune system is extremely important.

Mr Abbott had a herbal practice in Leigh, Lancashire. He saw everything in black and white and would share his philosophies in no uncertain terms (and not always in the most friendly way!), as he was very keen that his patients kept to his rules. I only had the pleasure of meeting Mr Abbott once. I was very impressed with some of his patients who came to see me in the clinic in Chorley and, as I had heard so much about his work, I wanted to meet him, but never had an opportunity to talk to him. What I was most interested in was that Mr Abbott had a sort of black box in one of his rooms. It looked like an iron cage, with a little seat inside and a few monitors. At that time, I had no idea just how advanced Mr Abbott's vision was: he was working with electromagnets, whereby he could greatly improve his patients' energy. This was not just a diagnostic tool, although he also learned a great deal about his patients while they were undergoing treatment.

Never did I think over 30 years ago, when I first saw this place, that I would ever become the owner. Mr Abbott, who had been married four times, had a great history. Growing up in a coal-mining area, where there was a lot of TB and chest problems, he started to search for ways in which nature could help him. When he discovered all the things that natural medicine had to offer, he started to study as a herbalist. He was a very clever man, and the books and recipes I found in that clinic are of the greatest value and are greatly treasured. Mr Abbott was very studious, which was why his practice was so big. People would come from as far away as London and beyond to his herbal practice in Railway Road. He was an active man but, unfortunately, due to a tragic accident when he was quite elderly, his life came to an end, which was a big shock for his patients, as he had helped so many. He too was misunderstood. He was threatened with prison and had a court case brought against him by a patient who wanted to sue him unjustifiably. Thankfully, as with Mr Napier, the verdict was in his favour and he was acquitted.

It is very important in life that whatever we do, we do it honestly. I remember my mother often said, 'You never need to worry about anything as long as whatever you do is done with honesty and dignity.'

Mr Abbott's recipes were even better than Napier's. His concoctions went a lot further and when I found his treasury of recipes and other things he had left behind, I counted myself the luckiest man in the world to have these in my possession. Today I still own Abbott's of Leigh, and people all over the country are helped by his recipes, which were long forgotten but have now been resurrected for the good of many.

It was a wonderful industry to be involved in. Through the media, knowledge about health food shops, herbal shops and herbal clinics became much more widespread and popular. Why was there such a huge interest in alternative health at that time? Personally, I think that people were growing concerned about the side effects of drugs and if they felt they could improve their health naturally, then they were very happy to do so. During my travels, which I shall speak about in the next chapter, I have been in many health food stores throughout the world and consulted there. When I think of Mrs Gooch's health food stores in America, which were probably between 25 and 35 thousand square feet, our health food shops in Britain seem like miniatures in comparison. The potential of those shops was enormous. I still remember, with the greatest pleasure, the times I consulted in Mrs Gooch's shops, especially in Hollywood and Wiltshire where I had consulting rooms, and where I saw some of the most famous film stars in the world. I would give them nutritional advice and remedies to balance their very busy taxing lifestyles. They frequently had little sleep and their bodies were screaming for harmony and nourishment. I was also encouraged by Sandy Gooch's desire to get this vital message over to people and to make them realise how important this was. I helped with school excursions to the shop, and we tried to instil in the children how important it was that they looked after themselves, building an immune system for the future, and the importance of good food instead of junk food. I was pleased that so many universities in the States had asked me to go and lecture on the importance of nutrition and health food.

Throughout my travels, I have been encouraged by seeing that people from all over the world now have an understanding of the things that I have been preaching about for so long. The other day I read that cardiologists were advising people to eat six apples a day for their heart problems. This is a very positive step, but has come just a little too late. For many years, we have been preaching this particular gospel, knowing that we have a live body that needs live foods – not dead ones – to exist. The body needs 91 nutrients, and it won't get them from a synthetic pudding or a tin of tomato soup that has never seen a tomato. One message that I like to give is, for goodness sake, keep the body as healthy as possible. The outflowing aura that I often see in people, and which has been scientifically proven on the Kirlian photography machine, can also show whether food is alive or dead. If we look at a black and white photograph of a dead piece of meat, there is virtually no aura, but if the same is done with an organic apple or other piece of fruit, we see an almost unbroken energy aura. I am thankful for the gift that God has given me. When I see a patient in front of me, look at that outflowing aura and see the breaks and the holes, I feel it is my responsibility to try and mend them – for goodness sake.

My very loyal and excellent bookkeeper, Mrs Nancy Buchanan, and I have often thought about how we could serve people better and quicker. A new idea came to our minds, and we are now trying to encourage people to help themselves to better health with guidance and information through Jan de Vries Health and Diet Centres. The idea originated in Troon, where we had a health food shop called Jan de Vries Health and Diet Centre, which included a great information bank that people found helpful. The new Jan de Vries Health and Diet Centres not only have remedy sections that are safe for people to use, but three also provide consultations where people can come and get advice. It is not always easy to find good practitioners, and I feel that these centres work very well. We started in Glasgow and have since added Dumfries and Stranraer plus the shops in Prestwick and Stewarton.

One important thing is that the growth of the health food industry must be controlled. Too many cowboys and charlatans have profited by exploiting this field, and that is not always to the benefit of patients. I sometimes see patients who have gone to see such people and have not been monitored while taking remedies. It is very worrying to see the effect this can have, and therefore it is very necessary that experienced people who have devoted their lives to helping others control the industry.

12

The Flying Dutchman

It has been a great privilege for me to have visited 61 countries over the years and lectured in 40 US states. Although this is a terrific honour, I have actually seen very little of these countries – mainly lecture halls and airports. The little I have seen throughout the world, however, is a real treasure to me. I often think back to the very heavy lecture schedules that I had, where I was sometimes travelling two or three times a day by plane from one place to another so that I could lecture and spread the message. When I get more time, I would love to see the places I have lectured in properly. Hopefully that will happen some day.

In the meantime, I have wonderful memories of the places I have been and, travelling through our own country, I have very much enjoyed and valued the villages, towns and countryside where I have given hundreds of lectures. Throughout Britain, I have admired the beauty of this country. Many of my memories go back to the days when audiences might vary from ten or twelve people to thousands. I am terribly privileged to have made so many friends throughout the world during the course of my work. It would be impossible to list all the places I have lectured, or all the good and bad bits of these travels. However, I will mention a few that spring to my mind and which I often think back to.

About 25 years ago I did a talk in Los Angeles in the Ambassador Hotel. Afterwards, a gentleman who later became a real friend of mine asked me if I would go to Canada and give a talk in Toronto to a small group who had started an annual health conference called Total Health. I talked to him and, as we were both going to a meeting of the Rotary Club in Los Angeles, we shared a lot of ideas and, being on the same wavelength, I agreed to go. It was a most revealing meeting, with about 12 speakers, of whom I am now the only one left. Over the years, a lot of these wonderful people have passed away – people who worked so hard for the sake of health and gave up their lives to this work. Some of them mysteriously died, like my friend, Leon Shelly. It is still a mystery to me how these healthy people suddenly developed strange illnesses and died in the prime of their lives. Although I have my own suspicions, I am sure that in time we shall find out what really happened to them.

The conference in Toronto was wonderful, with 500 visitors, and I really enjoyed it. It was not without problems, though, as the Canadian authorities and drug industry didn't like the idea of some of the alternative treatments being promoted there. People like Max Gerson, Dr Mendelson, Dr Kelley and many others who spoke that night are no longer with us. They fought hard to bring the message closer to the people and I remember the last time I visited my friend Leon Shelly, who fought against pollution and against the establishment as it then was. A mysterious illness took his life. I think of Dr Mendelson, to whom I spoke on the Saturday evening after his brilliant lecture on medicine; the next day, after he left Toronto, I phoned his daughter and was told that he had died suddenly. A host of questions surrounding these mysteries became a bit clearer to me when, on one of my visits, five minutes before I was due to go on the platform, by this time speaking to thousands of people (as Total Health had grown so fast by then) a letter was handed to me by the sheriff of Toronto. I was warned about what to say and what not to say, and told that if I did not keep to the rules laid out in that letter, I would be prosecuted. In other words, it would really be better if I didn't speak there at all. I went to my friends, Claus Schmidt and Hermann Geiger, and when I showed them the letter they said, 'Jan, what are you going to do?'

I said, 'I will speak. My mother taught me that when you have an honest message, you have nothing to fear.' I probably gave a better talk that evening than I have ever done before because this threat kept my adrenalin flowing. I believe in freedom of speech. We had a most wonderful conference and I went back year after year.

On my travels throughout the United States, I have given talks, seminars and conferences in over 40 states, and spoken on radio and television. I have often met with opposition and been threatened with imprisonment and prosecution, but I have battled on. I remember that on one visit to St Catherine's, Canada, an interviewer kept me on air for two and a half hours, telling me that his programmes were listened to as far away as Buffalo in the USA and that it was important that I give people the message. In Vancouver, we built up a wonderful conference and it is with great respect that I think of the people who worked so hard to bring health to people in that beautiful part of the world. At one of the highest points in Vancouver, looking over British Columbia and Vancouver Island, the views were breathtaking and ones that I looked forward to after very busy days. Gazing out over God's wonderful creation, I felt it was worthwhile tackling governments and health officials to keep this great world free of pollution and destruction.

In the United States, where I gave hundreds of talks and seminars, I met with a great deal of goodwill and a thirst for knowledge of what nature had to offer. I remember one morning having to go on television. It was in Portland, Oregon, and I was asked to give a talk on my book *Menopause*. I had been on television before with these particular interviewers, Jim and Mary, whose programmes had millions of followers. When I arrived, the drug industry had taken offence at a book I had written about food. Together with a few other carefully chosen people, they wanted to challenge me and attack me on the book I had written. When I had met Jim and Mary a year earlier I liked them very much. When I did an iridology on Jim's eyes, I asked him what had happened to part of his heart. In great amazement, he said to me, 'How do you know? I have had a heart bypass.' With Mary, I did a similar thing and asked her what was wrong with her neck as I saw problems there and that she had severe whiplash. Luckily, this couple were sympathetic and so we went on with the programme. The first lady who attacked me was sitting a bit away from me. She told me that she drank between four and six bottles of a special fizzy drink every day and felt very well on it; it also appeared to have cleared her asthma. Jim then asked me what I thought about this particular drink. I told him that it was a good window cleaner! Then I turned to a coloured lady and asked her why she was ill. She replied, 'I am not ill.'

I said, 'I think you are. From where I am sitting, I can see you are ill.' I used Chinese facial diagnosis. I said, 'Apart from everything else, your hair is in a terrible state, your nails are breaking, your skin is deteriorating and you really have to seriously look at your diet. I would advise you to read my book on food.' I was quite happy with that particular book, as one of the big Sunday papers in Britain had given it a great appraisal and one professor who wrote about it said that it would benefit everyone's health if they read this book. So, I told her I would present her with a copy of my book and she should look seriously at her health. In front of us, there was a table full of junk food – and I mean real junk food. Mary lifted a sort of bun, called a Susi Q, off the table. Susi Qs were very popular in America at that time and Mary told me that the next lady ate two of these for her breakfast every day and felt great, as they contained a lot of zinc. I lifted up the Susi Q, with its layer of artificial cream in the middle and a red cherry on the top. I asked the lady if it was true that she ate two of these every day, and she said it was. I then asked, 'And why are you ill?'

'There is nothing wrong with me' was her reply. I said, 'Yes there is, you have rhinitis, sinusitis and I am sure you have allergies, as well as being grossly overweight.' She then nodded her head. Later on, that lady came to see me as a patient. The attack by the food industry on my book came to nothing.

At the end of the programme, Jim said that I was to speak again in Portland that evening. When I arrived at the place, there were so many people there that I heard one lady saying to another, 'It looks as though Elvis Presley has been resurrected. Who is going to be speaking here?' I ended up in a mall, a very large open place, with three microphones talking to people regarding their health problems – these people had an enormous need to get help.

In Chicago, I had a similar experience. When I arrived in Chicago, at a pharmacy called Merz, a little bit of the United States's history was evident, as this was the oldest pharmacy and also lovely to look at. There was a big illuminated flashing banner draped across the street that read 'Jan de Vries is here'. The evenings were mobbed. They were wonderful experiences.

Going back to the days when Gaylord Hauser was alive, I remember a wonderful experience when he gave a very eloquent speech and I was due to speak after him. Gaylord Hauser was a health guru from America, who was not only greatly loved by the film stars, but was also a man who had the tremendous ability of getting his message across to the public. He was a picture of health himself, even when in his 90s. To continue with the story, I was extremely worried as I felt I could certainly not come up to his standards. I spoke for about an hour and my reward came later when a little man came up to the platform, put his hand on my shoulder and said, 'That was a wonderful Scottish accent this afternoon.' I told him that I was Dutch, but I was very proud of the fact that he could hear the Scottish accent in my voice and told him that lots of people in Scotland called me 'MacVries'. I have seen so many people in the health food markets – too many to write about in this book.

It was not always very easy as America is full of contrasts. Generally I met the most loving people, but there were exceptions. One afternoon, I was consulting in a very big store – 35,000 square feet – and in the vitamin department, some yards away, was the check-out assistant. Two men came in and demanded money, which he wouldn't give them. They then shot him, took the money and walked out. I was devastated because the poor man, who was only doing his job, was shot dead and the two men got away. Despite these terrible things, life has to go on.

Another lecture comes to my mind, this time in San Jose, in the US. It is a lovely place with beautiful scenery. I was at a big Jewish health food market. The owners had arranged that I should do a talk in the evening in a big hall belonging to the synagogue.

When we arrived that evening, the place was absolutely packed, but more and more people continued to arrive. When the rabbi came to listen to my lecture, he saw the crowd situation and said to me, 'You cannot hold all the people in here,' so I asked him what could be done. 'Well,' he said, 'you can use the synagogue if you are willing to put on a little cap and talk from the pulpit.' This was difficult because I am not Jewish. When I told him that I was partly Jewish, however, and had Jewish blood in me, his face changed and he said, 'Well, that changes the picture. Put on that little cap and go ahead.' I never saw a place so full.

In Tampa, I had a similar experience, as again we had a big hall for the talk and, in the afternoon, I had talked to a lot of people in a big health food marketplace. Again, when we arrived in the evening, the place was crammed with people. When the minister came, he said that I could not have my talk there and what I really needed was the church. I asked him if he would be willing for me to use the church and he said that would be fine, but it might be better if I could incorporate something about the Bible into my lecture. I said to him that I could probably speak a bit about herbs from the Bible and he thought that was a brilliant idea. It was a talk that I enjoyed because I racked my brain to think of biblical herbs. That evening was such a success, especially when I mentioned the advice given in one of the oldest books of the Bible, Ecclesiastes. In the last chapter there is a wonderful little story. It says that, as one gets older, one must remember the Creator of youth. In Ecclesiastes 12:3–6, it tells us what happens as one gets older:'the keepers of the house' (the legs) start to tremble,'the grinders' (the teeth) become fewer,'the windows become darkened' (the eyes) and 'the doors shall be shut in the streets' (our ears). Advice is given in some translations that one should look to the caperberry for help. In other words, the use of the caperberry will be beneficial when one gets older, when the memory (the golden ball) and the heart (the picture) start to fail. Everybody stormed into the chemists and health food stores to find extract of caperberry, which was not there because, again, it is one of the forgotten herbs. It was a wonderful story and, along with all the other biblical herbs I mentioned, contributed to a great evening. However, this lecture had an impact on me and I felt I should investigate the caperberry. When I finally found the extract of caperberry (which grows profusely in Israel), I realised that indeed it was of great benefit, aiding vitality and energy and, following some research, I incorporated it into one of my flower essences.

Another time that I often think about was when I was asked in Miami to open a large store. I had to arrive quite early and, of course, I was dressed up to the nines for this big opening because a lot of people from the health food world would be gathered there. We had a most wonderful time. Two boys who were with me asked if I had ever visited Miami Beach. I told them no, I never had, and they said,'Well, why don't we take some time off and go there?'

On a glorious day, when most people were lying half naked on the beach, I stepped between them wearing my Sunday suit, enjoying the wonderful sea views and experiencing the feeling of being on the sands of Miami Beach. Often, when I think of that occasion, I smile to myself and think,'Will I ever be able to enjoy sunbathing on Miami Beach?'

In India and Pakistan, when I lectured and worked in one of the main hospitals in Bombay, I also had some wonderful times, although there are enormous contrasts in those countries. When I treated some of the richest and most important people there, it drove me to try and work hard for the Third World and to help those in need, not only financially but also with their health problems. I treated world leaders and was greatly supported by the Sumaya family, who were a tremendous help to me in the course of my work there.

Back in the Scandinavian countries, I lectured, helped students leading up to their exams, visited universities and also the oldest medical library in Stockholm, where Dr Voll and I looked at records relating to original medicine. In the oldest department of books, it was recorded where medicine started. It is wonderful to see many aspects of healthcare returning to traditional treatments. Medical people all know about the Karolinska Institute. It is a marvellous medical library housing the most fascinating books. In the oldest part of that library, where there are thousands of books, one can read of old medical folklore from many centuries ago. We were especially interested to see that so much had been written on herbs, flowers, foods, barks of trees and leaves which were used in folklore for medicinal purposes. There was so much material contained within that library that we could spend years expanding our knowledge, and it would be quite beneficial for medicine to inspect these old writings.

In Sri Lanka, where I worked during the revolution, in the Kaliboa Hospital in Colombo, I saw the most awful scenes, but it encouraged me that traditional or indigenous medicine was promoted by the government. I saw the oldest forms of medicine practised in Sri Lanka. When I sold a house and gave a lot of the money to this particular hospital for development, I was sorry to see how some of that money was spent on erecting a statue and, with great honour, this was accepted. However, I would much rather have seen all the money being spent on medicine to alleviate human suffering. Nevertheless, great lessons were learned from what I saw in Sri Lanka.

From Sri Lanka, I went to Zambia, where I had to treat some of the most important people in the country. While there, I asked permission to see a few hospitals, which was granted by some of the leaders of that country, but I was shocked to see some of them packed with AIDS sufferers. It was heartbreaking to hear the cries for help from patients who were battling with an illness for which medicine had no answer. I had the privilege of staying for a little while in that beautiful country with its wonderful blue flowers along the streets.

When I left Zambia, I had the most horrific experience on the way home. We were told our plane was being hijacked. Luckily, everything turned out all right in the end, but the pilot had to land in a godforsaken place in Eastern Germany. When we landed, we were kept in the plane for six hours, where there was really no outlook at all, just a lot of nervous people. I managed to settle most of them down and kept the ones who were very nervous as calm as possible. It wasn't a scary business, except for the fact that no one knew what the outcome would be. Finally, after negotiations were finalised, we were allowed to leave and landed in Bonn. I ran for my life when I came out of that plane, and was so happy to see the British Airways desk. I asked them when the first plane to London was and was told that it would be in ten minutes. I managed to get a ticket and when the lady asked about my luggage, I said, 'Never mind the luggage. Let me go home.' I was so grateful to be safely back home again when we landed on British soil. It was a shattering experience; sunshine and shadows were keeping life very interesting.

I had a very nice experience during one of my plane journeys, however. I was asked by a stewardess to go to the first-class section. I never usually travel first class because it is basically against my principles but, as I was very tired, I accepted her offer. I sat down, had a wonderful meal, and was treated to champagne and everything that she wanted to give me. Then she suddenly said, 'Do you not recognise me?' I looked at that beautiful girl, and she told me that my best friend had given birth to her back in Nunspeet and now lived in Switzerland. This was her daughter, who had treated me to such luxury. Her mother had told her about me, she recognised me from the photographs and treated me so well. This was one of the nice things that happened during my travels.

Another time, I was sitting in a plane with two ladies who asked me where I was going. I told them that I was going to Belfast. Then they asked me where I had come from. I told them from Scotland. They asked me if I knew Jan de Vries, who had such popular programmes with Sean Rafferty – they were desperate to meet him! I told them he was sitting beside them. This is an uplifting story that very often helped in the work that I was doing.

Alfred Vogel once asked me to give a talk to medics in West Germany in a place called Freiburg. Because this talk had to be in German and he couldn't manage, he asked me to go. I enjoyed looking around that marvellous city with its universities and beautiful buildings before going to the big meeting, where I had to speak on viruses, allergies and the immune system. The talk went well, but as medics and students often like to criticise, or sometimes just be difficult, one student started to question the excellent remedy called Echinacea. Echinacea is a wonderful plant to help strengthen the immune system and I had already spoken about it. He was very difficult about it until one lady doctor stood up and said that she had been on holiday in Brazil and, during her holiday, suffered a bad throat infection which caused a swelling like a golf ball in her throat. She tried to find a pharmacy to get antibiotics, but instead found an old health food store that had one bottle of *Echinaforce* left on its shelf. She thought of getting some chamomile tea, but the health food shop owner advised her to try *Echinaforce* instead. She bought it and looked at the label, which read 'three times daily, ten drops'. She thought she would double that amount as she really didn't believe that herbal medicine was effective. She told the whole meeting that within three hours the abscess had burst and by the next day she was fine. She added that, as a result of her quick recovery, she was now very interested in homoeopathic and herbal medicine. She was most encouraging and a tremendous help to me at that meeting.

In South Africa, where I lectured in the main cities, I was criticised by a very well-known professor of pharmacology in Durban. I was to be interviewed by him, but I was wary about it as Earl Mindell, the man who wrote *The Vitamin Bible*, had returned following an interview breathing fire at the way the professor had attacked him. My anxiety wasn't helped by the fact that the evening before I had agreed to do an interview with black television. In those days, when apartheid was still rife, they didn't care much when I told them that we all have red blood and whether a person's skin is black, yellow or white makes no difference to me, as I see everyone as a human being. I was worried about this professor, as I knew he hated alternative medicine and was ready for a confrontation. I met up with him in the waiting room and I could see he took an instant dislike to me. Then he asked me where I lived. I told him in Troon, Scotland. 'Ah,' he said, 'where the famous golf courses are.' I said, 'Yes, and I live almost on Royal Troon golf course.' He told me he had played there. His focus immediately turned to golf and, when he heard that I had treated lots of famous golfers from around the world, he became extremely interested. We went on the programme and I can still hear him saying, 'Here is the most wonderful man who lives in my favourite place and with my favourite game – golf.' After that, we got on famously together, discussing different topics relating to health. So that was another victory for me. Afterwards I treated myself by going to the beach. While I was going in and out of the water, I got a shock when I saw a notice stating that this beach was only for the black community. Not that it made any difference to me, but I was supposed to go to the beach for the white community. Incidents like that were very educational.

I had a very interesting case, again in South Africa, when I was staying with a homoeopathic doctor and her husband, who was a surgeon. I really enjoyed that visit as I had so much in common with her, and had some very lively discussions with her husband, as he was so against alternative medicine – and not without reason. He saw many patients who ended up in hospital very ill because they had consulted witch doctors. The couple had a chauffeur, a very nice man, who was fascinated by my ballpoint pens. I got friendly with him, but I could see he walked very badly (one of his legs was shorter than the other) and told him that I would like to help him to walk a bit better. He said absolutely no way, because he was going to the witch doctor. I gave him all my ballpoint pens and managed to persuade him to take me with him to the witch doctor because I wanted to see what he actually did. I have never seen such a painful and awful experience as that which my chauffeur friend, of whom I had grown very fond, had to endure. I asked the witch doctor if he could put the man's left and right legs into a certain position. He said, 'No problem.' He took a very hot poker and went to four points in the shorter leg and told the man that it was now balanced, but there was no difference. I showed him. I wasn't allowed to touch the patient, but it was obvious that one leg was still a lot shorter than the other leg, and I asked him to put the ankle bones together so that I could show him. He then took a handful of wishbones, threw them in the air and prayed to his god to correct the problem, but nothing happened.

By luck, I had a few copper and zinc magnets in my pocket that I had taken with me, as I wanted to see this particular exercise working. In opposite directions, I put the copper and the zinc magnets on his sacrum, on the ileum and some on the left and the right legs. I too prayed very hard to my god, who never leaves or forsakes me, and is always with me. My prayers, in conjunction with the treatment, worked. One could almost see the left and right legs straightening themselves out. I asked the witch doctor which treatment he thought was best. He shrugged his shoulders and walked off. I am sure that my friend, the chauffeur, would still go back to him, as his belief in him was so strong. That was a nice experience that I shall never forget, and which I hold dear when I think of my visits to South Africa.

As I have said, it would be too much to write about all the countries I have visited and the many experiences I have had. I have been greatly encouraged by people's support. When I went to an enormous health food store in Richmond in America, a woman stood for a whole afternoon in a queue just to get my book *Do Miracles Exist?* When she finally got the book, I signed it and she told me that, as the queue was so long, she had had to wait four hours for her book. I expanded on this subject in *Do Miracles Exist?*, as I have often witnessed unexpected reversals in illness and disease through intervention. I have often asked myself in such cases whether this is divine intervention, or just coincidence.

In Cincinnati, I was greatly encouraged when a family came in with three children. I had been in that place about eight years previously and had first met this couple then. At our first meeting they were both very upset and emotional as they desperately wanted a child. Nothing had worked; none of the doctors they had consulted could help them and it was driving them apart. They asked if there was anything I could do. I hadn't a lot of choice, so I went and collected four remedies. I gave them some advice and as there were no obvious reasons – except he had a low sperm count and she had irregular periods – I told them what to do. Now, eight years later, here they were with their three children; the first remedies I gave them had worked and, every time they wanted another child, they had repeated the procedure and it had worked. What a joy. On that visit my public relations man, Peter Rule, was with me. He was so amazed that he sent his daughter and son-in-law, who had the same problem, to see me and, again, they were successful in having a child. These little miracles are an encouragement to keep going.

My travels also took me to Australia, which I dearly loved, as I spent my days lecturing at the Botanic Gardens in Sydney, Melbourne, Brisbane and Perth, and was especially pleased at the tremendous gatherings I had in Melbourne. Those days were absolutely wonderful. However, as I have said in so many of my lectures, man has three bodies, not one. They should all be in harmony and health is dependent on them all. The immune system is vital for the world we live in today. Unfortunately, on this occasion, I became very much aware of that fact. I was on my way to Australia for the third time, having just finished a very busy day at Harley Street. I was tired. I had also received a letter which had greatly upset me. When I arrived at Heathrow Airport, I was told that the only available seats were in the smoking section, unless I went first class. As first class is against my principles, I had to sit next to a lady who was very nice but smoked all the way. To summarise, my emotional body had been attacked by the letter, my physical body had been attacked by the very busy day I had had as well as the cigarette smoke, and my mental body was under strain because of the short time I had to prepare for the lectures in Australia. So my three bodies were totally out of harmony. When I arrived in Melbourne, I had no time to have a rest, but had to go straight in to take a big lecture. The next day, we had to go into the bush, a very taxing experience as I had to speak on the characteristics and the signatures of plants, herbs, flowers and trees that I had never seen before but, by their signs, I could tell what they should be used for. As we had an entourage of reporters with us, I had to be very sure of my facts. My body was under par and unfortunately, there in the bush, I was attacked by a virus to which I had no immunity. I managed to carry on for the few days, but became quite unwell. On the way back to Sydney, I had to do a talk in the evening on constitutional homoeopathy, which is not always the easiest topic. In the middle of that talk, I started to shake. I managed to finish and, luckily, met up with Juliet and Hayley Mills. I had treated their father and mother and, as they were very concerned about me, they were of great help. It was lucky that God had sent a few angels to help me, as I felt absolutely awful. I saw a consultant in the hospital, who said that it was probably a viral attack from an unknown virus and I had pneumonia, which I'd had before. I was very ill indeed. He wanted to give me antibiotics, which I cannot take as I am allergic to them, and he said, 'Well, you cannot stay in the hospital. Everybody has seen you today with your work on television and we can't have you dying in an Australian hospital!' That was, of course, true. I told him that I would go back to the hotel. That was a night I shall never forget. I prayed hard to God that I would not die in Australia and God answered my prayers. I used a whole bottle of *Echinaforce* that night and did all the cold and hot water treatments my grandmother taught me.

Early the next morning, the consultant came to my door. He said he had not slept all night as he was so worried about me and wondered how I was. I was in fact extremely ill. He helped me considerably and luckily I recovered, so that I was able to carry on with the rest of my work in Australia. By the next Saturday, when my niece and nephew came all the way down from Adelaide to see me, I was a bit better. Luckily, my wife wasn't informed, otherwise she would not have known what to do, but I told my niece and nephew that I was fine. However, the hospital consultant gave me a letter for my own doctor. Upon my return, I saw a doctor in Troon who was quite shocked and said immediately that I had to go to hospital. In the hospital, I met up with a very nice and understanding consultant who, in no uncertain terms, told me that I would need to spend a day in hospital as he believed I had developed diabetes. Indeed, the virus had attacked my pancreas and I had a blood sugar of 33 per cent (very high). I was given advice about injections, tablets and insulin, but I asked this doctor kindly if I could treat it myself and my blood sugar went from 33 to 16 per cent, and is now between 6 and 8 per cent (a good level is below 7 per cent). I have managed with my own remedies to keep this balanced, for which I am very grateful. Not that other people should do the same thing. With diabetes, it is very important to follow a consultant's instruction, although a lot can be done to bring the blood sugar down through dietary management and alternative medicine.

My illness in Australia taught me a great lesson: the immune system is very important and when the three bodies are under threat, one should be very careful. So, temporarily, I had to reduce my workload, but happily I can now continue lecturing throughout this country and others as I did before, and still raise thousands and thousands of pounds for charity to help wherever I can.

I had some funny experiences in Australia too. I remember one evening, when I was lecturing to a large audience and feeling very tired, that there was a lady in the front row who never took her eyes off me all night. She was keen to speak to me afterwards and said that as I had worked so hard, would I go back to her house because she was very anxious to give me a colonic irrigation in order to make me feel a bit better! The only thing I wanted that night was to go to my hotel and then go straight to bed – certainly not to have a colonic irrigation! Sometimes it is very funny when you go around lecturing and remember the things that people ask you. Following another talk, one lady, after listening intently to my lecture, came to me and asked if my hair was its natural colour or if I used hair dye, as she hadn't noticed a single grey hair on my head during my lecture that evening. One can never forget some of these little stories.

Lecture tours, which I mainly do for charity, have been a great help to those in need throughout the world. The most unexpected situations sometimes arise during these tours. I remember in Northern Ireland, in a place called Warren Point, around 600 or 700 people were packed into a hall on a very stormy night and all the lights went out. I did the talk completely in darkness, managed to keep the audience cheery and, shortly after the talk, when the lights went back on, there was great hilarity. When all these experiences are put in your path, it is a matter of trying to carry on and stand up and fight as best you can.

I had a great friend in Sir Stanley Matthews, and I always told him that he had feet like nobody else. His football talent was the gift given to him and during his last visit to me, I will never forget him saying, 'Whatever comes, keep going on.' That very often leads to victory and to the goal we want in life.

13

The Media – Friend or Foe?

While I was staying in the state of Indiana once, I was awakened very early one morning by the sound of a cock crowing. When, in the glory of that early morning, I looked out of the window and saw fields and fields without a soul, the sound of that cock crowing made me think of yet another full day of being with the media, for the strength of the media is indeed as powerful as the sound of that cock crowing far afield. Years after lectures and interviews on radio and television programmes, questions often come back to me: 'Why did you say this?' or 'When did you say that?'

One day, I was travelling by plane through three states of America, and was engaged in lectures, radio and television work. In the evening, I had a wonderful experience, as my friend, Roy Smalling, had hired a car to give me a fantastic surprise – or so I thought. He told me we were going to a place called Fort Worth Stock Yards in the state of Texas and that I would be in for a great surprise. It was very late at night when, after a fairly long journey, I looked around and saw that the streets were covered in sand, cowboys were walking around and it looked like something from the books I had read as a child. Roy eventually told me that this was the hotel. The horses were tied up against the wall outside. Everything appeared to be made of wood: when we went inside, the floors, ceilings and walls were all wooden and I thought, coming into the bar area, that it looked very rough. It all seemed like a dream after reading about places like this as a boy. It was quite an experience, but the surprise did not end there, and was something I shall not easily forget.

I was quite tired and, shortly after arriving, asked Roy if I could go to bed. Even my bedroom was all made of wood, including the toilet, but, although very simple, it had all the necessities. I was exhausted and fell into a deep sleep until, in the middle of the night, I awoke with a great shock. Two big eyes were staring right at me and, although it was dark, there was a glare in them that frightened me. So I thought I would use the ostrich policy of putting my head under the blankets and going back to sleep. However, my Dutch nature – which is very nosy – refused to let me get back to sleep and every time I peeked over the top of the blankets, all I could see were those big, shiny eyes. Eventually, I could not stand this any longer, so I put on the light – and then I laughed and laughed and laughed at what confronted me. The wooden shutters on the window were not closed very tightly. The moon had been shining through the slats of the shutters and directly into the eyes of a horse's head that was mounted on the wall; it was the reflected moonlight that was glaring down at me. It made me think that we are often afraid of things that are not there, and the power of the imagination can be very strong.

It is not always easy dealing with the media and one has to be very well trained in what can be said, which can be very daunting, especially in my line of work where there is so much criticism. Fear can be one's worst enemy and there is a very fine line between what one can say and what one cannot.

When Mr Collins from the well-known publishing and printing company was still alive, we spoke one day about various stories and he encouraged me to write some books. I told him I was not a writer, but he asked me just to tell my story, as it would be interesting enough for his company to print. He suggested that I should write about what I thought was the most prevalent health problem at that time. Well, at that particular time, I found that stress and nervous disorders were the most appropriate health problems to write about, not knowing that 20 years later these disorders would be even more widespread. I therefore embarked on my book *Stress and Nervous Disorders*, which is still one of the best-selling books. However, the Collins company did not publish it and I was lucky enough to be advised to speak to Mainstream, then the second biggest publisher in Scotland. When I arrived one afternoon at their office, the two owners, Bill Campbell and Peter MacKenzie, were present. They had a small room upstairs in the building, packed with books, notes and a desk full of papers. To be honest, when I saw the enormous bundles of papers there, I feared that they would not even look at my simple little book. However, Bill Campbell looked at the manuscript and handed it to Peter MacKenzie, and a discussion then followed between them. I was quite sure that, with my bad English and grammatical mistakes, they would not be interested. However, to my great surprise, luck was with me and they said they would give it a try. The book was printed, went on the market and was a success – and remains so to this day. When my youngest daughter read the book, she said, 'I hope my English teacher never reads this.' Twenty years later, the Northern Irish *County Down Spectator* reported that:

> At a glance, the Public Lending Right figures for 2004–05 paint a rather idyllic picture. Having a closer look at the figures, disturbing trends begin to emerge. While across the UK the most borrowed book in the medical category was *Self Help for Backs*, Northern Ireland's library users were more concerned with their mental health than with any aches or pains. The book most often requested, in fact, is the book *Stress and Nervous Disorders* written by Jan de Vries.

After my book was launched, the media became interested. Steven Williams, a London publicist hired by Mainstream, arranged several interviews for me, one of which was with Gloria Hunniford. Gloria was not very keen on alternative medicine at that time, but we managed to persuade her to do an interview on Radio 2. That was in 1982. The interview went well and Gloria often relates stories about my funny voice and the way I formulated my sentences. It made her smile and the public liked it. The programme was such a success that the BBC decided to do further interviews and, as it was a great way to reach out to the public, the publishers were very keen that I contributed to these programmes once a month or even once a fortnight. Those programmes became very influential and were listened to by millions of people. The letters we received provided clear evidence that listeners wanted to know more about alternative medicine and, from 1982 until 1992, I participated in these programmes. Later, I appeared with Gloria on *Open House* for television. I was pleased that despite her initial scepticism, Gloria and her family became real converts to alternative medicine.

Other stations then started to get interested and one of the first presenters to come on the scene was a great friend of Gloria's, the very popular Sean Rafferty who broadcast on BBC Radio Northern

Ireland. Sean and I often recall the first programme we did together, when I got held up in traffic and we had no alternative but to conduct the programme by mobile telephone from the car until I arrived at the studio to continue the programme from there. It was the beginning of a long and fruitful relationship. The programmes became very popular in Northern Ireland, and for years I was able to give people simple advice on home remedies and ways of maintaining a healthier lifestyle. We had a great rapport and Sean often helped me in my voluntary work when holding lectures for charities, by either opening events or helping to make these worthwhile. When the big choir, DEV, came over from Holland to do a concert for the Red Cross in Westminster in London, Sean introduced their music. That was a great media exercise, because DEV is very famous in Holland. We became a real pair of advisers and, after some time, I am sure that Sean knew what advice to give just as well as I did. It was great fun.

Because the programmes were so popular, the *Belfast Telegraph*, which is widely read throughout the world, became very interested and I wrote a weekly column there for many years, answering people's questions and giving them advice and guidance. I think it is very important that people receive guidance because they are often left in doubt, not knowing what to do and, for that reason, between Holland and Britain, I have written 40 books on the subject of health. Mainstream has been a tower of strength in this work and I shall be forever grateful for their guidance and assistance in doing this job. They have become real friends to me and have provided a mainstay when writing the books.

Magazines became greatly interested and asked me to write for them – like *Woman's Realm*, *Woman's Weekly*, *Hello* magazine, *Top Santé*, *Here's Health*, *Ulster Tatler* – I could go on and on. The feedback from these magazines was great as lots of people wanted to know more about alternative medicine. The thirst for additional knowledge in this field became just as big here as it was in the United States.

I eventually had 22 radio programmes and about 4 television programmes. The impact of the features I did on *This Morning* with Richard and Judy was quite amazing. I participated in these programmes once a month for a number of years. Not only was it really great fun, but it also helped a lot of people with their health problems. People asked me if I liked giving answers on television, probably because I was not used to it. I haven't even got a television in my own home as, with our busy lives, we need rest. Nevertheless, I realise that the power of the media is immeasurable and if it can help people and ease their suffering then it is a wonderful thing. I can well understand publishing companies' need for the media's help in order to sell books.

I sometimes feel sorry for people who are involved in this type of work because they are subjected to so much pressure and criticism that they need a nervous system made of iron and steel to withstand it. I remember once I was asked to do a tour of some of the old Dutch colonies – Curaçao, the Dutch Antilles, Aruba – all these places, including Guatemala. I was also asked to visit Bonaire, which was a quiet place. The beaches were white, the sand was glowing and the peace was almost heavenly. There, in that lonely place, I found a bundle of television stars and broadcasters, who had discovered a little oasis there. My old friend, Adele Bloemendal, so well known by the Dutch public, said, 'Come and join us here, Jan. At long last, we can get some peace.'

Relaxation is very important. I meet so many stressed people who drink too much coffee to keep them going, and too much alcohol for relaxation. Their busy lifestyles can put their bodies under enormous strain and it is comforting to know that they can sometimes find a place where they can rest and relax completely.

Anything that one does incorrectly can lead to big problems. I clearly remember on one of the programmes speaking about certain foods that are not good for certain illnesses, and trying to exclude certain foods from the daily diet that might be causing allergic reactions, or too much acidity or alkalinity in the body. Balance is very important. With rheumatoid arthritis and psoriasis, I often suggest eating nothing from the pig. This almost led to legal action from the British pig breeders, but, on the programme, I said that, although the pig was a very nice animal, in some cases it was not good for people's health. So I managed to get out of that.

Some broadcasters were absolute masters, like Alison Brown from Radio Lancashire who, in only half an hour, managed to ask 40 questions. A lot of skill is needed in the making of these programmes to keep the broadcasters on the right side of the law, while still answering questions from the listeners as well as they can. Most of the programmes are done via the ISDN line, so I don't always need to travel. One programme I dearly loved and personally took part in for a long time was that of Radio Kent. Barbara Sturgeon, not only a very eloquent broadcaster but also a great personality, made it tremendous fun and the people she worked with were absolutely wonderful. Peter Rule, my PR agent, and I always looked forward to that trip and the fun we had.

It really makes me smile to think back to the sort of questions that I was asked. As I have a great affinity with animals, at one point we landed up with real animal programmes and on one programme – which I shall never forget – people came to the studio with their cats and dogs and all their problems when they knew I was there and the management had to tell me that I was not allowed to see anybody there as, again, it looked like a surgery.

Another experience that comes to my mind was on the *Gerry Kelly Show* in Belfast, which I did regularly. On the show there was an entertainer called May McFetteridge, a transvestite. May entertains the public wonderfully and he is a very nice man but, funnily enough, when he is dressed up he looks just like a real woman. On the programme, Gerry asked me if I would do some iridology. I looked in the eyes of quite a number of people, told them what could be wrong and, to their astonishment, they said that that was exactly what was wrong with them. So, in front of the public, May asked me what I found wrong with her. When I looked deep into her eyes, I told her that I saw that she wasn't really a woman, but actually a man. This caused great hilarity and those shows have been a great success.

It is a wonderful thing when one can provide evidence of the work one is doing. For years, I prepared columns in the *Daily Record* and the questions were quite amazing, but I was happy when I switched over to the *Sunday Post*. I had not realised that that paper was so powerful. Today, the *Sunday Post* is still one of the biggest papers. I think it is so much loved and admired throughout the world because of its simplicity and the fact that they write the truth and do not sensationalise situations. The editor who did the pages with me at the start, Carolyn Smeaton, has great knowledge as a layperson of the whole field of alternative medicine, and she often improved on the articles I had written.

The media is very powerful. Over the years that I have written and broadcast in this field, I have received a great deal of feedback. One day, I was at Olympia in London where I spoke four times to absolutely packed halls with large groups of journalists. One of the journalists said to me, 'Remember when you started here that there was only a handful of people. Now there are hundreds and hundreds, if not thousands, who have become followers.' It was wonderful when one of the visitors stood up and said, 'I watched you on *This Morning* with Richard and

Judy for many years and was initially completely against alternative medicine, but you converted me and thank God you did, because I now feel like a new person and have a new lease of life.'

When people try to criticise and say there is nothing in alternative medicine, I ask them to just try it – try it for three to six months and then see how you feel. I know that most people will then come back and say that they have a new lease of life. Every broadcaster has his own style of working and yet, sometimes, one is surprised. A broadcaster from Canada comes to mind. With all my personal experience, I would say that he is the best broadcaster I have ever worked with. He was very well versed in his subject, had a great rapport with people, and yet, the last time I was over in Canada, he had gone. The station didn't want his services any more. It often saddens me when I have worked with people for so long, that they suddenly disappear, often without a word of thanks from their employers and colleagues. The world of the media is very cold and is one that I personally would not like to be part of. Today is everything, tomorrow is nothing. The media can also be extremely hard and twist words. They can take certain phrases from a book without giving the whole picture, thereby giving people the wrong impression, or they can attack you with something that, taken in the context it was written, probably has a totally different meaning but, given a twist, comes out incorrectly and can have repercussions. National stations, international stations – they all have their attractions and their listeners, but a lot depends on how the message comes across.

I once did a talk for a big group of ladies. There was a large turnout of journalists and I could see that the man who was to introduce me was very tired and probably bored. He told everybody that I was a great speaker and that he, for one, had looked forward to the talks I would be giving that day and knew that the rest of the audience would find them very interesting. After I started my talk, he fell into a deep sleep and, when his colleagues woke him after I had finished an hour later, he stood up telling everybody what a wonderful talk it had been. That is typical of my experience of the media.

I get an enormous number of letters following television programmes. One letter from a lady really surprised me when she wrote to say that she was absolutely glued to her television when I was on – but, instead of listening to what I was saying, she was more interested in my wavy hair! She asked me if I wore a wig as, at my age, she felt I couldn't have such dark, healthy-looking hair. I was sorry to hear this because I neither have a wig nor colour my hair, and would have been happier if she had been more interested in the topic I was discussing than in my hair!

Another story I will never forget concerned my great friend, Len Allan. I will write about him in more depth in the next chapter, but I had given a talk on the radio, after which there was time set aside for questions. A lady phoned up and told of her child who had weeping ears, which I know is very, very difficult. Being over-enthusiastic, I said to her that it was quite easily solved. I said she could do such and such, and I even said that she *should* do such and such. I got a phone call from my friend, Len, who had listened to the programme and was highly shocked that I had advised this lady that she must give her child this and that. He had been in practice for over 50 years and told me that in all that time he had never said to any patient 'you *must* do this and that', because it is forbidden by law. He was sitting shaking in his chair listening to the radio, wondering what the nation must be thinking of what I was saying. That, again, was a great lesson.

People constantly ask me to keep in touch and, especially after seeing my newspaper articles and hearing my radio or television programmes, want to be kept informed on the developments of complementary medicine. I am very pleased that, after a lot of hard work, I have established our own magazine, which comes out four times a year and is called *In Touch*. The circulation has grown fast and it is much easier to get my messages across to people this way. No matter where I am throughout the world, when I see new developments I am so very anxious to share this information with my patients and ex-patients. *In Touch* has made this possible.

I was involved with *Health Check*, a television programme in Belfast which became very popular. It was quite astonishing that enormous numbers of people wanted to be on the programme, either for advice or for diagnosis. The variety of problems was so amazing that the viewers were glued to their screens to see what advice I would give.

Thinking about the power of the media reminded me of a programme I was on in 1991 with Mrs Logie Baird, who was then in her 90s and whose husband invented television. She said that if her husband could have envisaged how people would become addicted to their television screens and what an enormous part it would play in the lives of families, he would have been ashamed. People who have an addiction to television should realise that it is not good for their eyes. To watch television once in a while is fine, but not – as one patient told me she did – switch the television on in the morning and switch it off at night when you go to bed. That is dangerous.

However, I am happy that the media has spread the message. For that reason, I cooperate with them so that people in this country have freedom of choice, whatever treatment they decide to pursue.

When the first alternative health conferences were held in this country, the media regarded them as some sort of quackery, whereas nowadays these conferences are of huge interest to the public. I was delighted to be asked by the magazine *Here's Health*, sadly no longer published, to present awards to the best companies from different countries that had produced the finest products in this field. There were many awards and what pleased me was that companies that would never have looked at alternative medicine previously now, thankfully, were recipients – companies like Boots, Waitrose, Sainsbury, Tesco and Marks & Spencer alongside small companies that had done their best to pioneer this market and had overtaken the giant companies when they realised the huge potential that was there to be tapped. It was with considerable pride that I gave out those well-deserved awards for the kind of products that we see on the market today, which are well promoted and so well received by the public. It was also a great honour for Alfred Vogel's company, Bioforce, to receive the top award.

I just wish that Vogel could have been alive to see how much his products are revered in this country and that his lifetime's devotion has been so worthwhile. Alfred Vogel and others who have followed in his footsteps have worked with an open vision to give freedom of choice to the public. Personally, this is also my mission and I am grateful to the media for their help, but this interest must start with oneself. Even if I have to preach it on the streets, I am happy to work for an honest cause to help alleviate human suffering.

Some time ago, when the alternative medicine exhibition in Edinburgh took place, I arrived to make two afternoon speeches. My talks there are always packed. We were told that there was no electricity and the public was not allowed to go into the building. Everybody was so disappointed and upset, until I suggested that we should go to Rose Street, behind the Assembly Rooms in George Street, where there were benches. I managed to find a big box and a loudspeaker and, in front of hundreds of people, conducted my lectures in the street. It was a glorious Sunday afternoon and, as more and more people came to listen, it was wonderful to be able to preach the message of health there in the streets.

One day, when I was speaking at a big yoga seminar, the hall was so warm that I advised the audience that we should go out onto the street. Hundreds of people joined us and we had great fun. Afterwards, the press wrote about this fantastic interest in the different forms of alternative medicine.

Sometimes the public itself is a great form of media. I was very encouraged by a small incident. On her way to my clinic in Troon was the wife of a very well-known doctor in Edinburgh. She had with her a consultant from one of the hospitals in Edinburgh. Both the consultant and the doctor (my patient's husband) were very against alternative medicine. In fact, they laughed about it. My patient, who was in great despair, had been improving and, reluctantly, her husband had to accept this. He said, 'Whatever this man is doing, just keep doing it.' That was the reason he agreed to bring his wife back to me. So, on that sunny afternoon, they were all on their way to visit my clinic, and also to see Royal Troon golf course. When they were near Lanark, they got a flat tyre. They were in the middle of nowhere, but managed to spot a farm. They went up to it and the farmer who answered the door asked them what they wanted. They asked if they could use his telephone. He said, 'Absolutely not. When I let people into this house to use the phone before, they stole some of my belongings. You will just have to go.' They told the farmer that they were on their way to Troon because the lady in the car was quite ill and had to see a doctor there. His face lit up as he asked, 'Is that the Dutch doctor?'

The gentleman said, 'Yes, I believe he is Dutch.'

The farmer asked, 'Is he small, and is his name Jan de Vries?' They said that was correct. The farmer then told them that they could use the phone for nothing. He added, 'That man cured my back some years ago and I have never looked back. Please use the phone.'

When young practitioners have just started in practice and don't have enough patients, I have often encouraged them to keep going and hold on. If they are good and know what they are doing, they will reach their goal. I have often repeated to them the words of Sir Stanley Matthews who said, 'Keep going, fight back and you will be victorious.'

14

Pioneers and Fighters
for Truth and Freedom

This chapter is about the pioneers of alternative medicine and, although I will write about the ones I have known personally, it would also be good to mention a few who, throughout the world, have done their best to open people's eyes to something that has become very valuable today.

Samuel Hahnemann, the founder of homoeopathy, had three principles that he preached to diagnose a problem: look at the image of a person, look at the life force in a person and don't just treat the problem, but also treat the cause of the problem. A lot of the people we know from history, such as Lust, Kneipp, Benjamin, Priestnitz, Bircher Benner, Vogel, Lindlahr and, later on, Thomson, Leaf, Jay, and many others who have gone before, pioneered different fields, and also laid the groundwork for a wonderful team who have carried on from them and are working just as hard today for justice, truth and freedom for what has now become complementary medicine.

When I came to this country 47 years ago, my very first visit was to the Kingston Clinic in Edinburgh. I met old Mr Thomson, who had very extreme ideas on nature cures. He treated patients with the four naturopathic principles, which are treating with food, water, air and a little manipulation and massage. Hydrotherapy was very important. Without doubt, the patients I spoke to were all quite happy. I was also pleased to speak to Mr Thomson a bit about the past and the difficulties he encountered with his views on medicine then. I asked him how high the cancer rate was in Scotland. He told me that it was 1 in 18 to 20 at that time, whereas today it is 1 in 3, with bowel cancer being the highest in the world – which is an enormous increase over that relatively short period. When I spoke to him about the past, he told me how Stanley Leaf, John Jay and he started a practice together in Hanover Street, and about the different paths they eventually took. First of all, Stanley Leaf went to England and later formed a very well-known clinic of nature cure called Champneys, while Thomson formed Kingston, the beautiful estate where so many people found peace and rest. Nowadays Champneys is run more as a beauty farm. Later on, John Jay, who was the assistant at Kingston, went to Ayr. His story is quite intriguing.

John was an excellent practitioner who had many followers, until something happened in his life that made his beliefs become very extreme, although he wrote intelligently about his views on medicine and how people could help themselves towards better health. My third daughter, Tertia, is a medical herbalist. She often saw a man who looked like a tramp walking barefoot in the streets of Ayr, with an old bike and a little basket, rummaging through dustbins for lettuce or cabbage leaves, and she became intrigued. Tertia had no idea who this man was, and one day asked him why he had so much seaweed in his basket. He told her he used it for his potato growing, which he did in a small field. He was homeless and living in the open air, but had small plots of land where he ate greenery and potatoes grown in seaweed. She asked him why he was so extreme in his views and if she could help him in any way. He asked her who she was, and she said her name was Tertia, the daughter of Jan de Vries, a naturopath. He shook his head and said to Tertia, 'I am a naturopath. Your father is not. He practises homoeopathy, herbalism and acupuncture but that is not the same as nature cure.' He was quite right, as a naturopath only uses the four methods that I mentioned. This man, a tramp, turned out to be John Jay.

Tertia got quite interested in talking to him and asked him what had happened. He told her a bit of his story. She then said, 'My father would love to meet you,' and he replied, 'I would love to meet your father.' Arrangements were made that he would come to Auchenkyle on the Sunday afternoon. Just before he arrived, I had a phone call from the police to say that a tramp had been seen around Auchenkyle and to ask if I was aware of this. I said that I was, and that I had been expecting that particular gentleman. Before he arrived, Tertia had warned me to put plenty of air fresheners in the room and, indeed, when he arrived, you could see that he was living like a tramp. We had a most interesting talk and I learned a lot about the British forefathers of natural medicine whom he had studied and worked with – people like Semple, of whom I had never heard, but who had such a wonderful history. My knowledge of the forefathers of British nature cure was very limited. I was also intrigued by this man himself because, although he was in his 90s, he still had some teeth and looked in perfect health. I asked him what had happened, but he did not want to talk about it. However, I later learned that his wife, who was a doctor, had left him and, because of the shock, he had become a bit peculiar. He insisted that people's immune systems would greatly improve if they lived in the open air and ate the greens from the field. This was actually what he did. Even on the coldest nights, he would sleep in the streets, still barefoot, and lived not only on the greens of the field, but also on the vegetable leaves he found in people's dustbins. He could not stand the wastage he found. He would rummage through bins for any vegetable leaves he could find, wash them in seawater and then eat them. Although his views were very extreme, his knowledge of naturopathy conveyed in his writing made very interesting reading. I wanted to stay friendly with him and help him with his work, but this became impossible as unfortunately he became absolutely obsessed with my daughter Tertia, who had to be very hard on him. From that day, he did not come near us again, so there was not much we could do about it. Not long after that, he wrote quite a big article in the local newspapers about interference with drinking water and the use of herbicides, pesticides and fertilisers. Unfortunately, when John died, nobody really knew what age he was, but I knew from his history that, when we met him, he must have been well into his 90s.

This was something I saw in Holland too; where some of the old fathers of naturopathy became very extreme and no longer had both feet on the ground. There were also some who became quite vindictive and dogmatic. Today, when I think of several practitioners I have known, I am grateful to them for the knowledge they have left us and the work they did to make naturopathy and the different methods of homoeopathy, acupuncture and other forms of alternative medicine better known. As I have often said, it is high time that orthodox medicine (yang) joined alternative medicine (yin) in a great marriage of complementary medicine. Apart from everything else, they are both trying to ease human suffering. I often think of Alfred Vogel, who did so much to bring this nearer to the masses and to help people understand his work. Although some of the work of the pioneers was understood, sadly they were sometimes hampered by the 'powers that be', who didn't want their message to succeed. It sometimes takes a battle to overcome negative attitudes in the media, which can be, as I said in the previous chapter, either a friend or foe.

Dr Hans Moolenburgh found this out when he almost lost his battle against fluoride being added to drinking water. He had so much scientific evidence on self-medication and the harm that fluoride could have in drinking water that he attacked the Dutch government and did what he could to keep it out of the drinking water. He nearly lost his battle, until he was allowed to appear on television, when he managed to convince the entire Dutch public that adding fluoride to their water could be harmful. It was not only because he was a doctor, but also because he had the scientific evidence to prove the harm that fluoride could do if it was added to the water supply. He had a great following and therefore won his fight and managed to get fluoride banned from drinking water. He too, even today, is a fighter for freedom and feels that every person should have freedom of choice in the way that they are treated.

Dr Benthem Oosterhuis fought for the freedom of homoeopathy and won. In a great example, he showed the Dutch people what the combination of good dietary management and homoeopathy could do for them. He was living proof of this as, even when he was over 100, he still bicycled. Together with him, I set up the Alternative Food and Drug Administration which controlled a lot of the foods that were not up to our standard.

I attended the last seminar of Keith Lamont, who died shortly afterwards. Although he was old and not very fit, it was still his wish to share a few of his ideas with those who were interested. Not only did I learn a lot from him at his last seminar about things that interested me and methods that I still use today but, above all, I admired his interest and enthusiasm demonstrated by the fact he still wanted to share some of his findings with his younger colleagues after being in practice for so many years. When I looked at him that day, I wondered how long he would still be here and how much it would take out of him to spend a day teaching, but his desire for others to understand the enormous wisdom that he had gathered over the years was so strong. I am grateful to people whom I have known, as teachers and as lecturers, over the years who have now passed away.

Apart from Alfred Vogel, I have given seminars myself to get his message across to others. One of my best teachers, who also became one of my best friends, was Dr Len Allan. Len wrote five very valuable books on his work as an osteopath and acupuncturist and, as a man who knew a great deal about nutrition, gathered knowledge from all over the world and incorporated this into his books. Today I am adding to and editing the great work that he did, in a book I will call *Dr Len Allan's Almanac*. This will be a valuable book for young practitioners of the future and will be a treasure for them to have in their practices. I often think of the amazing results that Len achieved and the value of his teachings and the knowledge that he gathered from all over the world. Even when I was in Australia and went into a doctor's surgery, I saw his chart, which he had put together so cleverly, in one of the consulting rooms. I was struck by what this man had taught me and I have been privileged to learn all the methods he practised for years. I followed many of his seminars and these were of great benefit to me. He did a wonderful job and had much success where others failed, and I am very grateful today that I have been able to help people because of what he taught me.

A very well-known lady from Belfast came to me. She had a problem with her coccyx and her husband told me that he had spent over £4,500 trying to help his wife with this problem, but to no avail. On one particular Saturday, I carried out one of Len's procedures on her coccyx and, on the Monday, she phoned to say that the tremendous pain and suffering she had endured had gone. Her husband returned two weeks later and asked me if I could take him on as a patient. This was one of the wonderful things I learned from Len, and something that I shall always be grateful for.

I am always disappointed when people who have taught so many and to whom we should be so grateful have been forgotten. Unfortunately, Len's mind went, and when I visited him not long before he died, I asked his wife, Doris, if some of the old students ever visited him and she said no, that I was the only one. Even though he was very ill, he still recognised me and the smile on his face reminded me of the many good jokes that he would tell us during his valuable lectures.

I think of Gonstead in the United States and his neuromuscular techniques and chiro techniques, especially for the adjustment of a hiatus hernia. When I think of the many people I have saved from operations by performing this adjustment, I am so grateful for the opportunity of attending some of his seminars and for the knowledge that he shared with us while I was over there.

I developed a tremendous friendship with Dr Willem Khoe, who used to be a surgeon but became interested in osteopathic techniques. He taught me many of these, in particular a jaw adjustment that only he could do. He showed me the procedure probably about 50 times before I mastered it, and I have since helped many people who have had problems with speaking, singing, sciatica, neuralgia and headaches, after the jaw has been put out of place during treatment by the dentist. I remember the tremendous interest that arose when I carried out this technique on television on *This Morning*, after which many people contacted me. A tremendous amount of expert help and knowledge was needed to perfect this technique, and a lot of research went into finding out the best and easiest ways to adjust the jaw. After all, it is vitally important to get the balance right. As is often said, when the wheel in a watch stops, the whole watch is no use, or if a ship is laden too much on one side, it will capsize – the same also happens with the human body, where harmony and balance is absolutely necessary.

In the summer of 1971, I had a letter from a professor in London. He said in his letter, 'I am a caller in the wilderness, nobody listens to me and yet I controlled my multiple sclerosis.' I wrote back and said that I had treated multiple sclerosis for many years but never had great results and would love to meet him. He wrote back and invited me to go and see him. Shortly afterwards, I went to visit him in Hampstead in London. I rang the doorbell and heard somebody walking very quickly down the stairs, when the door was opened by Professor Roger MacDougall. Very cheerily, he said, 'Come upstairs with me.' He took me into his lounge and told me his story. At a certain age, after he had written the scripts for two very well-known films, he developed multiple sclerosis. It was diagnosed as progressive and, a few years later, he was trapped in a wheelchair and was nearly blind.

One day, when he sat there feeling miserable, he said to himself, 'Roger, your name is up in Glasgow University as one of their most clever pupils. You have not used your brain.' He had heard that in Holland during the war there was no Crohn's disease, coeliac disease, and very little diverticulitis or diverticulosis. Looking into this, he discovered that the diet in Holland at that time was low in gluten, and people ate quite a lot of fruit, vegetables, nuts and natural foods. He decided to remove gluten from his daily diet and take some extra vitamins, and see what happened. After some months, he felt he had a bit more power in his legs. He looked again at his diet to see if he could improve it further and decided to cut out most dairy products, along with refined sugar. He then reviewed his vitamin intake and added evening primrose. Four and a half years later, his sight came back, he could walk again and he returned to normal.

As Roger was telling me this story, his neurologist arrived. Roger had asked him to come while I was there to confirm to me that he was a fully diagnosed MS patient and that he was not in remission. We had a very interesting talk. Afterwards I had to see some Dutch patients in the Hilton Hotel Park Lane. Roger offered to walk with me and I was very surprised when we walked the length of Piccadilly Lane from Piccadilly Circus, talking about his wonderful findings and the possibilities of helping so many people. He was fully convinced that people with MS could improve their condition if they adhered to the diet completely and took extra vitamins, minerals and trace elements (especially the B vitamins) to supplement it, and evening primrose. From that day on, I adapted his diet for use in my clinic and have, over the years, treated hundreds of MS patients. I became very friendly with him and his ex-wife, with whom he was still friendly, and who came to stay with us in our residential clinic, where we nursed her and helped with her problems. We met up many times after that, lecturing together at universities, to doctors, and abroad. His programme has been of great benefit, not only for people suffering from MS, but also for schizophrenics and patients with autism. Something that he did develop was the great desire to help his fellow human beings who were in the same boat as he was. It is impossible to cure multiple sclerosis, but you can control it – I have seen evidence of this many times.

With great admiration, I remember Dr Kelley, a dentist who was dying of cancer. Dr Kelley and I had a lot in common. We were always digging for the truth and he felt, like me, that the answers to many problems can be found by searching seriously. He used to say, and I will never forget this, that searching for answers is like the story in the Bible of the man who had a field. This man knew there was treasure hidden somewhere in the field, but he had to dig for it and make every effort to find that treasure. Once he found it, he knew how much he could do with it. We both felt we had found treasure in the course of our work, and that it could not be taken from us. Dr Kelley had to find how to look after his body when it was stricken with cancer. This was a huge shock to him, and certain emotional traumas that had happened during his life had made his cancer worse. He looked for an answer, and found that cancer was a metabolic disease. He started to study it and found that certain vitamins, minerals and trace elements were of benefit. He devised a naturopathic nutritional programme, very cleverly computerised, and worked out which remedies would help. This was a great achievement and he shared his knowledge with others, such as the Mexican doctors Gonzalez and Contreas. Others studied his methods and continued researching the illness, and many people were helped.

Others expounded great ideas, like Harold Manner and Virginia Livingston, who worked on a system that was vitally important in helping alleviate suffering. It takes courage to make a stand; I clearly remember a banquet held after a big conference, when I sat next to Ann Wigmore, the author of the book *Be Your Own Doctor*. While everybody else enjoyed the delicious food, she sat there with a plate of wheatgrass. She was the healthiest girl in the world and had found treasure in the use of wheatgrass and natural living. She helped cancer and AIDS patients and had great results, and it was a terrible shock when I heard that she had died in a house fire. She did so much for others – I would have liked her to have had a much longer life.

I think of Dr Heede's methods; he was instrumental in my writing the books *10 Golden Rules for Good Health* and *Healing in the 21st Century*. I think also of the Max Gerson Institute, continuing the work of Dr Max Gerson, which is practised even better today, with all the discoveries that have taken place in this big field of medicine. Many pioneers were involved in these discoveries and research, and many had the guts to tackle the industry.

I remember a great friend in America who had a wonderful farm. After a conference, she invited me to go there, and on the way bought two chickens from one of the large battery chicken factories. The chickens were big, and had been injected with water (amongst other things) to increase their weight. When we arrived at the laboratory, she did a blood test. The test showed that the blood contained cancerous cells in one of the chickens and pre-cancerous cells in the other. She then took a chicken from her own farm and did a blood test on it – the results were normal.

I learned a lot from the pioneers of complementary medicine I have known. Many have now gone, but they left a legacy of truth and freedom of choice. They did their best to work for causes that are still relevant today. There is the example of Wakefield, who had doubts about the MMR vaccination and had the guts to stand up and fight against it, while awaiting the evidence of the effects of the injection. A few times during my many years in practice, I too have had to fight for the freedom of choice in this matter, so that these inoculations can be administered in three parts and not in one combined shot. The little body that gets that shot is very often not able to cope with it. There is also the example of Dr Yehudi Gordon, who fought and won the right for pregnant women to take an active part in the birth of their babies, completely against the wishes of the establishment and after a long battle.

Every day, information trickles in from researchers. The pioneers in medicine are the ones who stand up in the fight against an establishment which finds change hard to accept; for example the New Zealand doctor who fought for the acceptance of the *helicobactor pylori* and the ones who fought for the official recognition of *Candida albicans*, a yeast parasite (the establishment often said there was not such a thing). Then there are the doctors who fought for the recognition of ME by the World Health Organisation, who diagnosed this wrongly by stating it was a disease of the nervous system – it is in fact a disease of the immune system. Our immunity is something that we all have to protect.

Dr Moerman, a Dutchman, had to fight after he lost his only daughter to the monstrous disease of cancer. He thought long and hard and, looking outside at his pigeons, thought, 'Why don't my pigeons have cancer – why don't *any* pigeons ever have cancer?' He looked at the lifestyle of the pigeons and what they were eating and, after a lot of research, came to the strange conclusion that it must be their diet. Like Dr Kelley, he recognised the importance of dietary management, as cancer is a metabolic disease. The Moerman diet became very well known, although the battle by the establishment to keep him quiet was fierce. There were a lot of powers at work that didn't like Moerman's ideas, but he kept fighting. When my friend Hans Moolenburgh became one of the ten Moerman doctors in Holland, I remembered the expression 'the truth will set you free'. Moerman's work became more widely known and he continued to fight for truth and freedom until finally the Dutch government recognised and accepted his ideas.

Nobody wanted to know when Professor Shamsuddin, an Indian doctor I met in London, recognised that IP6, a protein found in the minute inner wall of a rice grain, could block the growth of cancer cells and was a great boost to the immune system. I was very impressed with the work that Professor Shamsuddin did over the years in cancer research and with IP6. He has done so much for cancer research; I was very happy to talk to him into the small hours of the night. He worked so hard to discover what he did and I was very pleased when an oncologist wrote to me, having monitored some of his cancer patients, stating how impressed he was by the help the patients had received from IP6. He was hungry for more information and wanted to know all about it. Many of the pioneers in this area had the vision to work in a field that was virtually unknown, but learned how to control cancer cells. It is amazing to think that the minute part each of these doctors played can have such an impact in the war against cancer cells. Cancer is warfare between two armies of cells – regenerative and degenerative. Even with the aid of chemotherapy or radiotherapy, the army of regenerative cells must be as strong as possible to fight the cancer and, therefore, immunity has a very important part to play.

Today we should be grateful to the pioneers. When I started in this field in Britain over 35 years ago, I can think of a few people who helped me in the fight for health. Many have brought naturopathy into focus today, like Roger Newman Turner, whom I call the father of naturopathy, and Joe Goodman, whom I call the father of acupuncture. Joe worked with Sidney Rose-Neil, a very good friend of mine who also fought very hard to bring acupuncture to the fore in this country. Many other people also did their best to bring these methods into the public eye, and contributed to their popularity today.

My grandmother wisely taught me the secrets of nature when I was a young boy and, in her own way, talked to me about the importance of a balance of energy. My mother also fought for the truth. When she died, I sadly lost a good and true friend. My father lost his old set ideas and became an example and, as he often said, 'The best thing in life you can do is to be a good example.' There are too many people for me to mention here whom I have met in my lifetime and who have fought for freedom and truth, and despite a lot of opposition kept working for this, which was so necessary to improve our understanding.

When I think of that little army fighting against the big army of the establishment, I know that they all understood the biblical expression: 'Where there is no vision, the people perish.' (Proverbs 29:18)

15

The Other Side of the Coin

After the many years of criticism, abuse and insults of various kinds, the sun is rising above the horizon of what is now called complementary medicine. When I look back over the years, at the difficulties Alfred Vogel and I faced when we opened the first naturopathic clinic in Holland, the jealousies and misunderstandings, and the way practitioners of alternative medicine were provoked by the establishment and media, I am grateful that those pioneering years have passed.

I have received many letters, some bigoted, others very nasty, threatening me with legal action and sometimes advising me to stop practising alternative medicine altogether. Now there is more understanding and a wider view of what is meant by complementary medicine: using both principles of medicine, alternative and orthodox, to help and assist in alleviating human suffering.

Now we can finally contemplate the integration of alternative medicine into a complementary system. Many times I wondered if this would ever come about, especially when doctors lowered themselves to very public attacks on my work. Some doctors even went as far as placing articles in the local paper expressing their concern when I opened an X-ray centre above our health food store, claiming this had caused the whole street to be contaminated by radiation – this was complete and utter nonsense, as the X-ray centre was fitted by the best people in Scotland, HA West in Edinburgh. Every care was taken to ensure that it was not only totally safe for the patients, but for the whole area in general. As well as this, the benefit to patients of quick diagnosis was tremendous. It was an excellent service and I still value the support of all the neighbours who laughed at the doctors' scaremongering tactics. When the Inspector of Health was called in to investigate the complaint, he verified that the job had been done well, and, as he was leaving, I asked him to tell the worried doctor who initiated this inspection to stop such low attacks and become better informed before he sent articles to the local newspapers.

On another occasion, at a local Rotary Club lunchtime meeting, I happened to mention that I had been asked to lecture to doctors and nurses at a local hospital. During the course of that afternoon, I was told that the hospital had been instructed to cancel the lecture because some individuals in the medical field had heard me saying that I was giving this talk – yet another insult.

At a lecture I once gave on natural medicine, the person who gave the vote of thanks claimed that there was nothing of value in health foods or health food medicine. However, that very afternoon, the very same person was seen snooping around in one of our health food stores to find exactly the products I had been talking about earlier in order to sell them in his chemist's shop! No wonder, after so many years, I have a real laugh about it all. When I think of the many people who criticised me and sent awful letters (which have since become treasures to me), I realise just how childish this kind of behaviour was. People like that, who are full of their own self-importance and criticise alternative medicine without knowing anything about it, will go into history as being totally foolish in their objections.

At one point, I remember, I wanted to join a local club and two doctors fiercely objected to my membership. It was as if I was insignificant because I practised alternative medicine. One would never believe that such behaviour could exist, and it is pitiful. Those people showed themselves up as being very narrow-minded.

I will say that, although I could stand up to that behaviour, at times I felt sorry for my children, who attended local schools and were sometimes looked upon as odd because their father practised a very strange form of medicine – as it was then seen. Even when my children were older and some of them went into orthodox forms of medicine, I was conscious that, while they were growing up, I was not seen as a valued member of society. In those days, alternative medicine was often seen as quackery. When I was joined by my first proper assistant, a well-qualified physiotherapist, I remember her father angrily told her that she was not to work for a foreign quack. Little did he know that

I had an orthodox training behind me, training which to this day is recognised by the health authorities.

It is interesting to witness the developments that have taken place in alternative medicine over the years. When I think of the times I have been asked by hospitals to open units for acupuncture, the many lectures I have given to postgraduates at universities and the university talks and lectures I have given, I say, 'Well, isn't it amazing that we now have the same situation as Copernicus had in his day and age, when he expressed his views on the solar system and was made out to be a fool!'

Society has changed considerably over time and sometimes it is necessary to have an open mind to gain knowledge. Nowadays, after my early struggle, I see the other side of the coin; I receive complimentary letters from hospitals and, not so long ago, an oncologist from a research unit almost begged me to go to the hospital to give a lecture on a few of the methods I had been working with. He fully recognised that there had been positive results from the use of alternative medicine. I have also received letters from universities I have lectured at, and have often said that I am open to any discussion.

Not long ago I had a conversation with Prince Charles, and we both admired the way in which alternative medicine has become a very recognised part of our society. He was quite surprised that, during the time I have built up my clinics, orthodox doctors and alternative practitioners have come to work so well together in a complementary system that is beneficial to patients. I have often found a lot of understanding among the members of the Royal Family whom I have treated, as they have often looked into alternative medicine and researched it more fully than many other people.

Personally, I don't really care what people think of me – what I am concerned about is my patients, and I want the very best for them. Whichever method is used, my main desire is for them to get better. Orthodox, alternative or complementary – it doesn't matter, as long as the patients benefit, although I am happy that there is so much recognition and approval of the field of alternative medicine today.

I have been honoured with many titles over the years, but, to avoid causing confusion, I have never really used them. In all fairness though, it is with a certain amount of pride that I am able to use the title of 'Dr', as I was privileged to be awarded an honorary title in medicine from the most excellent International Academy Pax Mundi. I have never used my doctor's title, however, nor have I made much of the many decorations I have received, such as the Order de la Croix de Jerusalem, the Order of St John, the Order of St Brigitte of Sweden, the Creation Order and the Royal Knights of Justice Award, or the many certificates from my own profession, fellowships, etc. I could go on and on. I am very grateful for these, and very proud to have received them. These honours and the recognition they demonstrate are all very well, but the most important reward for me is that I have the approval of my Creator, who gives me the strength to carry out my daily work and helps me to try and make people better – that, for me, is the most important part of my life and as long as I have that I am happy. God's love is of the greatest importance, and it has also shielded me from the many dangerous situations I have been in during my life. It protected me from being shot in the Second World War, from danger when I was in a hijacked plane, from being involved in a severe traffic accident on the busiest road between The Hague and Rotterdam, from being a victim in a train crash when around 140 people were killed, from being nearly killed by a nasty virus in the bush in Australia, and from a traffic accident where amazingly my wife, Joyce, and I were saved from a monstrous lorry that stopped just centimetres from our little Peugeot. These are some of God's wonders, for which I am grateful, because I know that I am protected by the Creator who wants me to continue in my work to help the suffering.

Sometimes it helps to look back. When things were really difficult, because of jealousy and opposition from others in my own profession, I felt powerless against those who wished to destroy me because of my success. I phoned my mother to ask her what I should do in this situation. She said to me that you reap what you sow: 'This will not hurt you, but it will hurt those who do it. It is the only justice in life.' When I think back over the years of what has happened to those people, I now know that she was right. As she said, you get out of life what you put into it. The only justice in life is that one gets back what one gives, whether good or bad.

While I was sitting talking to a patient one day, my faithful housekeeper knocked on the door and handed me a letter. It stated on the envelope that the letter had to be opened immediately upon receipt and she therefore felt she had to disturb me to give me it. When I read it, I got a bit of a shock. I managed to finish my conversation with the patient, but afterwards read it again immediately. The letter actually said that I had to pay £50,000 at a certain place within two hours, otherwise

Auchenkyle and everything in it would be blown up. The blackmailer said he had written the letter because I had not treated his mother and sister to his satisfaction. There was no signature, but it sounded serious enough. He said he would phone and tell me where to go to hand over the money. I immediately phoned the police, who put me in contact with the CID. They took the letter very seriously and immediately phoned me back, as they believed this was the same character who had written similar letters to several other people, and who was only out to extort money. Indeed, it was serious enough that they felt I should act on it and do exactly what he said, if he was the same man, as one or two people had been victims of this particular person. So, when he phoned, I cooperated with him fully. He wanted me to go to a particular telephone box with a black bag containing the £50,000. I told him that I could not possibly get away, but would send my manageress, and she would meet him at the specified time and place to hand over the bag. He was happy enough with this arrangement at the time, but then started to make threatening phone calls every 15 to 20 minutes, which made the staff in Auchenkyle very nervous. When I asked my manageress if she was prepared to help, she said she had absolutely no objection to doing this and, because she was one of my best friends, I knew I could rely on her.

So she went, followed by plain-clothes police officers. When she arrived, there was a little man in the telephone box who, becoming suspicious at the various cars driving around, ran away and disappeared. The police couldn't catch him. Everybody was very nervous – nobody had a clue who or where he was. A search started. The police manned our phones all day and kept their eyes open for anything out of the ordinary. At that time, I had a very clever assistant who helped me with patients and she told me she had seen a blue van in the road next to the estate, with a man in it, writing something. The police were obviously very interested in that information, and they jumped into their car and sped away. Within half an hour, they returned with the happy news that they had caught him. They had been misled by others who had mistakenly thought they had seen the man in a yellow car, but when they found out it was a blue van they managed to track him down.

It was a very sad situation because the case would have to go to court, and it would be a very lengthy process as there were about 10 or 12 other charges against the man. I was very nervous because I could ill afford the time involved to sit through all those court cases. Luckily,

I was one of the first to go to court. I had never been involved with the police before, nor had I ever been involved in a court case in my life, and I was also slightly nervous that the mother and the sister would hold what had happened against me.

The day before the court case, Joyce took me for a drive. It was a lovely summer's day, and I can vividly remember coming across one of the nicest views in the world, at Tighnabruaich, at a high point looking out over the Kyles of Bute, and thinking it was heaven. There was a little plaque on the point where we stood which said 'I will lift up mine eyes unto the hills, from whence cometh my help.' (Psalms 121:1)

I felt very calm the next day when I went to court because I had nothing to hide, although the defendant's solicitor was very rough on me, and I always said if I ever needed a lawyer to defend a case for me, I would ask him because he almost made me feel guilty even though I had done nothing wrong. However, I had a very strong case and was touched when the mother and sister came to give evidence. To my amazement, they were completely on my side, and told the court how much I had done for them. That was a wonderful experience. The court case lasted a few days, after which time the jury came to the decision that the accused was guilty.

It is wonderful to have friends in life. Two old ladies whom I knew sat through the entire court case and it was reassuring to know that they were behind me and praying for me, so that this case came to a satisfactory conclusion. It was comforting to feel protected by a higher power who has the last word in everything.

It is often encouraging to see how conversations develop. I was once talking to Pat Kenny, the famous Irish broadcaster, and another doctor who criticised homoeopathy. He said there was absolutely no proof of its efficacy. I told him that a ten-year study had shown that the lowest potency in homoeopathy had affected mucous cells when tested, and it was proven that there was a scientific aspect to homoeopathy. The doctor muttered, and I will never forget Pat saying, 'Well, whatever, you can never argue with results.' This I have often said. Although homoeopathy and some forms of alternative medicine are often criticised, if the results are obvious, it doesn't matter what works, or how, just as long as it does. At many meetings, when certain subjects such as life energy and balancing energy are introduced, some professors put their hands up in the air and say, 'Prove it, show us and let's see how it works.' This is sometimes difficult, but over the years I have often put the ball back in their court. It causes a bit of a laugh, but nevertheless makes the point, when I ask them to explain to me how conception works. There are things that we can explain scientifically, and there are things we cannot. There are some areas where we have only scraped the surface but although they may sometimes be difficult to prove, they all have a purpose in this life-fulfilling plan.

This brings me to one of my experiences of how orthodox and alternative medicine can work successfully in a complementary system, where benefits can be seen. Back in the days when I did interviews with Gloria Hunniford, a little girl, aged seven, came to me with her mother. I saw them both very briefly in the George Hotel in London, where I had a short conversation with them. The girl impressed me by the way she so graciously accepted her very serious illness, which was thought to be an inoperable brain tumour. She had all the symptoms – drooping eyes and a very deteriorated state – and I could see that her mother was fighting hard for her only and beautiful little daughter. She asked for some advice as the surgeon wanted to operate. When she mentioned to the surgeon that they were coming to see me, he encouraged them to do so and also said that he would cooperate in every way possible with anything I suggested. I told the mother that, by law, only the oncologist was allowed to treat her child's cancerous state, and he would do this in conjunction with the neurosurgeon. I could only help boost her immune system in order that her little body would have the strength to cope with what she had to face, and back up the operation with treatment afterwards. The girl's father was in the service of Her Majesty the Queen, and he was in agreement with my treating his child, so I took the girl into my care, helping to boost her immunity, and strengthening her for all that she had to go through. I also gave her some remedies which helped to balance her white and red blood cells. Basically, that was how I treated her and, after the operation had taken place and I introduced some other remedies, the surgeon was very impressed with the speed of the healing process. He asked me what I thought of using laser treatment to divide the remaining particles left over in the brain, and I agreed that this should be done. Overall, the treatment of this lovely little girl was very successful and it is with pride that I see her now, as a young woman, just how well she has done, and how grateful she is for all the help she received.

The laser equipment being used in that particular hospital was becoming obsolete. The girl's mother wanted to raise enough money to buy a new laser to help other patients in their treatment. She asked for my cooperation which, of course, I gave, and then she told me there would be a big concert in Her Majesty's Guards' Chapel in London, which the girl's father would supervise. She was adamant that she wanted me to be there, but I told the mother that I was not very keen on these big occasions and, as I would be in London working all that day, it would be difficult for me to be there on time and also I would not be able to attend in formal evening wear. She still felt that I should be there. After work, I went to my favourite accommodation in London, the YMCA, where I always stayed because it was so central. The mother somehow managed to trace me and begged me to come, saying that her daughter thought the evening would not be complete if I was not there. I was very upset, as I felt I would not be properly dressed for this special occasion. Eventually, I agreed that I would go, but said I would sit behind a pillar. I managed to take a double-decker to Buckingham Palace but unfortunately, on leaving the bus, a piece of metal that was sticking out tore a hole in my trousers and I felt absolutely awful. I managed to get some tape to temporarily repair them and carried on to the Guards' Chapel. When I arrived, the guards who were at the gate asked me who I was and I was told to wait. The father of my little patient arrived with the guards and, flanked by them, I was marched into the chapel. Whatever happened, I did not want a fuss. Nevertheless, I was given a place of honour. I felt absolutely terrible as I saw the seats being filled by many of the Royal Family, our Prime Minister, other ministers, people of great importance and celebrities. Further attention was focused on me when my name was mentioned, and also when the little girl publicly gave the surgeon and me a kiss to thank us for all we had done. That was an honour I shall never forget but, nonetheless, I was quite upset and embarrassed by the whole situation. At the same time, I was very happy that complementary medicine had received so much recognition that evening, and that it had benefited my little patient so much. After the concert, when I met several members of the Royal Family and celebrities, I was very encouraged to see the other side of the coin and the growing recognition for something that potentially could develop into a real integration as, after all, the aim of both principles is to help the sick.

Some time ago, a series of articles appeared in the *Sunday Times*, written by Dr Michael Gearin-Tosh. The articles appeared following a book he had written called *Living Proof: A Medical Mutiny*. When I read the first article, I saw my name mentioned. Since that time, the book has swamped the British market and has been read by many people. After the publication of these articles in the *Sunday Times*, people throughout Britain talked of this spellbinding book that revealed the whole truth of the treatment of the doctor's cancer. It is a book that has been an eye-opener for many, but especially for the medical profession.

I remember this Oxford doctor and lecturer arriving in my clinic in the north of London. He had no appointment, so I did not have much time to spare him. When I saw him I could tell immediately that he had problems, but as there was no taste in my mouth and nothing visible in his aura, I knew that he was not dying, and could therefore put his mind at rest when he told me that he had a short time to live as he had quite an aggressive cancer. He was a very nice man who I could see was not only very well educated, but also had a wisdom that stretched further than I had thought. He was the first man since I went into practice to suspect that I had an extra sense of intuition that assisted me in my work, and he wrote about this. After many years of being repeatedly asked what my secrets were I decided, now that Dr Michael Gearin-Tosh had let the cat out of the bag, to reveal some of them in this autobiography, which I had been planning to write for some time. It is thanks to him that I have now written this book. I felt the time had come for me to share my little stories, probably due to the fact that I have been in practice for nearly 50 years.

Michael Gearin-Tosh wrote that, when he was on his way home after seeing me, his friend who accompanied him asked him what he thought about me. He told his friend that my eyes had been focusing on him for a whole minute and that I had said to him, 'One look at you and I know you do not need chemotherapy.' During the drive back home, his friend told him about doctors with extra senses in his country of Kurdistan. They could sense a patient's magnetic field and aura. He suggested that perhaps I had this gift, or that I might have been trained. Well, I had no training in this. I discovered my gift at the age of four, have worked with it all my life and never usually talk about it. That is why Michael Gearin-Tosh was the first person to suspect. I have humbly accepted this gift of intuition and premonition as a great help to me in treating patients.

Throughout his book, Michael talks about my extra sense. He wonders if it played a part when he had a breakthrough with his cancer through the wonderful Chinese breathing exercise I taught him, writing: 'Did he pierce some inner world ...Whatever, I feel I can climb a mountain.'

Everybody has a gift, but it is as I wrote earlier – a treasure in a big field that one has to dig for, find, cherish and use. I personally feel, as I have said before, that it has a lot to do with breathing. When a baby is born, it becomes a living soul, breathing for life through its nostrils and becoming a living being. 'The Lord God formed man of the dust of the ground, and breathed into his nostrils the breath of life; and man became a living soul.' (Genesis 2:7) This wonderful breath of life that God gave became the soul of man, alive and in harmony with its creation. Our health depends, however, on how we use that breathing. While an asthmatic breathes from the chest, a very relaxed person breathes from under the navel. This greatly affects the harmony between yin and yang, the streams of life and death, and correct breathing can bring relaxation and calm. We see with illness and disease that the way in which we breathe plays a very important part. This has a tremendous influence on the endocrine system (in other words the seven endocrine glands) and is in tune with the cosmos, thus making it very valuable. Other capabilities we do not know about may have been unlocked by individuals who have learned to be in contact with the cosmos and can use their gifts in prayer and meditation. These are very important tools which can be used to nurture this particular extra sense, as they can influence the electromagnetic field which emanates from every one of us. Everybody is surrounded by colours that should be in harmony and can be found reflected back in the eye retina. That is why iridology often plays an important part as an accessory in diagnosing patients.

Being in harmony with nature means being in harmony with one's Creator, and that means obeying the laws of nature, which will bring peace. One of the reasons that Michael Gearin-Tosh's treatment was such a success was that he perfected the Chinese breathing exercise, which I explained to him was necessary to bring new life into his system and also to overcome the negative thoughts surrounding his condition. He understood what it meant to unlock these positive powers within himself in order to overcome the negative powers. After all, as I have said before, cancer is a war between the two armies of cells and the more the army of regenerative cells is strengthened, the more chance of life there is. We also see this influence when visualisation techniques are practised frequently, even when one has come to the end of the road. Positive will always win over negative. I often tell patients to look at the battery of a car, where there is a positive and a negative. Right in the middle of that battery is a zone where nothing happens, which we call the neutral zone. This is also the case with people, and through the neutral zone, we have to use powerful methods to add positive energy and, in so doing, help strengthen the immune system. For almost 50 years, I have been looking after patients and have found that if I can unlock a patient's negative attitude by the use of just a positive word or thought, that patient is halfway to recovery. In this warfare, where there are all kinds of diseases, you need to keep fighting, hold on, and victory will come. There are tremendous powers in everybody that are unused or never discovered and which are of great value in making life worthwhile, by simply opening oneself to what the future holds. With this higher power and guidance, we can accept the saying I have used before: 'It is not in man that walketh to direct his steps.' (Jeremiah 10:23)

Sometimes things happen that we don't expect – we might have intuitions or premonitions, but life is always full of surprises. Bad things can happen in life, but if we look at the positive things, they often make up for it. The years of fighting for my beliefs in my profession have not been easy and yet the positive things that have happened during this time have given me the encouragement to carry on and made me realise how good it is to be alive. To be able to breathe in the powers of nature, to look all around at the wonderful things that have been established and then, without warning, to get a little pat on the back from an unexpected source, makes all my efforts seem worthwhile and are great reasons to fight on.

PART TWO

FIFTY YEARS FIGHTING

1

My Fight for Freedom of Choice in Medicine

One morning in August 1961, my three colleagues and I were all very busy, patients going in and out of our Naturopathic Clinic at Roode Wald, Nunspeet, Holland, which I had helped the Swiss naturopath Alfred Vogel to establish. It was the first of its kind in Holland. Everyone was happily going about their business when a registered letter arrived for me. It was from the Dutch Inspector of Health, who wanted to know precisely what we were doing. He was very interested in the roles of Dr Jan Kok, Dr Tine Kaayk and Dr Robert Koch, all established doctors in Holland, and also my own position as a pharmacist.

I wrote back to him clearly explaining our roles and another recorded delivery letter soon arrived summoning us to a meeting with him two weeks later. We were all very shocked by this ominous demand because we knew it could mean the end of our work at the clinic. Dr Kaayk decided not to attend but we three felt that we had nothing else to do but go. In a telephone conversation with Alfred Vogel in Switzerland he had encouraged me to stand firm, as right would always win through, and so, on a beautiful morning at the end of August, we went to Nijmegen. Everyone was rather nervous.

Being inexperienced in those days, I was in fear and trembling when we arrived at the very stately house at the Oranjesingel, Nijmegen, where the meeting was to take place. Years later, I took my family to live in that town and regularly visited the same area as it housed our bank. Every time I went there, I experienced the same feeling of dread.

The Inspector was not unfriendly but nevertheless it was a gruelling

135

experience. He told us in no uncertain terms that we had to resign our posts in Roode Wald. I still maintain that it was the best clinic I have known in my lifetime.

He told us that there was no way for us to carry on, as the Government would not allow alternative medicine to be practised in Holland. The Inspector of Health was completely against homoeopathic and herbal medicine, stating that the methods were unproven. In addition, alternative medicine had a very bad name in Holland in those days because it held too many echoes of the Nazi era – such remedies had been popular with Hitler and his lieutenants. The Inspector insisted that we agree there and then that we would give up our posts, as it was the Government's intention to close the clinic.

In answer to Dr Koch's questions, the Inspector admitted that the world of orthodox medicine was not perfect. Doctors frequently did not have enough time for their patients, sometimes deciding what treatment a patient needed before even visiting them, and that they did make mistakes. He also admitted that many people were in hospital unnecessarily, but he remained adamant. He worked for the medical establishment who had set rules and one had to abide by those rules or face the consequences.

I asked him what the consequences would be for us if we refused to give up our positions.

He looked at me darkly and said, 'If, by tomorrow, I do not have a letter confirming your compliance with this requirement, I will have no other choice but to strip you of your right to operate as a pharmacist [I had only recently graduated] and imprison you.'

Perhaps I was naive, but I could not believe what he was saying. I looked at him again and said, 'You say that if we do not stop, we will have to go to prison?'

He replied, 'Yes, and probably for quite a long time.'

'But we are doing honest work; we only want to help people,' I exclaimed.

He merely responded that he was carrying out the law and that we would have to obey it, as our kind of medicine would not be tolerated in Holland.

I have often wondered if this man ever witnessed the growth of natural medicine. Nowadays, a third of Dutch doctors prescribe our methods and our kind of medicine. Indeed, doctors in Holland now have to study homoeopathic and herbal medicine in their curriculum and can extend their university course by an extra year to study the principles of a multi-disciplinary programme. In addition, Alfred Vogel's name became renowned in Holland and he was adored by thousands of people for his philosophies and his principles.

When we left that meeting, I was still shaking. On the drive back to Nunspeet, my two colleagues told me that they had no choice but to comply with the Inspector's demand. Dr Kok, nowadays a leading professor in medicine, then had a young family and felt he could not risk his career. Dr Koch also decided to pull back, so I was left alone. I resolved to carry on and see what would happen. I had been taught from childhood that if you do the right thing, right will always win over wrong. A miracle happened and I was left to carry on at the clinic, unimpeded.

Over the years, many different means have been tried to reduce or prevent the growth of alternative medicine and so limit freedom of choice. It is very sad that certain remedies make headway and become known and much in demand by the public only to be discredited or withdrawn from the market, apparently because they are a threat to the large drugs companies. This continues to happen worldwide.

This thought brings to mind the story of a remedy that was a blessing for many people. While I was staying in Biel, Switzerland, Professor Kazuhiko Asai sought me out in my hotel room late one evening. Professor Asai was a well-known scientist who was greatly valued in his field. He immediately got my attention by telling me that he had been diagnosed with an inoperable throat tumour. His wife, a staunch Catholic, had taken him to Lourdes, where he drank gallons of the water and also bathed in it. He then discovered that his tumour had disappeared. Because he was not a religious man, he could not believe that it was as a result of the water of Lourdes but, nevertheless, he started to investigate and found it contained a high concentration of the oxygen-giving mineral germanium. This, he felt, was the real reason for his recovery. He came to understand that germanium, which is water soluble, releases a lot of oxygen into the body. With his scientist's mind he concluded that a cancer cell is an oxygen-poor cell. As a result of this research he developed a most amazing remedy called *Germanium GE32*. Many people were involved in his trials, with no recorded side effects.

Germanium proved to be very successful, having a positive effect on the health of ME patients, cancer sufferers and patients with other degenerative diseases. Unfortunately, in the early 1990s it was discredited in the media, where it was suggested that there were side effects associated with it that had caused the death of an elderly lady, although these were never scientifically proved. Equally, I am not aware of any of my patients having had problems with *Germanium GE32*. It was a very sad day when it was taken off the market in the UK and elsewhere, leaving many people helped by this remedy with no alternative. It continues to be sold in some countries, where it is still a blessing to many. However, research is ongoing and hopefully, one day, justice will prevail and this excellent product will once again become available to those who could greatly benefit from its properties.

And what about the simple amino acid called *L-tryptophan*, a food product which was of fantastic help to insomniacs, and *Melatonin*, used to regulate sleep patterns in people with jet-lag, for example. Both were withdrawn from over-the-counter sale, as the authorities decreed that there was insufficient proof of their safety.

Then, in this very stressful world, people were not even allowed to take *Kava-kava*, a popular herbal remedy used to ease tension and calm the nerves. Was there ever any real evidence that *Kava-kava* would cause any harm? Scientifically, we can prove that anything has the capacity to kill – even drinking too much water.

It was very disappointing to see such remedies withdrawn from the market and, during my years in practice, I have been shocked to see governments use their powers to take these God-given remedies away from the people who have a right to benefit from them.

A long time ago, I gave a lecture in Germany on the subject of vitamins, minerals and trace elements, which was attended by a large number of doctors and health practitioners. After I spoke about the many benefits of these products and of the people who supplied them, I was shocked later to hear how the German police had seized the entire stock from practitioners who had used these remedies sensibly and effectively for the benefit of their patients. Where is the justice and where is the people's right to freedom of choice?

Many of these innocent remedies prescribed by practitioners, when taken in the correct dosage and following the instructions on the packet, are much safer than certain painkillers available for sale in filling stations and supermarkets. In all my 50 years in this field, I have never heard of one single death caused by any of these natural products.

Not so long ago, my niece, a pharmacist in Holland, told me that certain homoeopathic and herbal remedies had been officially withdrawn from the market on the instructions of the Government.

Evidence that these remedies had helped people was not taken into consideration. I can well understand why the people who have been helped by these remedies were upset.

Despite all this legislative activity, I have seen a terrific growth in natural medicine over recent years. Homoeopathic and herbal medicines have come to the fore and slowly the public has begun to realise that if they can treat themselves with natural products, then why would they want to do so by artificial means? However, a side effect of the desire for freedom of choice was that suddenly the large drug companies began to recognise this growing trend and articles started to appear in newspapers warning of the possible deadly effects of very innocent natural remedies.

Such incidents raise a lot of questions in my mind: why are cigarettes so readily available yet each packet warns that smoking kills? Why is it possible that anyone can go into a filling station or a shop and buy as much aspirin as they like? Why is it that certain other drugs are so easily accessible in the supermarkets? With my pharmaceutical background, I cannot stress enough my deep and long-lasting concern at the way these drugs are made freely available to the public. It is the same with alcohol, which is also readily available in all manner of shops, making it possible for people to drink themselves to death.

Where is the evidence that natural remedies ever killed anybody, compared to the thousands of people who are killed by the use of tobacco and alcohol?

The explosion of pharmaceutical drugs has been a worry for me ever since I qualified as a pharmacist in 1958. One question concerned me from the start: where does medicine go from here? I looked at the vast and growing numbers of sleeping tablets, tranquillisers, antibiotics and long-term drugs on the market, and asked myself, 'Is there not another answer to this?'

Later, when hormonal products were developed and hormone replacement therapy (HRT) was thought to be the great new discovery of the age, I was horrified to realise that this treatment, devised to alleviate severe menopausal symptoms, was being used by some women purely to stop the development of facial wrinkles. From the start, I was deeply concerned about the potential side effects of HRT and lobbied against its use, but nobody believed me. I caused much anger in the orthodox world simply by pointing out that there are so many alternatives in nature, which do exactly the same as HRT, that we should be encouraging women to take the alternative, healthier route.

My concern increased as I found myself treating patients on HRT who were suffering from phlebitis, thrombosis and breast cancer. Still this was not enough to convince the medical profession that HRT was not the miracle they had assumed. I felt alone in the wilderness, where people thought I had gone completely cranky when I preached about the effects of this unnatural approach. It was not until recent confirmation of an increase in breast cancer in patients taking hormone replacement therapy that people started to listen.

Another battle involved a certain sleeping tablet that I knew to have serious side effects. I pleaded repeatedly with the Pharmaceutical Society to take this tablet off the market. When I heard from two Dutch ladies visiting my Troon clinic that that particular sleeping tablet appeared to have resulted in many suicides in Holland, I again appealed to the Society to investigate that drug, but to no avail as trials had shown that it was safe. Another ten years elapsed, during which this medication claimed even more victims. It was only when concerns were raised through the media that the situation came to a head and it was withdrawn from sale.

Some time ago, a tall, handsome gentleman came to see me. He was known in water sports circles as an excellent canoeist. He had been very unwell for three weeks and his skin was completely yellow. He told me his doctors were at a loss. I discovered that he had been taking a certain drug for the treatment of fungal infections that I had been fighting against for many years. It was this which had adversely affected him and in particular his liver. I gave him Alfred Vogel's *Milk Thistle Complex*, *Hepar Sulph* and *Echinaforce* along with a strict liver diet. Fortunately, these remedies helped to restore his health and he continues to be one of the top sportsmen in his field. He wrote to the drug company and to the medical establishment about his concerns, all to no avail. The reply he received was that his symptoms were listed in the leaflet detailing contraindications. It is very unfortunate that this same drug is still being prescribed. We have both tried to fight against this drug, even writing to the newspapers, but it was all ignored. It was claimed that the drug had been tried and tested, and that nobody would die from taking it. However, I must confess that this fellow was very near to death, and his wife and myself had to work hard to keep him alive and get him back to normal.

Again I would stress that in all these years of practising alternative medicine, I have never known of one single death attributed to the use of natural remedies. We have, however, seen many with so-called medicinal drugs. Fifty years ago, when my fight began, it was claimed that herbal medicine was of no benefit. Today remedies like *Kava-kava* are banned in Europe while the Irish Government has made *St John's Wort* and *Ginkgo biloba* prescription only, giving people the false impression that these remedies are harmful. Was that ever proven? Was there ever a case where those remedies did any harm if taken in the right quantity and by following the instructions? When the public does not adhere to the specified dosage, or exaggerates the advice given on the container, this is when problems may possibly occur.

A question mark is raised every time there is a challenge to natural remedies, when the orthodox world says there is not enough evidence that they work while on the other hand saying that they can cause death or disease! I have never experienced either outcome with the thousands of people I have treated. Certainly, orthodox medicine costs a vast amount of money and obtains all the necessary grants to prove itself, yet even after spending huge sums of money on research, usage can show that drugs are not as safe as first thought. Perhaps if similar funding was available to alternative remedies, we would finally be able to lay these misunderstandings to rest.

In nature, everything is in harmony, and it is only when Man disturbs this harmony of creation that problems arise. This was clearly illustrated by sheep belonging to my colleague and mentor, Alfred Vogel. One night they escaped from their field into his walled herb garden. Here Vogel grew many herbs and, in his methodical way, he had separated all the poisonous plants – such as digitalis, belladonna (also known as deadly nightshade), aconite and many others – from the non-poisonous ones. When Vogel found the sheep in the garden the following morning, he discovered to his horror that they had eaten their way through all his herbs. Yet not a single sheep died, as one plant had counteracted the effects of another.

Are natural remedies dangerous? No. It would take a large amount of a natural remedy to kill a patient. If we go about things intelligently, we can use these God-given methods and remedies for the benefit of all. One has to know what one is doing and that is the reason education is so important. Practice and experience are essential if we are to move forward.

Sometimes, when I see medical authorities, with the help of the police, going around as biblical 'breathing lions', I feel that we live in a police state rather than a democracy, where people have lost the right to choose for themselves. I saw this clearly not long ago when two official, well-dressed gentlemen entered a health food store, poked around and finally examined one single tube of ointment. There was an illegal medicinal claim on that tube, so they immediately asked to see the owner. Using their powers, they warned him that if he did not remove this product from his shelves immediately, he would be prosecuted.

This reminded me of a situation in which I was once involved. This was at a meeting about a particular natural medicine, which was attended by the Secretary of State for Health, health officials and a number of others who were invited by a very good friend of mine. This lengthy, difficult meeting had been arranged in order to try to gain some recognition for various natural medicines. Throughout the meeting, a gentleman in a smart, tailored suit sat silently in the corner. At the end of the meeting, my friend asked to be introduced. He persisted in asking this man what his job was, until it was eventually revealed that he was the president of a large pharmaceutical company. My friend realised then just how much the growth of natural medicine is influenced by the powers of outside organisations.

Some years ago, I was asked to do a series of lectures at the Bastyr University in Seattle in the United States, where people are trained in natural medicine. One particular morning, I spoke to the students about our identity as practitioners. I told them that they should be very proud of the profession that they had chosen. The founder of the university, Dr John Bastyr, was present that morning and, after the lecture, he told me that he could wholeheartedly identify with every word I had said. He agreed that we should indeed be proud of our identity as people who had learned to understand the needs of others and who wanted to help them using alternative methods, but, he said, it is a bitter fight. It is very sad how much opposition can be caused when certain therapies and natural medicines are found to benefit people. In order to learn to know one's identity, one has to face many character-forming experiences, but the path is not an easy one, as I have realised over the past 50 years.

From Seattle I went to another university in Portland, Oregon, and gave a similar lecture on identity. Amongst the many people present was a young man who had trained in orthodox medicine. He was of Scottish origin, so I had a nice talk with him. As we parted, he looked at me and said, 'I am going to fight to win recognition for alternative medicine,' and fight he did. When I see the work that he is doing today, the things that he has achieved and the methods he has established,

I am very happy that I was part of the reason he became involved in alternative medicine. I told him that whatever he did, if he did his job honestly and worked towards freedom of choice, he would be able to help people. It was a hard fight for him but, nevertheless, he won through and he has been very successful, becoming a well-known and respected practitioner.

I also remember the struggle experienced by Dutch GP Dr Moerman in developing his diet for cancer sufferers. The medical establishment made it so difficult for him that he sometimes thought of giving up. It took well over ten years to prove his findings, but he finally received the recognition he deserved from the Dutch Government.

The struggle is not always solely with the authorities. Regrettably, professional jealousy can also rear its head at times. I have never understood the reason for this, as I believe that we should love our neighbour as ourselves, especially in medicine where we have made the decision to help people.

Jealousy could have destroyed a very famous Dutch herbalist who had tremendous knowledge in this field. People went to him by the busload just to get a few minutes of his time. He was a great help to many people and he only prescribed mixtures of herbs which he had formulated. I have never heard of anyone dying from his treatments.

Orthodox practitioners resented his popularity. Soon, he started receiving letter after letter from the authorities demanding that he stop his practice. Even the threat of imprisonment did not prevent him continuing with his good work. He said, 'I am working for an honest cause. I want to help people. I want to make them better, and I cannot see that I am doing anything wrong.' After a number of warnings, the police came, handcuffed him and put him into prison. From there, he wrote that he was happy to be imprisoned if it meant that people would one day have the freedom to make their own choice as to how they wanted to be treated. He was detained in prison for a number of weeks, then released with a warning that he could not practise herbal medicine.

He ignored this warning and found a way to start in practice again. He brought an orthodox doctor into his practice, who first examined the patients and took their blood pressure before he himself treated them. Thus the authorities were able to turn a blind eye and he continued in practice for many years thereafter. His tenacity again showed that right will always win over wrong. To the day he died, he practised what he believed in – helping other people.

One way to help is simply to listen, even to the little things that someone has to say. Listening is a very great art and one we all need to learn. This brings to mind a case that made quite a stir in its day. It involved a Dutch gentleman of very impressive appearance. Whenever he was consulting, the streets around his house were filled with cars even though no one could quite explain exactly what he did. Sadly, when one old lady who went to him died – not as it transpired from his ministrations but from a combination of age and disease – her family took legal action against him. Witnesses were called from both the orthodox and the alternative fields, and I was asked to speak on his behalf as an expert in alternative treatments.

Everybody who was involved took the case very seriously but no one could find any evidence that he had done anything wrong. When I asked him what he did with his patients, he had one simple answer. 'I am only a listener. I am a good listener, and I give as good advice as I can. I have never taken anybody off medication they have been prescribed by their doctors, nor have I advised them to stop taking it. I have only given them advice for natural living.' This major case was a complete waste of money, because all that this good man did was listen to people's needs. Today, we have forgotten how to listen to the needs of others, particularly patients who seek help with the problems that are making their lives so miserable.

When I think of the misunderstandings and problems encountered, and the struggle to attain recognition for alternative medicine, I again ask myself, 'Where is the freedom of choice?' Bickering does not help people. After all, natural medicine is as much aimed at alleviating human suffering as orthodox medicine. Both groups of practitioners have chosen to help people in need. So why don't they get together to help people and end this ruthless attitude of withdrawing remedies that are known to be of benefit? The drive towards ever-greater profits must be put aside in favour of the only worthy motive: striving with all our hearts to help people in need.

I had occasion to lecture on freedom of choice many years ago in Toronto, which boasts the largest education centre for natural medicine in Canada. What a wonderful spirit was present, especially amongst the younger college students who wanted to fight for their profession, to understand their role and to work towards something that they believed in.

Two years later, when I lectured at the same college, a young fellow came to me and said, 'Do you remember two years ago when you spoke on the identity of the practitioner?' He continued, 'I was not a student. My friend had brought me to listen to you.' He said that he had been contemplating buying a photography shop, as he was a qualified photographer. However, the night after the lecture he could not sleep. He thought of all the things I had said about alternative medicine and realised that he had become interested in the field. The following day, he returned to the college and enrolled on a course of study to become a natural health practitioner. Today, he is one of the most successful practitioners in Canada, and for one simple reason – he did it from the heart. Only if we put our heart and soul into this work can we be successful.

Freedom of choice in medicine will be a wonderful thing, but we must go about achieving it with common sense and intelligence. People must be educated to make the right choices in what they eat and drink, and how they exercise. It is a major task to educate thousands of people on the dangers involved when they daily buy a packet of cigarettes, or drink too much alcohol, or go into a shop or filling station for paracetamol or other drugs. Let's be honest with each other and then we can help this world more effectively and help people to attain better health.

2

My Fight against
Degenerative Diseases

Just imagine the Underground in London on a Monday morning at around quarter past seven, when the congestion charge had just been put into operation and commuters were packed into the Tube like sardines. Imagine that confined, bacteria-filled space, some people coughing, some looking very ill, and imagine having to be part of that journey for sometimes an hour or more. One can imagine what effect this could have on the immune system. I boarded that Tube at Marylebone on the way to my Hadley Wood clinic, my last stop being Cockfosters. After a little while, I was able to get a seat. Next to me sat a fairly plump young lady with a child on her lap, both of whom looked very ill. This did not surprise me, as I saw the rubbish the mother was eating, while the child was obviously addicted to the nasty-looking coloured sweets that she popped into her mouth one after the other.

It was not long before the mother started to moan and groan. She rubbed her legs, stood up and was clearly in a lot of pain. Hearing her mother's distress, the child started to cry. It was a very difficult scene. Then, unusually for the Tube, she plucked up the courage to speak to me. She described the terrible pain she was experiencing. I could see from her joints that, young as she was, she was suffering from arthritis, which must have given her a lot of discomfort. I asked her what she would like me to do about it. She answered, 'You can help me. You are the television doctor – I have seen you many times. So, please, give me some advice.'

I felt very sorry for this mother and her child. When people ask for my help, I try to offer what advice I can. It is my vocation. I started to

146

question her about her daily diet, which I soon realised was appalling. The problems ranged from very irregular meal times to the type of food that she was eating. In this way, she had introduced toxins into her system, which had slowly affected her blood, resulting in the pain she was now experiencing. The body will cry out for help when it is not being treated properly. I started to tell her all about a natural wholefood diet and what steps she could take to change her lifestyle. I also told her that I was concerned about her child. One could see from the girl's behaviour that there were problems that desperately needed attention. She was almost uncontrollable, to my mind because of the amount of sugar that she had consumed during that short space of time, and the artificial colouring in those sweets was very detrimental to the child's health. I asked the mother how much sleep her daughter got and if she was a happy child. She told of a life where money was tight and of much unhappiness since her husband walked out to be with someone else. It was not a happy scene to start off a Monday morning but, nevertheless, she showed a willingness to listen. When we arrived at Finsbury Park, where she was due to get off, she asked if she could join me to my destination, as she wanted to talk further. So, as we continued to Cockfosters, I wrote out some simple dietary tips for her and her daughter, and arranged to send her Alfred Vogel's *Knotgrass Complex* and *Devil's Claw*, along with *Flaxseed Oil* to be taken at bedtime. I am so happy to say that with this help, possibly coupled by reading several of my books, including *Realistic Weight Control*, this lady began to take an interest in looking after herself responsibly and was able to reduce her weight. She wrote to me enclosing a photo of her child, who looked much happier. Her hyperactive tendencies, which were heading in a very negative direction, had reduced due to many changes to her diet, as well as taking *Child Essence*, which I had also advised.

I am not planning in this chapter to discuss at length dietary management or even lifestyle. In my many books, I have already covered this topic in great depth. However, I do want to say that over the years I have been in practice, I have seen the increase of many degenerative diseases and seen how these particular diseases are often misunderstood. Where did it all start?

By observing those commuters on that London Tube, we get an idea where things are going wrong, beginning possibly as far back as when they were young children, with childhood illnesses perhaps neglected or treated improperly. I touch on this in my book *Mother and Child*.

If we start to adopt an unhealthy lifestyle, we are just inviting more problems. The body is a wonderful device that tells us if something goes wrong. When children cannot sleep, are hyperactive or under par, it is all too easy to say things will turn out all right if we just give it time. However, it is essential to put things right at the time. We must look sensibly at our lifestyle when we realise that something is wrong. A willingness to listen and to make any necessary changes is very important, as can be seen with the lady on the Tube. She was willing to listen, willing to follow my advice and thus she leads a totally different life today. In her last letter, she told me how happy she now is and that she has a nice man in her life.

We cannot get away from the fact that our bodies are constantly under attack. Through the food and drink that we consume, we can come into contact with many chemicals and additives that are not good for us and, if we do not take appropriate precautions, we can lay our bodies open to problems.

I have often said that in suppressing disease, we create a nation of invalids. I saw that clearly in a patient who arrived at my clinic in a wheelchair. Two years earlier, he had been diagnosed with multiple sclerosis (MS). This is a degenerative disease that can often cripple one for life. I carried out a test on him and, on noticing he had nicotine poisoning, advised him that he must stop smoking. I explained the Roger MacDougall diet to him in depth and offered him advice about adopting a healthier lifestyle. Using a Dutch saying, I told him, 'It is not five minutes to twelve, it is five minutes past twelve.' In short, he must take action now. If he did not stop smoking immediately, his health would deteriorate to such an extent that the MS would cripple him for life. Fortunately, he followed my advice and his health slowly improved.

Let there be no misunderstanding – one cannot cure multiple sclerosis, but one can control it. I have often seen with smokers that nicotine has a terrific influence on the myelin sheaths, causing them to break or release their deposits and, thereafter, signs of MS will probably appear. That was the case with this young man. He made great improvements and carried out my instructions to the letter, until he had a major row with his girlfriend, which ended their romance.

He was so devastated by this that he started smoking again. I did not see him for a long time afterwards, until that day he arrived in his wheelchair and, in tears, told me what had happened. He asked, 'What can I do? I am now completely wheelchair-bound. Is it too late?'

Very often, once the damage is done, one can do very little. Sadly, in this case a lot of symptoms associated with MS were already apparent, like double vision, lack of bladder control, pins and needles, and little or no feeling in his feet. I felt sorry for this young man. All too often the spirit is willing, but the flesh is weak and, especially when a traumatic event occurs, the tendency is to give up, which is entirely the wrong thing to do. This always disappoints me greatly, and I feel so powerless to get the message over to the patient. It is vital not to give up when this sort of thing happens.

On the other hand, I am often encouraged. Some years ago a young, very pretty woman struggled into my clinic to see me. She told me that she had an executive post at one of the large banks, but, at the height of her career, was stricken with MS. The doctor had told her that she should give up her job as her MS was progressing. She was also quite well known in horse riding circles and found her illness was restricting her activity in this area too. She also told me she was on the verge of getting married and really wanted a child.

I looked at this charming young lady and told her that she must be very positive – that together we would positively handle this and positively we would do what we could for her. I could see from the determination in her eyes that she was prepared to do what was necessary. At that stage, she could hardly walk down the stairs and, in fact, she had suffered some bad falls. I could fully understand why the doctor had advised her to give up her work.

Although I usually agree with doctors, in this case I felt she should remain in her job. I asked her if she was willing to follow a sensible diet and if she was prepared to do all I advised. She nodded that she was, saying she would do everything possible. So she went on a strict gluten-free diet and I gave her a course of injections. These measures, together with monthly visits to the clinic, helped her to continue working. Her health gradually improved and, as I write, she is in remission, able to do anything she wishes. Her job was her salvation because it helped to keep her mind off her illness. She was also able to continue horse riding, which was a great comfort to her.

Her future husband was also most supportive. Once she was able to control the MS, they got married and they have a lovely daughter. She was so eager to adhere to all my recommendations that she even devised a lot of recipes that can be found in my book *New Developments for MS Sufferers*. In that book, she also relates a little of her own story. It is very important to realise that, with sensible advice and determination, one can often go a long way to improve one's own health.

We see this so often with cancer patients. This is another degenerative disease, which I often call 'a monster', yet with determination, one can do so much. I have helped many people – including some of my own family – through the trauma of cancer. I have also seen that by using that determination in not accepting cancer, one can do a great deal.

I was greatly encouraged by a man who came to me, having been told by his doctor that he had two months to live. He had prostate cancer, which unfortunately had spread. When I first saw this gentleman, he was very yellow and extremely tired, but he said that he could not accept his prognosis. He told me he had a wonderful wife and family, and he wanted to live longer. One can often do a lot to help oneself if one refuses to accept that nothing can be done and is determined to fight. I have fought many battles with people in this same condition. Victory is not always possible, but there are many who succeed. As I have often said, a cancer cell is like a brain cell. Visualisation and positive action are often of great benefit, and such was the case with this man. I told him that I felt there was probably some hope for him. I also told him that he should eat organic foods and that there were certain foods he must avoid, as I had established he had some allergy problems.

One has to treat each cancer patient as an individual. Even if there are 60 patients with prostate cancer, 60 with stomach cancer or 60 with lung cancer, every patient is different, and the problem has to be tackled individually, as so many characteristics, as well as the background to each illness, have to be taken into account in each situation.

The gentleman's wife later told me that he went home and thought about what I had said. The next day, she saw him digging up part of their beautiful lawn. He screened it off, fertilised it with natural substances and told his wife that he was going to grow his own vegetables and fruit. Fortunately, he had the strength to carry out this work and it also helped to take his mind off his problems. He worked hard and got the whole plot ready to grow fresh organic foods.

Seven years later, he looked a picture of health. With a smile, he said, 'My doctors are so happy with me. They don't know what has happened. I have to do a testimonial for the hospital.' He said he was delighted that he felt so well and would welcome my help in keeping it that way. He told me that his organic gardening had become of great interest to him. Just the day before, he had picked some of his broad beans and, an hour later, his wife had used them when cooking lunch. One could not eat vegetables that were fresher or that tasted better than that. He enthused about the enjoyment they got from the vegetables and the help he was able to give other growers. Most important of all, he said, 'I am alive and kicking, and, even at my age, can do what I like.' He beamed with happiness because he had achieved something in life, he had proved others wrong and had seen for himself what he could do to help himself to better health.

This is often the secret of the whole matter. I have seen it with other similar cases. One young girl particularly comes to my mind. She had developed a nasty ovarian cancer while studying hard. She was very determined to achieve her goal, but sadly, in the middle of her studies, she was faced with this tremendous conflict. Luckily, she was quite philosophical about it, saying she wanted to do the very best she could. I explained to her that the best thing was for her to back up everything that her oncologist advised with good dietary management and cancer-fighting supplements. Luckily, she did not need an operation and the specialists had agreed that she could benefit from some supportive complementary treatment.

I often describe cancer as being like a war: a battle between degenerative cells and regenerative cells. We often see with chemotherapy or radiotherapy that both types of cells are killed. So it is best to be positive and help with good dietary management and remedies to build up the army of regenerative cells in order to achieve victory over the degenerative cells. During our discussions, I told her of the tremendous findings of Professor Shamsuddin who, after years of research, found a wonderful protein, IP-6, on the inner wall of a grain of rice. Having isolated that protein, he found that he would probably be able to control cancer cells. After all, cancer is a condition in which cells are out of control.

This young lady was as eager to tackle this disease as she was in her studies. I was delighted by her attitude. I have often noted that, in the fight against degenerative diseases, the more positive one is, the better, and the more one wants to fight, the better. It was most encouraging to see this young patient go from strength to strength by fighting her way through. She even managed to continue her studies and, I am delighted to say, she has been successful in her battle.

3

My Fight against the Media

While I was contemplating this chapter, something happened that I will touch on later, which made me aware of just how influential the media can be. They can have a powerful impact on one's life, both negative and positive, with enormous implications for the present and the future, as indeed can any form of publicity.

While I was pondering this particular subject, a hairdresser came into my consulting room. I recognised his name as being very well known in his field and I have several patients who speak highly of him. I listened as he explained why he had finally decided to consult me with what appeared to be an incurable neck problem. Through his profession he had obviously put a lot of strain on his neck, which had led to restrictions in that area. X-rays revealed that he had severe cervical spondylitis.

Several of his customers had recommended me, but he was basically scared to let anyone touch his neck which, in principle, is a very sensible attitude as many mistakes can be made while treating neck problems. He asked an orthopaedic surgeon, a regular customer at his salon, what his thoughts were on alternative medicine. The surgeon asked him who he was planning to consult. When he replied, 'Jan de Vries', the surgeon said, 'Well, my advice to you is that if you have too much money, you go to him and he will certainly help you to get rid of it.' The hairdresser responded that many of his customers spoke highly of me and said my fees were very reasonable. The surgeon said it was up to him.

A few days later, another well-known consultant was in his salon, so he sought his advice. He said, 'These people do not know what they are doing. I would be very careful.' To this, the hairdresser said that he knew I had been in practice for a great number of years, so I probably did know what I was doing. Because of the conflicting reports, and not being satisfied with what he had heard, the hairdresser went to his own doctor and asked for his opinion. The doctor said, 'Well, if we can't help you, you should perhaps give him a try. I have heard about him and know that he has been in practice a long time.' At least this comment was unbiased.

When negative things are said, either publicly or in the media, they often come from people who have little or no knowledge of alternative medicine. Luckily, an editor from one of the major newspapers came into his salon. The hairdresser asked him what he thought. The editor spoke of me in glowing terms, told him that he had heard from so many people that I had helped them and advised that he should see me without delay. Based on that very positive report, the hairdresser came to see me. I helped him with acupuncture and soft-tissue manipulation, and prescribed Alfred Vogel's *Knotgrass Complex* and *Devil's Claw*. He now tries to convert the orthodox people who, he said, were probably only jealous because they had heard of some of my successes with patients they were unable to help.

It is often very difficult, even through the media, to make known what one is capable of until the proof is visible. Through the media and lectures, I have often shown what my work can achieve and how the results have proved a blessing to so many people. Positive publicity is wonderful and very often it comes through word of mouth – from people who have been for treatment and been helped who then tell others. I love to treat hairdressers because, if their treatment is successful, they will let their many customers know.

Nevertheless, I have had some serious fights with the media, often caused by jealousy or ignorance. The incident I touched on at the start of this chapter occurred when I was asked by a university to lecture to a group of some 500 experienced nutritionists and alternative therapists who were attending a congress. Everyone listened attentively to all I had to say and asked some very thought-provoking and stimulating questions. However, towards the end of the questioning, a group of people from the media – obviously totally against alternative medicine – started asking me some very awkward questions, which I believe I answered adequately.

They were obviously there to criticise alternative medicine and stated that there was no proof that it worked. I responded that one cannot argue with results and that a number of universities nowadays are producing evidence to show that it does work. They also claimed that homoeopathy was useless, whereupon I told them that at the University of Utrecht, Holland, it had been shown that even the lowest potency of homoeopathy still changed cells.

They were not satisfied with my answers and the inevitable happened. The local newspaper published an article stating that alternative medicine did not work. This was widely read and discussed, causing some very negative feedback. I phoned the reporter and asked if she would retract her comments, offering to send her evidence to show that it does work. I also advised her to speak to several specialists in this field who would corroborate what I had said. I told her that orthodox medicine was not always successful, and that it is fortunate enough to receive all the funding needed for research, whereas alternative medicine has had to prove itself by the successes gained with the patients themselves. The voice of the patients speaks loud enough to show that it does work. Fortunately, the reporter did retract her comments.

Alternative practitioners do their best to help with human suffering using remedies that have few side effects. On the other hand, we are often shocked when we hear of the contraindications of drugs. While writing this chapter, I was reminded of the time I got into deep trouble when Gloria Hunniford and I spoke on air on the subject of HRT. All I said was that, in the many years I had been in practice, I had never seen any side effects when using alternative remedies to treat the symptoms of the menopause and that I would gladly recommend them. I had, however, observed cases of thrombosis, phlebitis and breast cancer in patients who were prescribed HRT. So why not treat these troublesome menopausal symptoms with natural remedies? As we are natural beings, we should use a natural approach. I reiterated that I had seen many side effects with the use of orthodox medicine during the years I had been in practice.

This caused trouble with the medical authorities and I was asked to retract that statement, which I refused to do, because I was absolutely certain that I was right. Many years later, national and international newspapers, television and radio have now verified my comments. It is still an irrefutable fact that we are born in nature, we belong to nature and we have to obey the laws of nature, which will only benefit us.

On another occasion, I got into quite a bit of trouble with the British Federation of Pig Breeders, who lodged a serious complaint against me. They had followed some of my BBC radio broadcasts and had become extremely annoyed about my criticisms of the poor pig, telling people not to eat pork, sausages, bacon, ham or gammon. They took these remarks very seriously and I was informed that legal action would follow. One of the top people from the BBC asked to see me to discuss what they should do about it. I told them that there was not a soul in the world who can contradict the fact that the pig contains very high levels of animal acid and animal fat, which I have found to be detrimental to sufferers of rheumatism or arthritis. He asked me to clarify that fact on subsequent programmes, which I duly did. I made it clear to everyone that the pig may be a very nice and intelligent animal, but that its meat is very acidic and has a very high fat content. Therefore, if people have had problems of acidity during their lives, then they would probably benefit from eliminating pork from their diet. That is the only reason I often speak against the pig. Fortunately, no more was heard about that particular incident.

Another situation comes very clearly to my mind. At the time I had a regular and successful slot on the ITV programme *This Morning*, and I was asked to demonstrate methods of manipulation that I had found to be greatly successful. Someone – who I can only think was very jealous – played a very dirty trick. This person managed to get a letterhead from *This Morning*, wrote a letter to me and signed it from the researcher. In it he stated that my methods were totally unacceptable, that I would no longer be required to appear on the programme and that I would probably get into trouble because of the claims I had made. I was mystified because everybody seemed to be very happy with what I had done, so I went to see the researcher and showed her the letter. She immediately said that it was a fake, that it was completely untrue, that nobody there had ever written such a letter and that I would be on as normal the next time I was due to appear. This demonstrates the desperate lengths some people will go to when they are consumed with jealousy. I decided to ignore the whole situation as I thought it was not only childish, but that it would make no sense to take it further. Sadly, I have become used to such situations, which can occur when one is in the public eye. One day, this particular character will have to deal with the consequences of his actions, because one justice in life still prevails: you reap what you sow.

Now another battle looms large, which is being fought at least in part by the media. Although there have been many battles to promote the benefits of natural medicine and many criticisms of it made by the media, there has also been tremendously positive coverage. However, powers at work against natural medicine are now using other methods too. Potential EEC legislation seems determined to deprive the public of their right to much that is good in natural medicine, with medicine control agencies having the task of trying to withdraw remedies from the market, even though they have been available and beneficial to the public for many years. Remedies such as *Kava-kava*, *St John's Wort*, *Ginkgo biloba*, *L-tryptophan* and many others have already come under attack. When a friend of mine received a visit from two gentlemen who told him to remove certain remedies from his shelves, he asked, 'Have we landed in a police state? Do people have freedom of choice or is this all coming to an end?' How appropriate this question appears to be.

There appears to be considerably more interference than ever before, often from people who have limited knowledge, resulting in even trained and experienced practitioners in established practices being refused the recognition they deserve.

In the 50 years that I have been working in this field, I never believed that we would be up against such barriers. At an exhibition, television was used, perhaps unwittingly, to brand a product which many people had found useful as useless and expensive. Something that I have long fought against are the high prices that practitioners sometimes charge – the enormous charges made to the public for some remedies that cost so little to manufacture. However, that occurs not only in alternative medicine, but in orthodox medicine too. If we investigate the prices being charged for alternative remedies, then it would be only fair that the media compare both sides, as there are so many orthodox remedies on the market that are far too expensive in comparison to what it costs to produce them.

It is very sad that in the 50 years that I have been in practice, we have learned so very little from the past. Restrictions, rules and regulations are all necessary. One cannot oversee such a big field without disciplines and regulations, but what I have fought for during these 50 years is justice, freedom of choice and a melding together of the two principles that can often be combined to benefit the patients. I often get calls from a hospital or a doctor asking me what course I am following with a particular patient and, at such times, I am more than happy to explain what I am doing because the patient deserves the attention and cooperation to get better. So much could be done if all this bigotry and drive for profit was put aside and the patients were put first. During lectures, I always tell students that this is the most important thing we can ever do. It is this freedom I want from the media.

It saddens me so much when, in order to make a shocking story that would catch the attention of the public, a journalist will set out to strip away all the positive aspects of alternative medicine and twist the facts to suit himself. This is often the problem today – not only in alternative medicine but in all situations of life where, for their own advantage, newspapers often sensationalise articles to excite or shock the public. It is sad to see how little we have learned from the many mistakes that have been made in the past. However, we must hold on to the belief that right will always win over wrong. I often think that those people who tell lies are probably just out to shock the public, or have probably been set up. Such people will not benefit from their actions.

Overall, I have been very lucky with the media and they have not been too hard on me. On the positive side, I have had a lot of wonderful testimonials published in newspapers and magazines. I remember being packed out with patients after a young Celtic footballer mentioned visiting me in an interview with one of the main national papers. His doctor had told him he would never play again, but after two treatments from me he was playing better than ever and is still playing today. Such comments are always very welcome and much appreciated. I was very pleased that this young footballer did as I advised, following my instructions to the last detail.

The positive side of the media is quite encouraging, especially as they cannot deny the fact that many people who have been disappointed in their regular treatments and who have sought refuge in alternative medicine have benefited to the extent that they have progressed from a very handicapped life to a very happy situation. One cannot argue with the results in such cases, which do much to highlight the success of natural medicine. I will continue to ask why, if we can treat health problems naturally, should we do it artificially? We are born in nature, we belong to nature and we have to obey the laws of nature in order to be in harmony with our Creator and ourselves.

4

My Fight against Addictions Today

I am often labelled as addicted to writing books. Whilst I would disagree with that statement, I confess to being addicted to my work, for one very simple reason. When I was about 17 or 18 years old, I was both studying at university and working extremely hard in a pharmacy at the weekends to earn some money. At that time, I started my fight for something I thought would not only be beneficial to those with addictions but also something that was needed by society at that time.

One particular day, a man about my age came into the pharmacy and called me over. He told me about his terrific struggle against drug addiction and how he was unable to beat it. Around that time, various addictive drugs from the Far East were becoming more available in Holland, attracting interest mainly from the younger generation. This fellow had become involved with a girl who was addicted to cannabis. As he was very much in love with her, he wanted to please her and, in so doing, he started to experiment with drugs, getting mixed up in the drug scene. In the then non-permissive society in which we lived, drug addicts faced a tremendous struggle, and only limited help and understanding was available to people in their predicament. During our conversation, I became aware that, although this problem was not perceived as serious in Holland at that time, a lot of young people were being drawn into this increasing drug culture. When I realised the struggles they faced and the associated problems, it only reinforced my commitment to health. I started to fight to improve the health and well-being of addicts and to achieve a better quality of life for them and for all those still affected by all the struggles and deprivation of the Second World War.

When I investigated the whole issue of soft and hard drugs, I was amazed at what I learned and later I endeavoured to lend a helping hand with counselling, acupuncture and herbal remedies like *Ginsavena* whenever I could.

One evening, I went with a group of people to a dark and miserable place in Antwerp (a large harbour town in Belgium), which was lit only by candles. I shall never forget the distressing scenes I witnessed there, too horrific to describe here. I realised then that it would be an uphill battle to tackle a problem of such magnitude. I concluded that addiction was one of the worst diseases that I had ever had to help with and I knew that I had to keep up the fight. Today, I am deeply saddened when I see how this particular problem has escalated. When I think of the medical advances during my lifetime and how this problem has increased, I am extremely concerned that I have not been able to do more. This is especially the case when I see useful young lives being destroyed when people are drawn against their will into this underworld, which often brings to an untimely end a life which could have been so worthwhile, if only more support and help had been available.

In the town in Holland where I was born, certain drugs are freely sold in inconspicuous backstreet shops. When I observe the unhealthy, dishevelled people going in and out of these establishments, I fear that the fight against this problem is beyond anyone's control, even though we are part of a society where each individual has the power to determine his own destiny.

One case which really shocked me was when I was asked to see a girl whose parents lived in Scotland and whom I had known for many years. Both parents were extremely hard working and held responsible positions. Their daughter had had a good upbringing and, at that time, was working in London. Unfortunately, she had become acquainted with a group of people who introduced her to drugs. As she did not realise their addictive powers, the drugs steadily took over her life. She had changed into a self-centred, aggressive, nasty girl. When I went to talk to her, she was quite open and cooperative, telling me all about her situation. She mentioned her disappointments in life and how these people had a listening ear. She had felt very lonely after going to London and, as a result, had become heavily involved in the practices to which she had now become addicted. During our conversation, I discovered that she was pregnant, which worried her greatly. She also told me that she desperately wanted to make something of her life and she felt that this baby was probably the answer. She did not know who the father of her unborn baby was and, basically, did not want to know. As my eldest daughter was a midwife in London at that time, I sought her advice on what the outcome would be for a young baby born of drug-using parents.

It was a lengthy process to help this girl but, using acupuncture and with help from others, we managed to wean her off the drugs. Luckily, by the time the baby was born, the young mother was in quite good health. Although the baby needed some treatment as she grew up, everything turned out all right. The love that she had, and which had been misused, was now focused on the baby.

It was fortunate that everything turned out well in that instance, after many struggles, fears and problems – but how many similar cases end in disaster?

I once took care of a young baby who was born of parents who were heavily dependent on drink and drugs. The authorities decided that the mother could not care for the baby and, fortunately, another family member was willing to shoulder this responsibility. This, coupled with the help I was able to give the baby, enabled us to bring this child into a society where, although her intelligence was slightly impaired, she nevertheless has grown into a lovely girl who is managing to face the world.

The fight against addictions continues. In addition to the battle with drugs, another major addiction to be tackled is alcoholism.

How many people in the world today are dependent on alcohol? For recovering alcoholics, it takes just one small drink for things to get out of hand. Over the years, I have treated some of the finest people who, because they have been unwilling to seek help for this enormous problem, have become outcasts from society.

I have often managed to help alcoholics regain a normal life, but when I look at the destruction resulting from alcohol, I realise how this problem is escalating and becoming ever more devastating.

I remember a gentleman of whom I was very fond and who had done a very great deal for society. He devoted his time, energy and even his own money to helping those less fortunate, especially disabled or abandoned children. Sadly, however, he slowly got into the grip of that incredibly addictive drug, alcohol. He lost sight of what was important and lost his possessions. Things went from bad to worse until, finally, it affected his health. His very supportive family and I did all that we could. Alas, nothing could prevent his untimely death from liver failure.

Kampen, the little place where I was born.

At kindergarten – the building was not unlike my clinic at Auchenkyle.

At school, looking after the invalids. I am in the front row, first left, standing.

Just engaged!

Biohorma,
Holland. I was one
of the founders.

At Teufen in the
early days.

Preaching the message of
health in Edinburgh.

With Professor Geers,
the tallest man in the
Swiss Alps.

On one of my
world tours, at
the Botanical
Gardens in
Melbourne,
Australia.

Performing iridology in
New York.

In Chicago for
consultations.

On a vegetarian
cooking
demonstration
television
programme in
Portland, Oregon.

I travelled all over the world with Alfred Vogel and I was shocked by the evidence of apartheid in South Africa in the 1980s.

In conversation with HRH the Duchess of Gloucester.

In one of my meetings with Prince Charles.

In the Botanic Gardens in Glasgow launching the Jan de Vries Benevolent Trust with patron Hayley Mills, second from right.

The whole family.

Tamara, our Samoyed, whose story is told in this book, with her son, Raja. The smaller of the two is Tamara.

Opening yet another clinic.

With Gloria, fighting for recognition of complementary medicine.

Alfred Vogel – still
teaching me!

My great friend Joss
Lussenburg, who greatly
enjoyed his discussions
with Vogel.

Alfred and me
examining some
Crataegus berries.

As I stood at his grave, I recalled the many fights I had won during my life, yet this one I had lost. I had been unable to make his mind strong enough to overcome his disastrous alcohol addiction.

I have, however, often been victorious, helping people through such difficult times. If patients realise the damaging effects of alcohol on their health and agree to cooperate fully with any treatment I suggest, it is possible to overcome the problems and regain their quality of life.

A young woman who had been badly treated by her husband came to see me. Very lonely and unable to sleep at night, she had started taking what she called 'a nightcap'. Alcohol, being so addictive, soon took hold. Unknown to some of her family, she became an alcoholic. Her health had deteriorated and she had become quite weak. I had many conversations with her, some quite lengthy. When I was finally able to reach her conscious mind, making her realise how this addiction was damaging her health and her life, and frightening her children, she started to cooperate with the help and treatment offered, and eventually overcame the addiction. I shall never forget her saying, 'I did not know what I was doing, but I know life has become very meaningful to me once more and my children recognise me again as their own mother.'

It is always unpredictable how quickly one can reach the mind. Sometimes one little sentence is enough to change an addict's thoughts into positively wanting to overcome their problems. I have always said, 'Where there is a will, there is a way.' If one really wants to overcome a problem with addiction, it can be done.

Over the years, I have seen many unhappy, unlucky people who turn to addictive substances which are not only capable of destroying their hopes and happiness, but also their lives. Alcohol is both a threat to our bodily health and one of the biggest factors in carnage on the roads.

The lowering of oxygen in the tissue cells is a great danger and, whatever the explanation, one has to realise that with the long-term use and overuse of alcohol, brain damage will result, following which one is often incapable of seeing things in a clear light.

During this 50-year fight to help those with alcohol dependency, I have seen poverty, sadness and unhappiness, but I still must battle on to help human suffering wherever I possibly can.

It is not only our character but also our mind that can be altered by the regular use of addictive substances. We realise this when we look at the countless people who were constantly warned of the serious effects of nicotine. Nicotine, often more addictive than alcohol, can be a real problem. When nicotine affects people's lungs or even their joints, I again use the phrase, 'It is not five minutes to twelve, it is five minutes past twelve,' to remind them that they must take action immediately. Yet we have seen the most intelligent people failing in their fight to overcome their addictions. However, I have helped countless nicotine addicts over the years through holding counselling sessions, usually in groups of 12, and giving them acupuncture coupled with remedies such as *Craving Essence*. Many patients have written to me saying how grateful they are that they managed to conquer this nasty, dirty habit.

A hospital pathologist once showed me the lungs of a recently deceased smoker. I shall never forget seeing the black deposits in the tissue and black shadows on the lungs in the X-rays. The waste material that had totally congested the lungs of this patient had, yet again, caused an untimely death.

Do smokers not realise what they are doing to their health as a result of their addiction to nicotine? Even a visit to a hospital ward where the harsh reality of smokers fighting for life is clearly visible is still not a strong enough sight to discourage them. The message has to become clear in the conscious mind in order to influence the subconscious mind in the decision to stop. For many, that is where the great difficulty lies. To get this point over, they have to look forward and visualise a better life, where they will have improved skin, better health, improved breathing and increased energy. There is so much to look forward to. As I write, I am looking at a postcard I received from a patient that says, 'I am now enjoying a wonderful holiday with all the money which I would have spent on cigarettes when I was on the road to committing suicide with that nasty addictive habit.'

A great deal of self-control is needed to overcome engrained habits, which is not easy. It is much less work simply to give in. Nevertheless, the achievement gained from attaining self-control is better than the challenge of winning a football match. To emerge victorious in a battle against oneself is much more rewarding and worthwhile.

Fighting addictions can be a very hard battle, and can often be lost. However, I was reminded again recently of the tremendous reward to be gained by overcoming these habits. A gentleman had been coming to me for a long time with incurable psoriasis. It completely covered his body and he failed to make any progress. His joints were showing all the signs of arthritis, and I told him that in these joints were nicotine deposits. That shocked him. He promised me that he would quit smoking, although I warned him that it would not be easy. In the end, he was successful. I was absolutely astonished when, within three months, his psoriasis had cleared up. I commented how worthwhile it had been for him to give up smoking, to which he replied that he now had the chance of a new and better quality of life. That made me so happy.

Some time later, a young woman sat beside me, puffing, panting and gasping for breath. She had struggled repeatedly to give up smoking, but had been unsuccessful on each occasion, so she had decided to give in. I told her that her health could be improved greatly if she stopped smoking, as its effects were very noticeable. Although I offered to help her, she was unwilling to try again. I feel powerless and full of regret in situations such as this, but I understand the feeling so well.

It came to my mind a few weeks ago when a lady offered me a piece of Lindt bitter chocolate – something that I love. Inwardly, I was asking myself, 'Will I, will I not?' Then I failed. I took a piece, which I love to have with a cup of tea. This is a very bad combination for a diabetic like myself. However, when I imagined the lovely taste of that piece of chocolate, I felt guilty. I knew that I would pay for it later, because I realised that I would probably start to perspire minutes after eating it and feel unwell. I then told myself to consider my patients, because I knew I would be unable to give them 100 per cent if I was battling with yet another setback in my diabetes and not feeling myself. Fortunately, such thoughts are usually enough to stop me surrendering to any temptation.

During the many years I have been in practice, I have seen numerous battles against many different forms of addiction. One very particular addiction comes to mind.

A young lawyer once consulted me. Although he had a beautiful wife, he was addicted to other women. When he discussed this problem with me, he said that every time he had been with another woman, he promised himself that he would never do it again. Being religious, he prayed for guidance, but each time he failed. He asked if I could offer an explanation. This is very difficult because human flesh is weak and weaknesses can take over. Sadly, his actions ultimately destroyed his marriage. He asked afterwards, 'Was it worth it? Why am I so weak? Why can I not overcome this battle?' I told him that he could only do so if he talked to himself and, with a lot of prayer and meditation, he could overcome the weaknesses of the flesh. He said he wished I could give him an example, so that he could accept, in his subconscious mind, what he was doing. I told him that the only examples are those people who have total self-control, which enables them to overcome the problem. I have met many people from different religious backgrounds who have achieved success by meditation, or joining a group to practise yoga, and thus have been able to overcome their addictions.

The great King David won victorious battles. He was a wonderful, spiritual man who appreciated God's tremendous love for him. Yet, although the Psalms show what a great man he was, he lost the battle against the weaknesses of the flesh. He battled with himself when he took the wife of one of his officers and even let that officer die in battle. The punishment was great and this awful deed followed him throughout the rest of his life.

Addictions can even be manipulated to people's advantage. A famous London lawyer once pleaded with me to treat a young client of his who was addicted to gambling. He would even attack old ladies to get the necessary money to feed his habit. This lawyer said that if I could provide a statement that I would treat this man for his addiction, this could be sufficient to keep him out of prison. I told the lawyer that I would do no such thing, but that I would be prepared to treat his client and show him what he was doing wrong in order to bring him to his senses.

Addictions can be extremely strong and have to be recognised in order to treat them. The subconscious mind has to take on board the message from the conscious mind and realise that life can be damaged or even destroyed unless changes are made. It takes considerable effort and guidance to help deal with an addiction but the end results can be so worthwhile.

It is encouraging to see how we can succeed in overcoming addictions and our own human failings. This is not only the case with strong addictions such as drugs, nicotine and alcohol, but also with the addiction many children have to sugar. Mothers face a huge battle to discourage their children from eating cream cakes or sugar-laden chocolate bars that are so addictive. Sugar has brought many people to their knees, in particular because of the health problems associated with it. In my book *Realistic Weight Control*, I give many examples, especially of young, hyperactive or autistic children, who are addicted to certain ingredients within foods to which they might be allergic and yet which they crave. We see this with migraine sufferers when they crave chocolate while enduring a bad attack. The foods that cause the trouble are the very ingredients that one craves and eats during such times.

One encouraging point is that it only takes three weeks for the palate to become accustomed to the elimination of addictive substances. By withdrawing a specific item for three weeks, the palate no longer has any need for that particular substance. Consider people who take three or more spoonfuls of sugar in their tea or coffee. Withdraw the sweetener for two or three weeks and they will not like the taste of it when it is reintroduced. That is how we often have to look upon addictive problems. With children, we have to teach that it is not possible for them to have certain foodstuffs that are disastrous to their health. Psychological influence can help children overcome addictive tendencies while they are still very young. If, however, they continue along the path of addiction, it could result in disaster.

The worst offenders are refined carbohydrates (such as sugar and refined flour), food additives, chemicals and synthetic drugs, plus addictive and unsuitable drinks. Bad nutritional habits and an inadequate or uninspired diet, combined with other lifestyle factors, are very often the reason for addictive tendencies. I have regularly seen this when natural products are tampered with and turned into artificial products, which have nothing in common with the original. Products in their natural state help people stay healthy. The offending artificial foodstuffs are very often addictive. Some soft drinks even go so far as to contain addictive substances that encourage people to crave more of them.

A young girl who drank eight large bottles of a certain cola each day came to see me. Not only was she grossly overweight but, because of her addictive nature, her personality had totally changed. I pleaded with her to give up these drinks, although I knew it would not be an easy task. I finally had to give her acupuncture, after which she managed to stop. When her addiction ceased, I saw a changed girl. She had a different attitude and became much more active in her daily life.

A healthy body will metabolise natural sugars from fruit, raw vegetables and cereals, which contain all the original vital substances such as vitamins and minerals, without any problem. However, concentrated refined carbohydrates can cause a sudden sharp rise in the blood sugar level, which leads to an addictive condition that causes hypoglycaemia (a drop in blood sugar).

I realise that children like chocolate drinks. However, these drinks often contain 60 to 70 per cent sugar and, for this reason, they should be withdrawn from the diet. They also include indigestible cocoa that contains caffeine and saturated fats. Once a child becomes addicted, this can trigger allergies, and the degree of saturation can be so high that when children eat or drink chocolate, they can lose their natural appetite. The biggest problem is that these drinks do not contain natural complementary substances that enable chocolate drinks to be properly digested. The same applies to plain chocolate, which is a vitamin and mineral robber.

We live in a world full of addiction. Nowadays, people prefer to drink coffee, black tea, milk chocolate drinks, soft drinks, cola, alcohol or milk (which is also quite indigestible), instead of healthy water. Coffee and other drinks containing caffeine stimulate the taste buds in the mouth; they also stimulate the digestive juices in the stomach, increase the heart rate and the functions of the brain, help temporarily against migraine headache and stimulate urine production and bowel movement. It is no exaggeration to say that some coffee drinkers drink eight or more cups of coffee per day. I see this regularly in the television and radio world, where broadcasters need these stimulants to keep them going. However, in the long term, coffee is a nerve poison. Cola drinks containing a lot of caffeine are often the cause of children being highly strung. Sleeplessness and depression are also some of the problems associated with such addictions. Similar reactions follow the consumption of alcoholic drinks, and those who make a habit of drinking alcohol may be creating severe health problems for themselves.

Since the First World War, the consumption of coffee and sweet drinks has increased tenfold and the number of alcoholics is now frightening. Because coffee and alcohol stimulate kidney function and water elimination from the reserves of the body, these types of drinks can truly dehydrate the body.

It is often realised too late that an addiction needs treatment and, by that time, it is a struggle to stop. This is why I often tell parents and grandparents not to feed their children with these addictive products.

When I look at the world today and at my practice, and see how people so easily mistreat their bodies over and over again, I am disappointed that more has not been done. It is not, as I often say, the quantity of life that is important, it is the quality of life that counts. When we look at the staggering figures of the increase in degenerative diseases, such as cancer, multiple sclerosis, diabetes, arthritis and so many others, I am convinced, after 50 years fighting for people's health, that poor dietary management and addictions to the wrong foods, drinks and inappropriate habits can be blamed for the horrific problems we are faced with today.

So the fight against addictions continues. Old habits can die, but then come quickly back to life again. The slightest mishap or stressful situation can lead addictive people to seek solace by returning to their old ways. Very often, without knowing, they are drawn back to that downward spiral, from where they were once so happy to have escaped.

I shall never forget a gentleman whom I greatly admired. His wife was one of my patients. He was a wonderful person and basically a loving husband, father and grandfather, but for many years he had been an alcoholic. He struggled against it most of his life until it almost killed him. His wife finally managed to persuade him to see me and we had a long chat. To cut a long story short, using acupuncture, counselling and herbal remedies I was able to help him and he stopped drinking. It was amazing to see how his liver regenerated. This is the only part of the anatomy that will regenerate if influenced positively. He gained a new lease of life.

Sadly, after many years, he sat before me again. I looked at him and I knew that he was in trouble. He said, 'Believe it or not, for seven years I have been in heaven. Now, I am back in hell.' He was back in the grip of his addiction and felt very lonely. He told me that his son had returned from Paris at Christmas and brought a few bottles of liqueur. After dinner on Boxing Day, he poured out a glass of liqueur for everyone and, without thinking, he took a little glass himself. That same evening, he was back in the pub. He begged me to help him conquer this dreadful addiction once more and to help him understand that the minute he took another drink, he would be back on this downward spiral again. This is a lesson for all those I have treated and seen over the years. With an addiction, one has to put a stop to it very firmly, because the minute one develops an addiction – no matter to what – if a relapse occurs, one is fully back in its grip, which can result in disappointment and destruction.

5

My Fight against Poison and Pollution

After lecturing on this subject, I am often asked if we have reached the point of no return. I generally reply that we live by food, water and air. We have greater control of the first two if we take care of our diet but air is different. Here we need to become actively involved to improve matters, lobbying governments and environmental agencies, as I do, in the fight against air pollution.

We must all act now to protect the planet – this wonderful creation that God gave Man to enjoy. Time and again I have repeated Alfred Vogel's statement, 'In nature, everything is in harmony. What is out of harmony is Man's creation and we must do everything to make sure that what Man does is safe.'

While carrying out research for my book *Female Cancers*, I looked into the whole matter of poison and pollution, and concluded that it is not surprising that degenerative disease, for example cancer, has increased to the levels it has reached today.

While I was still working in pharmacy as far back as 40 years ago, at a time when penicillin and certain other antibiotics were freely available, and when farmers routinely came to collect ampoules of these drugs to inject into their cattle, I asked myself, 'How can this be good for Man?'

Years ago, I was quite intrigued to read an article on this topic written by Dr Benthem Oostrehuis, an elderly doctor from Amsterdam who, incidentally, lived to the remarkable age of 102. He claimed that antibiotics administered to animals were used too intensively and warned about their overuse. I travelled to Holland particularly to see this eccentric doctor and soon realised that we were both of the same opinion: it is not possible for these particular remedies to be freely used without harming people or animals. Together, we established an Association for Alternative Food and Drug Administration in Holland. A lot of people joined forces with us and we became very active. At one point I became suspicious about a particular factory and I urged the Dutch equivalent of the Milk Marketing Board to take a few samples of milk from its premises for analysis. When the tests showed the high percentage of antibiotics that were present in the milk and their possible poisonous influence, the Food and Drug Administration immediately ordered 650,000 pints of milk to be disposed of – and that was only one incident.

Consider the intensive use over many years of insecticides, pesticides and fertilisers to make grass grow more rapidly to feed cattle, together with all that Man has introduced (not only for himself but also for cattle). With these chemicals being slowly absorbed by the body through consumption of animal products it does not surprise me that such a monstrous disease as cancer is having its devastating effect on Man. I came to this conclusion many years ago when like-minded people and I discussed in depth how this would affect people's health.

I smiled to myself when I finally read in national newspapers that doctors were *now* warning against antibiotics being administered like sweets. Although I have nothing against antibiotics – Sir Alexander Fleming's realisation of the effect of penicillin on bacteria was indeed a great discovery – I am sure he would not have approved of people taking them so freely, or the extent to which they have gradually affected Man. For this reason, I have always said that caution must be exercised when using specific poisons or drugs as they could have a detrimental effect on health.

One lovely sunny morning, many years ago, a farming couple sat before me. I shall never forget them relating their symptoms to me. I listened carefully and found it incredible that the lady was describing an illness rarely heard of at that time, ME (myalgic encephalomyelitis). She was my very first ME patient. Her husband, on the other hand, showed all the symptoms of Parkinson's disease. The whole case puzzled me. They told me they lived in an area that was, by all accounts, a very healthy one. When I took a blood test from both patients my questions were answered as both revealed an accumulation of toxins in their systems. As the gentleman visibly showed characteristics of Parkinson's disease, I started to wonder about the whole situation.

Quite a number of years later, I heard that many cows in that same area were dying of cancer. Following investigations, it was discovered that large amounts of artificial fertilisers were being used and that the farmers had been using pesticides such as Lindane for many years. As I mentioned in *Female Cancers*, Lindane is an organochlorine pesticide that has been extensively used in Western Europe for over 60 years. Serious health problems have been linked to this chemical. Human poisoning by Lindane has been reported throughout Europe and children are particularly susceptible to its toxic effects. It has also been noted as a possible carcinogen and an endocrine disrupter. The acceptable daily intake of its residues is very often exceeded. This pollutant is highly volatile and, when applied, the pesticide enters the atmosphere and is deposited by rain. Because it is fat soluble, it can appear in the food chain and leaves its residues in the kidneys, liver and tissues – not only in humans, but also in animals. It is for those reasons that I have been campaigning hard to get Lindane banned.

The case of that particular couple interested me so much that I rose from my bed in the middle of the night and went into my library. I had recalled reading that, in a few tests carried out in Australia, certain post-viral syndromes were detected and also that Parkinson's disease had been linked to the use of various pesticides, insecticides and fertilisers. It was reassuring to discover that what I had believed throughout the many years I have worked in this field was correct. It is astounding to realise how much poisonous and waste material is present in people's blood. Even with the younger generation, when I have the slightest inkling that a lymphatic problem may be present, I carry out tests to find out what is happening in the body. Nowadays, with the more modern equipment like the Vegacheck machine, we can get an indication of how much damage is being done to the system by one simple check.

We are natural beings, we live in nature, belong to nature, are part of nature and we need to keep life as natural as possible, because we have finally realised that, scientifically, things have gone too far. For many years I have campaigned against spraying crops and have appealed to countless farmers. In addition, Alfred Vogel and I have both written at length in magazines on the dangers of pesticide poisoning. The many articles published on poisons and pollution are always present to remind us of their dangers, and that we must take these matters seriously or pay the price for them.

It is the same with dental amalgam in teeth. One would think it impossible that every time we grind our teeth, a small particle of mercury enters our system, but if we think homoeopathically with its smallest potencies, we can then understand how things can easily go wrong. One can either have an allergy to the mercury, which can lead to bigger problems, or the blood is being constantly attacked.

There is nothing better for Man than clean blood. That is the reason I advocate detoxification and the continual cleansing of the system. It is quite surprising just how much better one feels following a detox programme. An excellent one that I recommend is Alfred Vogel's *Detox Box*. I can truly say that, having been in this field of medicine for half a century, it is crucial to keep our bodies as clean and pure as we possibly can.

My mind goes back to the time 50 years ago when I assisted in the pharmacy in Holland. I recollect people reporting how much better they felt when taking two or three garlic capsules at night. They had been taking various drugs, etc., but when they started to take simple garlic capsules – and you could say there is nothing more simple than garlic – they felt so much better. Why? Garlic is wonderful for cleansing the blood. It is an antiseptic, a deodoriser and, although it might have an unpleasant smell, it is of great benefit to health.

I get exasperated when older people say that because things will not change during their lifetime, why should they concern themselves about the state of the planet, or that there is nothing they can do to change things anyway. Even though people sometimes criticise the younger generation, I admire those who do take action and are conscious that we have to protect this planet of which we are all a part.

It is very important that we consider ways to improve matters in order to protect our health. Sadly, we live in a world surrounded by drugs and materials that need to be cleared out. It is therefore essential that we keep active in our fight, looking not only at the harmful effects of poisons and pollution in the world today but also at the geopathic stress (from living under electric cables) that is all around us, in order to keep the energies in balance so that our bodies can function properly.

One patient asked me why people long ago believed in fasting. Fasting is a process of cleansing the system and giving the body a rest from its normal food intake, and, if undertaken sensibly, is beneficial to the functioning of the body. A blood sample taken from this lady revealed that a lot of waste material was present in her blood. She said she wanted to start on a fasting programme immediately, but I advised her against this course of action. Although I am keen on fasting, I recommended that we start by cleansing her system. I advised her to follow a sensible, healthy diet for a month and I prescribed a strong antioxidant and another brilliant remedy, now sadly no longer available to me. After a month, she returned and said she felt so well that she didn't really want to go ahead with the fast, but I advised her that then was the best time to do just that. I recommended that, if possible, she should aim to fast for a week by following a system I would devise for her, and then to come back and see me. She decided to do this for ten days, which would give her body a much-needed break. I understood exactly what she meant afterwards when she said, 'Now I feel clean.'

Isn't it a satisfying feeling when one cleans out a cupboard or a room and then, on inspection, is aware that it is a great deal tidier, a lot nicer and a much better environment? It is the same with the human body. It is a marvellous feeling when you are cleansed of everything that could possibly have damaged your system by healing the body's abnormalities. The problem could possibly have been constipation or even a constant cough or wheeze. There are so many ways you can cleanse your system and I have written at length in *Stomach and Bowel Disorders* and *Viruses, Allergies and the Immune System* on this subject. Over the years, I have dealt with many patients who have gone through the same treatment as that particular lady, resulting in their feeling really clean, healthy and able to cope with life's daily tasks.

It is all too easy to get into a rut, to take life for granted and plod along, not thinking of the consequences. Animals, which are almost invariably in greater contact with pollutions and poisons than humans as they are closer to nature, can suffer from their harmful effects, often more quickly than humans. Nowadays, we see so many people suffering from the mistakes made by previous generations. Certain poisons can trigger symptoms that can slowly lead to a dangerous situation and damage our body's cells. We need cell renewers, not cell breakers. We must therefore set aside time to take stock of what we are doing to our bodies.

I will never forget the dreadful consequences of the thalidomide drug. Pregnant mothers took it in good faith to prevent morning sickness. I remember the uproar in the pharmacy business in the 1960s when the terrible effects of this drug were made public – babies born with deformed or missing limbs. Even simple remedies that were used to treat travel sickness had to be taken off the market. Although many trials had been carried out on this drug, the body's reaction to it was devastating. It was interesting to read of the legal cases that followed its withdrawal from the market. I have often said that one cannot claim that a drug is not dangerous or has no side effects by merely undertaking a specific number of trials. We have to examine the long-term effects of such drugs.

I recall another drug that used to be prescribed for rheumatic conditions. When I realised patients were experiencing various problems while taking this drug, I started to question its safety. I voiced my fears to the Pharmaceutical Society and, after a few years, it was acknowledged that it had caused liver damage. I could list similar instances that I have witnessed during the many years I have been working in this field.

Nevertheless, it is not all doom and gloom. Nowadays, much more is being done to offer protection to patients and customers who are taking remedies or medicines. With prescribed drugs and, where permitted, with natural medicines, the possible side effects and contraindications are stated inside the packet. The controls on certain remedies are definitely much more stringent than ever before.

I only wish those same controls were applied to preservatives (in particular, the so-called 'E' numbers), pesticides and herbicides. Fortunately, when the directions for use are observed, then there will probably be no evidence of chemical damage. However, very often those instructions are not adhered to. All too often I see the consequences in the form of allergic reactions from the overuse of numerous substances.

I have great concerns about food allergies. If we look at the huge quantities of the additive monosodium glutamate, used simply to improve the flavour of particular foods, we can expect adverse consequences. Consuming foods containing such additives can cause headaches that are often ignored. Headaches should be seen as a friendly alarm bell to warn us that we must be wary of what we eat. A reaction to additives can result in an allergy or be a tell-tale sign that our body cannot tolerate such substances. These initial warning signals are often ignored. With prolonged use, the body becomes accustomed to the specific additive and, if one continues to eat a particular substance, it becomes poisonous to the body and can cause internal damage. This is often the case with babies. A baby, who cannot talk, will instinctively start to scream. This can be a warning sign that the baby's body cannot tolerate an ingredient in the food. Particular care has to be exercised with tinned baby foods to ensure that the baby can tolerate any additives.

There is a call for the increased consumption of organic foods. So often in lectures people have expressed the view that it is too expensive. However, if more people bought organic foods, then the prices would gradually fall to a more affordable level so that everyone could reap the benefit. The quality of food, animal welfare, environmental benefits and avoidance of GM ingredients are the main reasons why more and more people are turning to organic foods. However, the extra cost remains the biggest deterrent. I do realise that in order to feed the masses in a world with a rising population vast quantities of foods have to be produced quickly, but this is normally done without any consideration of the best or safest methods of cultivation. Unfortunately, the consumption of mass-produced foods leaves us asking ourselves, 'Is it safe?' The only way to reassure ourselves on that point is to consume, where possible, more organic produce, free of artificial pesticides, herbicides or fertilisers.

Because I have long been involved with organic farming, I have campaigned for safer pesticides. There are so many alternatives that can be used in order to control insects, and proper advice should be sought on the right way to go about it. It is unquestionable that those who eat mass-produced foods, which contain fewer vitamins, minerals and trace elements than good-quality organic foods, develop more deficiencies in their bodies. Organic farming calls for a lot of understanding, but if science would put more effort into its study, the true benefits would be more widely known. We only have to taste organic foods to appreciate the difference.

There are numerous ways in which we can improve our food and help the environment. When I studied organic farming, I once asked one of my old gardeners if we could grow better leeks than those I had seen in Holland. I shall never forget his words. First he showed me a bed of strawberries, grown with the help of pesticides, herbicides and fertilisers, and asked me to taste one, which I did. He then showed me a similar bed, which he had grown naturally using compost that was completely safe and had been approved by The Soil Association. These strawberries were a bit smaller than the artificially grown ones and he again invited me to try one. Both the smell and the taste of the naturally grown strawberry were absolutely wonderful. He said that we could do the same with the leeks. With the use of natural compost, our leeks were even bigger than the ones I had seen in Holland and, more importantly, the taste was far superior. This natural cultivation had resulted in the leeks being much higher in minerals and having a strong immune system. I was delighted to be able to report on our tremendous results with those organically grown leeks, which are especially beneficial to diabetics, so that others could follow suit.

When I examine blood tests to try to establish where a problem lies, it is alarming to realise that it is not only the obvious chemicals like mercury amalgam that are harmful. Cooking salt already has a lot to answer for and is often used far more than is necessary, as is white sugar. These two culprits are often responsible for problems I have to help conquer nowadays such as high blood pressure, diabetes and obesity. It is a struggle to discourage people from consuming such products and I often have to stress the harm they can cause. Metallic salts are also extremely hazardous. Many are used in old-fashioned 'preserving' and food products, and they will eventually arrive in the lymph system, where they can cause a lot of damage.

Many patients have lymphatic congestion. I only need to look at the lymph glands in the neck, under the arms or between the legs for signs of this. The poisons or waste materials which have become lodged in those lymph glands have to be removed. I have covered this topic in *Questions and Answers on Family Health* and *Female Cancers* but, basically, the lymph glands, which during the night cleanse waste material gathered in the body over the course of the day, are often overworked. We have to ensure that we do not overload them. When there is toxicity in the blood or one feels unwell, the alarm bells of the lymphatic system start ringing.

When we scrutinise the contents in the wide array of aerosols used in and around the home – like hair lacquers, deodorants or insecticide sprays – it should be noted that many of the ingredients are poisons. One way or another, these substances will affect the bloodstream. It is not only the obvious things like chemical sprays that should concern us – the obscure ones can cause the most damage.

All these factors make us look at the numerous poisons surrounding us – the pollution and poisons in the air or the pollution in the water caused, for instance, by the dumping of everything from old computers to dangerous waste, which not only affect us in the Western world, but people everywhere. If we look at pots and pans made from aluminium, it is easy to understand how this metal can get into our systems through the cooking process; or consider the synthetic fibres we wear, with which we are in constant contact, or the plastic containers in such regular use, while some materials even contain considerable electromagnetic energy. Body energies have to cope with a lot. If they are positive, they will be to our benefit. However, if these are negative, problems can arise. I have seen many patients over the years who, to put it simply, are victims of an environment created by Man. I have dedicated time and effort through my books and elsewhere to warning against pollution and asking for help in the ongoing fight.

When working in some underdeveloped countries, I have witnessed the results of ruthless management in the use of harmful or dangerous products and materials. Some time ago I visited Ghana and Sri Lanka, where I met with representatives from the Ministry of Health and had the opportunity to look around. Not only was I alarmed by the climatic influences in these countries, but also by the circumstances in which the people lived. In Zambia, I was shocked to see all the hospitals crammed with AIDS patients, as well as those crippled with rheumatic diseases. The latter may be caused by their hot and humid climate, or their unhealthy diet.

Yet I have visited countries where degenerative diseases are fairly rare. I once visited South-west Africa, where the people endure a constantly hot, sauna-like climate, yet there were virtually no rheumatic diseases. We learned there how *Devil's Claw*, which they were taking almost on a daily basis, was a great help not only in keeping their kidneys cleansed, but also providing the natural salts necessary for their daily diet. It is important to keep the balance right in order to maintain a healthy system. If one aspect is out of balance, the others become imbalanced, yet it takes so little to return the situation to normal. Therefore, with a little effort and guidance, one can reach one's goal of better health.

We can see the first signs of the greenhouse effect today – the summer of 2003 gave us an indication of what can happen. The effects of the sun's very hot rays were very noticeable. In a greenhouse, plants will soon wither and die from the effects of excessive sunlight if they are not watered at the right time or do not receive the correct amount of moisture. It is the same for human beings, as overexposure to the sun's rays can result in sunburn and skin cancers. Again, balance is essential or problems will arise.

One of the most difficult journeys I have ever had to make was to a cemetery where a young mother was buried. A few months earlier she had given birth to her third baby. She had become an innocent victim of today's society as, unknown to her, chemical poisoning entered her system and destroyed her nerve tissue before finally taking a beautiful young life that filled such a worthwhile place in society. This is what worries me today – that Man, who was entrusted with Mother Earth, is gradually destroying the beautiful creation in which we live, but I cling to the great hope that all will become new again.

6

My Fight for Complementary
Medicine Education

My primary school education was very disrupted, as the majority of it took place during the Second World War. Although nursery school went smoothly, difficulties arose during my primary school education, as there were frequently neither heating nor teaching premises available because of the conflict. Primary school started well and all was fine at first. But when our school was taken over by the Germans to be used as a pigsty, our schooling became very sporadic, as we were moved from pillar to post – an occasional day here and there in a church or in a hall. At that time, things were more geared towards fun than learning. Eventually premises were found where we could be given a more stable education. However, this was short-lived, as it emerged that the teacher was a collaborator and had been using the children as a means of gathering information for the Germans.

It was not until primary four, therefore, that I realised how hard I would have to work to catch up. I was lucky enough to receive a lot of encouragement from my teacher in primary six – Mr Nijboer – and we became good friends. One of the photographs in this book shows that particular class. I greatly admired him and he had an immense influence on my life. The headmaster, on the other hand, disliked me and was very rough with me. To make matters worse, I got little support from my mother, who always sided with the teachers. Once, when I had been naughty again, the headmaster lost his temper, threw me out of the classroom and beat me to such an extent that my mother returned with me to the school for an explanation of what had happened. The headmaster apologised profusely, admitted to my mother he had gone too far, but explained how I had disrupted the whole class yet again. My mother, in his presence, gave me another slap around the ears and said she would make sure I would never do that again.

By the time I started further education, I realised that if I was to make something of my life I would have to work hard. I actually became quite a hard-working student, which certainly made up for the lack of interest I had shown at primary school. I quite enjoyed further education after acquiring this thirst for knowledge. I even attended a wide range of courses until I was well into my 50s to achieve a better understanding of what education really meant.

It was after meeting the Swiss naturopath Alfred Vogel in 1959 that I decided to dedicate my energies to complementary medicine. I was fascinated by all he had to say, finding the principles of alternative medicine most interesting. Regrettably, there were then only a limited number of institutions in Holland where one could gain knowledge and understanding in this field of medicine. The Germans, on the other hand, were quite familiar with alternative medicine – sometimes called natural medicine. They had become more aware of homoeopathy and naturopathy under the reign of Hitler, and 'Naturpraktiker' was thriving there before the war because both Hitler and Himmler were extremely knowledgeable in this field. Countries such as Germany and Switzerland led the way and the theories of Carl Bilz, Sebastian Kneipp and many others were widely accepted. When the Germans invaded Holland, the Dutch homoeopaths and the handful of naturopaths were extremely keen on the Hitler regime simply because they finally received the help they had always wanted. To show their gratitude for this help, many sadly joined the NSP (the National Socialist Party). For that reason, when the war ended, anyone in Holland who was remotely connected to this field of medicine was virtually ignored and labelled a betrayer of their country. Therefore, when I started working alongside Alfred Vogel, it was very difficult to educate the Dutch people in the principles of natural medicine because its very name had been brought into such disrepute. That is why, in 1961, when the Inspector of Health became aware of what Vogel, my Dutch colleagues and I were doing, he called for me to be imprisoned and threatened to strip me of my orthodox certificates.

There was very little we could do until well into the 1960s when the understanding of alternative medicine became more recognised and young people's desire to study this branch of medicine became greater. When I bring to mind the changes that have since taken place and the hard work of pioneers to gain recognition, it is gratifying to see them now reaping the fruits of their labours.

Most doctors in Holland have some knowledge of natural medicine and most have undertaken courses in different disciplines to enable them to offer multi-disciplinary practices to their patients. Throughout Holland, education in alternative medicine is now much more advanced than in most other parts of the world.

When I arrived in Scotland in 1970, I realised that people's knowledge still had a long way to go and that was why I wanted to promote alternative medicine there. Realising how little was available in Britain, I knew a lot of work lay ahead of me if I was to succeed in integrating orthodox medicine with alternative medicine to create a system of complementary medicine. In order to do this, however, I had to study further to gain British qualifications. When I look back over the years since I came to Scotland, fighting for the recognition of homoeopathic and naturopathic treatments, it is gratifying that people have gradually become more aware of the immense benefits these healing methods can achieve.

I recall an evening in 1971 in the Turf Hotel in Ayrshire where my wife and her friends from boarding school days met for reunions. The well-known Scots actor Rikki Fulton – our wives had been friends since those schooldays – said, 'If you want to get anywhere with alternative medicine in Scotland, it will need a lot of education to show the benefits that it can bring.' The Turf Hotel's owner, a relation of Sir Alexander Fleming and known to all as Aunt Nettie, agreed, saying that I would need both to educate people and to have scientific proof that it really worked. Although I had just arrived in the country, I knew they were right. From that day, I have done everything possible to bring greater awareness of this field of medicine to Britain. There have been many misunderstandings surrounding alternative medicine, but we are steadily getting there. The immense thirst for further knowledge of complementary medicine, coupled with its growth and development, is proof of this.

In order to work towards my goal, I began giving lectures in hospitals. Back in the 1970s, it was difficult to convince medical students of the benefits of using alternative medicine and I faced many fights with critics, but I was lucky enough to lecture to postgraduates at the University of Edinburgh Medical School. As hardly any time was devoted to this field of study in universities at that time, they knew nothing about the topic and were often incredibly grateful for the lectures. Some of those students even went on to specialise in this field of medicine. It gives me such pleasure when I see throughout England,

Scotland, Ireland and Wales that some of those same students have flourishing practices today.

So, that was the beginning.

I consulted for many years at 10 Harley Street in London, with around 60 other orthodox and alternative practitioners. At our meetings, we often discussed the call for further education, and the recognition that documentary proof was needed to support our claims. Of course, that was exceedingly difficult, because while governments would grant funding to further research in orthodox medicine, similar financial assistance was not offered to alternative medicine. So, whilst the orthodox practitioners had sufficient money to prove themselves, the alternative practitioners had to do it themselves. Often the only proof that alternative medicine worked at that time was the sight of waiting rooms full of patients seeking help. The practitioners could then demonstrate its efficacy by saying, 'Here you are. These patients are better and one cannot argue with results.'

I continue to travel throughout the world educating people in the principles of alternative medicine. In America and Canada, I was able to help establish an appropriate teaching programme, lecturing in many of their universities and alternative medicine colleges (which have now become universities). It gives me great pleasure to witness this expansion, to the extent that I even joined several committees at some of these universities.

Whenever I took part in radio programmes on CHML in Hamilton, Canada, I would take the opportunity of lecturing at the neighbouring McMaster University to give students an understanding of my work. It was the same in America. The need to educate people was enormous and a lot of work had to be done to get the message across to as many people as possible.

Back in Britain, in the late 1970s and early 1980s, alternative practitioners were gradually starting to establish themselves. The BCNO (British College for Naturopathy and Osteopathy), which is possibly the most advanced in both disciplines, was steadily becoming recognised as one of the top colleges in Britain. The same applied to the field of acupuncture and other alternative therapies. At long last, some universities had wakened up to the fact that there was a need for further education and recognition in this field of medicine and they then started to introduce the first forms of alternative medicine, nutrition and many other therapies to their programmes.

There was a great need to make alternative treatments more freely available to patients. However, many people were sceptical and wanted to know how they could be sure if the practitioners were recognised in their field and had received a proper education in alternative medicine or if they were quacks. Those questions were asked many times when I broadcast with Gloria Hunniford on her radio programme, as far back as the 1980s. I discussed the issue with many people in the public eye, whom I had treated as patients, and I often asked them for their support in spreading the word – people like Cliff Richard, Donny Osmond and many other famous singers, sports people and supportive journalists. Still, it was a fight, but a fight that was, little by little, marching uphill to victory. Although we are not quite there yet, we are nearing our goal.

I remember one occasion when, feeling quite distressed about further misunderstandings from the orthodox world, I received a call to visit a well-respected oncologist in this country. When I arrived at his beautiful home, this gentleman pleaded for help because he had almost come to the end of the road in his own life. We talked at length and it became apparent that he was extremely interested in alternative medicine and was open-minded enough to encourage me to persevere in what I was doing and to find more ways of educating universities with a view to increasing their understanding of this field of medicine. Even our well-loved Queen Elizabeth offered me advice on how to tackle the difficulties I was facing and, in fact, many members of the Royal Family have encouraged me to soldier on. I am happy to say that although the battle has not been won – especially nowadays against the drug industry – we are still gaining ground. As I have said in an earlier chapter, honesty will always win.

There are some professors who are bursting with knowledge and scientific facts, but if they lack understanding or the human ability to recognise the needs of those patients who have come to the end of the road with regard to orthodox treatments, then they are of little help in the fight to alleviate human suffering. On the other hand, we have the simple, sometimes less well-educated practitioners who, through their hands-on work, can relieve the pain and suffering of so many. Throughout the world, I have seen uneducated people who possess this special gift – probably handed down from grandparents and parents – who through working with their hands, and with simple, safe treatments, are able to help so many people in need.

I have given hundreds of seminars to practitioners, throughout the country, to encourage them to study and educate themselves and gain recognition in their field. They need to become aware of the basics of how to deal with people and, in order to ensure the safety of the public, they must be totally aware of what they are doing. Many have gone down different paths in their field of study, whether it be massage, reflexology, homoeopathy, aromatherapy, or perhaps the most important one that I have taught them – sympathy and compassion for the patients seeking help. That need is massive and requires to be met.

A number of years ago, I was asked by Queen's University, Belfast, to undertake postgraduate training seminars in the Pharmaceutical Department. These were designed to provide basic information on the products that the public were seeking and on the disciplines used in complementary medicine. What I found unbelievable was that the Government instructed a locum to be present to evaluate my seminars. I felt it an immense accomplishment when looking at the evaluations after each seminar to note that I had scored very high levels of acceptance on each occasion, once almost 90 per cent. I believe the interest engendered by these seminars has been beneficial on many fronts. For example, one particular pharmacist increased turnover sixfold after becoming aware of what people wanted and recognising which remedies had proved to be particularly beneficial.

I decided to write *The Pharmacy Guide to Herbal Remedies* to assist them. Of all the many books that I have written on the subject of complementary medicine, that one is used almost daily in countless health stores and pharmacies as a quick and easy reference guide to the remedies people can take safely and those which have to be taken more cautiously.

Alfred Vogel and I organised several educative courses, as have others. The UK arm of Bioforce, under the direction of my daughter Janyn and her husband Dr Jen Tan, established an invaluable distance-learning course on Phytotherapy (plant medicine), which continues to be of immense help to doctors, pharmacists and practitioners who all have a responsibility to care for people's well-being. This course is probably one of the most valued courses in the industry and is one that I have personally endorsed many times.

I always gain great pleasure when I hold lectures throughout the world to see the enormous need and thirst there is for more information. We know that knowledge and education are vital to establish a recognised system. People here in Britain have fought so hard for this understanding – not just in my time but even as far back as 100 years ago. They have done all they possibly could to bring this knowledge into the field of education. A few I have admired immensely are Sidney

Rose-Neil, Joe Goodman, Keith Lamont, Walter Thomson . . . but there are so many others who have also done their best to share their vast knowledge with those who are eager to learn.

Whenever I meet my friend Roger Newman Turner, who has also done everything he can for complementary medicine education, we talk with admiration of those who have left the legacy of tirelessly working towards the goal of a multi-disciplinary system to ensure that human suffering can benefit from the diverse methods that have been practised over hundreds of years.

I was extremely encouraged when the principal of Queen Margaret University College in Edinburgh personally asked me to assist in developing the education of students of complementary medicine, a task already begun by Professor Anne de Looy and her staff. I have donated to them my large collection of books, inherited from Alfred Vogel, Dr Len Allan and many others who studied these subjects in great depth, which will find a home in their new Craighall campus in East Lothian.

When I look at the research work undertaken by the well-known practitioner Dr Allan, which he outlines in his books, I now realise what an extraordinary researcher he was. Establishing an extensive library, covering every aspect of alternative medicine, is of enormous assistance to students, who can only benefit from this man and others having put their wide-ranging knowledge and understanding down on paper.

Probably one of my proudest moments was when I was granted the Professorship in Complementary Medicine at Queen Margaret's – the first such chair in Scotland – in recognition of my work in the field of naturopathic medicine and the development and promotion of the wider field of complementary medicine to the general public.

It gives me the greatest pleasure when I think of the medical people who, having spoken with me or attended my seminars, have introduced some of these multi-disciplinary therapies into their orthodox practices. It is pleasing not only to see how busy and how outstanding they are but, above all, to know that the patients get the help they deserve to alleviate their suffering. Many of these patients have come to the end of the orthodox road and, as a last resort, they turn to alternative therapies, the benefits of which are often beyond human understanding.

It is an uphill battle to establish education in complementary medicine. At long last, after 50 years fighting, the goal is in view and there is a warm feeling in our hearts because, over the years, we have proved it really works.

7

My Fight for Understanding

Many times during my life I have been aware of the true meaning of the word 'understanding'. I have possibly learnt this the hard way, but, in so doing, it has enabled me to display a great deal of understanding when it is needed – although, when I have not met with the understanding I seek in return, I experience a sense of failure. One needs to be willing to cooperate with what is being offered and one must be prepared to show this same understanding in return.

Understanding is essential in the world in which we live. We are all conscious that the nation is becoming increasingly selfish – a matter of 'I'm all right, Jack'. We live in a world where we must offer support to each other and not act as though we are some of the first people to live on this Earth. When Cain murdered his brother, Abel, and God asked him where his brother was, Cain replied, 'Am I my brother's keeper?' Yes, we are. We have to help each other, but we must also have understanding from both sides, accepting the reality of life and recognising what we can and cannot do.

Whilst writing on this subject, I am reminded of the time when, a number of years ago, I was president of the British and European Osteopathic Association. We had quite a lot of members and, at one of our meetings, one member lodged a complaint concerning the actions of another, accusing him of trying to drum up extra business by handing out leaflets in which he made claims about the treatment he was providing and attempting to poach patients from the area in which this practitioner worked. As we were extremely strict on such matters and members had to abide by our rules and regulations, two written warnings were sent to him, without success. After a third and final warning, he was asked to attend a meeting. A number of those present asked why he could not build up his business by other methods, or if he was having financial problems. He said he had no financial worries, nor could he see any problem in handing out these leaflets.

I had to tell him in no uncertain terms that we had no alternative but to expel him from the Association. When he realised that he had gone too far and that I meant what I had said, he had tears in his eyes. He eventually admitted that he needed the patients. I tried to understand his problems. It was a Sunday and from the pavement under the window of the hotel room in which we were meeting I heard the Salvation Army band playing 'Jesus Died for Sinners'. I smiled inwardly and asked myself how we could be so hard as to take away this man's bread and butter. So, for a third time, we forgave him, on the strict condition that he would never repeat his tactics.

This is all part of life. It is wonderful to experience forgiveness, but if one repeats the same mistake over and over again, forgiveness will not be so forthcoming, and understanding will go out of the window. It is very important, though, to try to understand both sides of a situation.

It is wonderful to receive credit for one's work. Not only is it of great encouragement to have approval from reputable associations but it also offers the public peace of mind when deciding which practitioner to consult.

I experienced tremendous love and understanding from the Northern Institute of Massage and Manipulative Therapies. Not only are their study courses very well grounded but the sole aim of members is to help alleviate human suffering. At every meeting that was arranged – and I would like to give a special thanks to Ken and Audrey Woodward, who organised these – the welfare of the public was their top priority, then the practitioner, then networking. The Institute has stood the test of time for well over 80 years and maintains these fundamental principles. Our annual meetings were most enjoyable and I was often overwhelmed by the tremendous sense of love and understanding within the Institute and the enthusiasm to educate and protect the well-being of the public. It was therefore a great honour for me to be invited to become their president in 1991–2 and I was also privileged later to be made a Fellow of that very worthwhile Institute. When I think of all the good work that they have done and of the guidance they have given to many leading osteopaths in their chosen careers, I am thankful that I was once president of that Institute. It is with immense pleasure that today I can see the fruits of all their hard work.

The British Naturopathic and Osteopathic Association, founded by eminent people like Stanley Lief, John Thomson and many others, operated for many years before merging with the Osteopathic Association of Great Britain in 1991. They worked tirelessly to establish an organisation encompassing naturopathy and osteopathy in Britain. It is with great pride that today we still have the British Naturopathic Association, which basically follows the principles of the great forefathers in this field. When I see people like Roger Newman Turner and Joe Goodman striving to maintain the high standards of medical care in our profession, then I am extremely proud to be associated with those colleagues who, selflessly, do their best to alleviate human suffering.

A lot of these old-fashioned therapies have been tried and tested. We see this with the well-established British Acupuncture Association, of which I have been a member for many years, where they have worked diligently on educative matters and have succeeded in promoting public safety. There are too many to mention here, but when I think of people like Sidney Rose-Neil, Jack Worsley, Mary Austin, Eric Welton Johnson, Victor Foster, Keith Lamont and many more who have put every effort into fighting for their Association and its beliefs with the aim of establishing acupuncture as a much more acceptable and readily available part of medical treatment today, I am privileged to have been associated with them.

It has been with great conviction that those people, including myself, have fought for the acceptance and understanding of our disciplines, which now benefit from the vast amount of research and work carried out over the years. I have taken part in hundreds of television and radio broadcasts with the sole objective of getting our message across to as many of the public as possible.

It is so distressing to see money, selfish attitudes and misunderstandings being constantly responsible for a great number of rifts that could easily be avoided if everyone joined forces and worked together for a more understanding society. Sadly, jealousy can also play a major role in destroying what could otherwise have been so good.

This same problem is apparent in the drug industry, where the primary consideration appears to be profit. Regrettably, many companies, instead of ploughing back their profits to improve the quality of products, seem to have been reaping the benefits at the expense of the public, and are trying to destroy what was once good.

When I look at how ruthlessly those powerful industries go about their work, doing so little to further the research into what God has created for Man in his promise to give him the foods for his existence and the herbs for healing, my heart is deeply saddened. Their selfish attitudes are focused purely on economic growth and profits at any cost – even human lives – in a society where understanding and compassion is far from their minds.

Unfortunately, this problem exists in every country where people put profit before the well-being of others. I have sometimes watched with tears in my eyes as health inspectors have cleared the shelves of the natural products God gave Man to help himself. It is heartbreaking to see such powers destroying what was slowly building up to be such a great help to humanity.

I am so appreciative when I meet people who put their heart and soul into helping others and show understanding and compassion to their fellow human beings. The extent to which they are prepared to go to achieve this is often beyond human understanding. Once or twice in my lifetime, I have come across this wonderful experience.

Many years ago, when I was struggling to win for alternative medicine the recognition it deserved, I phoned practitioner and writer Michael van Straten to ask for help. When I told him about my problems, he offered support and sound advice, including a recommendation that I join the British Naturopathic and Osteopathic Association, which I mentioned earlier in this chapter.

It is comforting to know that there are some people we can turn to in life who have the ability to understand problems and are willing to help. I have always made an effort to correct myself when I have been too impatient about something, and cannot be faulted for striving to understand people's needs. I have always done my best to understand the great needs of this huge selfish world in which we live, where we ought to be each other's keeper.

Over the years, people have often asked, 'How can I learn understanding?' This is something we actually develop through time and it may be necessary to experience many difficult situations in life before we can truly show empathy towards others.

In the first part of this chapter, I consciously chose to relate the story of the osteopath who completely understood what we meant when he was told he could not continue as he was doing. The problem was that, because of his situation, and possibly greed, he initially made the decision to ignore the understanding behind our message. It is often difficult to accept and understand the message because it is not always what we want to hear.

I was aware of this on a visit to one of London's leading hospitals. The discussion focused on a certain product – *IP-6 and Inositol* – and its use as an extra boost in the treatment given to cancer patients. One doctor was totally open-minded and listened, trying to understand the message of Professor Shamsuddin who, having been in medicine himself for 30 years, researched this product and suddenly realised he had found what appeared to be a way of controlling cancer cells. This doctor understood that message, and was grateful for the little I could tell him about it and the literature I gave him on the product. On the other hand, his colleague was very negative. He didn't want to understand the message, because he was so locked into his own thoughts and the views cemented in his mind by his teachers so, without further investigation, he declared that there was nothing in it and it would be useless. He was not prepared to open his mind to this understanding.

Over the 50 years I have been in alternative – now more commonly called complementary – medicine, I have become so frustrated when I witness this narrow-minded attitude. When lecturing at universities both in Britain and abroad, I have often simply asked the questions, 'Do you know what I am talking about?', 'Do you understand the message in what I am saying?' I sometimes have to be quite blunt and almost rude in order to give students an understanding of something that they are either unwilling to come to grips with or to study. The Queen herself once said to me that it was necessary to have an open mind on everything and to make certain that no opinionated or predetermined frame of mind dismissed something from which we could learn so much. Would it not make more sense to give a particular remedy a chance, even to study it or perhaps try it, especially when there is evidence that it does work?

One cannot always provide total understanding. Here is a simple example. For many years I have taken part in radio and television programmes, and I have never felt embarrassed in recommending to those with painful knee joints that they place a fresh cabbage leaf over the knee, leave it there overnight and feel how much better the knee is the following morning. A long time ago, I was treating a hospital matron in the same way. I met her GP in a corridor and he looked at me and said, 'Jan, you are an intelligent man, so how can you possibly think that putting cabbage leaves on the matron's knees will cure her problem?' I told him it wasn't a cure, but a help. Immediately – as anyone else would probably do – he asked, 'But how does it work?' One explanation is that there is acidity in a cabbage leaf that draws out any inflammation, but there are all kinds of possible reasons. Simply put, one cannot argue with results. If something works, then I say that it does not matter how it works, as long as it is of help. Over the years, I have witnessed so many things that are beyond human understanding.

8

My Fight for Peace and Love

Those two little words – 'peace' and 'love' – are inseparable. Where there is love, there is generally peace, and vice versa. These emotional issues are very close to my heart and I feel that we all have the ability within us to achieve peace and to love others as we really should.

My struggle with the word 'peace' goes back more than 50 years, to a time when I was growing up amid the Second World War and peace seemed very distant. I witnessed the fighting that had escalated between the nations, the arguments that took place in people's homes and the tensions that broke out in the streets when starving townsfolk literally fought over a piece of bread. Hostility between people was all around us and, even at my young age, the seeds of hate were being sown against the enemy. This was something that was bred into us during the war and if we, as children, had the opportunity to play a dirty trick on the German occupiers we would do it, because we all wanted to play some small part in hampering the enemy's encroachment on our homes and country.

It was inevitable that the hatred being implanted in those young hearts would have repercussions in later life. I still see the hateful ramifications of that 'bloody war' today in my home country of Holland. We should have learned that if we all loved our neighbour as ourselves, then that war could have been avoided.

I have been lucky enough to travel to 61 countries and have lectured in 40 states of America. During my travels, I have looked around at what could be achieved by peace. I have often asked myself, 'What is peace?' and 'What sacrifices can we make to ensure peace throughout the world?' The great desire I have deep in my heart to be an instrument of peace is sometimes rudely disturbed when I see how seemingly minor incidents can easily trigger disharmony. By learning to understand ourselves better and by exercising the powers we have within us to exhibit peace and love, we will not only heal ourselves but we will also have the capacity to make a difference to the world – a world that is often deeply divided and miserable.

Making a difference does not need to cost money – we only have to understand a few points on how to show gratitude to our Creator. I often recount a short passage from the Old Testament when thinking of what our contribution should be to creation and to our Creator. When it was asked, What could we do?, the response came that it was not measured by great gifts, or in rivers of oil, or even sacrificing our firstborn – there are only three things necessary: first of all, to act justly; second, to show our merciful love; and third, to walk humbly with our Creator (Micah 6:7–8).

On the surface, these three requirements seem fairly straightforward. However, if we think about it methodically, it will probably take a lot of effort; but to strive for peace and love would be a great achievement. We perhaps only ponder these matters, but how good it is to know that when we put these thoughts into action, we will succeed, and we will then become an instrument of peace and love in this heartless world.

I often ask myself what the word 'peace' really means. Throughout the world, I have talked to many patients who probably became ill because they were powerless to create peace or unable to show or to accept love. To become a being or a spirit of love means healing. Every true and sincere desire to exercise healing is extremely important.

Love is the greatest force in the universe. It is the principle of all life and the basis of all existence. To love in the true sense of the word is to heal, and to love greatly is to possess immense healing powers. The soul of love is the pure and strong desire to bless, to share and to impart all our goods to others, and we need to have the capacity to show love unconditionally. Our ability to express love will grow through experience, and when we care for everybody with the same measure of love that we demand for ourselves, our power to heal will then become a natural emotion and unfailing every time.

Peace, however, is an atmosphere of the main essentials in our life. If we move into absolute silence and instil calm depths in our mind, then higher powers are found, as consciousness cannot enter into the deeper states of real life. The true being cannot be fully realised until a peaceful state is thoroughly established in mind and body. Silence is the great signature of peace, and the reality and understanding of silence will enhance our understanding of what peace is all about.

I became more aware of this during the revolution in Sri Lanka, when I was asked to help treat some of the refugees in one of the hospitals there. The hatred that spurred on the fighting between the Tamils and the Singhalese was so intense that they were bloodthirsty for each other's wives. But when they returned injured from battle and required hospital treatment, I witnessed some of those very hard hearts melting as they experienced love and care. It is of great help when the spirit is reminded of how wonderful love can be. In moments of tranquillity, I spoke to some of those ruthless fighters, when a sense of inner peace had eventually reached their souls. One can make a start in achieving peace by ensuring a tranquil environment during medical treatment, knowing that the deeper the peace, the more potent the healing force stimulated and, consequently, the greater the results.

This was very visible during the years I worked in Northern Ireland, where the hatred between opposing groups within its society caused hostility for almost 30 years and innocent blood to flow. Whether it was for religious or political reasons, the hatred was so fierce that the struggles they endured were visible. But wasn't it incredible that some of the parents of the innocents killed showed a spirit of forgiveness and love for their fellow beings, so that some of those intolerable conditions could be turned around? Astonishing transformations took place when some of those who were badly affected by this ruthless, senseless war became more forgiving and made a conscious effort to accept an almost unforgivable situation. By learning to acknowledge their circumstances, they forgave their enemies and, in so doing, created an atmosphere encompassing forgiveness, peace and love.

We see this in hospitals, nursing homes, hospices and other places where sick and afflicted people are nursed and cared for. Those peaceful and tranquil surroundings, combined with care, will help the weary sufferers more than any medicines. These experiences are often great healers. Conversely, I have witnessed situations in which hatred, jealousy or unnecessary quarrels have caused people's conditions to deteriorate.

I have pleaded repeatedly with many patients to try to find a harmonious solution to some of their troubles, and have explained how important it is to overcome their problems, no matter the cause, because anger, jealousy and hatred will always create an unloving atmosphere that will undoubtedly affect one's health.

I shall never forget the couple about whom I wrote in my book *Stress and Nervous Disorders*. They were arguing with each other during a consulting hour. They were really angry, swearing at each other and telling each other in no uncertain terms what they thought. The gentleman had asked me for some help in dealing with this problem. They were on the brink of divorce and, basically, I could not see either of them bringing their behaviour to an end. I told them to go home, take a piece of paper each and write all the negatives about each other on one side and, on the other, list all the positive attributes.

It appears that the list of negatives was the length of your arm, but sadly there were only a few positives. The woman sat down and examined her list. She wanted to save her marriage so she decided to change her way of thinking and disregard both the negatives and positives. She put her list on her husband's pillow, with a note which said, 'I want to forget about the negatives and positives. I love you unconditionally and I love you with all your positives and negatives, just as I loved you when we first met.' I am happy to say that they are still together and have seen their children mature in a happy atmosphere, thanks to a few well-chosen words, which helped determine their future.

It often does not take a lot to turn a difficult situation around. Where illness and disease are concerned, we have a tendency to focus purely on the physical symptoms to find out what could be wrong, but if we don't consider things from a holistic angle also, we may never find the answer.

We may say, for instance, that arthritic and rheumatic conditions can be the result of an infection, an allergy or an unknown condition, but when we examine the emotional part of life, and we experience hate, feeling unloved, jealousy or resentment, we often see that those degenerative illnesses – including cancer – can ensue from such unhealthy emotions. It is therefore extremely important that we look holistically at the body in order to establish the trigger for any of these conditions. If we establish possible causes, then work towards improving matters, a deeper harmony and better health can be achieved by simply adjusting one's thoughts to a more positive attitude of love and peace.

While writing about this, I thought of a lady who consulted me some time ago. She was very distressed, uptight and almost gasping for breath as she tried to tell me what was wrong. As she was crying inconsolably, I gave her some *Hypericum* (*St John's Wort*). It emerged that she was consumed with anger and hatred for her husband's secretary. Although she dearly loved her husband, behind her back he had become involved with his secretary and had unfortunately fallen in love with her.

The message she received from her husband was clear – he was going to leave her for his secretary and they planned to go away together. She was so full of hatred that she could hardly tell me the story and I practically had to drag the words out of her. I then gave her some *Heather* from Dr Bach. I have always found Dr Bach's Flower Remedies to be of tremendous help in dealing with a negative state of mind. Heather is a hateful plant. It pushes all other plants away and wants to take over. It is also a very jealous plant. This lady was not only extremely distressed about the situation she was facing, but the fact that this secretary, as she said, was so much more attractive and younger than she was, filled her with jealousy. Bach Flower Remedies are of tremendous benefit in such instances, as their characteristics and signatures tell us for which emotion they are helpful. It was quite amazing to see how her attitude changed after she took the *Heather*, so that we could talk calmly and rationally about the problems and how best to confront them. We often notice with those plants that 'hate' and those plants that 'love' that their extracts will be of great help in overcoming life's problems in order to gain better health, peace and love.

I have learned to value nature and it is often my best adviser. It is interesting when studying plants, herbs, roots and trees to see how they grow in nature and how they survive. The Essences that I have been able to produce are the result of spending many years in defining the nature of the plant, the herb or the flower. Flower Remedies can be of great help in boosting the positive part of one's nature and can be given when it is necessary to improve certain characteristics.

I will never forget a doctor's widow from the Shetland Islands who told me that long ago they knew which plants and herbs to use by simply looking at their signatures. This lady was almost 100 years old when she spoke to me about the terrific benefits obtainable from St John's wort. She said if you put it in some oil overnight, it would turn a blood-red colour, which is a clear indication that it is a wonderful remedy for blood circulation. If you examine its leaf under a microscope, you will notice hundreds of tiny holes filled with the extract of St John's wort, which wants to shout out to you, 'I love you, I want to heal and help you.' It is for this reason that it was named after St John, the apostle of love.

I often think back to the time during the war when my mother's help was needed in a home for the elderly in Arnhem Oosterbeek. Next to the home was a large monastery. At a time when bombs were falling around us, I became friendly with an old monk who tended the herb garden each day. During some peaceful moments, he told me about every plant and herb, and the signs that God had given them. He told me to look at the little wood pansy, a tricoloured flower with petals like satin. As our skin could be compared to a piece of beautiful satin, this little flower tells us to 'use me for your skin'. I cannot think of anything better than *Viola tricolor* to help repair damaged skin. It is even gentle enough to use for any skin blemishes on a newborn baby.

If we take a look at how mistletoe grows up a tree, clinging like a parasite, just as cancer grows like a parasite in the human body, it is saying to us, 'I am the plant of life and death. You will find the negatives and the positives in me. I am a parasite on this tree, like cancer is a parasite in the body.' I have seen many people in my lifetime being greatly helped by the homoeopathic extract of mistletoe, *Iscador*.

If we look at the artichoke, *Cynara*, and its form, we see how it can help the liver or, in combination with *Milk Thistle*, can be used as a liver tonic. Another brilliant remedy, *Ginkgo biloba*, comes from the ginkgo tree, one of the world's oldest species of tree. In China, this is known as the 'memory tree' because of its action in maintaining and improving one's memory. If we examine its leaf, we notice a peaceful harmony between its two sides – a heavy leaf, almost split in half and just held together by a thin stem – a perfect example of the human brain. God gave it the signature for how it should be used – keeping positive and negative together (as in both sides of the leaf) in a spirit of harmony that can be nothing but beneficial for mind, body and soul.

'Peace' and 'love' – two words which are so necessary in today's society, two words which need a lot of exercise to enable us to experience these emotions ourselves. Doesn't it give us a good feeling to love and help the less privileged? We often like to please ourselves but in so doing we weaken ourselves and others. It is only unconditional love that can facilitate peace and harmony.

To love and to be loved is very special – and this also applies to the animal world. It is amazing to see how much love an animal gives in return for the little care it receives. Because I have treated so many horses, dogs, cats and birds during my years in practice, I have learned to understand animals more. From the famous racehorse to the little stray dog, they have taught me so much, and the terrific pleasure I get from treating animals encourages me to help as many as I can. However, my hands are tied because, by law, only vets can treat animals. As I want to keep on the right side of the law, I always ensure that the vet is aware of any treatment I am giving, or that the owner has had the vet's approval before consulting me.

I have sometimes been able to treat successfully famous racehorses where conventional veterinary care has failed. This gives me the most pleasure, especially when those horses carry on to win further races which would otherwise have been impossible. When a horse is in pain and you relieve that pain, an amazing tenderness is visible in its eyes as gratitude for the way in which you have treated it. The honest eyes of animals, such as the many dogs I have treated, always follow you around.

Even when an animal has been hurt on the road or a bird has been brought in after being hit by a car, once their pain is relieved by treatment, they exhibit this thankful expression in their eyes that I often don't get from humans. Things are frequently taken for granted in the human world. Often we forget to show a little appreciation and love for the efforts made to help human suffering. With animals, it is different – time after time they show love beyond explanation.

I have seen this often with our own dogs. I remember Tamara, a 14-year-old Samoyed we had had since she was one. She was always very grateful for anything you did for her, and I shall never forget the day she died. We did everything possible to help her, as the whole family loved her so much and could not bear the thought of her leaving us. I well remember that morning when I said goodbye to her. Her eyes followed me wherever I went. I knew she was nearly at the end of her life and while waiting for the vet to arrive, I went back to comfort her one more time. Although she was very weak, she used all the power within her to lift her front paw as her way of giving me a last paw of thanks. It broke my heart because I knew that I had lost a very true friend. Love can sometimes be very difficult to express in words. It is often by our attitude or by the way we handle things that we show someone if we really have the capacity to love or to be kind in this often hard and cruel world.

Peace and love can easily be influenced, either negatively or positively. They are two very fragile emotions – as in a love/hate relationship or a peace/discord situation. I always feel so sad when peace is disrupted by seemingly minor mis-understandings that can spiral out of control. I have seen some of my best friends' marriages and the successful marriages of others going completely wrong because of this. It is so important to communicate with each other and to try to understand or accept certain situations to maintain peace and to keep love alive in a caring relationship.

However, there have been many times during my life when I have been encouraged by patients who, in some way, wanted to show their appreciation for the little I did to help, as with a very kind gentleman from Northern Ireland who happened to be one of my very first patients. I had a good relationship with both him and his wife. They were both ill and I tried to do all I could to help them. To those people who express their love and kindness to others throughout the world, I am happy that I can give them something back. I was aware of how much this particular gentleman had done, not only for the underprivileged but also for charities and many other worthwhile causes. He was a very wealthy man and wanted those in need to share in his good fortune. I think that is the reason he was granted such a blessed life. Many times he tried to pay me more than was necessary and I always said that I did not approve of that sort of practice. I can honestly say that I am not the sort of practitioner whose aim is to make money. I have always tried to give the best to my patients and to see them as a part of myself.

Because he was determined to show his gratitude, however, unknown to me he donated £5,000 to help fund a project on complementary medicine at Queen Margaret University College. When I later learned of his generous gift, I felt again the kindness of this loving man who had done much in support of peace in Northern Ireland. Many other patients, in their own way, think of ways of giving back some of the love I have shown them.

At a lecture, a lady enquired why I worked more than 90 hours a week to help so many people, and what my purpose was in doing so. It is certainly not for money. It is because I want to help those with problems, and the lengthy waiting lists at each clinic are evidence of this need. I said to that lady that when you give love, you receive love. It is a very simple fact, but it always works. There is always a place for peace if you want it to happen, and there is always a place for a loving, kind deed to help others in this often sad world.

A newspaper reporter who interviewed me some time ago asked an unusual question: 'What is the most loving thing that you have seen during your lifetime?' I must say that I was overwhelmed by the love shown when we all suffered at my father's departure. My father had developed cancer during the war, and at a fairly young age we had to say goodbye to him for the last time in this lifetime. He was a very kind man who helped a lot of people and had a loving word for everybody. In the darkest hours during his last few weeks on this Earth, my mother, brother, sister and I were so moved by the love shown to him. When he was in pain towards the end, one member of the family stayed with him in hospital overnight. Every morning there were three pairs of clogs outside the hospital entrance (a lot of people wore clogs in Holland at that time). For weeks on end, sometimes at five, six or seven o'clock in the morning, three men my father had known throughout his life came to offer him some comfort before going to work. The loving kindness I saw from those men, who greatly valued my father's friendship over the years, was so touching that I learned what real love means.

Real love, sitting in silence with an occasional kind or loving word, can mean so much during some of the darkest hours that one endures in life. It is during such occasions that we see this immeasurable love that makes life worthwhile.

I was once asked to take over the management of a pharmacy business in The Hague for a week so that a young family could have a well-earned holiday. Because I knew this family really needed a break, I was very happy to help. One day I had to go to the post office, which is in one of the busiest parts of The Hague. I rode quickly on my bicycle, but on the way back, although I was on the correct side of the very busy road, a car struck me. I was thrown forcefully over the handlebars and landed on the pavement, sustaining a bad head wound. Some onlookers carried me into a chemist's shop. By coincidence, one of my dearest and oldest friends happened to come in shortly afterwards and he was shocked when he realised it was me who had been hurt. He dropped everything, got a taxi and took me to the nearby hospital, where I was looked after with great devotion. When I was discharged in the evening, my friend took me back to his home, where his wife cared for me and insisted I stayed. She made a lovely meal and I shall never forget the love of those two elderly people who cared for me so well. This reminded me yet again of how wonderful this world would be if love were more freely given.

Just recently, I was deeply touched to receive a beautiful card from an elderly lady I had treated. She had painted the card herself and in it she thanked me for the way I had helped her during the last 30 years. Her words were very kind. She said, 'Your help does not go unnoticed and I have found great comfort in the genuine help and care that you have always given to me. I look forward always to seeing you, and think of the words of Oscar Levant, "Happiness isn't something you experience, it's something you remember."'

Happiness can be achieved if we produce the real love and real peace that are so necessary in this selfish, commercial world in which we live.

9

My Fight for Truth,
Honesty and Reality

What is truth? There is a story in St Matthew's Gospel (13:44) that I often think about in relation to that question. A man had a large field and hidden in that field was a treasure, but he had to dig for it and make every effort to find it. That treasure was the Kingdom of Heaven, which for me epitomises truth. I am fortunate to have found that little pearl, having searched for it since I was a child.

Listening to people's stories every day, I often ask myself what really is the truth. It is not easy to find. One has to search for it, and although sometimes one can easily say, 'That *is* the truth', one has to question oneself, 'Is this right?'

My struggle to find truth began when I was very young. In Holland, there are two types of schools: one has a choice of either going to a religious school where the Bible is taught or to a non-religious school. My problems started at kindergarten. Being an inquisitive five year old, as I listened to the Bible stories, I started to challenge what the teachers were saying, even questioning the existence of heaven and hell. Eventually, it was decided to transfer me to a non-religious kindergarten. Later, in primary school, I started asking question after question, which were never answered to my satisfaction. One day, the headmaster told us that the Protestants were better than the Catholics because the Catholics had burned heretics. I asked the headmaster how this could be so, as Calvin and other Protestants had also burned people, and why were they fighting when everybody should believe in the same God? He told me that I was a nasty, bad boy, and how dare I attack the Church fathers who had done so much for the freedom of religion.

My search continued for that treasure of truth until I realised it is actually quite straightforward. One only needs to consider a few values that the Bible puts forward simply in three principles: first, that one must worship God in spirit and in truth; second, that one has to be born again; and third, that everybody has to appear before the judgement throne of God. These may appear to be three simple principles, but they will take a whole lifetime to fulfil. Christ himself explained it so anyone could understand by saying that 'if one had the face of a child, it would be given to them'. When I recognised those three simple truths, a bright light shone. I have often spoken about the power of that light which will be experienced even more during prayer and meditation, a power that is bestowed on Man that he can use to great advantage. In my book *Female Cancers*, I wrote about some incredible case histories of people who had experienced that light and, through that light, how much healing they had been able to achieve, to the extent that some were even able to reverse their conditions. Once that light is discovered, life will take on a totally different meaning and, by following the second principle, 'to be born again', this re-creation will emerge as a new creature who will be a part of that great Universe that God has created for Man, if he accepts it.

The first thing that God created was light, but that was a spiritual light. If we discover that light and walk in that light, then we have a part in the almighty power that God will give to Man to keep him in contact with the great powers that He will freely give to Man during his existence on Earth. A new creature, a new creation in one's life then takes over, which has so much more meaning and is so powerful that truth can then be experienced by everyone if there is a willingness to accept it.

I have experienced many misunderstandings during my life, especially when I chose the lonely road of alternative medicine. I remember once giving a lecture on the truth of homoeopathy and the misunderstandings and the misinterpretations that were prevalent. Everyone is entitled to his own opinion, but when all those opinions have been put forward, it is advisable to then ask yourself, 'What is the truth of the matter?' or 'What is truth?' In the end, it all boils down to reaching exactly the same acceptance as Samuel Hahnemann, the founder of homoeopathy, achieved hundreds of years ago – that the truth is that it works.

Making an issue of the question 'What is truth?' can be very interesting. If one takes the trouble to discover the truth, no matter how small the issue, a very positive outcome can be reached. It is worthwhile taking the time to look into such matters and to realise that, if we make an effort, the truth can be found, just like the man working hard digging in the field to find that treasure. The treasure of truth in one's faith is without doubt the most valuable commodity that one can inherit in this life. It becomes part of an eternal life in the spirit that can continue to live in a different world where problems, difficulties and disease can be conquered.

When I was thinking about this, it reminded me of a boy of about 18 years old who lost the use of everything below the eighth dorsal vertebra in a car accident. Nevertheless, he had a strong determination to get better. The mind being stronger than the body, he put every effort into this and I helped him as best I could with counselling and homoeopathic remedies. Some feeling returned, as luckily everything was not totally destroyed. He was in a wheelchair after the accident, but because of his strong belief that he would get better, he managed to heal himself.

When he went to his specialist and said he had some feeling back in his legs, the specialist crushed his hopes by saying that he should stop dreaming, as it would be impossible for him to get better. He asked the consultant if that was the truth. The consultant said, more or less, that it was. The young man then said he had evidence that some life had returned to his legs, which had not been there previously. The specialist shrugged his shoulders.

It is very important that one always tells the truth. If that specialist was not completely sure – which obviously he wasn't – then he should have said to his patient that if he had some feeling there, then they would work on it to try to improve matters. When I see patients are putting every effort into helping themselves, I tell them to give it a chance and work on it, but without giving them false hopes. Praying and meditating and clearly visualising themselves as being well again will be most beneficial. The result for this young man was that he improved over time and is now walking unaided.

The power of truth and the power of faith can be strong enough to exercise the body to obey. It is extremely important that we look at the situation as it really is. One of my very best friends, who is a wonderful homoeopath, gave me a small extract from a book that her father, M.H. Abrams, wrote in 1953, entitled *The Mirror and The Lamp*. It gives an insight into 'the matter of truth' from every angle. He writes:

Of special interest to us are writers who, like Keats, contrast the poetic and scientific descriptions of a natural object, but use the instance to demonstrate that the two outlooks are compatible and mutually invulnerable. In a passage which Keats probably remembered while writing Lamia, Hazlitt admitted that, as a matter of historical fact, 'it cannot be concealed' that the progress of knowledge and experimental philosophy 'has a tendency to circumscribe the limits of the imagination and to clip the wings of poetry', yet, he added, scientific and poetic observations are not exclusive alternatives.

His example is of a glow-worm, which the naturalist carries home to find that it is 'nothing but a little grey worm'. The poet visits it in the evening when:

> it has to build itself a palace of emerald light. This is also one part of nature, one appearance which the glow-worm presents, and not the least interesting; so is poetry one part of the history of the human mind, though it is neither science nor philosophy.

Leigh Hunt preferred the lily as his example:

> Poetry begins where matter of fact or of science ceases to be merely such, and to exhibit a further truth; that is to say, the connexion it has with the world of emotion, and its power to produce imaginative pleasure. Inquiring of a gardener, for instance, what flower it is that we see yonder, he answers 'a lily'. This is a matter of fact. The botanist pronounces it to be the order of 'Hexandria Monogynia'. That is a matter of science ...
>
> The plant and flower of light, says Ben Jonson; and poetry then shows us the beauty of the flower in all its mystery and splendour.

I would merely add that I find it difficult always to express myself as I would wish. I love truth with all the simplicity of my heart, to be my all, the light to help and to shine for all time, which is a matter of truth.

It is that truth which will turn honesty into a reality, because as soon as that truth is found, then honesty becomes a very important part of life. Honesty will always win over dishonesty and although justice sometimes seems far away, the truth of the matter is that honesty will always win. If one twists the truth, then dishonesty will result. It is quite interesting to see that the spirit of honesty follows those people who have been honest in life and, in the end, it always pays to tell the truth.

I remember some 50 years ago being visited by two tax officers in the town where I was brought up. They wanted to inspect our pharmacy's books, and we welcomed them because we were quite sure all our records were in order. While chatting to these inspectors, one asked from which de Vries family I came. I told him that my father and grandfather had been in the tobacco industry, and the inspector said he knew them well. The older of the two gentlemen mentioned my grandfather by name and asked if my father was Hendrik de Vries, which I confirmed. Even in those days there was strict control over tobacco and tobacco tax. He told me that they never found it necessary to inspect my grandfather's business, because they felt he was the most honest man in town and everything was always perfectly in order when they carried out any small checks. He felt sure I would handle things in a similar vein. I agreed that I had to live up to the high standards of the family, being well aware that they had strong principles and that they did everything possible to keep a clear conscience. The outcome was that our business was in order and I was advised that no one would inspect any of our other premises.

Honesty will always pay and having a clear conscience helps to ensure a good night's sleep. I meet many patients suffering from insomnia, which often results from not having a clear conscience. This reminds me of a story that another great friend once told me, which he narrates as follows:

> This is a story of a man who had a qualification. His qualification was, 'I can sleep on a windy night.' The background of this was that, in mid-western America, farmers used to hire labourers by the season – summer or winter. A particular farmer and his wife went to town on the day when the hiring took place, but as it was rather late when they arrived, nearly everybody had been hired and the town was becoming deserted. But as they walked the streets, they saw someone leaning at a corner, and they asked him if he was looking for work. The man replied, 'Yes, sir.' 'What have you done on a farm?' the farmer asked. The man answered, 'I have done all the kinds of work there is, sir.' The farmer then asked what qualifications he had and what he

specialised in. The man replied, 'My qualification, sir, is that I can sleep on a windy night.' The farmer further asked, 'Yes, and what else?' 'Any job on the farm, sir, but that is my qualification,' the man replied. So the farmer and his wife walked down the street and wondered what he meant by that, as they did not think it was much of a qualification for a farm worker. However, as he was the only person there, and no one else could be found, they went back and told the man that they would hire him. They took the labourer back to their home and got him settled in. He lived with the farmer, ate with him and worked with him. He had his own little room at the top of one of the barns, where he went every night to be out of the way. He got up in the morning to milk the cows, and did all he was asked. Everything went well. But then one night, in the middle of the night, a terrific storm arose and the wind was howling and the rain was lashing down, so much so that the noise woke the farmer and his wife. The farmer sat up in bed and said, 'I wonder if everything is all right.' His wife wondered if the hen coops were all shuttered and if the sacks of corn and the sides of the barn were properly sheeted down; she also wondered if the door of the pigsty was wedged, because the pigs could easily push through it. The farmer said that he would get up and go and have a look. So he got up and inspected the whole place with his lantern and found everything in apple pie order: the sheets covering the corn were all held down with huge stones, there were wedges behind the pigsty door and the chicken coops were all well fastened and bolted. As everything was all right, he returned to bed with a peaceful mind. When they were having breakfast the following morning, the farmer said to the labourer, 'That was a terrible storm last night.' 'Oh, was it – why, what happened?' asked the labourer. 'Oh, the wind was terrible, so I went out to check everything.' The labourer asked if he had found everything to be in order, to which the farmer replied that everything was perfect. 'Well, sir, I did tell you that I can sleep on a windy night,' replied the labourer.

The moral of that story, of course, is that as the labourer did his job with honesty and was reliable, his clear conscience enabled him to sleep soundly.

It is important to realise that honesty follows when one exercises truth. I have seen this very plainly in the 50 years that I have worked in the field of medicine. There are, as I have said in the previous chapter, some medical people who shake their heads or shrug their shoulders and say quite firmly, 'We don't know enough about it, so we will leave it alone', or there are those who are dishonest and say, 'There is absolutely nothing in it. I don't know anything about it, but I would suggest that you don't give it a chance.'

I was very encouraged the other day when a patient told me that his doctor had sent him to our dispensary for *Linoforce*, which is probably one of the finest remedies for constipation. It was produced by Alfred Vogel and I have worked with it for an exceptionally long time. Apparently, this doctor had difficulty himself with constipation and had been advised to take this product, with great success. Because he had experienced that it worked he had no hesitation in recommending to his patient that he take *Linoforce*, saying it would help him greatly. That is being honest, and the evidence of the truth that it worked for him made him share this fact, as he knew it would also help his patients.

A patient told me a story recently of a time when he was in hospital. The consultant examined him thoroughly and advised him on several methods that might help him. The patient said that he already followed those methods, having been advised by me to do so, adding he did not expect the consultant would approve of Jan de Vries. The specialist looked at him and said, 'Look at that book. We catalogue a lot of his case histories because of his great successes. We record in that book what he has been doing and, when it is justified, we recommend our patients try his methods.' That is being honest. For the benefit of patients, we need to work together to make them better. I like that sort of spirit. It is not only a question of being honest but also of working for the well-being of patients. It is of no benefit giving patients false hopes whatever treatment they are receiving. The truth is that reality will speak.

Whilst writing this particular chapter, a patient handed me something that he had written about himself. I read it and decided to include it here because I know this gentleman as being an honest, truthful and admirable person. In his writing, he tells about 'That Other Way' he found to conquer his problems:

> One year past in September, I was dumped when I was told by a
> local doctor that what I had lost, I had lost. I had suffered with a

bad chest for some six years, having developed asthma, and the situation was becoming more chronic by the day. By this time I was on four inhalers that were not meeting the need and my war cry for a few years had been the phlegm that most sufferers know of only too well. My outlook was dismal to say the least and it seemed like the death knell had rung over me. I was in a very poor state of health and losing weight every day owing to constant sickness due to the phlegm.

Just about that time three people unknown to each other were serving me with the same advice, 'Why don't you try Mr de Vries?' My prospects for better health were very slim and in my mind I had nothing to lose, so I accepted the three-cornered advice as confirmation that I was meant to contact this gentleman in Troon. I did so and the date was coincidentally made for the very next day. 'There was another way' and I was about to give it a try.

I will never forget my first consultation, which offered me hope and confidence. Mr de Vries said confidently, 'I will make you a new man!' I freely admit that the first few months were really tough going and I began to wonder what was happening to me. However, in the back of my mind there was a mental picture of a lady from Devon walking the hills who had been as I was, but after about 18 months on the treatment was a changed woman. 'If he can do it for her,' I said to myself, 'he can do it for me.' By March, I began to feel myself turning the corner. I hasten to add that I was still attending my own doctor and visiting a chest specialist in the hospital and there were antibiotics and steroids but the outcome was that I was reduced from four inhalers down to one and, in the summer, I was discharged from the chest clinic as 'stabilised'. The hospital knew that I had visited Mr de Vries but sadly treated the matter as by the way. I don't think they took 'that other way' seriously. Thirteen months later, I am still on one inhaler; no more wheezing or breathlessness, the phlegm problem greatly reduced; no more sickness due to phlegm; I have put back about a stone in weight; look a lot healthier and have a sense of well-being that I haven't had in years.

In the event of passing on the good news, it is like preaching the gospel to the unconverted; I wonder in amazement at the unbelief of others in spite of the fact that my recovery and well-being is obvious. So many people are in a mind-set, conditioned by a wrong attitude and prevalent scepticism. There is another way. To the unbeliever, all I can say is that, 'whereas I was plagued by chest problems, today I am that new man! There is life after inhalers.'

That patient experienced the reality. I much prefer patients to be honest when they consult me. Over the years I have worked in Scotland, I have come to realise that the Scots are generally honest enough to tell me whether or not they will follow a particular diet or plan. Sadly, there are a lot of people who say they will do it and then don't, hoping that they will get better on their own. The patient who wrote that passage followed my instructions to the letter and consequently reaped the benefits.

Belief becomes very powerful and one becomes a new being when illness and disease have been conquered. So what is the reality of the matter? I am aware that if you break a leg or you have a burst appendix, then hospital treatment is required. The battle between orthodox and alternative medicine has been tremendous over the years. Misunderstandings, misconceptions, lies and all kinds of things have played a role in the fight to prove the efficacy of what is now termed 'complementary medicine'. The reality of it all is that many people who have taken the orthodox route and have not been satisfied with the results have found success when they subsequently followed the alternative system.

It is crucial that honesty should be shown to patients by hospitals. I admire those doctors, nurses and hospital staff who devote their lives to the well-being of their patients. The reality is that we should all be grateful for the research work that has been carried out over the years and practised at university and other hospitals, and honour that with appreciation. But then there is the reality that, in alternative medicine, so much research work has been ignored over the years, and the many doctors and professors who have been sceptical and have not given it a chance or a proper trial have squandered so much in the fight to relieve human suffering.

When I think of the indispensable machinery and instruments that are used today in alternative medicine to discover illnesses and diseases that were overlooked by orthodox methods, one can only be grateful that there was a school of thought that contradicted the orthodox system when questions were left unanswered, meaning that people could seek help from alternative methods and receive the treatment they needed.

I realise I was probably labelled as being a difficult and sometimes nasty little boy at school for asking questions. Even now, at my age, I still keep asking questions. I know there is not always an answer for everything, but one has to strive for it – one has to work, to dig and to plough in order to find an answer whenever possible.

If we look at the great discoverers in the world, the effort they have put in and the many times they have failed, we realise they could quite easily have given up. Instead, they left no stone unturned in trying to find answers. Because of their determination, we all benefit today from their hard work. Everyone should be grateful that those people who were classed as being 'difficult' have been a great blessing to others. That is the reality of it all.

How often do we get things out of context? Sitting down, thinking about it, then going back to find the truth of a particular matter often makes us realise how wrong we have been. Sometimes when my children were growing up they would make up some fantastic stories that obviously had no truth in them, and I would say, 'Please do get real.' Getting to grips with a situation is often very difficult, but it is so important. Yes, we have to get real and get organised in our minds to find out the importance of a particular subject.

These three subjects – truth, honesty and reality – make one think.

The reality is that alternative medicine is gradually becoming complementary medicine. During the last 50 years, I have striven to have the two systems of orthodox and alternative medicine working alongside one another. We still encounter many bigoted people who think 'there is no substance to it' and, unfortunately, this is the same on both sides of medicine. The truth is that nowadays we cannot manage without orthodox medicine but neither can we manage without alternative medicine. That is why we talk about complementary medicine, where the two systems can be used in conjunction to help human suffering.

I once met a wise elderly doctor, who said that it doesn't matter what system one uses, as long as it is of benefit to the patient. When patients cry out for help, it makes no difference what method they follow, as long as it helps them out of a bad situation. They deserve to get better if that can be achieved, and that is what we all strive for. We are here in life for only a short time and we want to enjoy it fully, but there are sometimes conditions that are beyond our control and, in such instances, one has to learn to face up to the facts and accept the inevitable, but not before taking every course of action possible to try to help the particular condition.

During the years that I have been in Scotland, I have heard too often of people giving up without a fight and thinking they cannot improve a situation. I am not a great believer in that attitude. I feel that when there is a problem, one has to do everything one can to solve it and not to give in by thinking, 'I will never get better.' Surprisingly, once we discover how powerful the mind and body really are, and the help that is available in trying to overcome a seemingly unbeatable situation, the outcome in reality can become something entirely different.

It is imperative to look for the right treatment. Over the years, I have seen the benefits achieved by homoeopathic methods, as well as other routes that have been taken such as osteopathy, naturopathy and acupuncture. It is essential to find qualified people who have the scientific knowledge. I find it most encouraging that the forefathers of alternative medicine had a very commonsense view – and let me say, there is nothing common about common sense – of their treatments and the application thereof.

Some newspaper journalists nowadays report that alternative medicine is something new, and write lengthy articles boasting of great discoveries that have been made. It must be emphasised that alternative medicine is older than orthodox medicine. It has been with us for a long time and it was brought to the fore by the pioneers for its acceptance as far back as 100 years ago. I have certainly pioneered for the acceptance of alternative medicine, not only in Holland but also in Britain, but I would never say that I was the discoverer of these treatments. The treatments have been practised around the world for generations and, particularly acupuncture, as far back as five or six thousand years! The success of a practitioner depends very much on gaining as much knowledge as possible in a specialised field and discovering what it is all about. If that is achieved, the success will be evident in the waiting room.

One day, an enthusiastic practitioner, full of good intentions, sat in front of me crying. He was young and so desperate to have a thriving practice, as I have seen with many others over the years. He told me that he had tried everything he could to attract patients and had even introduced a lot of other treatments, some of which probably had very little in common with what he had been trained to do and, indeed, some could even have been classed as gimmicks. I advised him to go back to basics with the treatment that he had learned, to concentrate on that and to give 100 per cent to his patients by putting his heart and soul into the work he was trained for. He would then probably become more successful. When I saw him again a few weeks later, he told me he was already seeing the benefits of my suggestions.

The reality of orthodox medicine and complementary medicine still remains – if we stick to what we know and we put 100 per cent into it, we will be successful. After all, we can only do our very best. Whichever treatment is decided upon – whether orthodox or alternative – it is there to help alleviate human suffering.

10

My Fight for Compassion

During the 50 years that I have worked diligently to give my very best to my patients, I have felt extremely guilty that, in so doing, I have often neglected my own family. Although I did all I could, the time I spent with my daughters while they were growing up was fairly limited because of the long hours I dedicated to my work. I realise how much I missed out on, not being able to devote more time to them at that important stage in their lives. Nevertheless, we are luckily gifted with ten wonderful grandchildren, with whom I try to spend more time, although, because of my exceptionally busy life, this is still something about which I feel guilty. However, I was so moved when a well-known magazine interviewed one of my daughters who is a successful businesswoman. The interviewer asked all kinds of questions. When asked what her husband had done for her, she said that he had taught her to be correct, accurate and tidy. Then he said, 'I believe that you are the daughter of Jan de Vries.' When she said she was, he said, 'I would really like to know what your father taught you.' Her simple answer was 'Compassion.'

When I read that article, I felt it a tribute to me and was really thankful because I have always believed that one of the most important aspects of life is our ability to show compassion. So often ruthless decisions are made without a thought for others, and many people can be harsh and show no understanding at all. It is always good to be able to exercise compassion, especially with people who are ill or who feel they have come to the end of the road. So I felt very content when I read that article. Although I still feel guilty about not giving my children the time they deserved while they were growing up, I have always tried to be a good example to them.

When I was around 18 years old and still busy studying, I was already taking my first step in helping people by working with an elderly professor in the nearby hospital. He donated all his consultation fees to the hospital as one way of showing his gratitude for the years he had been hidden there in the war as, being Jewish, the Nazis would have tried to capture him. A small man, with a long white beard, he had eyes as sharp as an eagle's and an incredible brain. He was one of the most eccentric people I have ever met but he had tremendous knowledge and many brilliant ideas in his approach to treating patients. Although his methods were basically very orthodox, he had introduced all kinds of homoeopathic and herbal ideas into his practice.

I recollect a lady who came in with a nasty-looking suppurating wound on her arm. She had been advised that her arm would have to be amputated. I will never forget the way he put snake poison into the festering wound and prescribed several homoeopathic remedies. It was miraculous how that wound healed.

People streamed in to see him with their various problems and a consultation session that should only have lasted an afternoon sometimes continued late into the night. It was quite incredible how he managed to carry out this difficult job. Witnessing this gifted man at work and learning from all his ideas and his vast experience offered me a golden opportunity, although all I was really asked to do was bring people in and out and give him whatever he needed. He treated people in a truly sympathetic way, which was almost unique, and I learned a lot about compassion from him.

I learned to exercise compassion very young, not only from my parents, who were extremely kind-hearted, but also when I lost my little school friend who died of cancer. I visited her every day to keep her company when she was suffering dreadfully from this monstrous disease. Following her death, another good friend needed a lot of care when he was stricken with polio. I took the task upon myself of helping him get to and from school each day and looking after his needs there.

I became even busier when I was about 18 when an elderly, crippled lady fell off the bus in front of me and broke her arm. I tried to ease her pain before she was taken to hospital and visited her when she returned to her old people's home. She was really a lonely soul and extremely grateful for my help. I realised that I was possibly the only human company she had and she became quite insistent that I visit her every Sunday afternoon, which I did, although I admit that I never expected that my free time would be as severely restricted as it was for the next few years by those weekly visits and by carrying out errands and other tasks.

By this time I had learned quite a lot about the vast subject of compassion. On my way to visit this elderly lady one day, I witnessed an attack by a ferocious dog on a tiny kitten. There, before my eyes, the dog savagely killed the kitten and then strolled off. Its owner never even scolded it, so I took the liberty of speaking to him. I told him I was deeply concerned that he had allowed his dog to viciously kill that defenceless little kitten. He shouted at me to mind my own business. I was extremely upset and felt something needed to be done to stop such a thing from happening again. I sought out the local animal protection society and became extremely active, helping animals and raising funds. We were able to open a home for mistreated animals in our town, which had an operating room and a local vet to do all the necessary work. I was pleased to be involved because I felt I had to do something worthwhile to protect the lives of neglected animals.

After I graduated and moved to a small village where we had our pharmacy shops, I continued in my crusade, raising money to open our own homes to protect animals. In this country village I again witnessed many heart-rending deeds. When kittens were born, I saw to my great sorrow how farmers put them into weighted bags and drowned them. It seemed to me that the farmers were heartless in destroying the litters, particularly as they liked to have cats around their homes. Here I became a committee member of the animal protection society, campaigned for regulations against such cruelty and opened a special unit to care for newborn kittens so that they would not have to face such an appalling death. Although this kept me extremely busy, I enjoyed the work and I have been pleased to treat animals where I can ever since.

When looking after my own animals, I could see that they suffered pain in the same way as humans. However, humans can describe their symptoms. It can be frustrating when dealing with animals because they cannot tell you what is wrong. I remember when one of my pigeons had a stone in its throat and it looked helplessly at me. I phoned the local vet, but as he was very busy I had no option but to operate on it myself and remove the stone. That was the only surgical operation I have performed in my life. All this took place on my kitchen table, and the pigeon went on to live for many more years.

We used to have French bulldogs, and kept the first two born in the litter. One was called Adam and the other, Bobo. They were lovely, extremely affectionate dogs and were very close to the family. However, Bobo had problems and the vet decided that a hysterectomy was necessary. I have never seen such a pathetic-looking little dog as Bobo after her operation, which had affected her emotionally to such an extent that she required great care and attention.

Compassion is a very strange thing, especially where animals are concerned. It is so rewarding when you are given such thankful looks by an animal in return for the help you offer. I saw that clearly with my Samoyed, Tamara, whom I have already mentioned. Samoyeds, often called 'the laughing dogs', are lovely animals, but before she came to us at one year old she had been mistreated and must have endured much hardship, which meant she initially displayed a nasty streak in her character. My second daughter, Janyn, worked incredibly hard with her and, with a lot of loving care and attention, she developed into a wonderful dog. We went through a lot with that dog, but she was very strong and even survived a parvovirus infection. I became fond of Tamara and I will never forget the months of suffering I endured after we lost her. I have written of Tamara's last moments with us in Chapter Eight. I was so upset when she passed away, and I have never witnessed such thankfulness from an animal in rewarding me for what I had done for her. I was so moved when we buried her. Unfortunately her son, Raja, had managed to get out and looked on from a distance. Raja instinctively did not come near Tamara as he normally would have done. Some people believe that animals have no feelings or that they don't understand, but they do – and often to a greater extent than humans.

Here is a story of compassion that is very difficult for me to analyse, as I was extremely fond of my father. He suffered the after-effects of the torture that he sustained during the Second World War, and when he came to the end of the road, he suffered terribly – much more than Tamara did. His agony lasted for a long time and we all prayed for his departure to free him from pain. The paradox of the story with Tamara and my father is that it is very difficult to explain compassion. We were all relieved when my father found release from his suffering. Although I suffered for months following the loss of Tamara, it seems hard to believe that I never shed one tear when my father left us. We were a close-knit family and very fond of each other, but there was such a difference in the way I coped with these two situations.

What is compassion and where do we apply it? I thought of the following story, which may make it a little clearer.

Last year an old lady was murdered outside a Glasgow tenement. The story interested me for the simple reason that there were five passers-by who witnessed this brutal attack but no one stopped to help. There was a lot of media coverage surrounding this murder as the police tried to piece together what had happened and asked for witnesses to come forward. When I read that five people had passed by and had not tried to help this elderly lady, it was obvious to me that there was a total lack of compassion. It seemed that three of those witnesses were afraid to do anything purely because they did not want a brush with the law, another one was frightened of the attacker and the fifth said he hadn't noticed what had happened. Law and order are vital, but the law needs to be changed if people are too frightened to become involved in incidents for fear of doing something wrong. It is for this reason that the old motto 'to love thy neighbour as thyself' is rapidly disappearing. It is distressing to think that people have become so blasé about compassion and friendship that being selfish and having an 'I'm all right, Jack' attitude has come very much to the fore. I have seen this in my own country of Holland. The pre-war people were very loving, compassionate and understanding. However, after the euphoria at the end of the war passed, I clearly saw this change in spirit to 'as long as I am all right'. Today, when I visit Holland I am ashamed of that attitude and of the aggressive and brutal behaviour that I encounter there. In my mind, I often blamed this on the young people, but I now sometimes wonder if today's society is responsible for cementing this sort of selfish attitude in their minds. If law-abiding people have come to the stage that they cannot be bothered to help their fellow human beings for fear of having a brush with the law – as I think they have – then isn't it time for a radical change? We have to examine and review this kind of attitude and ask ourselves, 'Where will this all end?' Life is very special when we learn that life means sharing.

Loneliness is probably one of the worst illnesses in the world and can lead to enormous problems. With the sort of selfish attitude that is becoming more prevalent today, the situation will eventually arise when little compassion is left, leaving individuals feeling extremely alone. This does not only affect those from less privileged backgrounds but also the most affluent in our society. This became apparent to me one evening when I was asked to go to a palace in London to see a young crown prince from another country. His father and mother were probably the richest people on Earth and were very keen that I saw their son, who, in time, would be educated to take over from his father and rule their large country. I spoke to this young fellow on my own for a short while. Although he was only about seven years old, it became obvious that his problems stemmed from loneliness, misunderstanding and missing the love that he desperately needed. Even with seven men in attendance to see to his every need, I could see that this little fellow needed some close monitoring, to experience some normal living and to be guided as to what life was really about. As I looked at him, I was full of compassion because, although he was a nice chap, he was well on his way to becoming totally disobedient. His slight hyperactivity needed control by dietary management and he needed some commonsense education. I took on the job of looking after him. I spoke to his nannies and left a message for his parents to say that if they really wanted to make something of this young boy, then he needed to gain some sound understanding of life. Luckily, the message was understood and now he is much better. The importance of that story is that compassion is not only needed when there is real trauma, but also in simple situations which, if left untreated, could get completely out of hand.

Both my wife, who used to work in education, and I tried our best to teach our children the real meaning of love and compassion. In their work today and in their daily lives I am very happy to see that they have exercised this in every possible way and have been of great help to many people.

My mind goes back many years ago to a nice hotel in Lochearnhead, Perthshire, called The Four Seasons, where we spent some special family time together. We stayed in one of the houses in its grounds and had meals in the hotel. When we were out for a walk one day, I saw an elderly gentleman having a nasty fall. I went as quickly as I could to help, but my four daughters – although small at that time – reached him before me. I was very touched to see the love and compassion they showed this elderly gentleman so that, by the time I reached him, they had already done all that was necessary. I was delighted that they were practising what they had learnt at home.

Small children in distress deserve great care and compassion. One day a lady came to see me with a young child. Weeping, she told me that while she was pregnant, her husband had been shot dead and that her parents lived far away. When the baby was born, it had uncontrollable fits and was diagnosed as being epileptic. The poor child had been prescribed all kinds of drugs, but these had not had a significant effect. The mother was at the end of her tether. I laid the baby on my bench and looked at this perfect example of creation. As I watched, she had a fit and I decided to work on her immediately. I asked if she had been born by Caesarean, which she had. That started me thinking. I was certain that the terrible trauma experienced by this baby while still in its mother's womb, followed by being brought into this world by Caesarean section, must have had some bearing on those uncontrollable fits.

When I began some cranial work on her little head, I discovered some slight damage, which had resulted in the fits. Her little eyes looked up at me as if pleading for help and she looked so insecure. She was a lovely baby and she let me work on her without crying. When I finally found where the problem was in the cranium, it only took two seconds to make the necessary adjustment, and a miracle happened – that baby never had a fit again. The mother was so grateful that this small correction was all that was necessary to improve the quality of her baby's life. It is reassuring to realise that often something can be done when one feels, like this mother, that there is nowhere to turn. It is often a question of being in the right place at the right time. I saw the girl again when she grew up, and I still see her mother who remains grateful for what I did for her daughter, who is the joy of her life.

While writing this chapter, I recalled a horse that stood 17 hands high. It was a lovely beast that had won many prizes, but it had become wild and uncontrollable. The owner cared deeply for the horse but feared it would have to be put down if nothing could be done. She said it had developed a sort of Jekyll and Hyde side to its nature after two things happened. First, it had become jealous when a pony encroached on its territory, as it had been accustomed to getting the attention. Second, it had developed allergies. Tests showed that the horse's dietary management needed to be changed, and, using iridology, I discovered that its nervous system needed drastic attention to achieve a positive result. I managed to change its attitude by giving it a few homoeopathic and herbal remedies and, by transforming its diet completely, it slowly returned to its normal self. The horse lived happily for quite a few years and even went on to win some important races. The negativity of a situation can often be overcome by showing compassion and by making necessary lifestyle changes.

Life can be much more fulfilling when there is compassion. To explain this a little further, I call to mind a case where endless compassion was necessary when a young man was reaching out for help. One evening, just as I was ready to leave after an extremely busy clinic, a worried father phoned me about his son, who was in a dreadful state. The father was a hospital consultant but did not know where to turn next. His son had been a very capable student who had already progressed quite far towards his PhD and was looking forward to a bright future. Sadly, this all came to an end when something happened that escalated into a chronic situation. The father begged me to go to see his son. As I was leaving the country the following day, I resolved to go there and then, and asked a friend if he could drive me.

When we arrived at their home, we found an extremely concerned father and mother. I listened as they told me how their son, once with such a promising future, now lay in a darkened room as he could not tolerate daylight. Nobody could offer any explanation other than that he was suffering from severe ME (myalgic encephalomyelitis). ME is often very misunderstood by the medical profession, so his parents had had a difficult time getting his problems recognised. They told me that their hard-working son had had a busy social life and a lovely girlfriend, but, a few months before developing these health problems, she had ended their relationship. He had then become quite depressed and more and more withdrawn. As a result, his work suffered and he became so tired and drained that he had no other choice but to return home to be looked after by his parents.

I was asked to see him in his room, but as it was in complete darkness it was impossible for me to carry out any iridology to establish what could possibly be wrong. He did not even have enough strength to talk. As he lay there, I checked his pulse, which was extremely weak. I spoke to him calmly and asked him if I could feel his throat and the lymph glands under his arms, which indeed were all very swollen. I managed to find out a bit about his medical history, and felt that a lot of compassion and time were needed to help this poor fellow. As I have so often said, Man has three bodies – a physical, a mental and an emotional body – and certainly with this young man, all three were in great disharmony. I promised I would soon return and, for months on end, I visited him in this dark room with its windows blackened out. I gradually made some headway in helping his condition. It was a very slow path and a lot of compassion was necessary to get him through the process.

After thorough detoxification and much counselling, he started to become accustomed to a little light. By that time, he was managing to eat some fruit and had become slightly more communicative.

His parents had also mentioned that he suffered from aggressive mood swings. I witnessed this for myself when I was having one of my regular deep conversations with him one evening. He was feeling very tired, as he had been out that day, and had found the light unbearable. He became very angry when I said something that touched a raw nerve. He suddenly stood up, slapped my face, punched me and then fell onto his bed crying. I remained calm and compassionate, and I think he felt ashamed of his behaviour. I then told him in no uncertain terms what his problem was and that we had to deal with it. When he was able to get that anger out of his system, I saw him slowly but surely improving, and today he is back to normal. Sometimes it needs a great deal of patience and understanding, but, above all, endless compassion is needed to understand human suffering.

On a lighter note, however, one has to be careful where and how to be compassionate. During my time with Alfred Vogel in Switzerland, his beautiful little house, with his laboratories, was home to my studies. In the third part of my autobiography, I will talk at greater length about my life and work with Alfred Vogel and describe more fully his home and the laboratories. Everyone who worked there was extremely industrious. My wife and I also worked very hard, clocking in at 7 a.m. and often clocking out at 8 p.m. There were few laws to regulate working hours, particularly in that region of Switzerland, and the Swiss took their work very seriously. As the controls and inspections of this type of work were of the highest standard, no one could afford to make even the smallest mistake.

My assistant was a 72-year-old lady. She was very diligent. Before she started work at 7 a.m. she milked a cow and then had to walk through the forest for an hour to get to Teufen where, on a steep hillside, she finally reached her workplace. She was a great help to me but, because of her age, I was concerned about her. I felt compassionate towards her, and I sometimes gave her some extra francs when she went home for the weekend, as she had told me how poor she was. She invited us to her home one Sunday afternoon. My wife and I walked to her little farmhouse and, when we went inside, we were shocked at what lay before us. Placed on the stone floor was a wooden chair, a wooden table and an uncomfortable straw bed – that was all she had. While we were joining her in a cup of tea, her young grandson came in, and we again felt moved by the plight of these hard-working people. At night, she walked us home in the dark, helped along the way by her little lantern, and then she returned to her bare farmhouse where we had left a small gift of money for her and her grandson. We felt full of compassion for their situation. We respected the hard work and help of this elderly lady who, although always friendly towards us, was quite reserved.

I decided to have a word with the laboratory manager, who was a personal friend of Alfred Vogel, to try to get a little bit more money for her by providing extra work that she obviously desperately wanted. He started to smile and asked if I had given her some money. I said I had. He then told me that while both he and Alfred Vogel might be considered quite rich, their combined fortunes were overshadowed by the money this 'poor' woman had. He pointed out the land and the farms that she owned and yet she lived in a world where she felt she could not spend one penny in improving her own or her family's situation. He told me it was a typical attitude of the elderly, reserved, conservative Swiss, who believed that they were poorer than the poor and had to live in this way to safeguard their inheritance. It was a revelation to me when I heard that story, which was later confirmed by Vogel himself, who told me that she would not even let him use any of her land for growing herbs. Instead of hoarding her money, she could have been using it to enhance her life and that of her family, thereby enjoying what had been entrusted to her.

This cautionary tale reminds us to ensure that help is given where it is really needed. It is necessary to be aware of the full facts.

I am never too tired to raise money. I have managed to raise hundreds of thousands of pounds for many charities during my life and I am aware that, when I do so, the money will go to where it is really needed. We have to show compassion by supporting the needy and sharing with them a positive vision of the future in this increasingly selfish world.

11

My Fight for Vision

It was in 1959 that, during my first visit to the beautiful city of Edinburgh, I found myself at the corner of Royal Terrace, clutching a bouquet of flowers for my host and hostess. As I stood, viewing the panorama of the city, I asked myself, 'What am I going to make of my life?' I did have a vision, however, and that vision was wholly focused on giving the public the freedom to choose which medicines or treatments they received – by offering them a natural alternative.

It has been a bitter fight during those years, and one that has often led to great misunderstandings as when, in 1961, I was threatened with imprisonment if I refused to stop practising natural medicine. In those days, it was seen as 'quackery', and you lost all your friends if you went into that field of medicine. I stood there pondering what would face me along the difficult road I had chosen – a lonely, yet fulfilling path. The idea of helping people who had been told by orthodox medicine that there was no hope greatly interested me. This was not solely because of the help I could give them but because of my great concern as a pharmacist at witnessing the number of new drugs flooding the market. I wanted to find a way of making people aware of the unwanted side effects attributable to these drugs. On that particular Saturday, I made my way to Hillside Crescent to be with my hosts, the Youngs, whose only son, Charlie, a navigator, had been shot down over Holland during the bitter fighting of the Second World War and whose grave I had had the honour to tend.

At supper the following day, my future was mapped out for me in that rich tapestry of life, ensuring that I would spend most of my life in my beloved Scotland – I met the girl who was to become my wife.

Things moved rapidly from that moment and we became engaged later that year. However, I once more became aware of the lonely path I had chosen, as the girl I was to marry had no time for alternative medicine. Again, I had to fight for understanding but fortunately I won. We got married in 1960 and, although she was still not keen on my chosen career, she stood by me and has helped me through what were some very difficult years.

My vision for the future was to fulfil the promise I had made on the tram tracks in Arnhem Oosterbeek during the brutal Second World War. Viewing the devastation of Operation Market Garden, after the horrific destruction of Hitler's bombardment which had cost so many young lives, I promised God that I would devote my life to helping other people if my mother and I were fortunate enough to survive. Seeing the destruction and death, I developed a deep desire in my young heart to help people in need wherever I could and to fight for peace, for life and for something with more value than all that could be destroyed in one moment.

Although I have always done my best to help people, I am saddened when I look around today and see how little people have learnt from that terrible war, and I ask myself, 'How can we find permanent peace? How can we stop terrorism and war?' The answer is that we can only put a stop to them if we all wake up and visualise ourselves as being part of the world that our Creator laid out so beautifully for us. We have a duty to protect His creation. We must realise that there is only one answer to this terrible, divided, uncivilised world where terrorism and war have caused such misery. If we want to take peace into our own hands, then we have to show by example how strongly each individual is prepared to work in this way to gain peace.

We are all aware of the horrific events of 11 September 2001 when terrorists hijacked four US planes, killing nearly 3,000 people in a matter of hours – a disaster which caused many people to despair for the future, not realising that destroyers will be destroyed. We get out of life what we put into it. With that simple thought in one's mind, there is only one solution – every person will be rewarded for the kind of work he or she does. That terrible disaster still speaks to us as a memorial to innocent victims whose lives were sacrificed when evil took over.

A very good friend of mine worked in one of the buildings totally destroyed. After a few days, trembling and in fear, I phoned her and was so relieved when I heard her voice. Why was she saved? Only God knows. The day before this disaster struck, she had terrible toothache and made an appointment to see the dentist the following morning. Her life was saved by that dental appointment. She thought of all the friends she had lost and she asked God, 'Why was I saved?' Was it coincidence or was she saved to work for humanity? She experienced the same feeling that I had on the day following Operation Market Garden when I was just a young boy.

It is possible to achieve peace if we all realise the formula: although each individual is only a drop in the ocean, we all belong to that ocean and everybody in that ocean has a place to fill with a love for peace and understanding. This can only come from the heart. There is no government that can truly protect against the heartless brutality of terrorism. It is sad to think that many of the monuments that have been erected throughout the world are reminders of evil deeds. Taking matters into one's own hands can never achieve peace. It can only be accomplished if everybody has a desire for peace and, by striving to achieve it with a vision that everything will become new, by God's great love, Man will one day be able to enjoy a peaceful world in a search to find that wonderful light that I spoke about earlier – to become a child of the light and to spread that wonderful message of truth, honesty and reality.

Although I often have had battles on my hands, time after time I have been encouraged by my vision to help others. I recollect the wonderful experience I had when a young doctor, Dr Sarah Marr, came into my clinic. She was very charming and I could see that she had a caring heart. She had sustained dreadful neck problems following an accident. She had really come to me as a last resort as she didn't have much faith in alternative medicine, but she had gained no benefit from other treatments. Fortunately, I was able to help her recover using acupuncture. Her mind was then open to the value of alternative medicine, having personally experienced the benefits. She adapted her totally orthodox practice and it was with the greatest pleasure that I went to work with her in Johnstone, near Glasgow. During those few years, we both witnessed the benefits people gained from a combined practice – which we shall call 'complementary' – with so many obtaining relief from their different ailments.

We once went to a research meeting in one of Glasgow's hospitals and listened to the different opinions being voiced on disease. When we came out, we agreed that both orthodox and alternative practitioners had a lot to learn. We were both open-minded enough to recognise that one cannot be bigoted where medicine is concerned. It is an untapped field where much can be learnt and where there is a need for understanding to develop the tools to make this world a better place. When we worked together I would often reiterate, 'Sarah, we still have a lot to learn', and after being in this field of medicine for 50 years, I am still of the same opinion. Because we both had that desire, her practice became a haven for many people and today I regularly hear from those we were able to help.

I encountered the same experience in the Elmfield Group Practice in Gosforth, Newcastle, where five doctors worked together in the orthodox field while I was the only one in the alternative field. Most of those doctors were honest enough to admit that they knew nothing about alternative medicine but were willing to learn. When a newly qualified doctor joined the practice and saw the fusion of orthodox and alternative treatments, she asked the senior partner, 'What is this all about?' The senior partner replied, 'Look and see for yourself.' This young doctor and I developed a wonderful working relationship by uniting to help people in need, and we learned so much from each other – that is what it is all about. We were all totally aware that we were there to help alleviate human suffering. I had a wonderful few years there and realised again what it meant to help people who were searching for ways to alleviate their distress.

Do we exercise the vision we need to help each other? Do we really understand what it takes to have that vision which is so pertinently expressed in the Bible, 'where there is no vision, the people must perish', by learning to understand each other and by helping, even without the other person realising what we are doing?

I recall the speech my Dutch friend, Dr Hans Moolenburgh, prepared for my youngest daughter's wedding. Mhairi and her husband, Marcus, both work in the field of medicine and he wanted to encourage them. He told them that although they had this difficult calling and had a great amount of professional knowledge, there was something that was more necessary. He started by explaining that he had known many medical professors who knew so much that they had become 'top-heavy and tumbled over' and yet were poor healers. On the other hand, he had known many humble therapists, who perhaps had only a little knowledge but, one after another, people were healed. He concluded that nowadays we do not really have the right idea of what is needed to help our sick fellow human beings for, whilst knowledge is necessary, there is that other imponderable that enters the equation:

Therapist + Patient = Help. He said that the best way to explain this was by recounting an old story about two brothers:

> Long ago, there lived in the Middle East two brothers. They were both farmers and they were also neighbours. One brother was married and had seven children, and the other brother was unmarried. In those times, long ago, that meant that you hadn't children either. Just after their wheat harvest, the unmarried brother could not sleep. 'Here I am,' he thought, 'with all that wheat, and there is my brother with eight more mouths to feed. I'll give him some extra wheat.' So he filled two bags with wheat and, in the dark night, staggered to the barn of his brother to deliver the bags. In the meantime, the married brother could not sleep either and thought, 'There is my poor, unmarried brother who has to go through life all alone. I will compensate his loneliness by giving him some extra wheat.' So, in the middle of the night, he staggered to the barn of his brother and delivered two bags there. Much astonished were both brothers when they discovered next morning that the amount of wheat had remained the same. They both thought that they had merely dreamt their good deeds, so that night they stayed awake and repeated their performance. Again, the amount of wheat had not diminished. So, on the third night, they took their bags and looked carefully around on their way to the other man's barn. So it happened that they bumped into each other on the border at their farmyards. They straight away understood what had happened, dropped their bags and fell into each other's arms, crying, 'Brother'. At that very moment, the Lord looked down from heaven and said, 'That is the way I meant people to behave towards each other. On that place, I will build my temple!' That happened where Jerusalem now is.

This complete and unconditional goodwill towards each other is the real ingredient of healing. Healers and practitioners need, apart from their knowledge, that basic love – not the love that says, 'If you scratch my back, I'll scratch yours', but the unconditional love known as 'agape' in the Bible. One cannot just whistle this up – one has to work for it and do one's very best to perform it in life.

One has to have a vision. I am tremendously encouraged by our own Queen Beatrix in Holland. She, like her mother, has done so much to strive for peace in this world. Although she is aware of the circumstances throughout the world, in her speeches she advises the nation to look forward, and not to be bigoted, but to have a vision. I often think back to the time she was crowned, when she was asked which king or queen she admired most. Without hesitation, she immediately said it was King David from the Bible who tried to lead very difficult people but admitted his mistakes and was prepared to learn from them. He too had a vision for the future and a vision of God's great creation, writing those wonderful Psalms to remind us of his enormous ability to work for peace and understanding but, above all, for the love of his Creator. Queen Beatrix, through some of her difficulties, has shown that her vision for the future is quite clear. She has lived with the people and is a great example to them all.

Before my grandmother said goodbye for the last time, she warned the family to keep a lookout, as the selfishness in the world would grow and grow. We live in a very selfish world, where it is often a case of 'I'm all right, Jack' and where we forget to love our neighbours as much as ourselves. That is important for the future. It is a sad fact of life, though, that some people learn this the hard way. The positive spirit that was so evident following the Second World War, when people displayed a willingness to work together towards peace and to prevent war breaking out again, seems far away nowadays. To work selflessly to fulfil that vision which is so dear to us may mean sacrificing material possessions in order to achieve improved economic situations.

I clearly recollect, on the day following my graduation, receiving a letter from the largest drug producer in Holland. A meeting was arranged and they offered me an excellent position, with the prospect of a wonderful future, and at the time I considered accepting the job. I was shown around the factory and saw the drugs that were produced there. However, when I came to the department where the animal experiments were carried out and I saw what happened to these innocent creatures in order to create more drugs, I asked one simple question of the man who interviewed me: 'If that is what happens to animals, what will happen to human beings if we pump so many of these drugs into them – could we turn them into zombies?' I realised I could not be part of that picture and, although it was a difficult decision (because I knew I would have had a bright future there), I decided to return to what became – especially in the beginning – my lonely path. Now I am so thankful that alternative medicine is receiving the recognition it so rightly deserves by being part of a complementary system that is extremely necessary.

I was president of the London and Counties Society of Physiologists during 1997–9. Because of my busy workload, I am sure that I wasn't one of their best presidents, but I enjoyed my years of service, being in contact with people who had one desire through their work – to help people in need. I met quite a number of the several thousand members, and they all possessed that united spirit which encouraged them to help relieve human suffering. I saw that same spirit among the committee members. Their founders had a vision, but the strongest vision came from Ken and Audrey Woodward, whom I mentioned earlier in relation to the Northern Institute of Massage. I admired and respected their diligent efforts to make that vision become a reality and their devotion to their hands-on work in educating people who sought proper training. They worked tirelessly to make this Society stand out, and they succeeded, because they had one clear view in mind: to help others. Whatever we do and wherever we are heading in this uphill struggle in life, we should establish a good foundation by visualising ourselves as giving our very best.

Not everyone's thought on vision is the same. We all have individual visions, as I learnt just a few Saturdays ago when a strikingly attractive young woman sat in front of me. She was probably in her 20s, and although she looked very healthy, she wanted to discuss a few minor problems with me. I looked at her and then glanced at her name on the piece of paper that lay before me. I said to her, 'Before we start dealing with your problems, you should know you were the best healer before you were born of anybody I know.'

Her eyes looked at me in bewilderment and she asked what I meant, so I explained what a wonderful healer she had been to her mother. I clearly remember the day her mother sat in front of me, gasping for breath. One of her lungs had collapsed, the other lung had a hole in it and she had great difficulty in breathing. It looked as though there was no hope of recovery. I asked her what her greatest problem was – whether it was purely her breathing or if there were other things troubling her. She said, 'Believe it or not, in my condition, I have also become pregnant.' I was extremely worried about her and told her that all I could do to help was to prescribe some *Echinaforce* from Alfred Vogel, which would possibly keep her clear of further infections. I also advised her to carry out the well-known Hara breathing exercises that I teach and, as many people will know from his book, *Living Proof: A Medical Mutiny*, were

229

of tremendous help to Dr Michael Gearin-Tosh. I told her to discuss the situation with her doctor but not to forget to do the breathing exercises. She was to contact me if there was anything further I could do.

A week later, she and her husband came to see. They told me that her doctor and the specialists had advised an abortion. This idea was completely against her principles, and she asked if I thought there was any chance she could make it through her pregnancy, as she dearly wanted a baby. I looked at her again, thought of the situation she was in and told her that it was not up to the doctor, the specialist or me to advise. It all depended on her own vision on the matter – the final decision should be made between her husband and herself. Her husband then said, 'Then there will be no abortion.'

The doctor in question contacted me and told me that we had to persuade her to have an abortion to save her from a lot of misery. I told him that although this might be his vision, the decision was entirely up to the prospective parents. The couple sought further reassurance that things would be all right. Again I told them that they must follow their own instinct on the matter. They decided to continue with the pregnancy and she asked me if I could see her regularly, which I did. To my great surprise, her health continued to improve. Of course, as most people know, encephalins and endorphins are released during pregnancy, which enabled her suffering to be eased. As time passed, with the mother-to-be's health improved and the baby progressing well, I wondered how she would cope during labour. She did everything she could to prepare, putting a lot of effort into her breathing exercises, which greatly improved matters. This method of Hara breathing has been a blessing to so many people throughout the world when practised in the way I teach. Thankfully, any fears I may have had about the birth were unfounded. A very healthy baby girl was born and that baby had cured the mother.

Nature will always overrule science. Science said, 'Here is an impossible situation,' and the answer was abortion. Nature said, 'Please give me a chance,' and it showed once more that nature overrules Man's scientific thoughts on the matter. I thanked God when I looked at this beautiful young woman sitting before me, who had been an amazing healer in her mother's womb. I could not help thinking again how remarkable vision really is, and that it is good to follow a vision with a mind that belongs to nature, as we need to obey the laws of nature and, in so doing, obey the laws of God.

I often think of another young girl who came to me following a horrific train accident. During this ordeal, her life flashed through her mind – her childhood, her family and her grandparents – as she thought this was the end. She had wanted to marry and have children, so as the train derailed and she saw it heading towards a tree, she focused her mind on stopping it. When the train eventually came to rest, a flow of energy suddenly entered her body. She felt that God had come to tell her that her life had been saved and she had been given this boost in energy for a reason. She looked around at the devastation, where even the table in front of her had collapsed, and the air was thick with dust and debris. Bodies had been thrown around in the two carriages in front of her, yet nothing appeared to be wrong with her at that moment. She was filled with this great love and a strong desire to offer help and compassion to her fellow passengers, which she did. As she often rationalised that event in her life, she said she was conscious that her guardian angel had been looking after her and, when she learnt that so many people had been killed in the front carriage, she often reflected on her miraculous escape. As she said, that experience was necessary to make her value life and to make her realise how quickly it can all be taken from us. It had freed her from all selfishness, as she so beautifully described it to me.

My friend Hans Moolenburgh told another story at my daughter's wedding about his favourite aunt, Corrie ten Boom. A lot of people have probably read her writings, but there is a great lesson to be learnt from the story that she told him personally. In Haarlem in Holland, the city where Hans works, there was a watchmaker's family who hid persecuted Jews during the war. In the end, they were betrayed, and two sisters, Corrie and Betsie, were taken to the concentration camp in Ravensbrück. There was a very cruel female guard there and, through her bad treatment, Betsie died. Corrie was miraculously released and, after the war, she gave a series of lectures in German. One day, a woman came up to her after a lecture and said, 'I've done terrible things during the war, but recently I have become a Christian and sought forgiveness for my misdeeds, but the Lord has said to me, "I will only forgive you when one of your former victims forgives you." Will you please forgive me?' Straight away, Corrie recognised that cruel guard and stood rooted to the ground. She simply was not able to do it.

Then she remembered that in the Lord's Prayer it says, '*Forgive us our trespasses, as we forgive those who trespass against us*'. Our sins cannot be forgiven when we do not forgive others. So, not because she felt anything, but because she obeyed the scriptures, she put out her hand and said, 'I forgive you, sister,' and only after she had acted in that way was she flushed with real compassion for the woman.

This is closely related to healing. Never ever think that we, as practitioners, can heal. It is always a smile from heaven. The only thing we have to do is to plant the healing seed; the rest is not our doing. Those patients who are not cured give us the necessary humility. For ourselves, we are nothing, and I have never ever said that I have cured anybody. Many times I have said, 'God cures, I only try to heal.' In that spirit, I have carried out my work now for 50 years, in the knowledge that I simply want to be guided by the only One who gives and takes life. It is comforting to think that I have been able to help many people. Yet we have to realise that it is only because of a gift that has been entrusted to us that we are enabled to help others.

Often, when we emerge from the dark experiences in life, we conclude that it has all been worth it. Also, we see individuals who have been helped to lead full lives once more, when those lives had almost come to an end, become more compassionate people – often because of their experiences. Such experiences serve as a reminder to us all to appreciate how fragile life is.

Following a morning clinic, my spirits were low after seeing so many discouraged patients who had been told they only had a short while to live. That afternoon, I had to give a lecture in a place that was almost packed to the ceiling, and I asked myself, 'How many people are there who need help?' Although I was quite disheartened, there are always people who can sense the right time to offer encouragement to move forward. A lady in the audience wrote me a little note, and she commented that when she saw all those people giving me their undivided attention, she wondered how I kept going at my age and how one small head could carry all that information. That is probably the secret of it all: knowing that we are one small drop in the ocean, yet so much can be entrusted to us to enable us to help others less fortunate than ourselves.

When I bring to mind the 50 years that have passed, when my life has been used to help others, I have one great desire – and that is to do even better, to work for something that is worthwhile, to try to steer away from the selfishness and the evil that surrounds today's world, and to realise that one can only stop this by taking into one's hands what is good and by enriching one's life by that which is light. Light has no communication with darkness. Once that great light is entrusted to us, and we walk in that light, we can become a shining example.

PART THREE

MY LIFE AND WORK
WITH ALFRED VOGEL

A Note from Alfred Vogel

This note originally appeared as a foreword to Traditional Home and Herbal Remedies *in 1986.*

It was a fortunate occasion when I met Jan de Vries in the Netherlands. With pleasure and conviction I spoke of my 40 years' experience in the field of herbal medicine and my views on diet and nourishment. I soon realised that I had an extremely interested listener who fully appreciated my acquired knowledge of the whole sphere of medical science.

Jan de Vries was not only interested to learn everything about my experiences of when, where and how to collect herbs, and which methods were to be followed, he also insisted on taking part in the actual process of extracting beneficial ingredients. As he was a trained and qualified pharmacist, he was already familiar with the world of plants and herbs, and had considerable knowledge in this field. He accepted an invitation to join our firm, which gave us the chance to establish a working relationship which has lasted for years. He was one of my best pupils, if not the very best, and he had the opportunity to further develop his given talents in the field of natural medicine.

I was very happy to share with him my enthusiasm for nature and the world of plants, as originated by the sovereign power of the Creator. He was also prepared to accept my principle that herbal medicine should always have priority in the treatment of illnesses.

As a result of our experiences, we both agreed that, through knowledge and advice on natural methods and herbal remedies, it was possible to improve one's health and keep illnesses at bay. Nature itself is capable of healing.

Drawing on my many years of experience, I was able to convince Jan de Vries completely that herbal medicine in combination with a natural diet could create positive responses in the body in order to ward off ailments. By creating the right conditions for the body and supplying it with the correct nourishment, one is able to activate one's own regenerative system. In this way it is possible to overcome, as well as cure, ailments. We realise more and more, and my experience over many years in practice has contributed to this, that we don't just have an important role to play in the curing of illnesses but also in the prevention of medical disturbances. This requires us to put emphasis on preventative medicine. Prevention is better than a cure.

This principle plays a major role in our programme. In an effort to clarify this for patients and other interested parties, I myself have written several books, such as *The Nature Doctor: A Manual of Traditional & Complementary Medicine*, *The Liver as the Regulator of our Health* and *Nature: Your Guide to Healthier Living*.

Jan de Vries was immediately prepared to share with his friends, and later with his patients, my experiences and he recommended these books for their information. He is, I am pleased to repeat, my most successful 'pupil'. His success from which many patients have benefited is, however, not only a result of his talents, it is also thanks to the Creator who has supplied so many plants with healing powers.

I am very pleased that Jan de Vries is making the effort to share his knowledge and experiences with us on paper. His books are written in a straightforward manner and can be readily understood by both patients and laymen alike. In them, he deals with natural ways and methods using herbal remedies to overcome ailments and illnesses.

It is important that not just the obvious symptoms are cured, as conventional medicine would teach us. We must look for the cause of the illness in order to continue the treatment and find a cure for the source. Very little benefit is obtained by clearing up an ache or easing a sensitivity if we are not able to eliminate the cause. In order to do this, we should study the whole person and attempt to recognise which factors have contributed to this condition. There could be very many reasons – for example, a breathing difficulty or a movement disorder, shortage of oxygen, rest or sleep. There can be so many causes of a biological imbalance.

Jan de Vries has acquired and developed a large knowledge in this area. With perseverance he builds up an overall picture of total health, not forgetting the physical and mental condition of the patient.

I am convinced that, in this book, he will show many sufferers the right way to recovery in plain and simple language. It is an excellent complement to my books, as we have both sincerely attempted to serve our fellow men and share with them our knowledge acquired from our understanding and experience of the bounty of nature.

Alfred Vogel

1

Good health should be treasured and never abused
– for good health leads to happiness.

Alfred Vogel, 1902–96

From reading the Foreword that my great friend Alfred Vogel wrote for one of my previous books (and which I have repeated here), it becomes apparent what a wonderful relationship we had. Vogel and I worked together for nearly 40 years and I still believe that he was brought into my young life to give it some direction – one that I have never regretted. We had very similar views in that we both wanted to promote good health and we realised the importance of maintaining a positive mental attitude, whatever the circumstances might be.

At the time of our first meeting at a lecture on homoeopathy in Amsterdam in 1959, I was sceptical about the benefits of complementary therapies. After talking with Vogel, however, he changed my way of thinking to such a degree that I went to visit him in Switzerland, where I was so impressed by his work that I decided to join him. From that date on, my life, like his, has been devoted to alleviating suffering in thousands of people.

He possessed a wonderful spirit. Not only was he a genius but he was also a man with a big heart who cared passionately about his fellow human beings and spent his life striving to achieve good health for everyone. Every single day I treasure the wonderful relationship I had with my great mentor and friend. When my mind is in a quandary, I often think to myself, 'Alfred, what would you do about this?'

The last time I saw him was when I travelled to Zurich just a few weeks before he died. I could see that his condition had deteriorated but he still retained a glimmer of happiness in his eyes as he made humorous remarks about life in general. We chatted together privately for a while, not only reminiscing about the wonderful times of the past but also discussing the present and the future. Although his time was coming to an end, he had an amazingly cheerful attitude and the contented look in his eyes showed that he had led a fulfilling life. Even at that point, he was still offering me advice and ideas.

So who was Alfred Vogel? From the first day we met, when he made such an impression on me, I realised he was a most remarkable, interesting man. He had an unshakeable belief, a great love of nature and a wonderful respect for his Creator.

Alfred was born on 26 October 1902 in a small agricultural village called Aesch near Basel. He was well cared for and his family instilled in him his great love of God and nature. Although he was not an only child, he was a very special individual and this was quickly recognised by his mother and grandmother. These women, who were to play such an important part in his life, were well known in the area for their knowledge of natural remedies and people would often go to them for help and advice. He was particularly influenced by his grandmother, who lived to the ripe old age of 103. Along with his parents, she offered him a lot of practical, sensible advice and put great effort into teaching little Alfred all about nature. His family led a sober life and respected his feelings for the animal and plant worlds; they applauded his vegetarian principles, which they also upheld.

While he was growing up, Alfred wanted to know about everything that was going on around him. Not only did he want to learn as much as he could about the healing properties of plants, he also wanted to research them. This was not always easy and his probing mind often got him into trouble, especially at school, where he sometimes contradicted his teachers. He never accepted anything at face value and would question their reasoning when something did not make sense to him. This was part of his character that drew me to Alfred, as I too was very inquisitive at school.

His enquiring mind also caused the local priest problems when Alfred started to question religion. When he was still young, the local priest said to him, 'Alfredli, do your best in your life, because you will either be a rascal or you will be an extremely good person.' I can certainly testify that he was the latter: he had exceedingly high principles, he always worked hard and he looked for what God had created in nature to help Man. He believed that religion is a personal matter and in order to have a relationship with one's Creator, one has to act from the heart. With that thought in his mind, he felt he had a duty to do everything possible to help his fellow human beings.

When he was younger, his views were quite extreme and not always appreciated by the local Swiss people, who were extremely conventional. Even though Switzerland was neutral during both world wars, Alfred caused controversy with his strong pacifist beliefs. He was a man who loved life and he could not understand why murder and war could be tolerated.

After he left school, Alfred was still eager to learn more about the world around him; indeed, this was part of his character that remained undiminished right till the end. While still in his teens, he visited Maximilian Bircher-Benner's renowned dietary clinic in Zurich. Bircher-Benner was a Swiss physician and a pioneer in nutritional research. At his sanatorium, a balanced diet of raw vegetables and fruit was used as a means to heal patients, and he is also known as the man who invented muesli. Vogel learned a great deal during his time there, and throughout his following career he remained convinced about the importance of food management, especially establishing a balance between protein and carbohydrates, and acidic and alkaline foods.

Following the opening of his first health food store at No. 1 Jurastrasse in 1920, word got around about who Vogel was and it was not long until he had gained a reputation as a great herbalist. As his fame grew, people would consult him when they were not satisfied with the results obtained from their own doctors.

He started to produce a monthly magazine to disseminate information about his findings, and eventually he would write many books. In this, he was fortunate to get some help from a teacher called Sophie – who was later to become his wife. She met Alfred as a customer in his shop and became fascinated by his work. They talked at great length about their mutual interest and grew very close. She also often helped with his lectures and once I got to know her I realised how intelligent and knowledgeable she was in matters relating to herbal medicines and their healing powers.

People came from all over to see Vogel, until his practice expanded to such an extent that he had to move to larger premises. In 1937, he managed to find a suitable place in Teufen, deep in the mountains, where he established his clinic. He became so popular that buses laden with people started to go up the hill to Teufen and it became necessary for people to make appointments well in advance to see this wonderful man. Although he was extremely busy, he always took time to talk and listen to those who were very ill. Doctors would also go to him for guidance and he was never too tired to share his great knowledge whenever possible. Not only did Vogel have time to help the ordinary man in the street but he also made himself available to those who genuinely wanted to study his methods. General Tito of Yugoslavia often asked him for advice and he never failed to help when he could.

I joined Alfred in Teufen to work with him at the clinic and together we achieved a great deal. During his consultations, he started to teach me about what he was doing and he would offer advice whenever possible on how we should treat people. Vogel adhered strictly to the principles of Dr Samuel Hahnemann, the founder of homoeopathy, who argued that Man is not one body but three: physical, mental and emotional. Using holistic methods, these three bodies must be treated together.

It was admirable to see how fervently he researched plants. Every plant, flower, root and even the bark of a tree has its own signature and characteristic. When we examine them and learn how they grow, they give us a message. Alfred studied as many species as he could and tried to establish whether the signatures of the plants gave an indication about which ailments they might be used to treat. He also needed to guarantee that when prescribing such remedies to patients, they would have no side effects, so a lot of research was involved in preparing his treatments.

It was always a delight to listen to Alfred as he explained the characteristics of different plants. When you step on arnica by mistake, for example, it flops back, telling you that it should be used to treat trauma, while the ingredients of a symphytum root – allantoin, for example – indicate the terrific healing powers of that plant, which is often used to treat wounds and broken bones.

Such was Alfred's relationship with nature that he knew virtually every plant that grew, every flower, every leaf and every bark. His senses were so developed that, even from a distance, he could smell which herbs were growing in a particular area. If he discovered something with which he was unfamiliar, he made every effort to find out about it.

Only the year before he died, I walked with him in the mountains. As he inhaled deeply, he said, 'I can smell wild garlic.' Alfred then went down on his knees and started to scrape at the dirty soil with his bare hands. When he reached the garlic, he pulled out the clean silvery bulb from the ground and not even one speck of dirt had adhered to it. He said, 'Look, even in all that mud and dirt, its silvery-white colour shows us that God gave this to Man to keep his body cleansed.' Alfred knew that garlic is a great antiseptic and should be used to treat viral problems and infections. At the time of writing this book, the newspapers are full of a 'new cure' for the horrific MRSA virus being contracted in hospitals and that 'new cure' is ... garlic! In fact, Alfred publicised its therapeutic properties as far back as 50 years ago.

Vogel's thirst for knowledge was unquenchable and he was so devoted to learning more from nature that I used to see him working in his herb garden at four or five o'clock in the morning, studying the plants. He often said that we had to dig deep and use the whole plant, thus avoiding the mistake sometimes made by the pharmaceutical industry when they sought a clear pharmacological action from a particular part of a plant or a herb, leading them to crystallise or extract only that part and make it into a remedy. One example of this happened with digitalis (foxglove). A remedy for heart conditions was made from this plant, but initially it caused some problems as the balance was incorrect. Following further research, *Digoxin* is used successfully as a remedy today and has helped many patients.

Alfred often spoke of his in-depth knowledge of Echinacea and of the terrific natural antibiotic properties of this plant. I was present once while a famous Dutch professor was interviewing him and I shall never forget Alfred's answer to one of his questions. When the professor asked Alfred how many medications he worked with, he replied that by his calculation there were roughly 360 but there was only one medicine which could be used to treat a large variety of illnesses. He then started to list all the benefits he had witnessed from this wonderful herb, *Echinaforce* (Echinacea), over the years. I can reinforce this statement because, throughout the years I have been in practice, *Echinaforce* has been of tremendous help and even saved my own life when I was desperately ill in Australia.

Vogel's life was totally absorbed in his great work. His energy rubbed off on me and even now, when I become tired, I recall how he used to soldier on to learn as much as he could about the healing power of plants. I would often find him experimenting with manure in order to produce the best organic blend he could, which, in turn, would produce the best herbs. If the manure was inferior, he would throw it away.

After I decided to work with Alfred in Teufen, one day he asked me to sign a legal document pledging that I would adhere to his principles and ensure that I prepared the remedies by meticulously following his recipes. I felt honoured to do so, having witnessed how carefully they had been developed, and I still strive to maintain the high standards and superior quality that were established by my mentor.

As our work progressed, Alfred began to travel around the world as part of his efforts to discover even more about nature and to look for solutions where science had failed. For example, he visited parts of the world where indigenous people maintained their traditional lifestyles in an attempt to find out why there was no cancer, multiple sclerosis or other such problems present there. I often travelled with him, along with his daughter Ruth, and I have wonderful memories of the journeys and friends we made.

I particularly recall trips we made to Holland to encourage the people in my home country to eat more sensibly. During the Second World War, the chronic shortage of food meant that Dutch people's diet was severely restricted. Interestingly, there was little evidence of colitis, diverticulitis or coeliac disease during this period, as the only foodstuffs freely available then were high in roughage. After the war ended, however, there was an explosion of such illnesses, as people began to eat anything they could get their hands on and, needless to say, these foods frequently contained limited nutrition. Thousands of people in Holland attended Vogel's lectures over the years, as this little Swiss man not only spoke a lot of sense but also educated people in how to lead a happier and healthier life.

If you ever visit Alfred Vogel's birthplace in the little village of Aesch in Switzerland, you will find a museum opened there in his honour which houses many of the artefacts he collected during the course of his travels around the world. He was unstoppable in his efforts to find out about growing plants and, while on the road, if we ever had cause to wonder where he had disappeared to, he could usually be found in the local markets – whether it be in Peru, Guatemala, the Amazon or whichever country we were in at the time. His energy for work was quite remarkable.

I clearly remember how delighted he was on his return from East Africa after finding out about the remarkable benefits of spilanthes. He handed me a small leaf and asked me to eat it. Immediately a strong astringent action took place in my mouth. He asked, 'Do you see how important this plant is for people who have thrush in their mouth or the chronic skin disorder lichen planus?' *Spilanthes mauritiana* is a weed that grows profusely in Kenya and Uganda. It is a complete remedy that is totally safe for animals and humans alike but, for insects and fish, it acts as a strong poison. The flowers of the spilanthes resemble chamomile in size and are used by the natives to alleviate toothache. The Zulus chew it as a treatment for mouth ulcers then rub it into their gums, which encourages this amazing sensation in the mouth. This feeling is so strong that you immediately know it will work. In Cameroon, it is used as a relief for snake bites and sometimes for bladder and kidney problems. *Spilanthol* is the quickest-acting ingredient in this brilliant plant and, externally, it can be used for the most seemingly incurable skin disorders or fungi. It offers almost instant relief and has been of the greatest help to many people. He was an expert in finding out about such plants from remote areas of the world.

Another discovery I remember was a little orange bud, which resembled a little lantern. When he opened up his hand, he said, 'Look, the seeds inside this bud are like your heart – this gives us a sign that this is a wonderful heart remedy.' Yet again, another incredible product was developed from one of his finds.

Many years ago he returned from his travels to the Far East with a small *Ginkgo biloba* tree. As he was telling me all the benefits of *Ginkgo biloba* and showing me one of its leaves, he said, 'Look, it almost resembles your brain – isn't it wonderful that this is beneficial for treating problems in that area.' He planted that little tree in the garden beside his house and researched it extensively. It was not until he was totally satisfied with the results that he put it on the market. Today, we would not know how to manage without *Ginkgo biloba*, which has been of tremendous help to countless people, for example in the treatment of strokes, headaches and depression. As Vogel says in his marvellous book *The Nature Doctor*, it is the only plant remedy we know that is so beneficial for the brain, central nervous system and vascular system.

During his life and travels, he had the opportunity to talk to the most wonderful teachers and professors who were interested both in his views and his in-depth knowledge of herbal medicine. The famous practitioners who influenced him include Bircher-Benner, Dr William Pfeiffer, Dr Ragnar Berg and Dr Klopfer – all extremely knowledgeable people. I was lucky enough to meet some of them, too, and we had a most interesting time when we visited the Bircher-Benner, Willmar Schwabe and Joseph Issler clinics. As we watched the staff there at work, we were amazed to witness what could be done to alleviate human suffering.

Before he died, Vogel kindly passed on to me some books which are now a cherished part of my own collection. One of these was by Vogel himself – a wonderful volume called *The Tropical Guide of Nature Cure*. Sadly this book is no longer in print but it has been helpful to many people affected by seemingly incurable tropical diseases. During a visit to the Royal Tropical Institute in Amsterdam, I once witnessed a man suffering from bilharzia who was near to death; the remedies that Vogel prescribed to sort this man out and get the condition completely under control were remarkable.

Another of the books that Vogel passed on to me was the enormously influential environmental treatise *Silent Spring* by Rachel Carson. Vogel took a great interest in what was happening around the world and was very concerned about environmental issues; climate change in particular caused him a lot of worry later in life. He was deeply influenced by what Rachel Carson had to say and he tried to share his concerns with as many people as possible. While in Australia, for example, we gave a talk on the dangers of DDT, which Carson had highlighted in her book as a dangerous pesticide that was having a detrimental effect on wildlife around the world. A group of young people came to speak to us afterwards and asked if there was anything they could do to help with this problem. I still remember Vogel encouraging them to tackle their government and to do all they could to try to get it banned. Eventually, due in large part to their campaign, Australia prohibited the use of DDT. Vogel spoke with such conviction that he inspired people to action.

Once, when we were in Biel-Bienne, he was asked to give two very important lectures. He prepared the gist of these in his mind, but when the organisers of the conference insisted that he wrote his lectures down, he was stuck! There would be people from 27 different nations attending that conference and so the translators obviously wanted a written lecture to work from; but as Vogel spoke from the heart, it was impossible for him to provide such a script. Although many lecturers require a lot of written material to prompt them, Vogel did his entirely off the cuff. His impromptu way of lecturing captivated his audiences and always received prolonged applause.

In 1982, Alfred's devoted and faithful wife Sophie died. Together with their daughter Ruth, she and Alfred had spent their lives exploring nature and developing helpful remedies, and he was devastated by her death. I could see that he was really suffering, so I asked him to come to Scotland – as I knew he had enjoyed previous trips here – and my manageress, Janice Thompson, and my wife spent a great deal of time trying to console him. In an effort to distract his mind from his great loss, they took him to places like Culzean Castle, where he was shown many of the native plants of Scotland as well as some more exotic species from other countries.

Later, after some time had passed, Alfred was fortunate enough to meet Denise, who spent time trying to lift his spirits, until eventually happiness arose again and they were married. She too was very much in tune with his ideas, his faith and his hopes for the future. What the future held for them personally was joy. Denise also helped with the vast amount of correspondence and writing that he did in order to help other people.

Alfred made his last visit to Scotland in 1992. He thoroughly enjoyed walking in our gardens at Auchenkyle and was delighted when he saw the organic nursery we had established. We showed him the foods that were grown artificially for research, the foods that were grown organically and also the reports from the Scottish Agricultural College at Auchincruive detailing the high quality of vitamins, minerals and trace elements found in our organic produce. That made him very happy but he could not resist telling our gardeners how to prepare the soil and how to protect it from the extremely strong sunshine (he told them to cover it with straw to keep the bacteria in the ground, so that the produce from it would be of high quality). Then he turned his attention to the amount of money we were wasting in heating the glasshouses. His mind was still so alert that he said, 'If you dig down about four or five metres into the ground, you will probably find hot water and that will heat your glasshouses.' Of course, he turned out to be right and thanks to him we developed a very cheap method of heating. Alfred was a very practical man and was often able to advise us of possibilities that we had overlooked.

I once visited the Bioforce factory in Roggwil in Switzerland when they were making *Santasapina*, one of the most effective cough mixtures available, which is made from pine kernels. Vogel was a very thrifty man and could not bear to throw away the residue after the cough mixture had been made. He said, 'We can use these remains to extract aromatic oils which will be very beneficial for skin problems.' As far as Vogel was concerned, no natural product should ever be wasted.

On one occasion, I asked to have his IQ tested. I can't remember the exact score but I do recall that it was very high and that the professor who carried out the test told me, 'You are dealing with a genius.' That is exactly what he was and in the following chapters, I will explain a little bit more about the work we did together and the help we always tried to give to the countless people who were in need.

2

Illness and suffering are caused by imbalance and disharmony, in whatever areas of our life they may occur.

Alfred Vogel

Alfred Vogel and I shared the view that it is vitally important in life to get the balance right. If we have a negative thought, then we must try and cancel this out with a positive thought. If there is an imbalance in one's health, then there are reasons for this and we must do everything possible to restore that balance. Just as an unbalanced wheel will cause a watch to stop, or an unbalanced load will cause a ship to capsize, so an imbalanced body will cause innumerable ailments in a human being. The centre of gravity of the body should always be in the correct position. The spine divides the body into left and right, and I often find it crucial to carry out spinal manipulation and spinal corrections to ensure the body is balanced.

In order to achieve balance for our patients, Vogel and I also agreed that, in many cases, they would benefit from a period during which they were under our constant care. In the late 1950s, Vogel had bought a lovely old house called Roode Wald in the beautiful rural setting of Nunspeet in Holland, right on the edge of the forest. I shared with him his vision of setting up the first nature cure clinic in the Netherlands and was delighted to join him in his work there. Roode Wald became a peaceful haven where many patients enjoyed the best care and attention. I have written about the clinic at length earlier in this book and I am still of the opinion that it was the finest place in which to look after people's well-being. As the patients were in our care for a set period of time, we were able to care for them holistically: combining a carefully monitored dietary regime with hands-on work such as massage and manipulation – and all treatments were purposely chosen to establish the balance between negative and positive.

I have often said that the future of medicine is in light and energy, and Vogel and I agreed that it was vital that the energy in all the rooms in the residential clinic was balanced. This became even clearer to us after we became familiar with the work of a gentleman called Nicolaas Kroeze. He was a well-known figure in Holland in his day, being the owner of a famous restaurant called The Five Flies. The Five Flies was widely acknowledged as being an outstanding and exclusive restaurant. It was wonderful to go there because every chair had a plaque on it giving the names of famous politicians, actors, film stars, sportspeople, etc. who had sat there. It had a great atmosphere and I can remember Vogel and I spending a most enjoyable evening there.

Nicolaas Kroeze came to Roode Wald to have a look around shortly after we opened. He had very specific ideas about negative and positive energy, and told us that, completely unaided, he had built a special glasshouse in his garden. He had thoroughly checked the energy lines under the glasshouse so that everything from the foundation upwards was in balance. After completing his construction, he saw his first patient there – a 12-year-old girl with leukaemia who, he told us, had been totally cured by the sun's rays and by the well-balanced energy that existed in that glasshouse. I am sure, as was Vogel, that Nicolaas Kroeze was another man who was ahead of his time. It was disappointing that he never got the backing to continue his work and substantiate his claims, and I still feel there is enormous scope for research into the work that he started.

This story made us realise that we should examine several rooms and areas in our clinic where we thought that the energy might be out of balance. We contacted another pioneering gentleman who arrived with apparatus that he had invented himself which could measure the energy forces in each room. He came to the conclusion that, apart from one room, the clinic was actually well balanced. The problematic space was a small room in which, he said, a faulty energy line from the earth went straight through the bed. He therefore advised us that it would be wiser to either change the position of the bed or not to use the room at all. We had, in fact, already noticed that people who used that room did not respond so well to treatment and we had made the decision not to use that room for consultations but merely for storage – that, incidentally, was entirely through our own intuition. This was a most interesting exercise and, as I have said, we had outstanding successes in that clinic.

When a geologist carried out a similar test in my own clinic, Mokoia, which I opened in Troon in 1970, he also found that there were two places where, as he put it, the 'holy energy lines were not in balance'. I refused to use these rooms to treat patients and I remain convinced that energy is the future of medicine.

Another pioneering step we took at Roode Wald involved colonic irrigation. This was a popular treatment back in the 1960s and has enjoyed a recent resurgence. An eminent Dutch professor, who had heard about our work, stepped into our clinic one day. After having a look around, he remarked how impressed he was and told us that he was keen to demonstrate his views on how to clear the 'inner chemistry' of the body. He asked if he could undertake some research work in our premises and when we pressed him for further details, he said he wanted to set up some apparatus to facilitate what he called 'higher bowel cleansing'. He told us that a rigorous detoxification programme would require the body to be thoroughly cleaned out.

We agreed to his proposal and so, for a short time, he worked with us on a voluntary basis to demonstrate the long-established principles of colonic irrigation, practised in his own, very thorough, way. He was busy for many weeks setting things up and, finally, when he was ready to start consulting, he showed us his fairly monstrous-looking apparatus and the procedure involved. Although this was something new to us, we trusted him because he was a professor of medicine.

His first patient was an extremely overweight lady. The process entailed having about 40 pints of chamomile water flushed through her system in order to totally cleanse her bowel. When he had finished, he showed us almost half a bucket of waste material that had been flushed out of her bowel and explained that the retention of such waste was a major cause of ill heath. Too much waste material in the bowel can encourage the excessive growth of a yeast or fungus, either of which definitely makes people ill. It is essential that the bowels are clean and that people have a motion every day. What you import in 24 hours, you have to export in 24 hours or even sooner; otherwise you are inviting problems. Our inner chemistry is most important.

The professor did the most wonderful job at the clinic, staying with us for about a year, and he told us that, just as people give their homes a thorough clean in spring and autumn, they should do likewise with their 'house of health'. This, he told us, would be extremely beneficial in helping to maintain health and harmony in the body. My own grandmother had also always stressed the importance of regular bowel movements and advised people when they had problems with their bowels, or even the slightest constipation, to take castor oil.

When I asked Vogel for his views on colonic irrigation, he said it was probably all right to carry it out every now and then but the danger was that people could become addicted, as they felt so well and energetic after it. In fact, he had a patient who wanted to carry out the procedure every day. This can have a detrimental effect on the function of the intestine, as it will flush out the healthy bacteria along with any waste matter. The intestine must be given time to recover after each treatment. If we eat a well-balanced diet and there is perhaps only a slight problem with constipation, then there are some excellent simple remedies, such as *Linoforce*, that can be taken to clean out the system.

Colonic irrigation was helpful for people who were grossly overweight and another successful method that we introduced to help weight control was our fasting days. Vogel was very keen on fasting but he always said that one had to do it sensibly. For those patients who stayed in the clinic, one day per week was a fasting, or juice, day. Interestingly, when people followed this regime – which involved having a glass of either vegetable or fruit juice for breakfast, lunch, dinner and supper – they felt so much better the following day. Everything in life needs balance, and balancing the human body is one of the most beneficial things to do to promote good health. Fasting allows the body to rebalance itself through detoxification.

Although the clinic in Nunspeet was a thriving business, it was by no means easy to manage. Vogel and I worked day and night to provide the necessary care but we struggled to employ qualified back-up staff to assist us. Finding other practitioners who were equally devoted to alleviating human suffering was much more difficult than we had expected. We encountered doctors who were unreliable and nurses who were often too busy with other things to do their job properly. We had no end of problems with domestic and kitchen staff, and some people stole from us – I could go on and on.

Vogel and I frequently held meetings to see if we could figure out how to improve the running of the business and I remember one such meeting that went on until nearly one o'clock in the morning. Vogel always rose very early – sometimes as early as four or five o'clock – and he always liked to go to bed between nine and ten o'clock at night or even earlier. He had an extremely long working day and that particular night I could see that he was beginning to get tired. Even though all the staff members had had ample opportunity to express their thoughts on the matter at hand, there was still no resolution in sight. Finally, he said, 'Let's reach a united decision. Let "yes" mean "yes" and "no" mean "no".' In other words, he wanted them to be decisive. He wanted things to be set out in black and white. They should consider their individual responsibilities and decide on the best course of action; then they should be resolute in their decision. Vogel had no time for indecision and never used half-hearted measures when tackling problems but dealt with them head on. Life would be much more straightforward if everyone stuck to the principle whereby 'yes' means 'yes' and 'no' means 'no'. Unfortunately, in today's society there appear to be so many grey areas and people often lack the backbone to stand up for their decisions.

As well as problems with staff, we also encountered resistance from the governmental authorities about the work we were doing in the clinic and in August 1961 I was summoned, along with three of the doctors who were working in the clinic at the time, to a meeting with the Dutch Inspector of Health in Nijmegen. At the meeting, the three of us who were able to attend were told in no uncertain terms that we should not continue with our work. The medical establishment was completely opposed to natural medicine and any clinics that did not follow the orthodox methods of treatment. The official threatened to take away our licences to practise and warned that if we refused to comply, we could face imprisonment. It appeared to be the government's intention to shut down the clinic.

When I told Vogel about our encounter with this bureaucrat, he encouraged me to stand firm and said, 'Good will always triumph in the end.' Unfortunately, however, my colleagues in the clinic decided to give up. They were too frightened to ignore the threats, as they did not want to risk losing their licences. For men with young families to support, this was an understandable decision but I myself resolved to keep going. This was not an easy decision to make and there continued to be a lot of governmental interference and threats. We incurred a lot of unnecessary expense due to these problems and, added to the terrific staffing problems that we were already experiencing, it became very difficult to carry on.

Eventually, as a result of all these problems, we were forced to change the clinic into one for day care only. I was determined, however, that whatever difficulties we were facing, the medicines developed by Vogel over so many years would not be allowed to disappear or be forced off the Dutch market and fought very hard for their continued existence. Thankfully, many of those medicines are nowadays being prescribed by a high percentage of doctors in Holland and are even being administered in hospitals. It was a tremendous achievement to win that fight.

Another product which survived was the famous 'Vogel bread'. This was an important part of the balanced diet which Vogel recommended to patients at the clinic. The bread was made from his own recipe, baked from whole grains, not crushed, and was absolutely delicious. This bread was already popular before a chance conversation in the clinic one day led to it being improved.

Our visitor on this occasion was the owner of a large bakery in Holland called Het Zeeuwse Meisje. Vogel asked me a few questions during this meeting and I joined in the conversation by telling both men a story about my youth. I must have been about six or seven years old, as the Second World War was still raging through Europe and Holland was occupied by the Nazis. There was very little to eat during the war years and one day my constant hunger got me into trouble. While I was out in the street, I saw a Nazi soldier eating some bread and watched as he threw the crust onto the street. My mother had told me very strictly never to take anything from the Nazis, or from the Dutch collaborators, but I was so hungry that I snatched that discarded crust of bread from the gutter and devoured it. I thought it was the best thing I had ever tasted. It had a particularly sour flavour but I was too young then to analyse what was in it. Nevertheless, it was delicious. When I arrived back home, I owned up to my mother what I had done and was punished severely.

As I told both men this story, the baker's eyes suddenly lit up and he said, 'I know what the Germans put into that bread during the war to make their soldiers healthy and strong – that was a very good recipe.' Vogel was so pleased to hear this story because he understood exactly what the baker was speaking about: the secret ingredient was whole rye. They both investigated this thoroughly and, as a result, Vogel adapted his bread-making recipe to make it even more beneficial for health.

Vogel's bread is still available today, providing an important part of a balanced diet, and it is with the greatest of pleasure that I can report that Vogel's cereals are also available in Britain. These formulas have been brilliantly put together by a company called Britannia Health and it is wonderful to see this nutritious, delicious and gluten-free cereal, which is of particular benefit to patients suffering with multiple sclerosis and coeliac disease, on the British market.

Grabbing a quick, nutritious bowl of cereal before rushing out of the house in the morning is the normal way to kick-start the day for much of the population. But this is not an option for an estimated 250,000 people in the UK with coeliac disease who are unable to tolerate the wheat, barley, rye and oats found in most cereals.

New VitaPro is a great-tasting, 'stay crunchy' alternative for coeliacs and others with gluten intolerance. VitaPro is a vitamin- and protein-enriched soy cereal, flavoured with natural honey and cinnamon. It is also the first breakfast cereal in the UK to contain Hi-maize, a unique and completely natural functional food ingredient rich in resistant starch, fibre and probiotic properties which significantly improve bowel health. Other fantastic products are Soytana and Ultrabran.

Alfred and I did some wonderful work at Roode Wald and we had great opportunities there to experiment and meet people from very varied backgrounds who shared with us some brilliant ideas. It was such a pity that the clinic was only open for a short time. We strove to help our patients achieve a healthy balance in their lives and were determined to carry on providing people with advice through our lectures and books. It is sometimes difficult for people to find the help they are looking for and that is why I have now written over 40 books dealing with many different issues. It is also wonderful to be able to back up this advice with the helpful remedies that Vogel devised and such products as his bread and cereals.

3

Happiness is the soothing balm for a sick heart and the best remedy for a wounded heart.

Alfred Vogel

It is over 45 years since Vogel and I first discussed in detail the subject of happiness and the importance of maintaining a positive mental attitude. While working in the clinic at Roode Wald one day in May 1961, I received a phone call from Switzerland to say that Vogel was urgently needed, as they were making an important decision there that required his input. He had gone to Amsterdam unexpectedly, so I was not sure exactly where to find him, but it was obviously vital that I did so.

After many fruitless enquiries, I eventually managed to track him down to the home of a very unhappy couple whose daughter had been told that she only had a few months to live. He had gone to offer them help and comfort, and was doing all he could for these people in their time of need. On my arrival, I relayed the message that he had to phone Switzerland immediately and so we had to leave. But even during the short time that I was there I could see that the family had derived reassurance and comfort from Vogel's personal visit. Fortunately, it would also transpire that the remedies Vogel prescribed had a beneficial effect on the daughter's immune system.

He felt extremely relieved that he had managed to help them but on the return journey to the clinic at Nunspeet he discussed the huge impact that the daughter's illness had had on the whole family. He explained to me that these people were worried to death about their daughter. We discussed the meaning of this phrase and Alfred explained that there are circumstances in life where worrying can spiral out of control. When this happens, it can have a serious effect on a person's health, causing stress which can lead to heart attacks, high blood pressure, strokes and so on. In severe cases, people can literally worry themselves to death. With the family we had just visited, not only were they dealing with the daughter's illness but also the effects of the intense stress that they were all under – and in some cases, worrying about an illness can actually cause more harm than the illness itself.

I wholeheartedly agreed that constant worry not only physically affects the body but also eats away at the soul of Man. In such instances, it is vital that people find some way to be positive about the circumstances in which they find themselves, however difficult this may appear to be. This is a vital part of achieving the balance that I discussed in the previous chapter.

I always admired the way in which Vogel coped with great problems by trying to remain positive and maintaining that glimmer of happiness which helped him through life's journeys. The quote at the beginning of this chapter has remained at the forefront of my mind over the years and he also told me that that happiness will be inexhaustible once you have found it.

There are many things in life that can make one *un*happy – selfishness, resentment, jealousy, envy, unhappy marriages, work and stress, for example. How often do I hear people moaning, 'Oh no, yet another day – I will need to try and get through it,' or 'Work again – I would rather be on holiday,' or 'I only look forward to the weekend.' There are many people who wake up with such feelings of dread and then turn over and try to go back to sleep for as long as possible. People like this are wishing their lives away.

I see the results of such negative attitudes every day in my clinics and I treat increasing numbers of patients for problems associated with their nervous systems. This is a sign that something in their body is not functioning properly but it is also often related to their outlook on life. If one makes an effort to go to bed at a reasonable time and waken up in the morning feeling and acting positively, then one can go to work in a happy frame of mind. It is also important to combine such a positive attitude with a healthy breakfast. If nerves are beginning to affect your life, then I would suggest having porridge for breakfast, together with plenty of fruit and vegetables, which will give the system a terrific boost to start the day. Only by being optimistic each day, working to the best of one's ability and finding satisfaction at the end of it can one experience real joy.

The other day I saw a recovered cancer patient. He looked at me and said, 'You know, I am grateful now for every day that God gives me, for the simple reason that I have been given an extension to my life and I am going to make the best of it.' That is really the most important thing anyone can do.

Each day should be seen as a gift and if we continue to be pessimistic, we encourage some extremely nasty diseases to develop. For example, I am convinced through research I have undertaken that cancer is influenced by the mind, both positively and negatively. Through visualisation techniques, meditation and positive thinking, a cancer patient can survive longer or, more amazingly, beat cancer entirely. The reverse side to this is that a negative attitude may well exacerbate the problem.

Back in 1961, during the journey from Amsterdam with Vogel, he described the physical effects that a positive state of mind can have on the body: for example, the pancreas will begin to function more effectively; the secretion of digestive enzymes increases, allowing the body to absorb nutrition from food more effectively; and, above all, it can improve liver function, as the liver is very sensitive to any emotional imbalance. Even if you feel unhappy, you should breathe in and out with the mental awareness that happiness is like warmth and can warm even the coldest heart. Happiness brings us peace, it improves attitudes and is a soothing balm that helps us to combat health problems. Happiness is also beneficial for the circulatory system. The sympathetic nervous system and all the organs that are related to it will gladly do their job if one is relaxed and happy. My grandmother always used to say that a patient will only get better if he is in a state of relaxation.

Following a virus I contracted while in the bush in Australia, which affected my pancreas, I sadly developed diabetes. It is vital that diabetics have a positive outlook and keep their spirits up, and one genuine comfort I have is that I am able to control my diabetes without the use of any insulin or other drugs. This is thanks to the natural remedies that I use and the healthy, positive way I try to lead my life. I feel very thankful for this wonderful creation in which we live – where every plant, every flower and every tree bark can tell us a story and often offer a solution to a problem. Although that viral enemy in the bush tried to destroy the contentment within me, I managed to overcome that force with the countless positive thoughts that I have put into my life and this buoyant attitude has also enabled me to continue to work 90 hours a week and remain happy.

One problem with a heavy workload of this kind is that it means that sacrifices have to be made in some other areas of life. Alfred Vogel dedicated himself totally to his work and helping other people. I can understand why he worked so tirelessly and have followed the same path myself. However, by devoting myself to helping others, this has meant that I have been unable to spend as much time as I would have liked at home with my wife and my children. Sometimes when I reflect on this reality it makes me very unhappy, but then there is often some light to follow such dark thoughts.

The other day, for example, I received a little thank you card from one of my daughters, which said, 'We want to thank you, not only for the hard work that you have done all your life to help others, but also in helping us, because we would not be where we are today if it hadn't been for your hard work.' Such thoughtful gestures make all the toil and sacrifice feel worthwhile and enable me to keep moving on, looking forward to everything that life still holds in store for me.

There are so many healing powers all around us and such a lot that we can do to help ourselves achieve better health by embracing happiness in our lives. Gloria Hunniford, with whom I worked on many occasions, gave me some good advice when we were facing certain difficulties. She told me, 'My dear mother always said, "If you have problems or worries, tackle them positively. If you cannot sort them out, leave them alone and they will sort themselves out."' Life's problems can often be resolved by adopting this kind of positive attitude and another thing that can help is having a good sense of humour.

When I arrived in Scotland in 1970, being Dutch I knew nothing about the dry Scottish sense of humour. Over the years, however, I have come to understand that style of humour and am now of the opinion that it is probably the best in the world. Often during the days when I am in practice in my clinics in Scotland I can be cheered up by the witty comments that patients make.

Vogel also had a great sense of humour, which came as a surprise to me because, like the Dutch, the Swiss are not renowned for their wit! Possibly it is because both nationalities are too conscientious. While this is a very good quality, if we lose our sense of humour, we miss out on an awful lot in life. In the evening, as we ponder the day's events, the parts that stick in our mind are probably those joyful instances that have helped improve our day and made us laugh. On the other hand, some people go a little bit too far in the other direction, by trying to laugh off any problems with forced humour. Laughter is a wonderful thing but it should come naturally and not be forced.

In 1961, when Vogel and I were first discussing the importance of happiness and positivity, Seasonal Affective Disorder (SAD) was unheard of. Today, however, it is becoming a serious issue with an estimated half a million people in the UK suffering from this type of depression every winter. SAD is caused by a biochemical imbalance in the hypothalamus, which in turn is caused by the reduced hours of daylight and lack of sunshine we have here in Britain, particularly between December and February. While I have a great deal of sympathy for people suffering from this condition, I often wonder whether part of the problem is that they have lost the ability to find simple pleasure in looking around at this great creation.

It is often the little things in life that make one happy. I frequently think of my own grandmother, who was equally wise as Alfred Vogel and equally happy. She often advised that when a problem or some unhappiness arose, then one should look out of the window at this wonderful world of which we are all part and, even at the gloomiest of moments, try to sing a song.

We must always remember that the sun is still there behind all the dark clouds. I advise people, if at all possible, to try to save up for a conservatory and expose themselves to as much light as possible. This exposure – particularly to natural daylight around midday – can be of great benefit to those suffering from winter depression.

Light is a very important part of life and while thinking about how to maintain happiness and defeat depression, I frequently turn to a biblical expression that I have discussed in many of my previous books: once we have found the light on our pathway, if we walk in that light, we will become children of the light. I once discussed this with an eminent scientist, Professor Arthur Ellison, who said that he believed that light and energy would be significant in the future of medicine. We need to energise ourselves and be aware of the ways in which we can improve our way of life. This will enable us to attain a much deeper, more satisfying joy, which will help us as we carry out our daily duties.

When I was only 18, more than 50 years ago, I was fortunate enough to assist a renowned professor in a local hospital. The matron who worked there always appeared to be happy and smiling. She kept the whole place running like clockwork, and, unlike modern hospitals in the UK, there were never any problems connected to hygiene because she ensured the wards were spotless. She used to paraphrase an old biblical expression, saying, 'Be careful, because unhappiness is a rotting of bones.' There was a wonderful atmosphere in that hospital because even though this matron had an extremely responsible and stressful job she still displayed such a happy attitude that it rubbed off on the staff and others around her. It is encouraging to see that, when we are happy, we touch the hearts of others and then this happiness, in turn, is passed on.

Back on that journey from Amsterdam all those years ago, Vogel explained how negative influences such as ignorance, inexperience, bad attitudes, neglect and evil thoughts can dampen our enthusiasm for life and lead to sadness and depression. He stressed how important it is that we continue to be optimistic, and quoted an old saying: 'The happiness we give to others will return to make our own hearts rejoice.'

Happiness for Vogel that day had been achieved by making the effort to find that simple little house in the middle of Amsterdam and helping to relieve the family of some of their burden of sorrow. It was instances like that that Vogel found so fulfilling and, no matter where he was, he would do whatever he could to bring happiness to others.

4

This is really the essence of life — by trying to help others, we, in turn, help ourselves.

Alfred Vogel

While emphasising the importance of being happy and maintaining a positive attitude, it is also necessary to recognise that sometimes events in life overtake us and even the most positive people can succumb to the effects of depression. Some of the most enlightening conversations about this problem and the ways to overcome it took place between two of my best friends, Jos Lussenburg and Alfred Vogel.

Jos and I became great friends when we lived in Nunspeet. My whole family adored him and while my children were growing up, he was like a grandfather to them. He would come to visit me every morning on his bicycle and we would have long talks. We had a special bond of friendship that helped both of us in dealing with our respective problems in life. I therefore understood him very well and when he mentioned his interest in talking to Alfred Vogel, I was very happy to set up a meeting between these two great thinkers one beautiful summer evening. They hit it off very well and were able to talk freely to one another. I felt privileged to be there and was greatly encouraged by many of the different things that they said.

Jos was a very talented artist and musician, and he was a pillar of the community, carrying out a lot of charitable work in the small town where we lived. But behind Jos's wonderful warm face, not everything in his life was rosy.

Jos had harnessed his musical talent and worked hard at his craft to become a famous professional violinist. When he was at the height of his music career, however, he lost two of his fingertips as the result of an infection. This did not diminish the love that he had for music, and indeed he was still able to play and conduct, but the fact that his ability had been impaired devastated him to such an extent that he became deeply depressed.

Today, when I see portraits of Beethoven, I can understand how artists struggled to capture the expressions on that great composer's face, as he was equally depressed when he lost his hearing. Like Beethoven, music was Lussenburg's great passion and, possibly as a result of his disability, he was able to express more powerful emotions when playing his violin or piano than many able-bodied musicians were capable of.

After the accident, not even aware that he could draw, Jos decided to take up painting. As he developed his skills, he began to realise that although one can put one's thoughts into one's music, one can express oneself even more deeply in painting. Jos became an extremely successful artist, with his paintings being sold for tremendous sums of money.

That evening, as he spoke to Alfred Vogel about his health and the several depressive periods that had darkened his life, it was fascinating to hear Vogel tell Jos that he had met several famous artists – using the term to cover those gifted in music, painting, singing, etc. – during his career and they all had one thing in common: because of their exceptional gift, they sometimes suffered from bouts of deep depression.

Fortunately, though, Lussenburg was not the type of man to stay depressed for long and while at times his talents could lead him to frustration and desolation, at other points they brought him great joy and comfort. He told Vogel that, whether painting or just sitting by the riverbank, he experienced a terrific release from life's tensions when he thought of Beethoven and all that he achieved. He proudly claimed to have all his symphonies, but felt that the Fifth was a particularly wonderful piece and declared that he knew the Seventh off by heart.

On that warm summer evening, when the three of us were in Lussenburg's home, we talked together about the disharmonies in life and how music, and, for Lussenburg, also his paintings, managed to bring it all back into balance. Lussenburg often said to me that depression is a state of mind and you need to muster up as much strength as possible to overcome it. We agreed that one's outlook can be positively changed by the therapeutic influence of music, even by singing a song when depression surfaces. Although they both suffered from this affliction, Mozart's and Beethoven's wonderful melodies have helped countless others overcome depression. It is important, though, to choose the right type of music to deal with each individual situation. The tranquillity of a soft melody can make the stormiest heart calm and possibly happy again.

Jos also enjoyed going sailing and he told us that when he went out on his boat, he sang a song that went, 'When my ship went out of the harbour, roll on my ship, roll on my ship, back to the home haven again'. His house was actually called Thuishaven (which literally means 'home haven'). As Lussenburg grew up next to the sea, he understood it very well and could paint seascapes like no one else. Vogel was very interested in this story, and as they were talking about life's problems and whether one could find peace in music or in painting, Lussenburg gave one of his paintings to Vogel.

That night they talked about the significance of life and how important it was for everyone to be grateful to the Creator. As Lussenburg said, 'God rules the traffic and it is important that, as we all move around, we remember that the great captain will determine the course of our lives.' In this great universe where we can be compared to a small drop in the ocean, we should realise that we are still part of that ocean and belong to it. Perhaps we are all guilty of not fully appreciating gifts that we receive. We should be thankful every day for those wonderful gifts of light, sunshine, air and nature that so many of us take for granted.

We all agreed that one has to be realistic by facing the problems we encounter along the way and making the best of them. Life is a miracle, and if we accept it as such, then we will be able to embark upon each day as a new challenge. Even when in his 90s, that is what Vogel did, and Lussenburg too, when he was in his 80s.

'How can an ill person be happy?' was one of the questions that was discussed that summer evening. It is often remarkable to see how some people, once they have come to terms with their illness, can be such a positive example to others and can spread much happiness to those around them. I have personally seen many critically ill people who, although accepting that they were coming to the end of their lives, still endeavoured to maintain a positive attitude and it is comforting to think that such people, no matter how little they have left to give, can still be such a help to others. To have a desire to help others is a commendable attitude.

My mother used to say, 'If you look around, you will always find somebody who is worse off than you.' I feel great sympathy in my heart when I see people struggling with their health problems – particularly those with degenerative diseases such as cancer, multiple sclerosis, muscular dystrophy or those crippled by osteoarthritis or rheumatoid arthritis. Although life can be particularly miserable for many such people, moaning and groaning about it cannot change things, whereas having a happy attitude will not only help oneself, but also those around us.

When one exerts oneself to find inner harmony in the three bodies that Man has, then one is equipped to find unending happiness. It makes such a difference when we open our windows in the morning with a happy heart. We should realise that we are all part of this great creation and see each day ahead as a challenge.

When my two friends talked about their trips around the world, Vogel told Lussenburg all about his great experiences in Peru. While there, he observed some of the world's poorest people but, surprisingly, they still appeared to be happy. When they suffered from illnesses and diseases, they took it into their own hands to regain their health, harnessing the power of the wonderful natural ingredients around them. When he went to the herbal markets in Peru and saw the huge variety of herbs being sold there, Vogel realised that the power for healing that God had provided through nature made these people happy and appreciative of the little they had. Their gratitude was written on their faces and, when Vogel went amongst them to offer advice, it made him happy that he was able to assist these underprivileged people. As he said, 'This is really the essence of life – by trying to help others, we, in turn, help ourselves.' The simple saying 'You get out of life what you put into it' is also, in most cases, so true.

We talked that evening about some wonderful remedies that Vogel found throughout the world – not only in Peru but in many other countries – and the relief that such treatment could have on balancing nervous anxieties and depression. Of course, Vogel and Lussenburg thought highly of St John's wort, which has lifted the spirits of many people. Even Paracelsus, the great sixteenth-century physician, recognised that it was a mood enhancer. What a wonderful gift this plant has been. Today, however, some St John's wort remedies are seen as a great threat to the powerful tranquillisers and antidepressants produced by the drugs industry and have, astonishingly, been banned in some countries.

When we went out into Lussenburg's peaceful garden, Vogel pointed out such plants as the sweet chestnut, clematis, rock rose, honeysuckle and gentian, the oak and the elm, all flowering and growing profusely – and he told us of the tremendous healing powers of those plants, flowers, herbs and trees. They are a valuable part of creation and, by their signatures and characteristics, they show us what they should be used for. I was able to harness the power of many flowers in my range of flower essences. These are liquid extracts of flowers in a base of grape alcohol. They can be taken orally and can have a beneficial effect on the emotions – which, in turn, can be beneficial for the health of the whole body.

While listening to Alfred and Jos in the surroundings of Lussenburg's studio, I counted myself blessed to be in their company. They were both recalling memorable occasions and were thankful that they had been given the opportunity to experience so much during their busy lives. Both had many interests and so much to do in their work that they never became bored, and the inheritance they left behind and their wonderful spirits are still with us today, helping many people.

I really like the word 'enthusiasm'. In one dictionary I have, it gives its meaning as 'God in you' – and this enthusiasm was clearly evident in those two special gentlemen that evening. Enthusiasm for helping others in today's world is very important, as is recognising that God can work within us in this great creation to bring happiness and good health into all our lives. That was the important lesson I learned that evening, and I shall treasure it to the end of my days.

5

Foresight is the source of health and happiness.
Alfred Vogel

At the time I graduated in the late 1950s, there were revolutionary changes going on in the pharmaceutical industry. The world was witnessing an explosion in the production of drugs such as antibiotics, tranquillisers and steroids, and these were being seized upon by the medical profession as some kind of panacea or holy grail. We were told that this was progress and that there would soon be a drug to treat every kind of ailment. While most people were very enthusiastic about these developments, I had serious reservations about the road the medical profession was travelling along. As far as I could see, these new drugs were created to treat specific symptoms that patients presented but little attempt seemed to be being made to establish why those problems had occurred in the first place. I worried that the widespread administration of such drugs would mean that major health problems in patients would merely be suppressed rather than addressed successfully. I foresaw a situation by which we would create chronic invalids who were dependent on synthetic drugs and I believe that today, with the spread of diseases such as ME and cancer, my predictions have been proved correct.

For obvious reasons, having such foresight often brings more frustration than satisfaction. It can be very difficult to get others to listen to your advice and you can feel helpless as you watch the problems that you have foreseen proliferate.

Vogel was a man with great foresight. When I look back to the work that he did when we opened the clinic at Nunspeet, I am always amazed at the way he was able to identify disorders that at that time were practically unheard of. He investigated problems that could arise in the body's yeast processes, such as the excessive growth of candida albicans, and he also conducted research into the pathogen *helicobacter pylori*, which can cause intestinal problems such as ulcers.

One of the most effective remedies Vogel created for sufferers of *Candida albicans* and other yeast infections was developed from spilanthes, one of his African discoveries which I have described previously. He would prescribe this along with a strict dietary regime. The juices had to be prepared from fresh vegetables and fruits using a juicer, and everything that was to be eaten had to be chewed thoroughly, so that it would mix properly with the saliva in one's mouth – a vital part of the digestive process. After following this regime, patients could slowly return to a more varied, natural diet. The programme he set up was very simple but very effective and I have detailed it below:

> *The first two days started with*: Chamomile tea at 8 a.m.; freshly prepared fruit juice at 10 a.m.; vegetable juice at noon; Chamomile tea at 4 p.m.; and, at 6 p.m., fruit juice.
>
> *The following two days were made up of*: Chamomile tea at 8 a.m.; yogurt at 10 a.m., together with some separate fruit juice; quark (soft white cheese) at noon; Chamomile tea again at 4 p.m.; and, at 6 p.m., quark with some separate fruit juice.
>
> *The next two to three days were*: Chamomile tea and some Ryvita at 8 a.m.; fruit juice at 10 a.m.; buttermilk with some separate vegetable juice at noon; Chamomile tea and two pieces of Ryvita spread with a little butter at 4 p.m.; and, at 6 p.m., some muesli.
>
> *The next two to three days consisted of*: Chamomile tea with two or three pieces of Ryvita at 8 a.m.; fruit juice with some separate quark at 10 a.m.; fruit juice and yogurt at noon; Chamomile tea with two slices of Ryvita at 4 p.m.; and, at 6 p.m., some muesli.
>
> *To be taken the next two to three days was*: Chamomile tea with two Ryvitas spread with a little butter at 8 a.m.; muesli at 10 a.m.; raw vegetables with some boiled rice at noon; fruit juice and an egg at 4 p.m.; and, at 6 p.m., muesli with some Ryvita.
>
> *The subsequent two to three days were*: Chamomile tea at 8 a.m. with Ryvita spread with a small amount of butter; muesli at 10 a.m.; raw vegetables with some boiled rice at noon; Chamomile tea plus two or three slices of Ryvita spread with a little butter; and, at 6 p.m., muesli and Ryvita.

I understand that people who followed this diet enjoyed relief from their symptoms and rarely suffered from any further problems with *Candida albicans* or yeast-processing difficulties. While I have now identified other ways to treat *Candida albicans* and *helicobacter pylori* which are less restricting for patients, it is nevertheless fascinating to see how far advanced Vogel was all those years ago in dealing with uncommon problems that have become so widespread today.

I have taken this opportunity to include in the following pages some further examples of the balanced diets devised by Vogel for patients at Roode Wald.

I apologise for the fact that these diets are still in Dutch and German, but I wanted to show a snippet of his work to demonstrate how much effort was spent in putting those diets together.

Such strict dietary programmes highlight the importance which Vogel attached to nutritional advice – an area in which he was, once again, ahead of his time. As a pupil of Bircher-Benner, Vogel focused on creating a balanced diet for his patients and so everything that was done in the kitchens at his clinics came under his close scrutiny. I often heard him becoming extremely annoyed when the dieticians hadn't done something properly. He examined every diet personally to ensure that the carbohydrates and proteins were perfectly balanced and that the acid/alkaline balance was also in order. He was particularly concerned that all foods be organically grown and naturally produced.

He achieved great successes with this approach but it wasn't always easy to persuade people to follow his methods. I can still hear him saying, 'People can change their political party, religion or even husband or wife, but if you want people to change their diet, you have a tough job on your hands.'

When we worked together, he always took time to impress upon me the importance of the dietary aspect of any patient's treatment and stressed that this was the first thing that should be tackled. And I have found, like Alfred, that this is not always a popular approach. Over the years, I have received a lot of verbal criticism during my lectures when I have spoken on diet and dietary matters. I clearly remember one lecture, which was filled to capacity, where some men were standing at the back of the hall waiting for their wives. They started banging on the doors, shouting that I had to stop going on about my bl**** diets! I have often been subjected to people swearing and cursing at me when I try to convey to them the importance of the dietary aspect of daily living. This usually happens when I recommend that people give up something that they are particularly fond of.

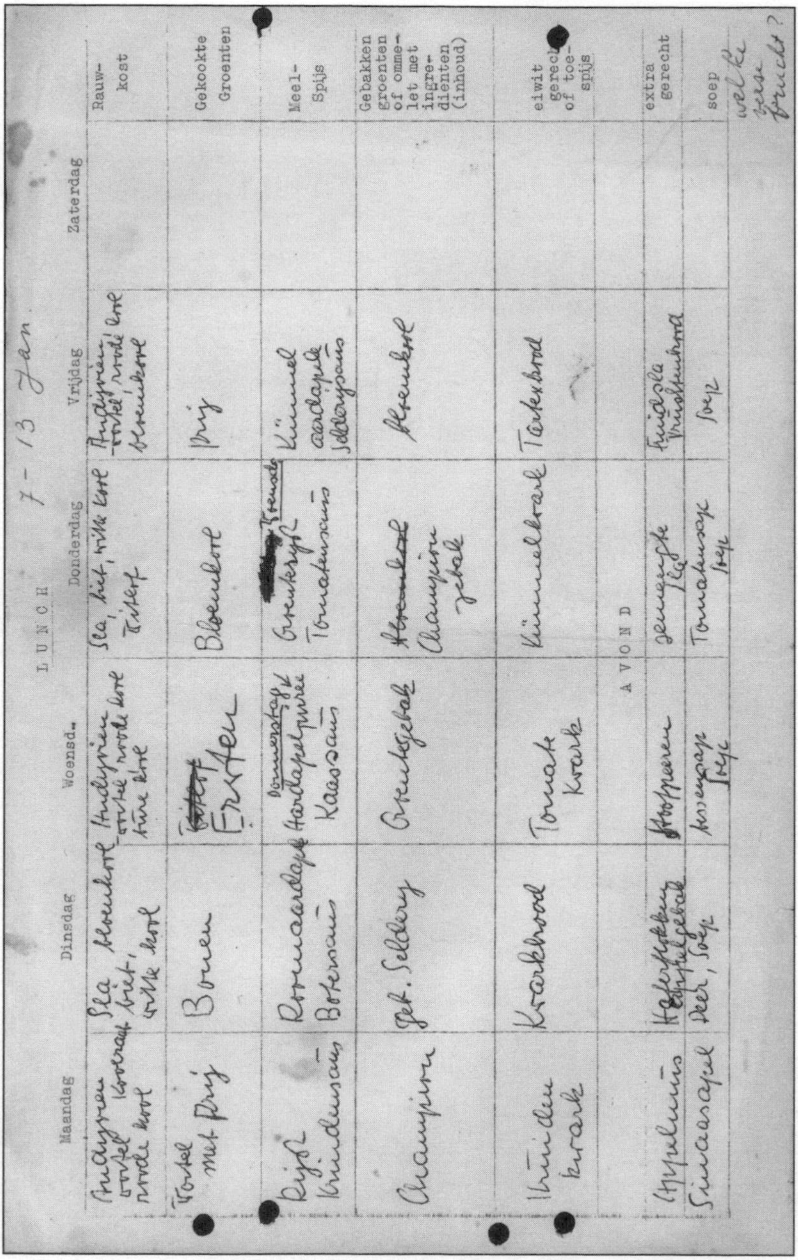

Figure 1 – An example of a dietary regime drafted by Alfred Vogel.

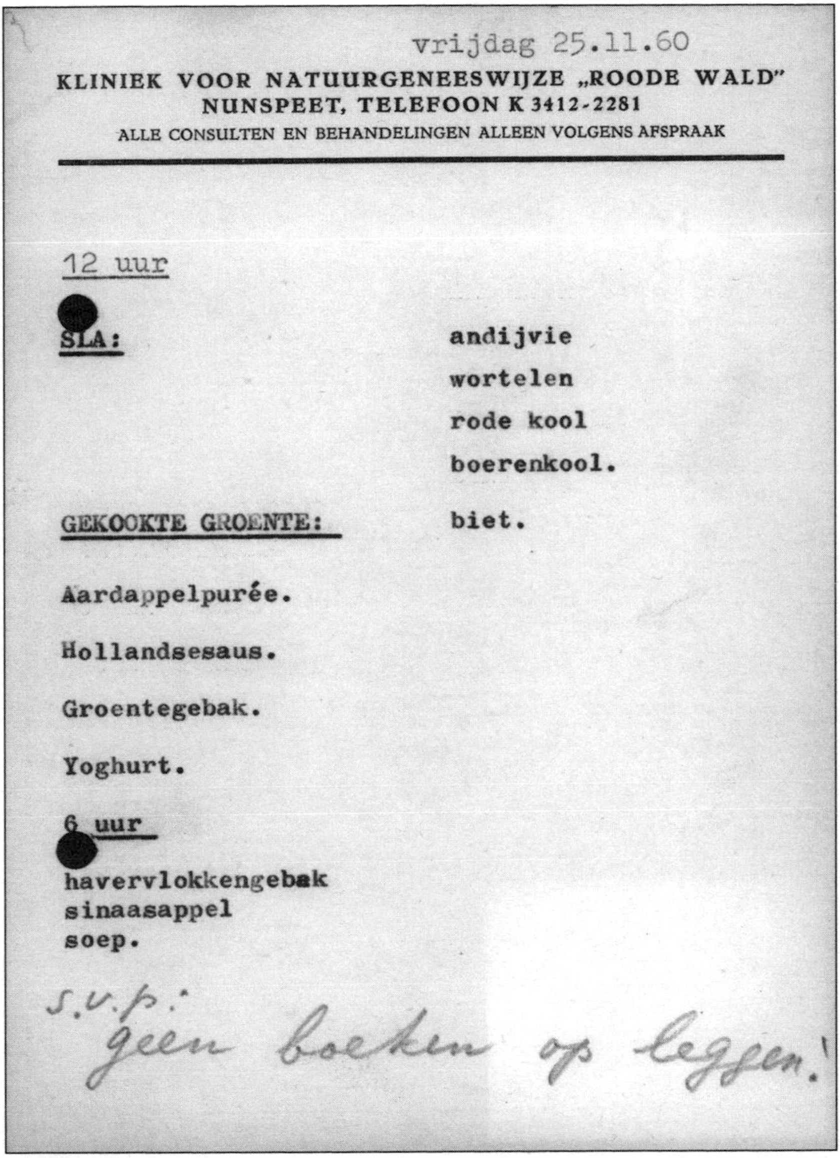

vrijdag 25.11.60

KLINIEK VOOR NATUURGENEESWIJZE „ROODE WALD"
NUNSPEET, TELEFOON K 3412-2281
ALLE CONSULTEN EN BEHANDELINGEN ALLEEN VOLGENS AFSPRAAK

12 uur

SLA:

andijvie
wortelen
rode kool
boerenkool.

GEKOOKTE GROENTE:

biet.

Aardappelpurée.

Hollandsesaus.

Groentegebak.

Yoghurt.

6 uur

havervlokkengebak
sinaasappel
soep.

s.v.p.: geen boeken op leggen!

Figure 2 and 3 (over) – Examples of patients' daily diets at Roode Wald.

KLINIEK VOOR NATUURGENEESWIJZE „ROODE WALD"
NUNSPEET, TELEFOON K 3412-2281
ALLE CONSULTEN EN BEHANDELINGEN ALLEEN VOLGENS AFSPRAAK

maandag 5.12 '60

12 uur
rauwe groenten:
Andijvie
Wortel
Rode kool
Koolraap
Boeren kool
gekookte groenten:
Bonen

Rijst
Kruidensaus
Groentegebak
Kwark
Tomatensap

6 uur
Fruitsla
Noten
Soep

Vogel was aware all those years ago about the detrimental effects that a bad diet could have on people's health but, once again, such valuable advice was not heeded. The result today is that levels of obesity in the Western world are at almost epidemic levels. Our children are getting fatter and fatter, as many of them are brought up on diets of convenience foods full of fat, sugar and additives. The level of allergies is increasing rapidly and the health problems caused by this situation are quite frightening.

Western governments are now making attempts to address the situation but it is like trying to shut the stable door after the horse has bolted. Here in the UK we are being bombarded with gimmicky programmes and books about diet, but people should be careful about the advice that they follow. Faddy diets should be avoided and instead people should find a sensible, balanced eating regime, such as those recommended by Alfred Vogel throughout his long career to promote good health.

One condition for which diet is particularly important is multiple sclerosis and by considering two different methods of treatment for this disease, the benefits of using organic produce – another prescient recommendation by Alfred Vogel – also become apparent.

When I was an 18-year-old student in Holland, I worked as an assistant to a medical professor and one day I told him about a particular patient whose symptoms were puzzling me. After I had relayed the details of the case to the professor, he told me that he wanted to see this patient for himself. Although multiple sclerosis was practically unknown in Holland at that time – I had never before heard of the disease – following some diagnostic tests, he said, 'This is a typical MS case.' In those days, the only thing he could recommend to the patient was Dr Evers' diet. Dr Joseph Evers, a German physician, believed that many illnesses were due to artificial methods of producing and processing foods. He recommended that only unprocessed foods be consumed, such as raw root vegetables, wholewheat bread, cheese, raw milk, raw eggs, butter, honey and so on. Salt and sugar were banned, as well as leafy greens and certain vegetables such as rhubarb, asparagus and cauliflower. Vital to this diet was the daily consumption of germinated wheat.

When I later discussed the Evers diet with Alfred Vogel, he confirmed that he had noted some degree of success with patients who followed this approach, but as my career has progressed, this has proved a bit of a puzzle to me for reasons that I will now explain.

In the 1960s, I met a man called Professor Roger MacDougall, who had developed his own dietary methods of controlling the symptoms of multiple sclerosis. He had worked out his own regime after being told that he was suffering from the disease and that nothing could be done for him. The puzzle for me lay in the fact that the diets devised by the two men seemed to have fundamentally different principles. Roger MacDougall's findings were that gluten could cause inflammation on the myelin sheath – leading to problems with the conduction of nerve impulses – and should be avoided at all costs, while on the Evers diet, patients were advised to consume daily rations of wheatgerm – wheatgerm, of course, containing a fairly large amount of gluten. Both approaches were apparently successful to some degree in containing the disease and with examples like this, it is not surprising that people become confused when one person says they should eat this and another person says they should eat that.

When comparing the two diets, however, I found far greater success with putting patients on the gluten-free programme. And Alfred Vogel confirmed that in countries he had travelled to which had a very low rate of cases of multiple sclerosis, such as Japan and Iceland, the gluten intake was extremely low. But this still did not account for the fact that any success was noted amongst patients following the Evers diet and this is where the importance of organically grown produce becomes apparent.

I noticed that when MS patients ate normal bread grains purchased from supermarkets, their health deteriorated more rapidly. In contrast, the grains used by Evers in his diet were completely organic and freshly sprouted. Under examination, it becomes apparent that the gluten content is significantly lower in such organic grains than in the artificially boosted grains that we consume today, which have been subjected to artificial fertilisers, insecticides and pesticides. After testing both theories, I found that each achieved a measure of success, but I saw a quick deterioration from those consuming what I called 'artificial' grains.

This was also relevant when considering allergies (which can easily lead to multiple sclerosis). It was often observed when a patient had an allergy to wheat, it was usually because the wheat was not organic and that was where the problems lay.

Once again, Vogel had shown remarkable foresight with his views on natural, organically grown foods. I remember about 20 years ago when he compared samples of food bought in a supermarket with produce from our organic nursery in Troon. He was greatly interested in the in-depth research that was being carried out at the Scottish Agricultural College, Auchincruive, near Ayr, and this inspired him to carry out his own investigations. When these tests were completed, it was remarkable to see how superior the organic foods were and how much richer they were in vitamins, minerals and trace elements than those from the supermarkets which were grown with the aid of fertilisers, insecticides and pesticides.

Vogel had strict control over his own gardens and it was not unusual for him to be heard shouting at his gardeners when they did not adhere to his totally organic processes. Anything with even a hint of a chemical smell was banned. It was fascinating to see the array of produce that Vogel grew in his own gardens – and also in ours when he came over to train our gardeners. He always seemed to be at his happiest when he was working outdoors.

Vogel was also ahead of his time in recognising that there might be a link between diet and behavioural patterns. This was an area that was also of great interest to me after I spent some time working in a psychiatric hospital while I was a student. After studying many of the patients, I was convinced that what they ate affected their behaviour. In particular, many of the patients reacted adversely to sugar and became hyperactive and disturbed after consuming any sugary food or drinks.

At the beginning of the 1980s, I was given a fascinating opportunity to conduct more research into this area when I undertook a study of criminals in British prisons. I wanted to ascertain whether violent behaviour could be traced back to poor eating habits. I was convinced that allergies to certain foods could trigger disturbed behaviour and was delighted when members of the Prison Officers' Association were willing to let me conduct research inside their institutions. They were obviously hopeful that my research would help them find effective ways to maintain order. Vogel was most interested to hear of this work and I kept in close contact with him throughout this period.

My first study involved the inmates of a female prison. I asked these women to keep daily diaries of what they ate and I also asked them to keep a note of problems they experienced due to hormonal changes. It became apparent through these studies that some of the women were affected by the poor quality of the food they were eating. Their diet was high in animal protein and sugar, and the effect this had was to turn them into Jekyll and Hyde characters. Many of them had also eaten poorly before being sent to prison and in some cases their violent behaviour (some had assaulted or even murdered their partners) appeared to have been exacerbated by what they ate. After committing such crimes, many of the women were full of remorse, as they had acted completely outwith the bounds of their normal behaviour. It is my belief that it was their diet that caused them to lose control to the extent that they even attacked the people they loved the most.

Women are particularly vulnerable at certain points of their menstrual cycle and there are some well-publicised incidents of women becoming violent when suffering badly from pre-menstrual tension (PMT). Following a balanced diet is very important for sufferers of PMT, in order to avoid fluctuating blood sugar levels, for example.

In another institution, one of my subjects had committed a number of murders. After spending some time with him and learning about his dietary habits, I became convinced that his appalling diet had affected his mind so much that it had caused him to lose all control and exhibit extremely violent behaviour. In my opinion, his problems had started when, as a young boy, his mother would give him candy-coated chocolate drops or coloured sweets to keep him quiet when he had been naughty, not realising that this was only exacerbating the situation and making him even more hyperactive. By the time he had grown up, he had become totally addicted to chocolate and biscuits, and there were many things to which he had become allergic.

When I first met him, it was clear that he found it difficult to control his temper and he was also asthmatic. When I talked to Vogel about this man, he listed all the foods to which the subject could possibly be allergic and when I undertook tests, Vogel turned out to be absolutely correct. Before carrying out his last horrific murder, I learned, the man had drunk six cups of milky coffee (and he was allergic to milk), each cup had six spoonfuls of sugar, which made him extremely hyperactive, and although he did not normally drink alcohol, he had some strong drinks which had a high gluten content. He then ate half a loaf of bread (the tests also showed that he was very allergic to wheat). He then ate a lot of chocolate and became so high that he totally lost control. When he cut out all the foods to which he was allergic, his character altered completely. When Princess Margaret visited some time later, she asked him what had changed him. He said that he had omitted all these allergens from his diet. Before this, he could even have murdered his guard, but now he wanted to change and to make up for all the things he had done wrong. He didn't ask her for his life sentence to be shortened. He asked her to understand that he wanted to live differently.

I carried out similar tests on many criminals and, having built up a considerable body of evidence, I have repeatedly asked for more consideration to be given to dietary management in British prisons, and for prisoners to be taught what to eat and what to avoid. Not only would it be good for their general health but it would also certainly save the lives of many innocent victims. I have pleaded with many MPs at the House of Commons and with peers in the House of Lords for action to be taken on this matter but, on the whole, my words have fallen on deaf ears. Is it really so unreasonable for us to pay close attention to a good balanced diet when people's lives are at stake?

The first people on earth mainly ate fruit, vegetables and nuts, and, later on, added some goats' milk. This does not sound much but, nevertheless, one could do much with such a diet. Vogel was a pioneer in this area and even when staying at the best hotels, he would arrive with his packet of muesli under his arm and plenty of fruit or vegetables in his bag for his breakfast. During our many travels together, I often admired him as his case would be laden with his home-grown organic apples and pears, and while I often offered him a meal, he would usually prefer to eat his own produce.

He was never ashamed to make people aware of his strong beliefs, his healthy diet and his natural medicine. I had a lot of respect for him as he continued preaching to his audiences that if they did not pay careful attention to their diet, then their health would fail. Unfortunately, of course, even when you are speaking the truth it is sometimes difficult to get people to listen to you.

6

The physician or therapist is like a mountain guide: he leads and shows the way, but he does not carry the patients – they have to make their way themselves.

Alfred Vogel

A tremendous crowd of people turned up for one of my lectures in Arbroath in 2004. The audience seemed engrossed as I talked about my chosen subject, 'How to be in tune with your body', and after they had all listened intently, there was a lengthy succession of questions. The final question, from a particularly astute gentleman in the audience, was, 'How would you deal with patients who were not willing to follow advice or could not see the point in their treatment, and how much effort would you put into guiding such patients?'

There is no easy answer to this question, although the situation that he described – in which patients ignore the advice given to them – is a familiar problem for all health practitioners. I found it was only possible to respond by giving various examples.

I told the gentleman that each practitioner, of course, has the same responsibility – to ensure that they give the best possible help and guidance to their patients. At times, however, it can be extremely difficult to get people to follow this advice, especially, for example, where dietary management is concerned. One often has to rely on one's power of persuasion and one thing that I really admired about Alfred Vogel was his ability to convince people to do the correct thing. When we talked to people, he would often say, 'It is not mathematics, it is common sense – start by looking at your lifestyle, then try to correct what is necessary.'

The man who had asked the question was, quite understandably, not satisfied with such a vague answer, so I then quoted the old adage that although you can lead a horse to water, you cannot make it drink. As Vogel said, and I quoted at the beginning of this chapter: 'as

278

practitioners, we are like mountain guides – we can lead the way but we have no control over how people will react to the advice they are given; they have to make their own way themselves.' While it can be frustrating when people fail to follow the good advice that they have been given, this would not lead me to turn them away or to stop trying to help them.

Another problem encountered by practitioners arises when patients expect to see quick results. If this does not happen, and they have to wait a long time to see any improvement in their condition, they can often lose faith in their practitioner and lose the will to carry on with their treatment. When this happened with patients of Vogel, he would acquaint them with the saying that an illness or disease usually comes to us on a horse but can leave us on a donkey – in other words, you need to have patience. When a patient has tolerated a longstanding illness for, say, more than a year, then it could possibly take a few years to be completely free of that particular complaint. As a practitioner, it is vital that you are able to convince your patient that you will be able to help them, as this is perhaps the only way you can persuade them to continue with treatment when they often feel like giving up. A positive attitude is essential. Euphoria can often lead to a good recovery. I saw this once in a young girl who was getting married. Although normally she could not walk very well, she walked perfectly down the aisle on her father's arm.

Alfred Vogel had a special ability whereby he could motivate people to believe in themselves and to become aware of what they were capable of achieving to help themselves. I discovered this when my wife Joyce and I arrived in Teufen to study with him. I have already mentioned the rather cold reception we received when we disturbed him at his work but when we did eventually get to speak to Vogel, I found him inspirational. He made me believe in him, and in myself, and after that meeting I felt as though my whole life was undergoing a revolution. He was so convincing in his belief that one must be in tune with nature in order to be in tune with oneself.

When Professor Geers, a famous professor of geology, came over from Finland with a group of students, I went with his group into the Jura mountains to study with Vogel. It was an amazing trip during which I came to appreciate even more how closely Vogel lived to nature. He was able to identify all the species that we saw on our journey and describe the attributes of each plant and flower. He picked up plants with such tenderness, examining the way they were growing and explaining why the leaves grew from the stem. He was so knowledgeable about nature and this was also displayed in his research work, where he crossed different species of plants to achieve tremendous results. Not only was he in tune with himself but also with nature, and that special gift enabled him to produce the exact remedy he was aiming for. It was because he believed so passionately that he wanted to be like a mountain guide. He wanted to share his enthusiasm with others and point out all the beauties to be found in nature. He wanted to show people the way to make changes in their lives that would be of great benefit to their health.

In this he was similar to a Scotsman called Dugald Semple, who shared many of Vogel's philosophies. Semple was a loner who travelled from one place to another in his small horse-drawn caravan. He felt it was his responsibility to investigate the quality of the soil being used to grow plants and foods, and also to find out which chemicals were being used. He did so by working and digging in the fields around him. Like Alfred, he too had a message to preach and later on, when he had his own little property, he held lectures to try to encourage people to discover their inner strength and explained how this strength could be built upon. Although he was seen by many as being very eccentric, he did develop quite a following and he was very influential in the vegetarian movement in the UK.

Vogel also believed it was vital for people to find inner peace. When he held lectures, for example in London, he took advantage of every opportunity to tell listeners that they did not need to belong to a religious sect or a political party to find inner peace. It was something that everyone could discover within themselves and once they found it they could use this power to overcome many problems and obstacles.

During his lectures, Vogel tried to persuade people to live according to the laws of nature and he did the same with those people who came to visit him at his little clinic in Teufen. It was not an easy task to reach him on that mountain, far away from all the hustle and bustle. But life there was calmer and enabled him, as a guide, to show people how to find inner peace. It was then up to each individual whether they followed his advice or not. Throughout our work, Vogel and I continually emphasised to people the importance of following our advice carefully and persevering until their problems cleared up. Unfortunately, people can so easily lose faith and quickly be led astray.

As well as providing guidance for individual patients, Vogel tried to use his powers of persuasion to influence change on a much larger scale. As I have already mentioned, he was very concerned about the damage that Man was doing to the environment and he took every opportunity to highlight these problems to governmental bodies and international authorities.

He attended inter-governmental congresses on environmental matters and tried to impress upon the authorities the damage that was being done to nature and the problems that mankind was creating for the future. He asked people to take action and to do something about the situation. One particular congress sticks out in my mind, as Alfred made a notably impassioned plea. At this important meeting of the Swiss Association for the Protection of Nature in 1972, Alfred spoke so persuasively that he even succeeded in convincing one of the managing directors from the chemical corporation Ciba-Geigy that changes were needed to stop large conglomerates from harming the environment. His charisma really was remarkable.

At that same congress, another speaker highlighted an issue that was also of vital interest to Vogel. Professor Picard, the well-known French professor of chemistry, said that, on this beautiful earth that was entrusted to us, we have to do our best to safeguard all that is natural and warned that if we did not stop adding poisons to the foods we were consuming and adding rubbish to the soil to make produce grow bigger, then one day we would reap what we had sown.

This, of course, was a subject about which Vogel was passionate. He was terribly worried about the quality of food and constantly pointed out that while the artificially fertilised and treated produce on sale in supermarkets might be big and might look nice, it is of little benefit to people's health if it doesn't contain the correct vitamins, minerals and trace elements. Vogel worked tirelessly in his herbal gardens day and night to guarantee that high quality was reached and to give back to humanity what he felt he owed because of the life that he had been given. He was also conscious of his own mortality, wanting everything he learned to go on being of benefit to others, and he often said to me, 'One day I will not be here and it will then be up to you.' So, today, that responsibility lies on my shoulders as I carry on Vogel's hard work.

As part of trying to get the message across to the younger generation, I often invite them to accompany me when I confront governments or those people in charge to try to impress upon them the harm that is being done by the proliferation of all these chemicals in the food chain. As I said in a previous chapter, things have to be in balance.

When a weighing machine is in balance, then its negative and positive are neutral. The same is the case with the cells in the body – but if we do things that adversely influence them, then those cells will become negative. We must therefore stop and think of the damage these harmful additives are causing. We are all born with cells of regeneration and degeneration but when the cells of degeneration (as in the case of cancer) rapidly take over from the regenerative cells, then problems arise. However, there is still a lot that one can do to regain that balance. The food we eat, the water we drink, the air we breathe: these are all important elements in helping to keep our cells in balance. As I have often pointed out, a cancer cell is an oxygen-poor cell, so it is therefore crucial that we strive for purer air and reduce the levels of air pollution.

As previously mentioned, Vogel also stressed the importance of adhering to a diet with a proper balance of carbohydrate and protein but he went further with his advice in this area. The optimum daily amount of protein is between 40 and 70 grams, and it is crucial that this is derived from the best source. It makes a vast difference whether we get our protein from a pig or a soya bean. The same goes for carbohydrates – if they are from the correct sources, then we will reap the benefit. Vogel tried to put this point across in many lectures and, as he was also concerned about the poor quality of bread being produced, he decided to make his own.

He was totally opposed to white sugar and used to warn about the harm that it would do to people's teeth. Vogel was always surprised to see that people from the West Indies had white, healthy teeth but although they had sugar in their diets, this was of the dark brown, unrefined variety. They extracted this fresh liquid, which they called 'pillo sillo' (this is how they pronounced it, I'm not sure how it would be spelled) from sugar cane. One problem today is the amount of hidden sugar in processed food and drinks. For example, a lot of sugar is added to processed fruit drinks, making them unhealthy. It is much more beneficial to drink freshly squeezed fruit juices. Fruits are naturally sweet, so there is no need at all to add refined sugars to them. If we want to eat something sweet, then it should take the form of natural sugars from good-quality fruits, but at the end of the day, it is our choice whether we eat refined sugar or natural sweeteners, such as honey.

Even though Vogel gave this advice many years ago, and pointed out the problems that would arise if it was not followed, little notice has been taken and we are paying the price with health problems today.

I was very intrigued when Vogel once took me to a factory that produced a wonderful remedy called *Molkosan*, which is naturally fermented concentrated whey made from the residue of cheese-making. Not only is *Molkosan* a great antiseptic (which can be used in the treatment of such problems as verrucas and fungal infections) but it is also of tremendous help to diabetics in assisting with the production of additional natural insulin. It can also help weight loss, when taken together with kelp, as this helps to regulate the body's metabolism.

The process of making *Molkosan* is very complicated but it is one of the finest products prescribed by me on a daily basis. Once again, however, I cannot force my patients to follow my advice.

The problem with the original *Molkosan* is its slightly unpleasant taste. But people should be able to overcome this if they are aware of how beneficial it can be for their health. It makes a nutritious drink, and yet many people find it unpalatable. Each individual therefore needs to experiment to find a way of including it in their diet to suit their own individual taste. When combined with other ingredients, *Molkosan* makes a rich and delicious salad dressing, for example, or you could mix it with a combination of fruit to make up a morning drink. Also, for those who really cannot take the original liquid, *Molkosan* is now available in powder form, called *Molkosan Vitality*, in which *Molkosan* itself is combined with green tea and dietary fibre to create a most beneficial prebiotic.

I cannot believe how short-sighted some people can be. I decided to try and make this product in Holland to help overweight Dutch people, so I went to a factory with my bottle of *Molkosan*. I told the managing director that if he agreed to produce this on my behalf, then the number of people with weight problems in Holland would probably be reduced by about half. He smiled as he visualised the money already rolling in to his company and asked to try the product. As I handed him the bottle, I advised him not to taste it in its pure state but he proceeded to do just that. He was so put off by the taste that he refused to make it for me. So I went to another factory in an effort to find someone willing to produce this excellent remedy.

I eventually succeeded but when I see it on the shelves today and it is not sold as readily as it should be, I often think of the many people, like myself, who are obtaining great benefit from it. Being a diabetic, it has helped me to stabilise my condition without taking the medication that would otherwise have been necessary.

Molkosan is a wonderful remedy in the treatment of so many conditions and yet, if one does not search for the underlying cause of the problem, then one can never wholly treat it. Many times Vogel said, 'Pain is like an alarm bell. The body will tell us that something is not in order, but we then have to take a look at what is wrong. We cannot stop the clock or allow the problem to continue. We have to investigate matters and find the source of the problem.' Today, the big problem is that people are dosing themselves with drugs to treat the symptoms of their problem instead of getting to the root cause of what is wrong.

On one occasion when Vogel was visiting me in Scotland, he sat in on a consultation I was having with a local fishmonger. This man had been feeling very unwell for a while now and was experiencing difficulty with his breathing. He had been given various drugs by his own doctors but nothing had been effective and he was desperate for help. Although he didn't totally understand what the fishmonger was saying, Vogel turned to me and commented that the man had a lot of toxicity in his system and that he needed something to help him breathe, as he was gasping while sitting in the consultation room. Vogel suggested giving him four tablets of kelp a day and monitoring the situation. Sea kelp works like a sponge, by somehow helping to mop up the waste that is dumped in the sea, and kelp tablets help the body in the same way, mopping up some of the rubbish in our system and improving blood circulation, while the iodine it contains gives the endocrine glands a boost. It is also effective in controlling weight problems. We rarely see overweight fishermen, as even the smell of kelp will help keep their weight under control. I remember back in the 1970s, one morning while I was working at my clinic in Ayrshire, I received a phone call from a professor in Edinburgh, who invited me down to look at some sea kelp. It was fascinating, like a glowing mass.

The fishmonger followed our advice and whenever I met him after that, he always told me how grateful he was for the improvement in his condition. He said that he would never have believed that a simple kelp tablet was capable of giving him a new lease of life. The drugs he had been given by his doctor had been aimed at alleviating his obvious respiratory problems but they did not address the underlying problem of toxicity in his system.

As I have said, Vogel was very practical and learned a lot from the many people that he met. One day he took me out for a run in his big car. Like me, he was not a competent driver and the journey was quite stressful but, after some time, we eventually arrived at a farm where harvesting was taking place. Vogel knew this particular farmer and asked him to tell me what he did with the first cut of the harvest when it was brought in. The farmer told me that, first, he gathered together the tops of some of the oats and took them into the house, where some brandy or other alcohol was poured over them. The mixture was then stored in a cupboard and when his mother became a bit nervous or when his father was overworked, they would take a sip of this liquor. In homoeopathy, this remedy is called *Avena sativa*, the Latin name for oats, and what a wonderful remedy it is, because the grains contain an ingredient called *avenine*, which is a marvellous tonic for the nerves. When discussing this remedy, I often think of my oldest patient who, at the incredible age of almost 108, has porridge every morning for breakfast. That is why she has such a wonderful nervous system – because she feeds her nerves with the oats in the porridge that she has made almost every morning during her remarkable life. Apart from those who are intolerant to oats, I would recommend porridge for breakfast to anyone. Unfortunately, however, it is not seen as being as tasty as the sugar-laden cereals that are regularly advertised on television, usually aimed at children.

Vogel also tried to spread his message through his lecture tours or by taking part in radio and television programmes. When I joined him, I always admired the way he always seemed to have an answer ready for any of the questions that might be thrown at him. I particularly enjoyed it when he told the audience stories about the many discoveries he had made. On one occasion, he was asked a question about the importance of calcium. This was a subject which Vogel had studied very carefully and he told the story of his battle to obtain calcium in a form that the body would be able to assimilate. Calcium is one of the most important minerals in the human body. As most of us know, it is vital for our teeth and bones but less well known is the fact that it is important in helping our bodies to fight off infectious diseases. There had been various calcium preparations available for some time but none of these were particularly effective. Vogel had considered this problem over a number of years and he received inspiration from a well-known chemist that he met in Davos in Switzerland. This man had experience in producing calcium milk but was searching for a better way to deliver the benefits of calcium to the human body. He was utterly

285

convinced that this would be possible and his conviction inspired Vogel to continue with his research. He looked to his beloved plants for the answer and finally succeeded in his quest. Today, in my own country of Holland, *Urticalcin*, which was the successful formulation, is one of the most frequently prescribed calcium remedies.

One of the plants that was most helpful in this preparation was the stinging nettle. Vogel knew what a wonderful plant the nettle, Urtica, was for a range of ailments, including anaemia, rickets and respiratory diseases, but one day he realised that if he mixed Urtica with calcium, then it would enter the bloodstream more quickly. What an excellent remedy he had produced and what a friend I have had in this preparation over the years in my practice.

With his incredible knowledge, Vogel wanted to impress on me that, as a practitioner, we have a duty to help people in more ways than one – not only by what we prescribe but also by leading and showing people the way through sharing our life experiences. The responsibility then passes to the patients to do as much as they can to help themselves with the advice we impart to them. Whenever he had a problem with his feet due to travelling or from standing too long, he would walk barefoot in the meadows. The healing properties of the earth always helped him, and he was never embarrassed to be seen doing seemingly unorthodox things, as he loved being outside with nature.

I remember one day when he asked us to do some translations for him after returning from having spent a few days in the Engadine. He had slept in the mountains overnight because he could not find anywhere suitable to stay. He did not believe in staying in upper-class hotels, as he was a man of simplicity. He would prefer to sleep outside in nature than somewhere that possibly wasn't clean and tidy or was too expensive. He also disliked staying anywhere with concrete or artificial flooring, as he said that they 'block the assimilation of cosmic energy'. He claimed that a cat or a dog will seldom lie on a concrete floor, even if covered by a blanket for them to lie on, and pointed to the example of his big black Newfoundland dogs. He told me that they would not go into the laboratory to sleep at night but were much happier to lie outside, even in the snow, or on natural stone floors. They never lay on concrete floors, as they intuitively knew it was not good for them.

He never pampered himself with life's luxuries and, like myself, loved simplicity. That was one of the reasons I was so much in tune with him and that we worked so well together, as we were both on the same wavelength.

Vogel was ahead of his time in so many ways and he tried through various methods to spread his ideas to as many people as possible. But he was also aware that you cannot force other people to adopt your ideas or follow your example. Sadly, as life today grows ever busier and more stressful, people have less time to listen to what their bodies are telling them and look for solutions in nature as Vogel advised.

7

My home is our planet.
Alfred Vogel

One of the many things I miss about Alfred Vogel now that he is no longer with us is his stories. He had so many anecdotes about the memorable events he experienced during his lifetime and his experiences during his extensive trips all over the world. I paid particular attention to those from the 1950s before we met. Later on, I was often lucky enough to accompany him on his travels and it was always a most enlightening experience.

As Vogel was continually on the lookout to discover more natural and traditional remedies, this tireless traveller journeyed throughout the world to further his knowledge of the age-old healing methods used by the indigenous people he met. He was always eager to visit museums and study people's lifestyles in an attempt to establish a link as to why in certain countries some diseases were virtually unheard of, while in others they were rampant.

He put a tremendous amount of energy into his travels and always liked to talk about his adventures at sea when he went to countries like North America in the days before air travel was widely available. He enjoyed experiencing the different climates and studying the soil of each country. I remember after I had been on a trip to South Dakota, I mentioned to him the volcanic soil that I had noticed. I knew that Alfred had travelled to that area previously and he told me that when he smelled the earth there, he realised that this wilderness had existed long before people started to discover it.

It was in the 1950s when he was visiting a remote part of South Dakota that he met a Sioux medicine man called Black Elk. This man introduced Vogel to the wonders of nature in that area of the world and

Vogel was fascinated to discover how long the trees that he could see had been growing there. Most importantly, Black Elk also introduced Alfred to the power of *Echinacea purpurea*, which was a plant well loved by the Native Americans. They had a mutual respect for nature and forged a friendship which Black Elk sealed by gifting a handful of Echinacea seeds to Vogel. Vogel took these back to his herb garden in Switzerland and nurtured them. Then he studied them carefully and, as we have already heard, *Echinaforce* became one of his most successful remedies.

He would talk to the old medicine men of the tribes about their traditional methods of treating human suffering, the secrets of which had been handed down from father to son. He considered the Navajo Indians to be a very healthy group of people and believed that this was due to their use of herbs. They had a clear philosophy and maintained the traditional forms of medicine that had been handed down through the generations. He was interested to learn what foods these people ate and discovered that their diet was almost totally vegetarian; he also learned how they baked their bread and tried to establish what their average age was as a way of gauging how healthy they were.

Sadly, over the past few decades the lifestyle of these people has changed dramatically due to the encroachment of the modern world and its effects on their diet and the amount of physical activity that they undertake. In 1997, the US *Journal of Nutrition* published data from the Navajo Health and Nutrition Survey study which showed that 22.9 per cent of Navajo adults age 20 and older had diabetes. Fourteen per cent had a history of diabetes and another 7 per cent were found to have undiagnosed diabetes during the survey.

I remember, during lectures, that Alfred referred to a meeting he had had with an old Sioux Indian who was 118 years old, and how four generations of his family lived together in one small hut. With sadness, he would tell the story of how the white people sent the Sioux Indians into the wilderness where they were forced to work like slaves.

He also learned a lot from the Papagos Indians when he visited Arizona and was amazed at the fantastic array of herbs that they grew and the way they made use of these herbs to eradicate insects. He commented that the Papagos were attractive people who had a very healthy lifestyle.

During the years 1950 to 1952, he lived for a short time in Pipeline Avenue in Pomona, California, where he learned a great deal about acupuncture, reflexology and other methods of treatment. While there, he became friendly with the well-known actress Gloria Swanson, who wrote a number of articles about his book *The Nature Doctor*, which was first published in 1952, remarking that every household in the United States should have a copy of it.

He also lectured at several colleges in the area on chiropractic, osteopathy and naturopathy but, after a while, felt he wanted to travel further. So, next he headed to Iowa.

When he arrived there, he saw enormous towers of corn being doused with petrol and set alight. When he asked the farmers why this was happening and why they did not seem to be concerned that their crops were being wantonly destroyed, they told him that they were being given large subsidies by the government as they were, in fact, growing too much corn. Vogel was appalled by this. He thought it was an absolute disgrace for perfectly good food to be destroyed in this way when there was so much hunger in the world. He was so annoyed that he wrote to Congress and the Senate and managed to make some headway with them, the burning being stopped at that time. He was always very friendly and open and had a positive outlook. Even during his darkest experiences, he kept a clear vision and even when confronted with problems such as a sandstorm in Nevada he was never discouraged from travelling.

I always had the feeling that he had a great love for Mexico, as he spoke warmly of the wonderful time he had spent there. When talking about the native people, he would say, 'As long as you remain friendly, they will be open and tell you what you want to know.' His passage through the country was not always easy, though, as people could be very suspicious of strangers. In the village of Lagos de Moreno, for example, he encountered problems with the head of the village, who thought he was a spy and wanted to imprison him. Alfred's wife, Sophie, and his daughter, Ruth, became so distressed that they clung to Alfred and pleaded with this leader to let him go. All three then started to sing some old Swiss songs as a way to try to show these people that they were not a threat. Luckily, as Vogel could speak Spanish, he was eventually able to convince them that he was a Swiss naturopath, not an international spy, and they let him go.

Another memorable experience Alfred had in Mexico was his visit to the gardens of Xochimilco, where he walked around the herbal gardens and inspected the beauty that nature had to offer. When he showed me some photographs he had taken, I could see what a wonderful place it was. In Mexico City, he realised again there was a lot to learn from people in different countries as he studied their metabolic therapy method of treating cancer.

During some lectures, Alfred would talk about Guatemala and I can remember him advising people that if they wanted to eat honey, then they should choose Guatemalan. According to him it was the purest available, as it was free of insecticides and pesticides. The Guatemalan people, especially those from the Ministry of Agriculture (MAGA) were very friendly, and in the east of the country, he spent some time with a Swiss family, which he thoroughly enjoyed. In 1976, Vogel was very upset to hear of the horrendous earthquake that had devastated Guatemala but he was relieved when he received news that his Swiss friends had not been badly affected.

After Guatemala, he then travelled through Colombia and Ecuador, where he carried out a lot of good work, and when he arrived in Peru, he was so impressed by the country that in 1958 he bought a farm where he proceeded to grow potatoes, bananas, cherries, papayas, etc. He sold these to the local people at the markets and he used the herbs that he grew to produce his remedies. Not only did he toil barefoot in these fields himself when he was able to visit the farm but the local Peruvians also helped him tremendously. In turn, he helped them with his research and application of *Tormentil Complex* to help with common bowel problems that the people were suffering from. He also used *Molkosan* to help combat the effects of poor hygiene.

He travelled extensively throughout Peru during his visits there, making the most wonderful videos and taking spectacular photographs. He thought it was such a beautiful country and loved to go downriver on expeditions. One story which I will always remember was about an Indian tribe who had built their huts out of tree trunks. He tried to converse with them as best he could as they sat around a small fire. He learned how they would pound the poisonous barbasco root and, when this substance was put into the river, the fish would come to the top, gasping for air, thus enabling the fishermen to easily scoop them up. They would then cook the fish, often in the liquid from palm trees and citrus fruits. It was quite amazing how tasty they were and how, in this remote part of Peru, people were very healthy.

One thing he never discovered was how the Indians of South America prepare curare. They used to coat the tips of their arrows with this substance and, using their bows, would fire them at their enemy or prey. Curare produces paralysis in muscles. In fatal doses, death is caused by respiratory paralysis. Although Alfred managed to get a small jar of it, he never actually found out what exactly it was made from.

He had some near escapes during his travels and I remember the story he told about one plane journey through the mountains in Peru when they suddenly flew into a dense blanket of cloud. The pilot of the very small 16-seater plane was forced skilfully to guide the plane above the clouds but at this altitude the oxygen levels in the tiny craft were greatly reduced. Although the passengers were sick and felt miserable when they eventually landed in Cusco, there was also great relief that they had managed to land safely. Luckily, Alfred had some *Crataegus*, *Echinaforce* and *Ginseng* with him and managed to help the passengers by administering these remedies. He always took *Echinaforce* with him wherever he went and, if he came across any problems, he would use it to help the local people, especially with any skin or bowel problems.

From Cusco he travelled to Machu Picchu, which is a remote settlement perched high in the Andes mountains on a steep-sided ridge. He was amazed by the remains of the ancient Incan civilisation that had been discovered there at the start of the twentieth century and felt that it was a very spiritual place.

He learned so much from the people and the plants in South America, and it was with tears in his eyes that Alfred told me that he had been compelled to sell his farm in Peru after the government legislated that outsiders were only permitted to own 15 acres of ground.

When he travelled to Africa, he wanted to find out what illnesses were prevalent on that continent and also about how the diet, which he believed to be high in protein, affected people's health. He did a lot of research there into problems affecting people's kidneys, lungs and bowels, and also into infectious diseases.

I remember how enthusiastic he was when he returned home in 1973 with some Harpagophytum (Devil's Claw), which he had discovered on meeting the Ovambo tribe in the wilderness in Namibia. I have often written about how these people used Devil's Claw as we would use potatoes and Vogel personally witnessed the tremendous benefits to those people who used this plant daily. They obtained all the natural mineral salts they needed from this source and even although they lived in conditions similar to a sauna, they still had no kidney problems or rheumatism. Vogel brought this plant back to Europe, where it has been used to treat, among other things, fevers, skin lesions, gout, rheumatoid arthritis and conditions affecting the gall bladder, pancreas, stomach and kidneys. When in South Africa, he held a lot of lectures on the healing properties of herbs and plants. He was very interested in the Dutch and Germans who had settled in that country.

In addition to the aforementioned countries, he also travelled to Israel, Jordan, Lebanon, Syria and Iraq several times, and he accumulated a lot of facts about the people living there and their history. He talked to the Muslims about their beliefs and, while travelling in the mountains, he learned a lot about people's attitudes, their clothing and their lifestyle. He was interested to find that as there were no refrigerators, the people in these areas used olive oil extensively as a preservative for their foodstuffs.

I was fascinated when he told me about the mountain he climbed, Mount Nebo in Jordan, where Moses died. It is my opinion that Moses must have been the greatest leader ever to have lived because, for a period of 40 years, he led the Israelites through the wilderness so that they could enter the Promised Land. Alfred had visited the place where Moses ended his tremendous journey and I was eager to hear all the details of this trip.

In Lebanon, Vogel was particularly keen to see the cedar trees there that were over a thousand years old. He was surprised to see how healthy the Druze people were, particularly their strong teeth. He was fascinated to witness how these people lived and was excited by the culture of the Middle East.

He also travelled extensively through India, Indonesia, China, Taiwan, Thailand, Korea, Japan and the tropics. He witnessed many problems in the tropics, which prompted him to write his invaluable book on tropical diseases, which, as I mentioned earlier, is now an invaluable addition to my own library. He also visited institutes of tropical diseases to share his knowledge on the different methods that people could use to treat these conditions and to stress the importance of good hygiene.

In Thailand, he was very interested in the rice-growing process, and always believed that brown rice from Thailand is the finest and most beneficial for one's health. He took careful note of the diets of people in the various countries that he visited, notably of the bread and cereals that they ate, and many of these products are luckily now available throughout Europe. Once again, he stressed the importance of achieving balance and pointed to nature for an example. In Thailand, he witnessed how one animal will kill another to keep nature in balance, as exemplified by the many snakes he witnessed killing the rats and mice that were destroying the rice fields.

In Korea, he was particularly interested in the ginseng found there. The Koreans use not only the root of the ginseng but part of the plant itself in order to maintain a strong nervous system. This is the perfect illustration of Alfred's belief that it is sometimes necessary to utilise the whole plant to obtain the optimum benefit.

During Alfred's lectures in countries such as Holland, Germany, Switzerland and also America, his listeners were always captivated by the stories of his exotic travels. I remember one time when we were in the United States when he talked about his magazine, *Gesundheits Nachrichten*, which continues to be published today and to which I have contributed a lot of articles. On this occasion he spoke about one of his own articles, in which he wrote about Ceylon (now Sri Lanka), where he came across many people with elephantiasis, a grotesque hardening and thickening of the skin which was particularly prevalent in people who lived around Mount Lavinia. Elephantiasis occurs when the sufferer has become host to parasitic filarial worms that lodge themselves in the lymphatic system. Female worms release millions of microfilariae (immature worms) that circulate in the blood and the disease is transmitted by mosquitoes. At one point during their trip, his daughter started to present signs of this condition and it was amazing to see how *Echinaforce* helped her overcome it. As a result, he recommended it to the local people and whenever he travelled to Sri Lanka, he often made use of that particular remedy. During his many travels, he often came across dangerous situations and diseases, so Vogel always went prepared!

During his lectures, he repeatedly spoke about the importance of life and when he spoke about the suffering that he had witnessed or the way that Man was destroying nature, he would often have tears in his eyes. For example, he always became upset when he thought of the tragic events that took place in Hiroshima and Nagasaki, and how, as a result, people there are still dying of cancer and leukaemia.

Alfred often said that being interested in what is happening around the world keeps you young. I try to follow his example and I shall always treasure the things he taught me following each excursion. Alfred thoroughly enjoyed his travels and this is why he so often said, 'My home is our planet.'

In his book *The Nature Doctor*, Vogel relates a lot more about his travels, but the ones I have mentioned here are those that are special to me. It is with the greatest joy that I think of the journeys we made together, mostly in Europe, and what we learned from the beneficial remedies that we came across, many of which I have written about in this book. It is wonderful to think that this small man shared his great knowledge so as to help alleviate human suffering. From the days of his youth, through his many travels, his one aim in life was always to help people. He managed to do this not just through his clinics, but also through his magazines and then the huge factories that eventually followed to produce the remedies that he devised.

8

Each plant is complete in itself; it proceeds from a formula based on intelligence, forethought and wise planning. The precious value of the individual plant is jeopardised if its delicately balanced structure is torn apart. Every substance contained in a plant has purpose and significance. They complement each other and act as a whole.

Alfred Vogel

On my last visit to Holland, I was taken to see some Echinacea plants that were growing on what was once the floor of the sea. The Dutch have made a great achievement by reclaiming land from the sea and in doing so have made available some of the most fertile soil in Holland.

The fields that I was looking at belonged to our company Biohorma, the Dutch arm of Bioforce, which Vogel and I established to enable the manufacture of his remedies on a larger scale.

The majority of plants used to produce Biohorma products are grown on site, allowing us to maintain complete control over the cultivation of the plants – from planting to harvesting – and ensure that Vogel's principles are still applied today. As the company was continually expanding, it became necessary to reclaim land and these areas proved to be particularly suitable for the cultivation of herbs.

As I stood in the middle of that field of Echinacea plants, my mind wandered back many years to the day when we opened the first clinic for natural treatments in Holland, and to the many obstacles we faced in importing the remedies that we prescribed. The bookkeeper came to me one day and said, 'Jan, we cannot expand any further. Importing goods from Switzerland has become so costly that the products are too expensive to sell.' Taxes were rising and transportation costs were escalating to such a level that we had to consider alternatives. We managed to persuade Vogel that my wife, Joyce, and I should go to

Switzerland to become skilled in the processes involved in making the remedies and, thereafter, return to Holland and put our newfound knowledge to good use by making the same products there. I have already given a brief account of that period in my life in the first part of this autobiography, but I would like to expand on this a bit further now.

When we arrived in Switzerland in 1961, we received a great deal of support from Dr Reinmalt and the then general manager, Mr Metler. Those two gentlemen possessed the same dedication and precision as Vogel himself but my greatest admiration was reserved for Alfred, whose knowledge in this field was second to none. I was amazed at how intelligently he had concocted those medicines. He had recorded all the formulae in a large ledger, which he kept with him at all times, and I have illustrated here an example of one such creation.

The combinations that he blended, added to the detailed advice he provided to treat each illness, were remarkable and of great benefit to so many people. He always ensured that he obtained the total picture of a patient's medical history and lifestyle before starting to combine remedies to suit their individual needs.

During our lessons, we learned how important it was, when we were making the tinctures, that everything was correct, right down to the smallest detail. The Swiss were meticulous and everything had been taken into account in each stage of the production process. Close attention was paid while growing the herbs, after which the factory workers macerated them with the greatest care through the final processes until the remedies were produced. I always felt proud when the Americans said they considered these remedies to be the Rolls Royce of herbal medicines. Many have tried and failed to reproduce them. Vogel's techniques were in tune with the natural products he was working with and that is what he tried to pass on to me. The following information from Bioforce UK explains a little bit more about the processes involved:

> Holistic Standardisation is the process by which we ensure that every batch of Bioforce herbs is as potent and effective as it should be. We look at every ingredient within the plant and test each batch of herbs to confirm that the full spectrum of ingredients is present to the necessary level. This process differs from Chemical Standardisation, whereby one component of the plant is selected as being responsible for the action of the

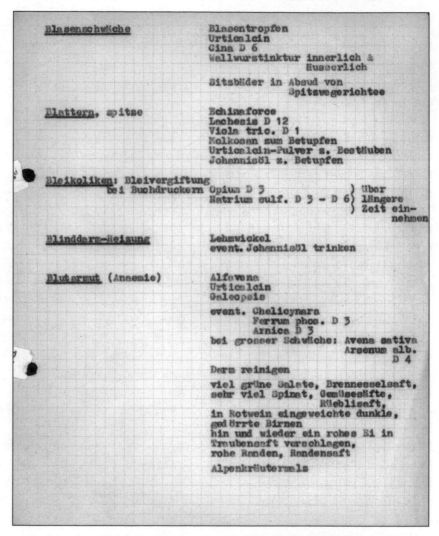

Figure 4 – Recommendations from Alfred Vogel
for the treatment of various diseases.

plant, and only the levels of that one component are measured. Bioforce believes that every element within a plant contributes to its overall effect and should be present in a tincture in the amounts found in the original herb.

We worked extremely hard during our visit to Switzerland and were fortunate to receive a lot of cooperation from the staff. We also went into the mountains with Vogel to widen our knowledge of the plants and herbs.

When we returned to Holland, we were able to start manufacturing some of the plant-based products, although, initially, only on a small scale. We realised that we were taking a big step but, as someone said to us, 'You need to start somewhere and people who have the courage to start will reap the rewards once the process becomes established.' Thankfully, after we entered into a legal agreement with Vogel for the recipes in his ledger, we had all the formulae we needed to get this new venture off the ground.

As the business expanded, we moved to Elburg. Under the management of Mr Bolle senior, things ran more smoothly and, together with my previous colleague, Mr Arie Drenth, we were able to open a manufacturing plant. Today, that has grown into Biohorma as we know it.

As my mind returned to the field of Echinacea plants, and I looked at those vast buildings and fertile fields, I was filled with pride at developing this important business. It was not without hard work, though. There were many times when things were extremely difficult and everything seemed to be against us. Favourable publicity from magazines such as *Beterschap* and leaflets such as 'Remedies from Nature' (of which I have illustrated the first pages) brought our work to people's attention and, from then on, our business expanded greatly and is still going strong today.

The Echinacea plants at which I was staring with such pride, were, of course, descendants – if that is the right word – from those seeds given to Vogel by Black Elk all those years ago in South Dakota. The Prairies of America are a long way from the foothills of the Swiss Alps, but it was in those Alps that Alfred Vogel tended Black Elk's seeds in the wholesome soil and healthy fresh air at his Teufen clinic. Those seeds, so carefully husbanded all those decades ago, provided the foundation for the now glorious fields of those wonderful purple-headed stems which grace the Bioforce fields in Switzerland and Holland. Each is still carefully sown and gently harvested as Vogel always wanted.

BETERSCHAP

AMERIKA	AUSTRALIË	BELGIË	NEDERLAND	DUITSLAND	CANADA	ZWITSERLAND
565-35th Avenue	29 Ghelmford Ave	25 Rue Henri de Seegher	BIOHORMA	Vogel & Weber	1188 Berritreet	Bioforce
San Francisco-Cal. USA	Epping NSW	Bruxelles 8	NUNSPEET	München	Montreal-St. N.	Teufen AR

Hulp uit Zwitserland

Loop niet door met uw klachten

Dank zij de medische vooruitgang in de laatste jaren is het sterftecijfer van tuberculose, kinderverlamming en verdere infectieziekten sterk gedaald. Wat een steeds groter aantal artsen nu grote zorg baart, is het ontstellend hoge cijfer chronische patiënten, dat ondanks hun harde werken niet daalt, maar integendeel nog dagelijks toeneemt.

Natuurlijke hulpbronnen

Astma, reuma, bloedsomloop- en spijsverteringsstoornissen zijn maar enkele van de vele plagen. De pijnen en direkte ziekteverschijnselen kunnen wel bestreden worden, maar het ziektebeeld zelf blijft praktisch onveranderd. Met een gevoel van wanhoop vragen vele patiënten zich af of er niet méér gedaan kan worden om te helpen.
Natuurlijk kan er meer gedaan worden!
Kruiden hebben al van onheuglijke tijden af genezing gebracht. Oude kultuurvolken kenden aan kruidendranken, die bereid waren door kundige handen, hoge waarde toe.

Verbluffende resultaten

Zij die reeds lang geplaagd worden door een aandoening, kunnen blij zijn dat er nieuwe mogelijkheden voor hen zijn. Laboratorium Biohorma te Nunspeet importeert namelijk de Zwitserse kruidentinkturen van ██. A. Vogel. Deze geneesmiddelen hebben internationale bekendheid gekregen, mede door de vaak verbluffende resultaten. Alleen al in Duitsland zijn er honderden artsen die ze geregeld voorschrijven. In de korte tijd dat deze geneesmiddelen in Nederland en België verkrijgbaar zijn, hebben zowel artsen als patiënten ze leren waarderen.

Waardevolle adviezen

Vele ziekten vinden vaak hun oorzaak in kleine voedings- en levensfouten. Iedereen die een kuur van Dr. A. Vogels geneesmiddelen bestelt, ontvangt daarom in een begeleidende brief uitgebreide medische adviezen. Deze zijn geput uit de grote ervaring die ██ A. Vogel en buitenlandse artsen hebben opgedaan. Eenvoudige waterbehandelingen, het al of niet eten van bepaalde voedingsmiddelen, enz., ondersteunen de goede werking der kuur. Vanzelfsprekend zal een en ander geschieden in overleg met de huisarts.
Dit zal nu werkelijk een hulp zijn voor mensen die misschien al lang de hoop op beterschap hebben verloren.

Hoe groene planten u kunnen helpen

De Zwitserse natuurarts Dr. Alfred Vogel, één der grote kruidenkenners van onze tijd, is van mening, dat men niet ongestraft chemische geneesmiddelen in het lichaam kan brengen. „Het lichaam is geen chemische fabriek", zegt Dr. Vogel in zijn door duizenden gelezen blad „Gezondheidspost". De enige juiste manier om een ziek organisme te helpen is een beroep te doen op de natuurlijke hulpbronnen die in duizenden kruiden verborgen zijn.
Wanneer men, zoals meestal de gewoonte is, kruiden na het oogsten droogt en in pakhuizen opslaat, gaat er veel van de natuurlijke geneeskracht verloren. ██ Alfred Vogel laat de in het wild verzamelde kruiden direkt koud uitpersen en het genezende groene sap wordt dan één van de kruidentinkturen. Dit koude bewerkingsproces is mede oorzaak van de hoge geneeskracht van deze kruidengeneesmiddelen. Door oplettend en nauwgezet te werk te gaan, kunnen alle natuurlijke hulpbronnen voor de patiënt behouden blijven.

Zwitserland, vindplaats van waardevolle kruiden

Geneeskrachtige kruiden worden hier verzameld op een hoogte van 1600 - 2500 meter. Ze groeien weelderig op de vaak steile berghellingen. Zwitserse kruiden bevatten méér geneeskracht, omdat ze profiteren van de natuurlijke bodem en intensere zonnestraling. Ervaren verzamelaars zoeken de plantjes in de tijd, dat ze net volgroeid zijn.

Kruiden brengen genezende werking

Figure 5 – The front page of the first edition of *Beterschap* (*Health News*).

Remedies from nature

Wandering in sumertime through the Bernese Highland, along the foot of the Matterhorn, or in the many side-valleys of the Engadin, yes, even upon the heights of the limy Jura we come upon a colourful flora of various herbs, many of which are well-known, proven medicinal herbs.

But not only in our country, in far off continents as well, in the highlands of the Andes of South America, in the tropical jungle of East Asia there plants are growing the curative effects of which are useful to mankind.

Since antiquity, the herb-medicines derived from them belong to our faithful helpers.

A. Vogel, the well-known Specialist for Phyto- and Nutritiontherapies, brings into full view to you some of his proven herbal remedies which – wherever possible – are prepared from fresh plants. The preparation is carried out in the new, up-to-date factory of the BIOFORCE LTD., in Roggwil TG. Your special shop where you will receive this prospectus will be pleased to let you have further information. Allow Vogel's fresh-plant preparations to become your helping friends. By these quite a number of health troubles can be removed.

In case of need we are recommending you the following products which have been well proved for many years.

Bioforce
A. Vogel

A. Vogel's Fresh-Plant Preparations

Bioforce LTD
ROGGWIL/TG
Switzerland

Bioforce
A. Vogel

BIOFORCE

Figure 6 – This was one of the first brochures that we produced.

When I looked at those Echinacea fields on reclaimed soil in Holland, that story – along with many others spanning the long number of years I shared with Vogel – came to my mind. If he ever discovered a plant of which he had limited knowledge, then he would think about its possible characteristics and signature before extensively researching it. As his work continued, so the pharmacy of natural herbal medicines in that little place of Teufen flourished.

Vogel had initially found it difficult to acquire arable land of the highest quality in Switzerland so I was delighted when in 1963, full of pride, he told me of some ground he had found that was of exactly the standard he was looking for. He felt it was like a gift from heaven, as it was well known that the likelihood of acquiring land in that area of Switzerland was remote.

The memory is so clear in my mind when I think back to that special day when he took me to see the wonderful new place in Roggwil where, in perfect peace and tranquillity, the medicinal herbs continue to be cultivated today according to Alfred Vogel's principles. As he stood there, he asked, 'Did you ever imagine that things would have expanded to this extent?' and he told me about the negotiations he had had to go through to acquire the land and continue with his quest to help his fellow human beings. You could see how humble he was about how he had managed to get everything to come together. His great desire was to offer people more help in their fight against illness and disease and to repair what Man had destroyed so easily.

When Vogel started his work he was fortunate to be able to have a lot of freedom in the remedies that he prescribed. Nowadays, our work is restricted by red tape and there is a proliferation of legislation outlining what practitioners are and are not allowed to do. People in authority have withdrawn some of the most valuable remedies from the market, which were more beneficial than many of the prescribed drugs with proven side effects. Sadly, their interference has not been in the best interest or well-being of the public but geared more towards increasing the profits of the giant drug companies. In contrast, Alfred Vogel was an individual who always put his patients' welfare first.

It is a great worry to me that, in today's society, the world is heading in the direction whereby people care more about money and materialistic possessions than for their fellow human beings. My grandmother was a wise old lady. At the age of 98, as she lay on her deathbed, she took hold of my hand and that of my cousin, who was a matron in a hospital, and said, 'You have both been called to help people. The biggest enemy you will face in the world will be the selfish attitudes of people who become lovers of themselves.' Vogel disliked such people. His compassionate heart always went out to those in need.

When he visited us in Scotland to offer advice on running our clinic, I often wondered if any of the patients realised what a brilliant man was in their midst. I remember one occasion when I was attending to a patient who was in a lot of pain. Vogel took off his jacket and started to work on this man using an old German practice called *Baunscheidt*. This is a very rigorous treatment and involves puncturing the skin with needles and then pouring oil over the area, which becomes very red and inflamed. It was invented by a German mechanic in the nineteenth century as a counter-irritation measure and it seemed very effective in relieving this patient's discomfort. Vogel told me of the people he had treated using such old, established methods in instances when patients had difficulty walking or were completely immobile. In cases where people had become totally lame and modern medicines did not offer any answers, he would turn to those old methods. He sometimes achieved the most amazing results by using the seemingly bizarre technique of rubbing bulls' testicles into the spine!

During one of his visits, when we held a lecture in Ayr, he selected a few people in the audience who were really ill and tried to offer them some guidance. He had that intuitive gift of being able to sense those who were unwell and to be able to talk to them with compassion. He focused on one particular lady, who was almost crippled with rheumatoid arthritis, and said to me, 'You have to treat this patient. You have the same gift as I have, and that is the gift of intuition. You will know how to treat her.' I went on to take care of that lady for quite a number of years, during which time she improved greatly. She said to me, 'Wasn't it a blessing that I was at that meeting and that Alfred Vogel picked me out and brought me to you, so that I now no longer need my wheelchair but can walk.' Instances like those make my work worthwhile and make me more eager than ever to continue.

I can recall one consultation I had with a 12-year-old girl while Vogel was visiting. He listened carefully to our consultation and I noticed he had tears in his eyes as he sat in the corner. Alfred realised that, as she had a very aggressive form of cancer, there was very little hope for this girl and her young life would soon come to an end. With deep compassion, he spoke to her and her parents and offered some advice to make things easier for them all. He shook his head when they left and said to me, 'It would be wonderful to think that one day illness and

303

untimely deaths will be a thing of the past.' I have always admired the loving attitude of that great man who worked diligently, harnessing the forces of nature, to help his fellow human beings and, indeed, together we worked hard to ease people's burdens. Until the day he died, he was completely true to these principles.

Today, Vogel's philosophies have come much more to the fore, with many of his ideas being replicated and a lot of his views being repeated. His favourite remedies are still sold worldwide and I am sure that he would have been proud to see the 'A. Vogel' name on them today – not only those that he worked on totally by himself but also the ones that we worked on together.

Seeds from cultures.
This guarantees us
the greatest possible
genetic uniformity.

Cultures are planted
according to
biological principles.
The use of chemicals
is replaced by the
expensive use of
manpower: weeding,
composting and
manual harvesting.

From planting
through to the
finished product,
constant checks and
laboratory analyses
help to ensure
the quality of our
products.

Figure 7 – The process of making *Echinaforce*.

9

In all your striving, let love be your guide for it is the greatest power in the universe.

Alfred Vogel

Quite a number of years ago I accompanied Vogel to New York, where he addressed an audience in a large, packed hall. He spoke on a variety of subjects and ended the evening on a very unusual note by quoting the words above.

He told his listeners that we were living in a world that had become so selfish we had no consideration for the welfare of our fellow human beings. To emphasise this point, he mentioned the biblical story of Cain and Abel. When Cain murdered his brother Abel and God called him to order, Cain asked, 'Am I my brother's keeper?' It is that spirit that Vogel warned us to beware of in the modern world, and it is certainly one that is unacceptable to those who believe in God. In every walk of life, God demonstrates his greatest love. When we look at the universe and all that He has created, we come to realise that love is the greatest power and will be the strongest force in achieving peace.

That lecture was actually held not far from the site of the appalling disaster of 11 September that took place many years later in 2001. When I heard of that horrific tragedy, I thought back to the words spoken by Vogel that evening. I realised that people had learnt nothing from the story of the beginning of creation, or the devastating events of two world wars that destroyed the lives of millions of innocent people. It is regrettable that we have not learnt that lesson to love each other and to realise that we *are* each other's keepers. A conscious effort must be made to help each other in this troubled world of which we are all a part.

I remember when I travelled by train with him and his wife, Denise, from Newcastle to Glasgow during one of their visits to the UK. As he looked at the sheep peacefully grazing on the hills during our journey, he started to tell me about the benefits of sheep eating certain herbs that were freely growing there. He then repeated one of his favourite sayings, 'In nature, everything is in balance.' He looked sad, however, as if thinking about what human intervention was doing to upset that balance.

During that journey, I told him a little about the history of Hadrian's Wall and how the Roman soldiers had built it to protect the northern boundary of the Roman Empire from hostile tribes that then inhabited Scotland. It is astonishing that sections of that wall are still visible and accessible today, which is a testament to the builders' skills. As a good road system made it easier for the emperors to control their empire by being able to send messages and orders more quickly, the roads had to be well constructed and straight. Excellent examples of these straight Roman roads can still be seen in the Newcastle area today.

Vogel agreed what a mighty empire it had been in its day. He then asked me, 'Do you know what caused the fall of that mighty Roman empire?'

I replied, 'Yes, I do know. They lost their empire as a result of immorality.' He informed me that, many times during his lifetime, he had seen how important and famous people had lost the battle with immorality. It is important that we keep our lives on a straight path. As he was a man to whom 'yes' meant 'yes' and 'no' meant 'no', he was as straight as the Roman road to Newcastle.

We discussed the importance of keeping order in life and about the tremendous hatred and jealousy that taints the modern world. He acquainted me with the story of an Indian prince who marvelled at one of his fellow believers – a poor man who, in spite of his poverty, rejoiced in the prince's wealth and his graceful wife. When the puzzled prince questioned him, the poor man happily explained, 'Why should I not rejoice in beauty, especially if it does not occasion me any worry or responsibility? You have the burden of overseeing all your wealth and of providing for all your wife's needs, while I, on the other hand, can rejoice in just looking at your treasures without any worry.' In *The Nature Doctor*, Vogel said, 'Those who can enjoy the good fortune of others without feeling envious have passed their first big test which will ensure them happiness and peace throughout their lives.'

Vogel always looked at the positive side of things and remained optimistic even in the face of some very negative situations, such as when he had been deceived or people had taken him for granted.

Many people in life tried to imitate him. Many tried to copy some of his wonderful recipes and his philosophies, and even went so far as stealing some of his possessions. He never complained much about it, though, and on the contrary, would remark, 'As long as it benefits other people.'

Vogel and I concurred that sharing is one of the most rewarding things in life. As with Vogel, I have often come across dishonest people and have had things cunningly taken from me but I really believe that those people who steal will never prosper. Being honest in life will not only benefit oneself but others as well. You reap what you sow in life and that is possibly the only justice there is.

He devoted a great deal of time to each individual who was in need of help. I remember a lecture he held in Zwolle, a city close to where I was born in Holland. A small man who came to chat to Vogel after the talk was so influenced by what Vogel had said that he sat down and cried. He told Vogel that his life had amounted to nothing and he explained that he could never be forgiven for the many sinful things he had done. As so often happens in such instances, his great sense of guilt had affected his physical, mental and emotional health. The things that we do wrong in life, or the dark secrets that we keep, all have a detrimental effect on our well-being. Guilt, jealousy, hatred and selfishness are some of the negative emotions that can gnaw away at our normal healthy existence.

Vogel spent a lot of time counselling this man and explained that forgiveness is unending. He said it could be compared to the sea, which was so vast that his sins, in comparison, would be forgotten about. He tried to lift the man's spirits by offering him advice and explained what an enormous help *St John's Wort* (*Hypericum perforatum*) could be to him. In addition, he prescribed some *Avena sativa* to calm his nerves. He suggested that he should ask for forgiveness and repent, and then start his life anew. The man replied that his life was so dark that he could not see any glimmer of hope but Vogel reminded him that behind every dark cloud there is sunshine. He directed him to put the past out of his mind, to look forward, be positive, to get his health back on track and then start over again.

It is an awful situation to be in when you cannot see the light at the end of the tunnel. Thankfully, however, it sometimes only takes a small event in life to lift one up and turn things around, so that we have the strength to carry on and start a new life. That man looked much happier as he said goodbye to us and I realised that I had learnt yet

They are carrying on his work

Alfred Vogel's "ambassadors" throughout the world

Nowhere else in the world have the thoughts and philosophy of Alfred Vogel fallen on such fertile ground as in the Netherlands. "The Nature Doctor" alone will soon have reached a circulation of one million copies, thus becoming one of the most widely read Dutch books of all. Alfred Vogel's ambassadors are particularly active here, with specialist courses, a visitors' centre and the "Alfred Vogel Prize", awarded every five years for scientific contributions in the service of natural medicine. The ideas of Alfred Vogel are also being propagated in many other countries by delighted patients who pass on their positive experiences to others, as well as by doctors, heads of clinics and research workers.

"Alfred Vogel's contribution to our understanding of medicinal plants and their effects has been outstanding", explained Dr M. O. Bruker, the internationally renowned doctor and head of a respected clinic for holistic medicine in Lahnstein, Germany. Recently, at the final session of a conference of the Society of Medical Advisers Dr Bruker introduced Dr Alfred Vogel to the delegates in the following way: "He has always argued passionately for a re-awakening of an awareness of the forces that lie within nature. In long, steady work with his patients, the readers of his journals and books and the audience at his lectures he has defended the use of medicinal plants and argued for a return to a simple lifestyle close to nature. Today, he is in a position to note with satisfaction that he is no longer a lone voice in the wilderness."

Dr Bruker, who has been a supporter of Alfred Vogel's for decades, is known to the public for his many scientific publications in which he has demonstrated, above all, the links between the "diseases of civilisation" and a diet and lifestyle that has become unnatural. Nowadays, among doctors, the significance of Dr Bruker's knowledge and experience for the future development of medicine is being recognized more and more.

The message of the advantages of a lifestyle and of a medical treatment in harmony with nature is also making itself felt in teaching and research. In Germany there are already some chairs of natural medicine at universities. In Switzerland the necessary political moves have been taken in Bern and Zürich, and similar efforts are afoot in other countries. Dr Silvio Jenny, long- serving head of the Bircher-Benner clinic in Zürich, commissioner for the professorial chair in Natural Medicine in Zürich and President of the Swiss Society of Practical Medicine said at a recent conference, in the presence of Alfred Vogel, that it was time to undertake "a further step towards the integration of plant medicine in modern medicine." Phytotherapy, as it was represented by Alfred Vogel, had limits set by nature. Within these limits, however, there was still an extremely extensive area for research and discovery. Because of this, felt Dr Jenny, the discipline of phytotherapy had to reclaim its rightful place in the medical system.

Shared work and shared goals: Alfred Vogel and one of his followers Jan de Vries

Figure 8 – Vogel's work attracted worldwide interest.

another lesson from my old friend, this time in how to offer guidance to people who feel they have come to the end of the road – it was another example of how Vogel tried to be his brother's keeper.

I shall always remember when I said goodbye to Alfred Vogel for the last time in this life. I spent a wonderful day with him in his home in Switzerland. Even although I could see that the end of his life was approaching, I was astonished at how sharp his mind was. We reminisced about some of our experiences, the different countries we had visited, the advances in what we refer to as 'complementary medicine', the changes that he had witnessed during his lifetime in people's lifestyles and society in general.

We were able to look back on many important achievements that we had made and I told him that I had recently seen a patient whom I had previously discussed with him. This girl had been suffering from cancer and had been told by conventional doctors that nothing more could be done for her, but I was delighted to report that, thanks to the advice he had given, she was now very happy and healthy.

This patient also represented another great achievement – as the wonderful methods he had researched and developed had now gained the respect of many orthodox practitioners. I don't think I ever witnessed a prouder moment in Vogel's life than when I handed him a letter written by an eminent consultant from one of London's foremost hospitals, who asked, 'What did you do to make this girl better? You have certainly accomplished something that we could not do.'

Science is a wonderful thing. We cannot survive without knowledge but, in so many situations, common sense is also necessary. This girl was probably examined scientifically from every angle and yet the scientists and conventional doctors had forgotten that she was just like any other human being – a part of nature. If she was ill, it was because there was an imbalance in her body. So, where did the imbalance lie when I first saw this girl? After delving into her medical history, I was able to piece together where the problems lay. Love and compassion were required to understand where she had been so misunderstood. First of all, her physical, mental and emotional bodies had to be put back into balance. We prescribed different remedies, examined her diet and also offered her counselling – and these sensible treatments made it possible for this girl to regain her health.

Even when we faced a barrage of criticism and misunderstanding of our work, I always said to Vogel that we owed it to mankind to carry on. It can be very difficult to continue to strive to do one's best for others in the face of hostility and contempt but it is always worth it in the end. If we possess love and compassion, and if we tackle life's problems with some common sense, then hopefully we will be rewarded by success, as was certainly the case with our work with this girl.

Vogel was very happy that day as I left and, knowing that it would be the last time I saw him on this earth, I was comforted by the fact that he knew in his heart that he had done his best. The love and compassion that he had demonstrated to his fellow human beings during a lifetime of hard work and dedication had definitely paid off.

10

There is nothing common about common sense.

Jan de Vries

One day when I was in Dublin, my eyes were drawn towards some bookmarks that were on sale in a bookshop. Imprinted on them was the above inscription, followed by my name. I never knew that these bookmarks were in circulation, although I regularly use that expression in my lectures. My parents taught me this lesson while I was growing up and I have applied it many times in life. Common sense is vital, especially in the approach to good health or in looking for answers to life's uncertainties.

I recall one particularly difficult, tiresome day when Vogel and I had had to face a barrage of unforeseen problems. It was not until we were leaving work and Vogel said to me, 'I really don't feel like doing this lecture tonight,' that I realised how much the day had drained his energies. That was very uncharacteristic of Vogel, because he never allowed anything to beat him. Even in his advancing years, he was always eager to tackle a problem head on. Looking at me, he then continued, 'I think you should take the lecture tonight.' This rather surprised me and I replied that it would not be the proper thing to do, as the hundreds of listeners who would be attending the lecture that night were going there to listen to *him* – not me.

I decided to try and lift his mood by telling him an amusing story about Albert Einstein. On his final lecture tour, Einstein apparently told his chauffeur that he did not want to do a particular lecture, just as Vogel had revealed to me that evening. His chauffeur, who had a white moustache and bore a close resemblance to the famous physicist, said, 'I shall do it, Professor. I have listened to your lectures so many times that I know them off by heart.' Amazingly, Einstein agreed to this unusual arrangement.

The lecture in question was being held at the Institute of Science in New York. Einstein decided to sit inconspicuously behind a pillar at the back of the hall to listen to his chauffeur. The chauffeur actually delivered the lecture very well, until it came to the moment where the audience could ask questions. As students like to grill guest speakers, a very difficult question was put to him. The chauffeur looked at the undergraduate and ingeniously replied, 'You must be a fool. Even my chauffeur who sits at the back of this audience could answer that question.'

Well, there was great hilarity in the car as I told Vogel that story and it appeared to cheer him up a great deal. I said to him, 'We may both be small but I don't have a moustache, and even although we do look like each other in many ways, I would definitely not be able to fool the audience into thinking I was you!'

When we arrived at the lecture hall, I asked Vogel if he was feeling a bit better. Although he said he was, he added that, because he was tired, he was going to deviate from the usual routine of his lectures. As it transpired, the lecture that followed that evening was the best he had ever given, although he never repeated it.

He started by telling his audience that, although he was there that evening to speak to them, he wanted to spend the time with them answering their questions. I actually wrote all those questions down and happened to come across them while I was writing this book. What amazed me about his answers was that a lot of them were basic common sense. I would now like to share some of them with you.

One of the first questions was, 'How long do you need to take the remedies for?' Vogel replied by wisely stating that, ideally, the body should be able to look after itself and should be allowed to repair itself. It is only when some extra help is needed that medicines should be used. Remedies for acute problems such as colds and flu should only be taken for a limited period – to give the body a boost. People who have a low immune system can benefit greatly from taking such remedies as *Echinacea* and *Urticalcin* to help increase their protection against ailments. But these remedies should also only be taken for a short time, then stopped for a spell before restarting if it is felt that a further boost is needed. With conditions like multiple sclerosis and rheumatoid arthritis, the remedies would probably have to be taken continually, though, of course, each case would have to be looked at individually.

As I have said, common sense is required. Women who are

experiencing physical symptoms associated with the menopause, for example, can gain welcome relief by taking *Salvia* and then discontinue it once their symptoms have either subsided or disappeared completely. In the case of fungal infections, however, it can often take a long time before they are brought under control and it is sometimes necessary to keep taking particular treatments for a prolonged period. In these instances, Vogel stressed how important it is for people to be patient and to believe in the remedies they have been prescribed. He repeated one of his favourite phrases about illness coming to us on a horse and leaving on a donkey, and stressed that patients should consult their practitioners rather than stopping a remedy when *they* feel they should.

I came across such an instance not so long ago with a patient who had been consulting me about her rheumatoid arthritis. She was actually progressing well and, because of her improvement, she wanted to stop taking the remedies I had been prescribing. I asked her if she had any financial concerns that would prevent her from continuing the treatment, to which she replied, 'No, but I want to stop.' I advised her to keep taking them for a little longer, because her condition would most probably improve even further. However, she did not heed my advice and, when I met her three months later, she was almost crippled and begged me to take her back as a patient. All those months previously, I had advised her to keep taking the remedies as I wanted her to be well again, but she failed to use her common sense and pay attention to my advice.

Another question that was quite interesting was, 'Is it safe for pregnant women to take these remedies?' Vogel said something that I always emphasise to pregnant women, 'Please be very cautious when pregnant, as you should not take anything unless you absolutely need it. Talk to your doctor, practitioner or midwife and make sure that you read any labels thoroughly.' If there is any risk at all, then the labels usually warn against taking a particular remedy during pregnancy, but it is crucial that women pay extra attention in such instances.

During that lecture, a small, crippled lady stood up and asked a question relating to rheumatism and arthritis. Without delay, he asked her if she was anaemic, but she did not know. Unlike me, Vogel had never studied Chinese facial diagnosis and I could see that her facial expressions definitely revealed the outward signs. When she came to speak to us at the end of the lecture, I gently pulled her bottom eyelid down and said to Vogel, 'Here is the evidence of a tired, listless, anaemic person. We need to help her as much as possible.' We did so by giving her vitamins, minerals and homoeopathic remedies.

Then another man stood up to ask a question about his health and I smiled to myself as, straight away, Vogel asked him if he owned a castle. He looked rather puzzled and replied that he did not. 'Well,' said Vogel, 'the "walls" around your eyes show that you must live in a castle. The very first thing we need to do is to break down those black walls under your eyes. It is possible that your kidneys need some attention.' The man asked Vogel if he had second sight, to which Vogel responded in the negative. He then asked if there was anything that could be done so that his kidneys could perform their job more efficiently. Vogel started by enquiring if he was fond of salt – to which he replied that he loved salt and that the salt cellar was never far away from him. The first bit of advice Vogel gave him was therefore to reduce his salt intake. He then recommended that he drank plenty of water – not sparkling mineral water, but good clear water – and, with the addition of some *Solidago Complex* and *Golden Grass Tea*, the 'walls' around his castle would soon disappear.

A lot of questions were asked that particular evening on the issue of dietary management. As I've already made clear, Vogel was a true campaigner for a healthy, balanced diet and he was a wonderful advertisement for the benefits of such a regime. At the age of 92, he bought himself a new pair of skis so that he could glide more quickly over the Swiss mountains – at the time he told me that vegetables and fruits (especially salads) were his favourite foods and he believed that if he didn't eat those things, he would not be able to participate in his favourite sport.

A lot of people asked what his main recommendation would be for a healthy diet and I was happy with the response he gave. He said he believed in an individual diet for each individual person. That is something I have always advocated. His main suggestions were to eliminate as many additives, E-numbers and artificial colourings as possible from the diet; to eat a lot of wholegrain products, rice and fresh fruit and vegetables; and to be sparing in the consumption of animal protein – soya, as an alternative, would be preferable. Care must also be taken with the three 'Ss' – salt, sugar and saturated fats. These fats should be eliminated from the diet and replaced with cold-pressed fats, such as olive oil, safflower oil and sunflower oil.

It is essential that greater emphasis be placed on increasing the consumption of alkaline foods and limiting the intake of acid-forming foods – this became evident when I was approached by the Dutch Health Service to carry out double-blind trials on patients suffering from arthritis and rheumatoid arthritis, in order to prove the efficacy of integrating alternative and orthodox medicine. These trials were also monitored by one of the universities in Holland and, at the beginning, I felt that the rheumatologist who headed the orthodox side of the research was negatively disposed towards complementary medicine. He often asked me bluntly why I was hassling patients to adhere to the diet I was giving them. But, once again, I was applying common sense in recommending a diet that would lower the acidity in their bodies and I was able to prove the benefits of my recommendations when the results of most urine samples from these patients illustrated complete over-acidity in their bodies. When this acidity was eliminated from their systems, the participating patients from my section were given a lot of relief from their pain.

Gout, for instance, results from an overabundance of uric acid in the body. Eventually this uric acid crystallises and settles in the joints, resulting in swelling, inflammation and unbearable pain. A diet that is more alkaline than acid can only improve the situation. Other conditions, such as arthritis, rheumatism, eczema, psoriasis and duodenal and peptic ulcers also develop from an overly acidic diet, so it is an important issue to address. In the trials, it was demonstrated that the patients who followed my dietary regime had more long-term success in treating their conditions than the patients treated by orthodox means who were given strong drugs. Although the conventional approach did work quickly to alleviate the symptoms of pain and inflammation, it did not address the root of the problem and so these patients remained crippled. It is therefore a matter of common sense to follow the correct diet in order to achieve long-term relief.

The foodstuffs that lead to the creation of acid in the body include meat (especially anything from the pig), cheese, citrus fruits, coffee, tea, alcohol and nicotine, whereas vegetables, fruits and even potatoes are more alkaline-based. Another benefit of cutting out acidic foods can be to lower one's cholesterol level – so it is certainly worth trying out these new eating habits.

Another question asked that evening was, 'Can eating a lot of raw food cause stomach problems?' Common sense again prevailed as Vogel explained that not only do raw foods (such as salads, vegetables and fruits) contain the most vitamins, minerals and trace elements but they are also rich in enzymes which aid absorption by the digestive system. Of course, however, if one suddenly starts to eat a large amount of raw food when the body is not used to it, this might cause a stomach upset. It is only sensible when a decision has been made to change one's diet to do so gradually in order to allow time for the stomach to adapt.

Other tips that Vogel gave were to eat slowly and chew your food thoroughly before swallowing. Whenever you experience acid reflux or problems with indigestion, make a conscious effort to chew your food extra thoroughly, so that the saliva (which is your best aid in the digestion of foods) can mix with it, thereby assisting the process.

It was also stressed, in response to a few questions, how imperative it is to ensure that recurring problems are investigated, and never to be concerned about going repeatedly to your doctor if you are at all anxious. As Vogel said, 'Your doctor should be your best friend, as he has a responsibility for your well-being.'

11

Questions lead to wisdom.
Jan de Vries

As I mentioned in the previous chapter, a lively discussion unfolded during an evening lecture when Alfred Vogel answered a series of interesting and unusual questions that were put to him by an attentive audience. Although I had listened to him countless times and, in my 40-plus books, have written extensively about the many ailments that afflict people, because that particular evening was so memorable, I felt it would be a good idea to highlight some more of the issues discussed, as those queries are similar to the ones on people's minds every day. As I have often said, questions lead to wisdom.

One question came from an elderly lady who stood up and said that every single night, after just a few hours' rest, she would waken up and could not get back to sleep. Consequently, when it came time for her to rise in the morning, she was so sleepy and tired that she felt unable to cope with the day's events. Her doctor had prescribed sleeping tablets but she commented that these made her feel like a zombie.

Vogel replied that there were many reasons why people might have difficulty in getting to sleep or experience irregular sleeping patterns. He said that if people waken up at roughly the same time each night, then this may be as a result of tension, worries, drinking caffeine-laden beverages (such as coffee or cola drinks), sleeping during the day, lying on an uncomfortable mattress or eating a meal too late at night. He even commented that watching an exciting television programme just before going to bed could stimulate the mind and keep people awake. His advice was to try not to have a nap in the afternoon, to go for a walk in the evening and definitely not to drink alcohol, tea, hot chocolate or coffee at night, although a cup of Bambu coffee would be an acceptable substitute. Drinking this half an hour before retiring, with a spoonful of honey added to it and 25 drops of *Valerian Hops* can often rectify sleeping difficulties.

On the same theme, another lady stood up and asked how she could wean herself off sleeping tablets. She explained that she had been prescribed them for years and when she tried to come off them, she had difficulty sleeping and experienced other symptoms such as palpitations and heavy perspiration. Vogel informed her that, although sleeping tablets might have a calming effect, as they are basically tranquillisers, they contain ingredients that influence the central nervous system, which has a knock-on effect on other parts of the body. To take a drug like this can give rise to many problems. It can especially affect the endocrine glands and sometimes the lymph glands, where waste material can lodge. He urged her not to stop taking this medication suddenly but to gradually reduce the dosage. In the meantime, to help alleviate any withdrawal symptoms, she could take some natural alternatives. He also suggested that she either went for a walk or perhaps a cycle ride in the evening; or, if she had a dog, she should take it for a walk before going to bed.

Looking rather embarrassed, the woman then told Vogel that she had an irrational fear of going out of doors and asked if there was anything he could recommend that would help her to overcome this phobia. Vogel advised her to take the remedy *Avena sativa*, which has a restorative action on the nervous system, and not to give in to the fear but instead strive to overcome it. He recommended that she went out with a friend who could offer her support and, each day, to go a little further away from her home. He tried to offer reassurance by saying that the feelings of panic she experienced would gradually lessen until they no longer troubled her. He also suggested that she took some herbal remedies, such as *Ginsavena*, which is of great help in such circumstances.

The manager of a large company asked the next question. He had tried to get extra sleep but found it impossible unless he smoked several cigarettes before going to bed. He continued by saying that, although he had tried to stop, he was unable to sleep without them. Vogel informed him that, in dealing with any addiction, it takes approximately three weeks for the palate to become accustomed to the elimination of the addictive substance. He stressed to this man that if he could abstain from smoking for that three-week period, then he would most probably be over the worst of any withdrawal symptoms. He acknowledged that the first few weeks would be difficult but if he also examined his diet to ensure that he ate healthily, this would make things a bit easier for him. He was aware that a great deal of effort would be needed but said that the end result would make it worthwhile. He recommended he take five drops of a homoeopathic remedy called *Tabaccum* twice daily, and boost his diet by eating foods rich in calcium, magnesium and sodium. It was a pity that, at that particular time, I did not have the necessary knowledge of acupuncture, because I have helped many people to quit smoking using this therapy. This has been confirmed by the many testimonials I have received from people telling me how their health and lives in general have been greatly enhanced since they stopped. There is so much pollution in the air caused by smokers; I always tell them they were not brought into this world with a chimney on their head!

Another excellent question put to Vogel was, 'Is it a responsible act to carry out self-doctoring?' When I look in shop windows or browse in shops, I feel that there is a remedy for everything and, as a lot are available without prescription, one can often treat oneself. I liked Vogel's answer because he said that there is no need for anyone to go to a doctor with everyday ailments such as nasal catarrh or a cough. As simple problems like this have been alleviated with remedies at home for a great number of years, then this is perfectly safe. However, it is always advisable to consult your own doctor when problems do not clear up, or if they recur. He said that one has to be cautious when self-doctoring by not taking over-the-counter medications for too long a period and to seek your doctor's advice if symptoms persist. He also gave some examples of when medical attention should be sought immediately, such as for continuous coughing, coughing up blood, an ulcer that does not heal, difficulties in swallowing, a lump in any part of the body, blood loss, change in stools or pain when going to the toilet, difficulty in emptying the bladder and a whole host of other symptoms.

During this part of the discussion, someone asked why homoeopathic doctors and naturopaths are so against antibiotics. It is accepted that antibiotics are necessary in some situations and, as Vogel admitted, some antibiotics can be a real salvation. But one should not take them like sweets, as has been the case for many years in the Western world. The problem that arises through the overuse of antibiotics is that the bacteria they have been developed to combat become resistant and the drugs are therefore no longer effective. We are seeing the frightening results of this situation today with the spread of superbugs such as MRSA. It is also common for antibiotics to disturb the bowel flora, as they kill the good bacteria that aid digestion as well as the bad bacteria causing the infection. If an infection does appear, then you must consult your own doctor. The benefit of taking a natural antibiotic, like *Echinaforce*, is that the white blood cells increase but it does not attack the good bacteria in the bowel. If it has been necessary to take antibiotics it is advisable to take *Milk Thistle Complex* or *Acidophilus*, as these will help the bowel to recover. The questioner seemed quite satisfied with Alfred Vogel's response to his enquiry.

Another lady, in her 80s, said she had taken antibiotics for a considerable period of time and was now left with a tremendous noise in her ears. She wondered whether this could have been caused by their long-term use. Vogel said that there are four major causes of tinnitus – an ear infection, fungus, a vertebrae problem or congestion – and great care has to be taken to avoid this condition leading to deafness. If one also suffers from attacks of dizziness and severe nausea, then Ménière's disease may be the diagnosis. One can do a lot in such circumstances with the use of acupuncture and also by taking the excellent remedy *Ginkgo biloba*, which stimulates the circulation of blood to the head and brain.

A gentleman then had a rather unusual query in that, when he awoke in the morning, his eyes were completely closed and he could only open them with great difficulty. He asked Vogel for some advice as to what he thought could be wrong. He said he had no discharge but Vogel and I agreed that he certainly had conjunctivitis, which can take a long time to clear. Vogel suggested he tried the old-fashioned remedy of chamomile compresses, which could be of tremendous help in such circumstances.

Another lively discussion then developed when a young lady said that it was not unusual for her not to go to the toilet for ten days. Although she was not unduly worried about this, Vogel was. He said that constipation can have several causes but when the large intestine is subject to metabolic changes then this can indicate a serious problem and everything possible must be done to alleviate the situation. The first thing he asked her to do was to study her diet, starting with what she ate for breakfast – which, in her case, was appalling. He recommended she eat muesli with the addition of some cooked prunes and prune juice, and to add to this a teaspoonful of *Linoforce*. This effective remedy offers relief by combining the gentle bulking action of linseed with the stimulating effects of senna leaves. As I mentioned in a previous chapter, if you do not export in 24 hours what you have consumed during that same period, then you are encouraging problems. Time must be taken to chew food thoroughly and, as Vogel said, your best digestive aid is saliva. Never postpone going to the toilet. Drink at least two glasses of lukewarm water first thing in the morning and make sure that you take plenty of exercise (whether it be in the form of walking, swimming or cycling). If the problem persists, then you should consult your doctor.

Vogel also commented that having a normal motion every day would have a beneficial effect on her weight and, as she had problems controlling her weight, she was pleased to hear that positive information.

Next followed a question from a lady in her 60s who suffered from daily nosebleeds. She said it was impossible for her to stop the bleeding and, although she had been to the doctor, she was still having problems, often at the most inopportune moments. Vogel believed that her blood vessels were weak but suggested a useful technique would be to press firmly on the relevant part of her nose until the bleeding stopped. If that failed, then she could take the rather bizarre step of placing a piece of fresh chicken meat up the appropriate nostril and then the bleeding would stop immediately. However, he said, a much simpler way would be to take *Bursa pastoris* tincture, which often proves to be most effective. This particular woman said she would try anything to stop this problem – even if it meant going into her fridge for a piece of fresh chicken meat!

Another woman said she was becoming forgetful and asked if anything could be done to improve this worrying situation. I was pleased that Vogel recalled the time we spent in Korea, as he told her about an elderly man there who chewed *Ginkgo biloba* leaves every day to keep his mind alert. As Vogel said, it is vital that the brain remains active. He asked her to ensure that she had ample relaxation and plenty of exercise, and also stressed the importance of keeping an eye on her cholesterol levels. He pointed out that a cholesterol level above 5.2 was not acceptable and that a lot of avoidable problems could develop if she didn't keep an eye on that. To lower cholesterol levels he recommended porridge in the morning, chewing the seeds from grapes, taking some *Milk Thistle Complex* and eating plenty of garlic.

This led to an elderly lady asking if anything could be done to combat osteoporosis. Vogel explained that a loss in bone mass can be experienced from the age of 40 onwards. There can be many causes, for example drinking too much alcohol, smoking, or having too much salt, animal protein, coffee, tea or chocolate in the diet. Vogel strongly advised people with osteoporosis to take the homoeopathic preparation *Urticalcin*, which I discussed earlier. If taken daily, it provides extra help in maintaining strong bones.

Another listener asked about hay fever. Vogel informed him that cases of hay fever were increasing annually, due in large part to the widespread growth of rapeseed. Those who suffer from hay fever should also be aware that they run the risk of developing arthritis or rheumatism. The first thing to do is look at the patient's diet and reduce their intake of milk, cheese and salt. It would also be of great benefit for them to start taking the remedy *Luffa Complex* from the end of March until the hay fever season is over. If one knows a good homoeopathic doctor, then an injection of a homoeopathic remedy can be given before the season starts but, as I have said, one of the finest things to take is *Luffa Complex*. From extensive research into this excellent product, it has also been shown to be helpful to those who are allergic to dust mites.

A tremendous range of questions were asked that evening. Another listener asked what could be done to ease the pain from wasp stings. Wasp stings can be very dangerous if the person who is stung is allergic to them. They can develop anaphylactic shock, displaying difficulty in breathing, swelling in the throat, itching or fainting. If someone exhibits any of these symptoms, it is imperative that they are taken to hospital straight away, as this condition can be fatal. In less serious cases, where the symptoms are swelling and discomfort, the quickest way to alleviate this is to take five drops of *Apis D4* straight away and repeat a further two times a day. Great relief can also be achieved by dabbing some tea tree oil onto the sting. But, above all, try and keep away from wasps! Citronella oil or *Po-Ho Oil* are good deterrents for bees, wasps and midges.

Another question was from a young girl who had tremendous problems with halitosis – in other words, bad breath. She told Vogel that she made sure that her teeth and gums were very healthy and she took great care with oral hygiene but, nevertheless, her boyfriend wanted to end their relationship because he found the situation repellent.

Many people suffer from this problem and Vogel told her that the most common cause is a disturbance in the bowel bacteria. He advised her to eliminate white sugar and white flour from her diet, to chew her food thoroughly, to keep her consumption of milk and cheese to a minimum and to take a teaspoonful of *Molkosan* twice daily, together with 20 drops of *Milk Thistle Complex*, also twice a day. He reassured her that, by making these changes to her diet, she would see a definite improvement. I would add that it would also be a good idea to take 15 drops of *Peppermint Complex* twice a day and to take 3 garlic capsules last thing at night, as this is an excellent deodoriser.

A man then put up his hand and pleaded with Vogel to help him because he had to rise five times during the night to go to the toilet. As he said, 'When I have to go, I have to go.' He explained that he had been to see a urologist and was told he had prostate problems but, because of his advancing years, he felt it unwise to undergo an operation. Vogel answered him by saying that if help is sought quickly, then prostate problems can be easily treated. If left untreated for a long time, however, the situation becomes more difficult. He recommended the man take a handful of pumpkin seeds every day, together with some *Saw Palmetto Complex* (also known as *Prostasan*), which, he assured him, would help a lot. He also said to make sure that he took enough exercise and kept his body moving, by walking, swimming or cycling, and emphasised the importance of keeping constipation at bay. He also urged him to keep a careful eye on such culprits as herbs, strong spices (like chilli), coffee and alcohol, and to restrict his intake of fluids after 6 p.m. Additional relief could also be achieved by rubbing *St John's Wort Oil* over the bladder area and between the legs.

That particular lecture proved to be such a success, with many people leaving much wiser than when they arrived. From the various questions that were asked, I too gained a lot of practical wisdom, which I have put to good use in helping people with their different ailments throughout the world.

12

Man has not one body but three – a physical, a mental and an emotional body.

Jan de Vries

In the eighteenth century, a man called Samuel Hahnemann travelled all the way from his homeland of Germany to visit the oldest medical school in Europe, which is now part of Edinburgh University. Hahnemann is credited with being the founder of homoeopathy as we know it today and while in Edinburgh he had a lively conversation with his peer, Professor Merridge. When the professor asked him, 'What is health?' Dr Hahnemann immediately fired back at him, 'What is illness?' Basically, illness is disharmony wherever it surfaces in the body, 'an aberration from the state of health' – whether physical, mental or emotional.

Vogel subscribed to many of Hahnemann's beliefs. He too was conscious of the fact that in order to achieve the best result for patients, it was not solely a matter of treating the physical symptoms; the mental and emotional state of a patient also had to be taken into account in order to harmonise the entire body. As I learned while I was studying in China, this principle is also fundamental to Chinese medicine, especially acupuncture – the aim of which is to harmonise that which is out of harmony in the body. The importance which the Chinese have long attributed to this state of being becomes gloriously apparent when you visit the Forbidden City in Beijing. One of the most amazing rooms in this breathtaking complex is the Hall of Supreme Harmony, which was used for important state occasions such as the enthronement of the Crown Prince, the celebration of the Emperor's birthday, and so on.

Today, many serious health problems are resulting from a lack of harmony in people's bodies and their lives in general. Sadly, problems caused by emotional imbalance are increasing at an alarming rate as people's mental health is under sustained attack in the modern world, with the result that more and more people are seeking relief through strong pharmaceutical products that can be very addictive. The side effects of drugs such as tranquillisers and antidepressants have received a lot of attention in the media in recent years, and of course these drugs only treat the symptoms of the problem rather than getting down to the root cause. It is very important when treating patients that we achieve harmony between the three bodies, and this is where complementary medicine, with its use of herbal or homoeopathic remedies, is of great benefit.

Over the course of his research, Hahnemann developed four fundamental principles. The first of these is '*similia similibus curentur*' or 'like cures like'. This means that a remedy that produces symptoms of a disease when given to a healthy patient can alleviate the problem in a patient suffering from the disease. This discovery can be applied to any condition and to any individual – in measles, for instance, the principle is not to suppress the illness, but to bring it out of the body. A homoeopathic remedy will probably make the measles a little worse before they are out of the system. Instead of assuming that symptoms represent illogical, improper or unhealthy responses that should be treated with drugs or surgery, Hahnemann believed that symptoms are positive, adaptive responses of the body to deal with an imbalance that has occurred. It is often said that God's creation, the body, is very intelligent – in fact, supremely intelligent.

The second principle is 'the minimum dose', which resulted from Hahnemann's attempts to work out a way of administering therapeutic doses of medicines while avoiding side effects. He believed that large doses of drugs actually made a patient's condition worse, while small, diluted doses enabled the body to fight off the disease. The way that he produced medicines was called 'potentiation' – the third principle. Homoeopathic remedies are made through a process of serial dilution, and the remedy is vigorously shaken through each stage to ensure its dynamic nature. Finally, the fourth principle is 'the single remedy', meaning that only one homoeopathic remedy should be administered at a time.

Homoeopathic practitioners believe that people differ in the way their bodies react to an illness, according to their temperament. Consequently, this calls for the need to match the characteristics of the patient (i.e. taking into consideration their temperament, personality, and emotional and physical states) with the remedy to be prescribed (whether it be a plant, mineral or other substance). A homoeopath therefore studies the person as a whole, treating the individual rather than just the disease. As a result, patients suffering from the same illness may actually be prescribed different remedies, which many people find difficult to comprehend.

Vogel and I were certain that God had created a remedy in nature to treat every illness and disease but believed that it is up to man to find the particular remedy that should be administered. It is, therefore, vital that the practitioner treating the patient is educated in the ways of homoeopathy, because one incorrectly prescribed remedy – even in its lowest potency – can cause a great deal of damage. Throughout our many years of practice, both Vogel and I unfortunately came across many cases where such damage had been done by wrongly prescribed medicines. One woman who stands out in my mind came to see me while I was giving a talk in a health food store in Kent. She had been suffering with various problems for over two years and told me that she had been prescribed the constitutional remedy *Sepia*. While this can be a wonderful remedy and has helped many people, it was completely unsuitable for this woman's symptoms, which had continued to get worse. I immediately prescribed *Ovarium* and she soon contacted me to thank me, as she was feeling so much better.

I cannot praise Vogel enough for the extensive research he carried out – even to the extent of testing remedies on himself – before prescribing a product. He went to great lengths to ensure that his remedies had no side effects and, as part of this process, he considered the effects that the treatments would have on all three bodies of Man. As described earlier, these brilliant remedies have provided the backbone for my work throughout the world.

Vogel and I talked a lot about Hahnemann's methods, one of which was to form an image of a person – and by looking at that image and talking to the patient, it becomes easier to determine where the problem may lie. I recall a mother and her little girl who came to talk to us following one particular lecture. I immediately sensed which type of characteristics this child had and realised that she was very much what we would term a '*Pulsatilla* child'. The person usually in need of *Pulsatilla* is a blue-eyed, blonde-haired individual, has a sensitive disposition, bursts into tears easily, needs comfort, hates quarrelling, has difficulty in digesting fatty foods, sometimes has poor circulation and, because the *Pulsatilla* type is often over-conscientious, has problems with the ears, bladder infections and diarrhoea. When answering Vogel's questions, the mother confirmed that these were precisely the problems affecting her child, who particularly suffered from recurrent bladder infections. Vogel and I had come to the same conclusion about this child without exchanging a single word. As her whole constitution pointed to the fact that she really needed to be treated as a *Pulsatilla* child, I wrote down on a piece of paper that her mother should give her *Pulsatilla D6*. A very grateful letter later followed from her, stating that, within a week, her daughter's problems had cleared up.

In homoeopathy, the combination of an individual's physical and mental characteristics is called their 'constitution', and *Pulsatilla* is what would be described as a constitutional remedy. When such a remedy is applied, one has to be extremely careful, as sometimes the symptoms will initially get worse. This is because, as Hahnemann advocated, there is a requirement to stimulate the body's own defence mechanisms to fight the illness and remove it from the body rather than, as in conventional medicine, suppressing the symptoms and, thus, keeping the illness within the body.

As was stressed to this child's mother, it is important when a constitutional remedy is prescribed that the patient gets plenty of fresh air, lots of rest and is kept warm. With the older *Pulsatilla* types, we often come across additional ailments such as headaches and menstrual problems.

This brings to mind another case that Vogel and I worked on together, where we had confirmation of Hahnemann's principles being so appropriate in this day and age. In this instance, we were consulted by a young policeman's wife. She was totally despondent when she first came to see us. Not only had she been on the verge of ending her own life on several occasions but she had also almost ended the lives of her husband and two children when she lost control and tried to drive her car into the river in an attempt to drown them. Various specialists had diagnosed her condition completely incorrectly – with their opinions varying from depression to ME – and some even admitted that they did not know what was wrong with her. When we saw her, however, I quickly remarked to Vogel that she had many characteristics of someone in need of *Gentiana*.

After finding out a bit about her medical history, Vogel and I were in total agreement that she had serious problems. Her lymph glands in her neck, armpits and groin were all swollen – and I commented to Vogel that her whole system seemed to be poisoned. Our diagnosis was confirmed when the results of a blood test showed high levels of toxicity within her body. Her lymph system had become completely congested with waste material, which had infected her blood and, as a result, her system had become very toxic. She had a lot of amalgam in the fillings in her teeth, her diet was appalling and, due to her prolonged ill health, a great strain had been put on her relationship with her husband.

We both looked at this woman who was so poorly and distraught. She was physically, mentally and emotionally imbalanced. I suggested that we started by giving her a combination of *Gentiana* and the homoeopathic remedy called *Arsenicum*, and then carry out a thorough detoxification. We started to treat her with the two constitutional remedies – one to be taken for the first month, then followed by the second – talked to her at length about ways of improving her diet and, following that, detoxified her system with the *Detox Box* of Alfred Vogel. This is a ten-day elimination programme during which the patient takes *Calendula Complex*, *Frangula Complex*, *Milk Thistle Complex* and *Solidago Complex* in regulated amounts.

As her immune system had been given a tremendous knock, it took us some time before we were able to make a breakthrough but eventually she made a steady recovery and has never looked back.

The Vogel *Detox Box* arose from a discussion that Alfred and I had during a trip to Canada in the 1970s. One morning while we were eating breakfast in the hotel restaurant, we looked around at the variety of different foods people were eating. When we noticed what one particular family had selected, we both shook our heads. Because I practise Chinese facial diagnosis, I commented to Vogel that the entire family had liver toxicity. We then discussed the best way in which to give the body a thorough spring clean. As a consequence of that talk, the *Detox Box* was conceived, which is now recognised all over the world as being one of the finest products on the market. Detoxification is not only a great way of spring cleaning the gall bladder, liver, bowel, kidneys and stomach, but it also starts the detoxification process of the lymph system.

During a later trip to San Francisco, when I conducted a consultation in a health food store, I learned that this treatment was particularly popular there because in that part of the United States there was a lot of pollution in the air and people wanted to do everything they could to clear it from their system. Later on, I devised a diet to be used in conjunction with the *Detox Box* and, today, I am happy to see that this treatment is still sold all over the world.

To find harmony between the physical, mental and emotional bodies is not an easy task. We have to contend with a lot of negative influences such as pollution, which undoubtedly has played an enormous role in the escalation of many modern illnesses and diseases. Now in the twenty-first century, we are witnessing a daily increase in the number of people suffering from allergies, as their immune systems are unable to cope with the poisonous chemicals that are all around us. As well as pollution, allergic reactions can be caused by such things as artificial food colourings, but whatever the cause they should be seen as an alarm bell indicating that something in the body needs attention. This situation is only made worse by the increase in stress caused by pressures at work, unforeseen circumstances and unhappiness. Health problems resulting from asthma and bronchitis are also increasing by the day.

I remember when a girl, aged about eight, came to see us. She was in complete turmoil. Not only did she suffer from hyperventilation and panic attacks but she was also slightly asthmatic. When we started to dig into her medical history, we soon discovered where her problems lay. Her system was being attacked by three obvious problems, namely, (a) her living conditions, (b) her unhappy family life, and (c) the most appalling diet. That unfortunate child was taking three different inhalers, in addition to other medication, just to keep her condition under control. The house in which she lived was filthy, exacerbating her allergy to dust, and her life circumstances in general were appalling.

In an attempt to get her condition under control, we first looked at ways of improving her diet, which entailed the withdrawal of cow's milk and cheese, and the introduction of supplements of B, C, D and E vitamins. We prescribed the anti-allergy homoeopathic remedy *Luffa Complex*, which is also ideal for desensitising the system, together with herbal *Drosinula Syrup* and some *Passiflora* to make her calmer. I also taught her some exercises to help her relax and gave her some acupuncture. Importantly, I was also able to talk to her parents about the home situation and gave them advice about diet and lifestyle. Later on, I also added some homoeopathic remedies to her treatment. She was a lovely girl, who thankfully followed our advice to the letter. Today, when I still sometimes see her, I think back to what her circumstances once were. Her case is a perfect example of how it is important not just to treat a patient's physical symptoms but also to look beyond these and get to the root of the problem as best we can.

I am aware that we all lead busy lives today, but it is now more important than ever that we make time to look thoroughly into the background of illnesses and diseases to try and find out how they started and in what circumstances they developed. This reminds me of a young woman who came to see me while Vogel was working with me in Scotland. Although this girl consulted us about a minor problem, we both became aware that, deep down, there was more to it than she had led us to believe. It was only when we examined her situation in greater detail that we both became aware that she was suicidal. She finally confided in us that she had personal problems – and this is where homoeopathy often comes into its own. When we carefully delved a bit deeper into her background, we realised that she was actually suffering from a severe emotional imbalance. It emerged that she had been in a relationship for many years but the relationship never really progressed and, when she finally realised that her boyfriend had been stringing her along, she became extremely distressed, as she was very fond of him. Sadly, women often take relationships far more seriously than men and it is easy to appreciate how such an emotional incident can have a detrimental effect on a person, like this girl, who was actually slowly dying of a broken heart. This might sound implausible but I have actually witnessed this happening once during the years I have been in practice.

When we chatted a little bit more to her, and Vogel and I pointed out certain things to her, sharing with her a few things we had learned about life and relationships along the way, she nodded, and I could see that she was starting to take in what we were saying and beginning to trust us. It became apparent that she was also consumed with jealousy, as this particular fellow had been seeing other women while involved with her but, even in spite of this, she still loved him so much.

We realised we had our work cut out in getting this emotional upset completely out of her system but, thankfully, we were eventually able to help her. In addition to some homoeopathic remedies, we also prescribed some flower remedies and after she had recovered from this whole unpleasant experience, she asked me to explain how we had been able to treat her. I told her that the symptoms she had were not the disease, only evidence of a disease, and that one of the benefits of homoeopathy is that it goes to the source of the problem. I told this young lady that she had been completely out of tune with her body because of her failed relationship and, as mentioned earlier, the three bodies (mental, emotional and physical) must be in tune with each other to bring harmony. The constitutional remedy that we used in this instance was *Aurum* and she listened intently as I told her that, in homoeopathy, we have learned the precision of a healing system which conceives all symptoms as part of a larger whole, which appears to stimulate the body's natural force, rather than attacking parts. Homoeopathy will work with us, not against us.

Unfortunately, many people are still sceptical about homoeopathy. I remember when I was invited to attend an important talk given for health insurers in Holland. As the main speaker was one of the most eminent pharmacologists in Holland, this generated a lot of interest, which was evident by the number of professors, doctors and scientists who attended. I wasn't terribly pleased at having to be present at that particular talk as I felt this professor was opposed to homoeopathy and herbal medicine. This was confirmed when he started the discussion by saying that the benefits of homoeopathy could be likened to the situation where a little boy fell in the street and his mother gently kissed his wound to make it better – it offered comfort but not real results.

A very lively debate developed and at the end he admitted that I had managed to make him think again. Not long after that discussion, which was covered extensively in the Dutch media, Vogel had an interview with that particular professor. I was very interested when the professor told him that most doctors in Holland were major users of herbal remedies. Vogel told him that even in countries where the governments were opposed to natural medicine, herbal medicine was taking over, as people wanted freedom of choice. As Vogel and I often said, you cannot argue with results.

There is a growing consensus in the world that the massive amount of money allocated to medical research has failed to achieve any significant improvement in Western societies' levels of health. The incidence of major, chronic diseases like cancer, diabetes and heart disease continues to climb, and homoeopathy offers a time-tested method that meets the need for additional non-toxic therapy. It is reassuring to know that, when homoeopathic remedies are administered properly, there are no side effects. This is a very important part of the whole concept of homoeopathy, which encompasses all areas of medical care, from prevention to emergency and acute care, as well as the treatment of chronic diseases. It offers the individual improved health and quality of life. As I stated in *Fifty Years Fighting*, I cannot understand why medical practitioners would resist this system, or why they would insist on administering aggressive drugs instead of looking for a more natural solution.

Luckily a change of attitude is now taking place all over the world with more and more scientific tests being carried out to prove the efficacy of herbal and homoeopathic remedies. As we are gaining ground, it is greatly encouraging to see how natural medicine works in instances where orthodox remedies might have failed. I often mention one of Vogel's sayings in lectures, 'We are born in nature, we belong to nature and if we obey the laws of nature, then we obey the laws of God.'

13

It is very important to be in tune with your body.

Jan de Vries

Nowadays, many people in the Western world are obsessed with body image. It would, however, be more beneficial if they became familiar with the way their body works rather than just the way it looks, as it is vital that we learn to recognise the warning signs when something may be going wrong. The last thing I want to do is turn people into hypochondriacs or neurotics but we need to pay attention to our bodies when they tell us to 'STOP'. A lot of people, including myself, often ignore the warning signs and try to carry on regardless. If this is allowed to happen, then the body will draw on its own reserve energies, and as soon as these energies become low, our immune system is laid open to attack. This is what happened to me in Australia when I contracted a virus and then developed diabetes. I had been working too hard, preparing for Alfred's arrival, and my resistance to infection was low. Contrary to general opinion, you cannot catch a virus easily; the body must be susceptible to attack, and this can have disastrous results.

It is most annoying if we hear a few notes at a concert that are out of tune. We then say, 'That is not right.' I wish it was possible to deal with the body's imbalances as easily as we can deal with an out-of-tune musical instrument.

The other day, I had a visit from a lady who was 103. It was apparent that she was incredibly alert and intelligent from the questions she asked me and she also told me about the daily duties she was still able to attend to. I was so impressed at how sharp-witted she was that I knew there must be an explanation, so I explained to her that I was in the process of gathering a wide variety of information for a new series

334

of books that I was going to write called *Jan de Vries's Health Secrets*. I told her a little about my great friend Alfred Vogel, remarking on how fresh his mind had been right up to the end and how he had given me many tips, and then I asked her if she would mind letting me into her own secret. She told me the same thing that my grandmother had told me when she was 98 years of age: 'The secret to good health and a bright mind is to keep yourself up to date with everything'. Although by that time in her life my grandmother could no longer see and needed the help of an assistant, she still made sure that she kept her mind active by doing daily crosswords.

This lady told me that as well as keeping up to date she kept in tune with her body and whenever something went wrong – even if it was something like a minor cold – she took action straight away. She is one of the countless people who believes that *Echinaforce* from Alfred Vogel is an outstanding remedy and, like Vogel (who used *Echinaforce* throughout his life because of the fine composition of this remedy), she didn't believe in discontinuing it. She informed me that she had been taking *Echinaforce* for the last 30 years, 'to keep me fit and healthy'. I am often asked if there is any reason why *Echinaforce* cannot be taken continuously and my view is that *Echinacea* is an immune booster while *Echinaforce* is an immune balancer. *Echinacea* should be taken when immunity may be low to give the system a boost, while *Echinaforce* helps to maintain a high level of immunity. During the 50 years I have been in practice and in all the years I have worked with *Echinaforce*, I can honestly say that I have never come across a single side effect and I have witnessed the tremendous benefits that people have obtained from this excellent treatment.

This elderly lady was very well informed, as she told me that she had read about Samuel Hahnemann's belief in the vital force in the body and wanted to ask me about it. He said something along the lines of, 'I make sure that my vital organs are taken care of and that the vital force is in tune.' It is this vital force and its healing mechanism which are stimulated by homoeopathic or herbal remedies, and naturopathic therapy is used to release blockages which sometimes can occur in this vital force. Hahnemann put a lot of emphasis on the fact that the vital force should flow freely. In my own practice, I have often seen in acupuncture that, by relieving one small energy blockage, the whole body is then allowed to strive to get back into tune.

We see with homoeopathic remedies that they often work as an adjunctive and supportive mechanism to standard medical therapies.

They are certainly not a replacement. The medical establishment, however, sometimes believes that this is the aim of complementary therapists – to replace them – and there are those who would like to see homoeopathy banned for that reason. Although this medical art has been used for centuries to treat illness, it was not designed for severe or chronic conditions, and we really have to try and understand how they work. My 103-year-old patient was completely familiar with that fact and I was amazed how, even with some of the constitutional remedies that she told me about, she was able to control some pain that she experienced.

It is quite amazing what one is capable of achieving with the use of homoeopathic remedies. This lady mentioned to me how she once managed to clear a nasty allergy by taking Vogel's *Luffa Complex*, and as I had a little time to spare, I told her the story about the development of this remedy, in which she was totally engrossed.

I am still acquainted with the Swiss chemist who had a tremendous input into Vogel's remedies. He worked on *Luffa Complex* with his team of co-workers and they developed this marvellous preparation by combining seven healthy plants from various parts of the world, though, of course, Vogel was involved at every stage. The first ingredient used was *Cardiospermum halicacabum*, which was later discovered to be extremely valuable in the treatment of allergies and skin problems, and is found in large quantities in Madeira. It also contains a North African remedy called *Ammi visnaga* (or *Khella*) which comes from the bark of a tree and is used to bring relief to those suffering from cramps and spasms. In addition, it contains a natural histamine which makes it invaluable to hay fever sufferers. *Okoubaka* is another component, which is taken from the bark of a tree in West Africa and is regularly used to neutralise poisons. *Aralia racemosa* comes from North America and is of remarkable help in treating respiratory problems and troublesome coughs. Mexico is the source of the next two ingredients. A plant called *Galphimia glauca* grows there, which greatly helps strengthen the tissues in the body, while the *Larrea mexicana* plant, which has quite a pleasant scent, can be found in the north of the country. Finally, there is *Luffa operculata*, one of the main ingredients in *Luffa Complex*. This comes from Colombia. So, natural resources from around the world have been brought together to formulate this excellent remedy, which I have often prescribed with great success for those whose bodies are slightly out of tune.

While writing this chapter, I recalled an elegant young couple who came to see me one busy Saturday. They made such an attractive pair and yet I could see by the expressions on their faces that something was bothering them. They were certainly in tune with each other, but their body energies were completely out of tune. It does not take a lot for this to happen and everyday incidents can easily accelerate this imbalance. The man was almost in tears as he told me that everything had been fine until one day when he was at work he got a phone call to inform him that his mother had died that afternoon. The person who conveyed this message was certainly not diplomatic and this news had a devastating impact on the fellow. The following day, he felt unwell and started to cough (which was probably a nervous cough). With each day that passed, he became more ill, and his wife became worried when she realised that he was still not right after his mother's funeral.

A series of little incidents occurred which caused his health to go completely out of tune. Unfortunately, he didn't want to communicate with anyone and had become totally withdrawn. On top of that, his sexual desires had diminished to such a level that he no longer felt capable of having a loving relationship with his wife. He was a sad young man but, as he said, he had an attractive wife who showed him great compassion and they would do anything possible to get things back in order.

There were a lot of things that needed to be done. First, he still had not come to terms with the grief he felt for his late mother and, to offer him some help in this direction, I prescribed *Ignatia*, which greatly assists in taking the sting out of bereavement. He had an extremely unhealthy diet and had started to drink excessively as a way of drowning his sorrows, which, of course, had the effect of further reducing his sexual appetite and he felt he had come to the end of the road. I went over all this with him in detail, then adjusted his diet and, because he was desperate to get well, he was very willing to cooperate. I introduced wheatgerm into his diet and even included some wheatgerm capsules from Alfred Vogel. I managed to cleanse his liver with the introduction of *Milk Thistle Complex* and then stimulated his prostate (as he also had problems in that area) with the fresh herbal extract *Saw Palmetto*. I also prescribed some *Vitality Essence*, together with some extra Vogel vitamins. He reported to me three weeks later that things were starting to improve, except he still had many problems with his sleep pattern. We managed to rectify this with some *Valerian Hops* (25 drops taken half an hour before going to bed).

Surprisingly, within a very short space of time, he was back in tune with his body. This, in turn, made him see things more positively and he was able to appreciate his wife again. I saw them some time later while still writing this book and they reminded me of the importance of being in tune with your body.

14

Nature always overrules science.
                              Jan de Vries

A middle-aged lady came to see me at my London clinic one day looking extremely healthy and happy. Although she lives abroad and I had not seen her for a number of years, I instantly recognised her. Her friendly smile now lit up her face but I could not help but remember a very different picture, as we had experienced a particularly anxious time when trying to treat her as a young girl. She smiled at me as she said, 'Can you believe how well I am? I now have three children, and I just wanted to come to tell you how grateful I am for everything you have done for me.'

I was so pleased to see her because I sometimes get depressed when I dwell on the many illnesses and diseases I see every day. It is very heartening when one is able to see the evidence of how nature can help people, particularly those who have come to the end of the road in terms of what conventional medicine can offer them. This particular patient had been crippled with arthritis at a very young age. Her doctors were unable to help her but, thankfully, with the application of acupuncture and the prescription of some remedies, I was able to turn her situation around.

I was once called to a London hospital where I found the distraught parents of a young girl sitting helplessly at her bedside. They had come from Nigeria in the hope of finding help but the doctors were baffled as to what was wrong with their daughter until they eventually diagnosed systemic lupus erythematosus (SLE). This is a chronic, multi-system inflammatory disease that can affect any and every organ, and by the time the diagnosis was made, she was in such a bad way that she was not expected to live more than a few weeks.

From her bed, the young girl looked up at me with big brown eyes as if pleading, 'Please help me.' I talked to her and, indeed, I too was worried because, after carrying out some iris diagnosis, feeling her pulse and looking at her tongue, I could see that her system was being poisoned. She had an extremely congested lymphatic system and a lot of skin problems, both of which are indicators of SLE. I took a blood sample, which was extensively researched and, from that, it was concluded that a lot of poisonous material had been accumulating in her system, probably for a few years.

I immediately set about prescribing some remedies for her – such as a strong antioxidant, *Petasites*, very high levels of vitamin C and as much beetroot juice as she could drink. After I saw the results of her blood test, I also phoned Alfred Vogel and explained the situation to him. As luck would have it, he said that he was actually going to be taking a break from his travels to visit London and he would be willing to see her.

A week later, he joined me at the bedside of this young girl in one of London's foremost hospitals. Vogel was also shocked at what he saw and said that we would need to use a strange, old-fashioned remedy that his grandmother regularly used when faced with serious problems. I was fascinated by his story of how the roots of couch grass were extremely helpful in cases such as this and immediately went to get some fresh couch grass juice via a friend in London who had agreed to help us. Vogel looked at her compassionately, took her pulse and said, 'I am sure she is going to make it.' Although she was critically ill at that time, he was right.

As soon as she awakened each morning, this young girl was given a small glass of fresh couch grass juice to drink. Fortunately I had planned to be in London for a few days and was therefore able to call on her after she had taken the initial dose. As her temperature continued to rise, the doctors were becoming increasingly alarmed that she would not pull through but, nevertheless, they were all willing to help. Once she started to show signs of improvement, they began to have faith in what we were doing and became so supportive that they left it up to us to do what we felt necessary as, scientifically, they could do nothing further to help this young girl. The end result was that she survived – with a simple helping hand from nature.

I have experienced many times in practice that nature can overrule science. Often it is not until we give nature a chance that we discover the solution to a problem.

I have told the story many times of when I was in a quandary over a patient's needs and Vogel advised me to go to the seaside or into the fields to ponder over what nature could offer to help. I am pleased to say that I have never been disappointed by the many answers that have sometimes been literally lying at my feet. The answer often becomes clear when I can actually see the herbs, plants or even trees which might offer me a clue, through their signatures or characteristics, as to what I should use to help a patient.

Situated across from Vogel's house was the Ida Wegmann Institute and I vividly recollect when we went there to study what they were practising. Vogel reminded me of one of their main remedies – Mistletoe (*Viscum album*) – and explained why they had chosen mistletoe preparations to help treat cancer patients. When he saw mistletoe growing in an oak tree, he used to say to me, 'Look what that is doing. The mistletoe is growing like a parasite on the tree just as cancer grows like a parasite in the human body.' It has been proved that *Mistletoe* can stimulate cell metabolism and, as this is generally weak in cancer patients, mistletoe preparations offer a valuable treatment. It is sometimes known as 'the plant of life and death', as it has both negatives and positives. It gives a clear message – 'Please use me. I am growing here like a parasite, killing this tree, just as cancer does, in this tree of life, which is what Man really is. Use me homoeopathically so that I can attack and kill off the cancer cells in the body, which are slowly killing this life within us.' During my years in practice, I have repeatedly been amazed at the remarkable results that can be achieved by using this parasitic plant.

Sometimes we are blind to what is going on around us. We must open our eyes to find the herb, plant or tree created by God that can help us. I am a firm believer that God has kept his promise by supplying us with everything in nature that we need to heal and protect our health – although it is up to Man to discover how these plants can be used. Instead of spending millions of pounds in finding out what happens on the moon or in examining the stars, we should be investigating and researching what is out there in nature and how it can be used to alleviate human suffering. After all, that is our greatest responsibility. Vogel used to say in his lectures, 'We are each other's debtors. We have to help each other in this often difficult life, and by sharing in each other's difficulties, we are helping wherever we can, which is of the utmost importance.'

A well-known gentleman entered my consulting room recently. I immediately recognised him and was aware of the high position he held. He looked sharply at me and, before even sitting down, asked, 'Do you practise intuitive medicine?' As nobody had ever asked me that before, I pondered over it for a moment. I asked him to sit down and enquired what he really meant by his question. He explained that he had followed my work for a long time, had read my books and was of the opinion that I must do a lot through intuition. He then asked if I believed in the sixth sense. I replied that I believed there are five tangible senses and, indeed, I did believe that intuition was a sixth sense. This response seemed to reassure him, as he then said he wanted me to treat him. I proceeded to examine him, carried out the necessary tests to confirm what was wrong and, fortunately, his treatment was successful.

Whilst writing this book, and thinking about that particular gentleman, I recalled an incident that took place an extremely long time ago when Alfred Vogel and I were waiting for the arrival of our train. A young family of five were also at the station – the parents and their three children. In that dank station, Vogel focused his attention on one particular child and became eager to talk to the family. Eventually he went up to them and enquired what was wrong with their child. The mother started to cry and said she was so pleased that we had approached them, even though she had no idea who Vogel or I were. With Vogel's knowledge and experience, he intuitively knew that there was something seriously wrong with that child and he wanted the mother's confirmation that he was correct. As it turned out, the parents stated that their daughter had leukaemia.

While Vogel spoke to these parents, he asked me to take down some notes. He then explained who he was and offered his help. He asked me to send some medicines for this child, free of charge. He assured the family that we would keep in contact with them and help their child to the best of our ability. After we had all the information we needed about this young girl, and received her parents' agreement to treat her, their train arrived and, as it pulled out of the station, I caught a glimpse of the happy expression on Vogel's face as he had yet again given help where it was needed. Many years have passed since our encounter at that dark station when everyone showed concern for that lovely young girl. Her parents wrote faithfully to me and, today, it is comforting to know that their daughter is alive and well.

There are often outward signs of what is happening inwardly. It was for that reason that I studied Chinese facial diagnosis and also the type of outgoing energy each individual possesses. Scientifically, that can be difficult to explain, but when one is close to nature, one often finds the answers.

Vogel was also blessed with a seventh sense. When he was faced with tremendous worries, he tried to look at problems from a humorous angle. That seventh sense – the sense of humour – was something that frequently helped him through difficult times. Like Vogel, having a sense of humour has helped me when things have not been easy, as I have written in *Fifty Years Fighting*. It is therefore important to look forward and never to lose that sense of humour. After all, it takes much less effort to smile than to frown.

When I helped to launch Vogel's first book, *The Nature Doctor*, in Holland, I was very aware that he had written it as he wanted to share his knowledge with others. It soon sold over 500,000 copies. Virtually every household in Holland now owns a copy and it has sold over 2,500,000 worldwide. This book, however, is only the tip of the iceberg in relation to the knowledge Vogel had. It provides first-hand advice on natural healing methods but he ends this informative book by saying:

> On the other hand, let me say that there is one little 'herb' I do not know either, the one referred to in an old proverb: 'There's many a herb to cure, Not one, however, for death, to be sure.' I am fully aware that my medical advice is but a help for dealing with the times in which we live.

We only have one chance at this life and so we must make the most of it. No one wants to live with problems, so we must do all we can to minimise or eliminate difficulties. On a daily basis in my practice I hear patients say, 'Oh well, I have a problem. I will have to live with it.' This is not true. If you have a problem, then you must make every effort to eradicate it, in order to have as fulfilling a life as possible.

It is said that 'you get out of life what you put into it', or 'you reap what you sow'. When we invest in our health, it is essential that we do so sensibly. As I have said in a previous chapter, there is nothing common about common sense. We should all set aside some time to sit down and contemplate where we are going wrong. Our own intuition will guide us and help us to restore balance. If we have lost that sense, then we have lost everything. My mother used to stress the importance of listening 'to your inner voice', which will tell us what we should or shouldn't do. By being in tune with our bodies, we will achieve greater happiness and enjoy good health.

In coming to the end of this autobiography, I would like to add how grateful I am to my Creator for letting me be a little part in this life. Although I am only a small drop in the ocean, it is comforting to know that everyone on earth belongs to that ocean. I am also grateful to those who have shown me the way to truth, reality and understanding. When I look at the sun, the moon and stars, the fields, the trees and flowers – in fact, all that is around us – I am thankful that I am a small part of that great creation, where I have seen that nature will always overrule science.

Although we live in a world of great unrest, terrorism and unhappiness, we have to look forward to the future that lies before us, to a time when we will be able to conquer illness and untimely death.

The last time I met with my great friend Alfred Vogel, we reflected, with grateful thanks, on the many years we had worked together and the part we had been able to play in alleviating human suffering. Looking back over the many positive results we had achieved made us both feel very humble that we could be used to show a way forward in a world where so many systems have failed. And nearly 40 years after we first met, we both agreed that nature is still our best friend.

AFTERWORD

Not long ago, on a beautiful Sunday afternoon, I picked up my bicycle and cycled around the edge of the golf course until I almost reached Prestwick. On my return journey, I looked at the construction which was under way for the new clubhouse and then cycled passed Mokoia, the first clinic we opened. Mokoia has since been converted into seven flats, but it has retained its charm and beauty. As I stood by the outside wall, a flood of memories came rushing back into my mind. It was at this very building that we arrived in Scotland on 2 January 1970. Although many years have passed since then, those memories are still so clear in my mind.

People from all over the world came to Mokoia to be helped, not only to consult me, but also the other practitioners who followed the principles set out by Alfred Vogel and me. I received thousands of testimonials over those years from patients who, having gone through the normal orthodox channels and felt they had come to the end of the road, decided to give us a try. I also thought of the failures and the possible reasons for them; they are the reason I am still dedicated to studying and working to improve people's health wherever I possibly can.

I asked myself if there really is a need for complementary medicine. Then I thought of the many people from all walks of life who have come to me for help: famous film stars, sportsmen and women and singers, the rich and the poor, all with a similar story to tell, who finally consulted me in the hope that another form of medicine might bring them the relief they longed for. They had become disillusioned and did not know what to do next or where to turn. I am like a Scottish collie that never lets go but tries and tries again. Sometimes this can take a long time, but sometimes all it takes is one simple adjustment to improve a situation which, if left untreated, could have persisted for years. As I always say to students during lectures, 'Medicine is not difficult. It is often common sense.' I have learned through undertaking specialist studies, particularly in manipulation and manipulative therapies, that it often takes only one small adjustment to enable a patient who has come into my clinic almost crippled to then walk out of my door unaided and onto the golf course to play their game!

As the years have gone by, I have encountered a lot of jealousy, both from those involved in orthodox medicine and from those in my own profession. Why should such ill feeling exist when we are all here to help people lead a healthier life? The selfishness in the world is getting worse. Everything nowadays is focused on money. As I sat on that small wall at Mokoia, looking up at the magnificence of the clouds and the sky and the beauty surrounding us in nature, I felt so sad that people had become so motivated by financial gain. I try to encourage people to use the strength that lies within them. Most of us are unaware that we possess this inner strength. We have only scratched the surface when it comes to understanding it. It must be remembered that positive attitudes need positive action.

While resting there, I thought about the day I spent with the psychic Uri Geller, when we took part in a lecture together. Although I was always very sceptical about his work, while he was demonstrating with the aid of several objects, I could see by the enormous concentration he displayed that there was nothing gimmicky about what he was doing – it was simply that he had discovered the secret of energy and the strong powers that the mind has to overcome terrific problems. Before he performed a certain exercise, he produced a few packets of tomato seeds that he had bought that day and, as proof, he showed me the receipt from the shop where he had made his purchase. He said he wanted to show me something. He took one packet of the seeds, placed some in the palm of his hand and told the seeds to grow. Almost instantly, those seeds began to sprout. Then he asked four children from the audience for their help. He gave the children some seeds from the same packet, asked them to place the seeds in the palms of their hands and to shout at the seeds that they should grow, and again, within seconds, they grew. He repeated the demonstration with the second packet of seeds, and it was amazing to see that those seeds also sprouted. In other words, he had used his positive mind to tell them to grow – and it worked. It wasn't a trick; it was a straightforward exercise to show how powerful the mind is. He said that you need to believe and to tell the brain what it needs to do. If you do not have that belief, you will get nowhere. If you believe that the seeds will grow, then they will, but if you have doubts, they won't.

This is what life is all about. We often doubt. We often don't believe that the treatment we get in hospital or from the doctor will be successful. I see this with patients who have given up and believe they will never get better. This is not the case. Our energy is much stronger than we think. It is possible to do the impossible if our belief is strong enough and by using our energy so that we can, with God's help, increase our own energies. It is quite remarkable what we are capable of doing. I was again amazed at the realisation that God will work with you, but not for you. We have to play our part and discover how wonderful this energy is. In several of my books, I have tried to share my studies and views on this matter.

As my mind returned to the present, I picked up my bike, and, as I cycled further, I thought of the 50-plus years during which I have been working in this field. My mind wandered all the way back to the beginning of my journey, to when, as a student at the young age of 18, I assisted a well-known professor in a Dutch hospital. He was an extremely intelligent man who shared a lot of his knowledge with me and who created in me that great desire to help other people.

I then cycled to Auchenkyle, which became our second clinic in Scotland. I felt at peace and at rest that Sunday afternoon – as the Americans would say, it was awesome. I rested my bicycle against the wall and sat down on the front steps, turning my mind to the beautiful old tree beside the coffee shop. I then wondered what that tree would say if it could only speak, if it would tell its age, its size and its strength. That particular tree had been planted in sandy soil covered with good-quality topsoil. I pondered again how it was possible for that enormous tree to have grown to its present size without having had the best feeding. Its widespread roots are close to the surface of the ground, and it is quite remarkable how it is able to withstand the strong sea winds and the storms that have battered it over the years. According to its size, I estimated that it must be around 150 to 200 years old. It shows the enormous energy within the tree and the strength that it has, even although it has not had the best nutrition. This underlines the fact that the strength in nature is immeasurable. Think of those tomato seeds sprouting in Uri Geller's hand at the conference.

On a daily basis, people from all walks of life flood in to Auchenkyle.

In the over 40 books I have written, and in contributing to magazines such as *In Touch*, I try to get the following message across: when people say to me, 'Thank God, you have cured me', I always reply that I have never cured anyone; it is God who cures, I only treat, and it is the strength within the patient that helps to cure. Positive will always win over negative, but it depends on how these are balanced. I turned my head to the side to look at the tarmac as I sat on the steps and was reminded of the time when I showed a psychiatrist's wife how strong we really are. I pointed out to her that some small crocuses had enough energy and strength to push their way through all the rubble and the tarmac on the ground so that we could see them in all their glory.

What was meant, then, when the Dutch national poet, P.A. de Genestet, said that God was mindful of him? He said that we are all wonderfully made, but we often abuse our bodies by consuming rubbish and by the way we live. How grateful I was that Sunday afternoon to experience not only the beautiful sunshine but also the thought that I was a small part of this world. A lady in despair once said to me that she felt absolutely worthless, and I told her that although she felt like just a small drop in the ocean, she still belonged to that great ocean of God's love.

How strong are we really, though? It is sometimes quite amazing to discover, by observing our own experiences, how strong we really are and how often we actually depend on that strength. Such was the case when I went to Australia about eight years ago, the story of which I have given an account of in Part One, 'A Step at a Time'. To recap, I was struck by an unknown virus, which was largely my own fault. We sometimes believe we are like a machine or a long-life battery. When I went into the bush, I caught this virus, which caused pneumonia, resulting in the destruction of half my pancreas. The consequence of this was that I became a diabetic overnight. Over the years, to the astonishment of my diabetic specialist and my own doctor, I have managed to keep this completely in hand through diet, although initially I did have an extremely high blood-sugar level. To this day, I still adhere to a restricted diet and take some natural remedies to keep it under control.

As I have always said, a person does not have only a physical body but three bodies: mental, physical and emotional. When some jealous colleagues conspired against me and tricked me, my emotional body was given such a knock that not only was my diabetic condition upset but the emotional turmoil also took its toll on my heart, resulting in a lot of damage. This injustice affected my health to the extent that I had to attend a cardiologist. He was very understanding but, as the damage had affected me badly, he spoke about the possibility of open-heart surgery. This shocked me as, although I had understood that the situation was not good, I realised then that this was in fact very serious. Once I picked up the pieces, I started to work on this problem and created a very good programme for myself. It took nearly six months before I was over that scare, and, luckily, at a recent check-up, the cardiologist was surprised that I no longer required surgical intervention, and he was quite happy for me to continue taking the remedies I had chosen for myself. Once again, I was grateful to nature for the benefits I obtained from *Crataegus*, which is a widely used herbal remedy for the heart. I took this in combination with garlic and some remedies chosen to lower both my blood pressure and my cholesterol, such as *Blood Pressure Factors*, *Cholesterol Factors* and *CoEQ10*, along with a few homoeopathic remedies. When I left the hospital that day, I thanked God once more that I had been able to get this condition under control without the need for surgery.

As I sat at the entrance of Auchenkyle and thought of the thousands of patients who have walked through that door, I was grateful that, with my own health, I have proved to be a good example of what natural remedies are capable of achieving. As a result, I understand even better the vital role that complementary medicine fills. I have really been thankful for the cooperation of consultants and my GP, and the understanding between orthodox and complementary medicine. In working together, they can be such a blessing to people in need.

I then cycled over the bridge at Auchenkyle and around the golf course to my home. I sat again for a moment on the wall of my neighbour's house to ponder a little over the years we have been neighbours, when my thoughts turned to a St Bernard dog we used to have, called Sheba. Sheba always depended on me for her Sunday walk. She taught me many lessons and was very wise. I remember once we went for a walk on the golf course and came across two small dogs fighting with each other. Sheba ran up to them and growled, which gave them such a shock that they parted company and went their own separate ways. That is something we often see in life. I remember that during practical chemistry lessons in school, we often made such a noise that it disturbed the rest of class. When a certain teacher entered the room, all he needed to do was to bang on the table for everyone to go back to their places. That is an admirable gift. Today, in this life, we see that those gifts are missing. Where is the respect? Where is the discipline? Where is the humanity? Indeed, do people respect life?

As it was such a beautiful day, I decided to go a bit further, when my thoughts turned to the days when I was one of the best cyclists in Holland. When I was young, I was able to build up an enormous speed, but nowadays, because of my age, I am a bit slower. When I think of the speed of life, I am glad that as I, thankfully, grow older, I am trying to take things a little easier. I am grateful for merely being part of life and just filling, with some responsibility, a necessary place. I am especially grateful that, after all my years fighting, I know there is a space for what we now call complementary medicine. I clearly understood from the cardiologist and diabetic specialist that I had abused my body through many years of hard work. I also knew that my case was very serious. I can remember my specialists' faces when I asked them if I could treat myself with natural medicines and how surprised they were that I was able to overcome what could have been disastrous and that, in so doing, I also avoided surgical intervention.

It is wonderful to be alive. As I said to a lady the other day, when we wake up with the thought that we are still part of the world, we want to share and contribute as much as possible. A lot is changing in the world of medicine. We have to look forward to the future of healthcare, which is perhaps in energy and time and the different cycles in which we take part, and as a result of which we can often be amazed at how situations work out in ways that are beyond our human understanding. Nature is still the best healer, and nature will teach us how to live in harmony with it if we just give it a chance. Life is becoming increasingly busy and opportunities are growing, but we sometimes need to stand still, look around and correct any imbalance in our lives. Patients often ask me what their first step should be to achieve a healthier life. That is not difficult. You just need to sit down and, with a good dose of common sense, look at your lifestyle and decide what you can do to change. Your health could be improved by dietary management, increased rest and relaxation or, above all, adopting a positive attitude and aiming to do your best.

I am really looking forward to the years ahead. I often think about my old friend, Linus Pauling, with whom I lectured many times. At the age of 67, he felt he had accomplished everything. He was a two-time Nobel Prize-winner. He then took stock of his life, and, although he accepted he had done a great deal to benefit the scientific world, he wondered what more he could do for his fellow human beings. So he decided to study health as a whole and, in particular, how much could be done by using vitamin C. He would often say to me, 'Jan, tell me your story again about the Second World War and how you all kept going by taking a simple little vitamin C tablet that the Red Cross gave you.' From the age of 67 until he was 92, he had yet another lifetime to look forward to. It is never too late if we use our capabilities and the strength that God has given us in the use of humanity.

When I look at my ten grandchildren, I see how they are all gifted in different ways, although they are all related to each other. They are all individuals, with the ability to benefit from the opportunities available to make something of their lives. I am encouraged by how much enthusiasm they have. Every day, with each new life, it is up to everyone to decide how best to make use of their time on this earth.